4th Edition

Children, Play,
and Development

With love to Bonnie, my wife and best friend, and to
Peter and Jon, the two young men who were once my playful little boys.

4th Edition

Children, Play, and Development

Fergus P. Hughes

University of Wisconsin–Green Bay

⑤SAGE

Los Angeles | London | New Delhi
Singapore | Washington DC

This book was previously published by Pearson Education, Inc.

For information:

SAGE Publications, Inc.
2455 Teller Road
Thousand Oaks,
   California 91320
E-mail: order@sagepub.com

SAGE Publications Ltd.
1 Oliver's Yard
55 City Road
London EC1Y 1SP
United Kingdom

SAGE Publications India Pvt. Ltd.
B 1/I 1 Mohan Cooperative
   Industrial Area
Mathura Road, New Delhi 110 044
India

SAGE Publications Asia-Pacific Pte. Ltd.
33 Pekin Street #02-01
Far East Square
Singapore 048763

Printed in the United States of America.

Library of Congress Cataloging-in-Publication Data

Hughes, Fergus P.
Children, play, and development / Fergus P. Hughes. — 4th ed.
      p. cm.
Includes bibliographical references and index.
ISBN 978-1-4129-6769-3 (pbk.)
   1. Play. 2. Child development. I. Title.

HQ782.H84 2010
305.231—dc22   2008044057

This book is printed on acid-free paper.

12   13   10   9   8   7   6   5   4   3   2

Acquisitions Editor:	Diane McDaniel
Editorial Assistant:	Ashley Conlon
Production Editor:	Brittany Bauhaus
Copy Editor:	Melinda Masson
Typesetter:	C&M Digitals (P) Ltd.
Proofreader:	Dennis W. Webb
Indexer:	Rick Hurd
Cover Designer:	Candice Harman
Marketing Manager:	Christy Guilbault

Brief Contents

Detailed Contents

Preface

When she decided to retire, my colleague, friend, and mentor, the late Ruth E. Hartley, asked me to assume responsibility for teaching her course on children's play. Ruth said that a person should not presume to understand children's development without having a complete understanding of children's play. I agreed enthusiastically, and I still do.

I faced a problem when I began to prepare my course on play. There was a complete absence of reading material suitable for the type of course I wanted to teach. The course was housed in a human development department, the aim of which was to provide students with a solid grounding in developmental theory and research. Students enrolling in the course were typically majoring in human development and were planning careers in such varied fields as psychology, education, social work, recreational therapy, and nursing. Therefore, I wanted to assign a book with a strong developmental approach that would provide a broad and thorough review of the current research in the field of children's play and extensive coverage of the theories that inform so much of the research. In addition, the book I needed would have to present material in such a way as to be engaging to undergraduate readers. It would have to very readable while still being a scholarly work, and it would have to be mindful of the desire of undergraduate students to know about the practical significance of scholarship. Unfortunately, no such book was available.

Most available books on children's play had a practical orientation and were intended specifically for teachers. This is still the case today. For teachers, such books may offer excellent practical advice on planning play activities for children, but they rarely attempt to explain the rationale behind the planning. They rarely offer a social, cultural, or historical context. However, knowledge of history, theory, and research in a field is extremely important, as is knowledge of the larger social and cultural context in which the research is done. Teachers who use play will use it more effectively if they fully understand its purpose and its numerous benefits. If they do so, they will be able to move beyond the use of programmed play activities and create activities of their own.

Knowledge of theory and research can empower teachers to be creative in their practicality. I decided then that I would write a book of my own, and the result was *Children, Play, and Development*.

Because an understanding of play is critical for an understanding of child development, the audience for this book includes anyone who works with—or plans to work with—children. This book is appropriate for undergraduate or graduate courses in children's play, child development, life span human development, child psychology, early childhood education, recreation and leisure, and pediatric nursing. It has been or could be adopted in courses with titles such as "Child Psychology," "Child Development," "Play and Creative Activities in Childhood," "Play Development and the Assessment of the Young Child," "Social Relationships and Peer Play," "The Role of Play in Learning," and "Developmental Play."

ORGANIZATION OF THE BOOK

The book is divided into 10 chapters, which are contained within four parts.

Part I. The Context of Play

1. Historical and Theoretical Viewpoints

2. Ethological and Cultural Perspectives

This section sets the stage for a discussion of the topic of play by defining it and differentiating it from other childhood activities such as exploration and work. The significance of play and the reasons for its occurrence are then explored in a section on traditional and contemporary theories. We then place play in its historical context by examining the ways in which past cultures viewed the activity and illustrating how the historical threads interweave to form our modern perspective on play. The context of play is further examined by comparing human play to the play of other animals and finally by reviewing the most often observed differences in play across human cultures.

Part II. The Development of Play

3. The First Two Years of Life

4. The Preschool Years: From 2 to 5

5. Play in Later Childhood and Adolescence

This section highlights the developmental emphasis of the book by describing play at different ages and, more important, by relating play to normal physical, social, intellectual, and emotional development. It is not sufficient for students of play to know what children do at particular ages. They must also realize that play both reflects and enhances development. In this section, play is discussed within the framework of developmental theories, such as those of Piaget and Erikson, as well as the major trends in developmental research, such as research on the development of social relationships.

Part III. Individual Differences in Play

6. Gender Differences in Play

7. Play in Special Populations

In this section, we highlight some of the major factors related to variations in play within our own culture. Among the most heavily researched areas related to variations in play are gender, physical impairment, intellectual differences, and emotional problems that range from chronic conditions such as autism to temporary life stresses. We address the question of why these variations exist and how an adult who works with children can effectively respond to them. A review of the current literature on play reveals that a large percentage of studies deal with the play of children who differ from the typically developing child. It is rewarding to realize that regardless of their life circumstances, all children want and need to play.

Part IV. The Benefits of Play

8. Play and Intellectual Development

9. Social Benefits of Play

10. The Uses of Play in Therapy

This section specifically addresses the benefits of play for all aspects of children's development. The chapter on intellectual development describes the ways in which some of the most commonly found play materials and activities can enhance children's intellectual functioning and the ways in which play is related to emergent literacy and problem solving. In the following chapter, we deal with the benefits of play for parent-child attachment and social integration with peers. Finally, we address the emotional benefits of play by discussing the uses of play in therapy. It is not anticipated that users of this book will seek careers as therapists, although some may. However, anyone who works with children is a therapist in the sense that he or she provides a climate that fosters emotional well-being.

Major Emphases

Unlike other books on the market, *Children, Play, and Development* has the following combination of five emphases.

1. **An extensive examination of the historical, sociocultural, and ethological context of play.** No human behavior can be examined out of *context*. We study the history of play in order to recognize that historical trends influence the behavior of children and to realize that much of our own uncertainty about the value of play has historical origins. We study play in other cultures to get a better sense of what is universal in play and what is influenced by society. When we discover, for example, that in many cultures a child's elders see little value in play, we can then ask why we value play as we do and what happens to children who are not encouraged to play. Even within our own culture there are variations in opportunity to play, a fact that is recognized by anyone who works with children.

2. **A strong developmental emphasis.** The *developmental emphasis* is essential because, like all childhood behaviors, various forms of play do not appear suddenly at a particular age but emerge gradually from earlier forms of play. For example, representational play emerges early in the second year of life, but elementary forms of representation are observable late in the first year. Representational skills follow a specific and predictable path during the second year, which we describe in Chapter 2 as gradual changes in decentration, integration, and decontextualization. As children become increasingly social—and increasingly able to assign thoughts and feelings to other people—their representational play is transformed into sociodramatic play. In the book, I tried to demonstrate these developmental patterns. I believe that students of play should learn enough about child development to predict with some degree of accuracy the play behaviors of children of any given age.

3. **Thorough coverage of theoretical perspectives on play.** *Theory* is important because it is a framework for interpreting and making sense of play. It is particularly important in this book since no one has ever been able

to fully explain why children play. There are no definitive answers. There are only theories. Students need to know that no one theory is correct or incorrect but all contribute to our understanding of play. They also need to know that theories do not necessarily contradict one another but often emphasize different aspects of human behavior. For example, there is no direct contradiction between psychoanalytic and cognitive theories of play, but one emphasizes the emotional benefits while the other focuses on play as a stimulus for intellectual growth. Theory is covered extensively in Chapter 1, as well as in Chapter 10, which deals with theoretical approaches to play as therapy.

4. **An up-to-date review of the literature.** An *up-to-date review of literature* is essential in any scholarly book but particularly in one in which the state of our knowledge is changing rapidly. Research on play is increasing exponentially as psychologists and educators recognize its central significance to child development. As pointed out below, nearly half of the references in this edition did not appear in the previous edition. Approximately 200 reference citations were deleted from this edition because the studies are dated and no longer reflect the current state of our knowledge. The reader can be assured that he or she is reading about the most recent studies that were available at the time this book was going to press.

5. **Suggestions for application.** I have made great efforts to include *practical implications* of the research findings. In my years of teaching, students often asked me why they needed to understand a certain concept or body of information, and I always believed that it is a fair question. We should be able to explain why the findings of a particular study are important for practitioners in the field of child development. Answers are not always easy to provide, but I have tried to do so when possible, either in the body of the text or in the "Putting Theory Into Practice" inserts described below.

Pedagogical Features of the Book

Key Terms

The most important terms are presented in boldface type and are listed at the end of each chapter. All the key terms, with their definitions, are also listed at the end of the book in the form of a glossary. This is intended to draw the attention of students to the key concepts in the book and to make it easier for them to study for exams.

Learning Objectives

The learning objectives that open each chapter represent the main points of the chapter, the core of the information that is presented. They can be used as guide-posts during the reading of the chapters and to measure levels of achievement.

Chapter Summaries

Each chapter concludes with a summary of the main points, which can serve as a reminder and a review for the reader.

Putting Theory Into Practice

In each chapter, there are two instances of "Putting Theory Into Practice," which contain practical applications of the information provided in the text. For example, we point out in Chapter 2 that aggression is a normal element of play. In one of the instances of "Putting Theory Into Practice" in that chapter, we indicate ways in which those who work with children can distinguish between normal aggression and aggression that is destructive and even dangerous.

Issues for Class Discussion

At the end of each chapter, there is a list of questions that might be used to stim-ulate class discussion of the ideas presented in the text. Discussion is sometimes difficult to generate, but the suggestions listed here are those that I found most effective in my 30 years of teaching a course on play.

New to the Fourth Edition

An obvious reason for revision is to update the material presented. Play contin-ues to be a heavily researched topic, as evidenced by the number of articles that appear continuously in psychology, child development, and education journals. To present the student with an accurate picture of the field, it is necessary to incorporate the newest research, and to that end 336 new reference citations have been added to this edition. Nearly half the references in this edition are new. I would like to point out, however, that much of the seminal work on chil-dren's play has stood the test of time very well, and there are many classic stud-ies included in this book. This is because they have never been improved upon.

A new edition involves updating, but it should also include a willingness by the writer to totally rethink every aspect of the book. Research takes new directions over the course of time. Therefore, while every chapter was updated to reflect the most current research, most chapters were also revised to include new information, often in the form of significantly expanded or totally new sections. The major changes were the following:

Chapter 1

- Inclusion of the contributions of Froebel, Montessori, and Dewey.
- Expansion of the section on Vygotsky's theory.

Chapter 2

- Information on brain correlates of aggressive play in humans and animals.
- New section on cultural differences in object play.
- New section on critique of experimental research on play across cultures.

Chapter 3

- New section on the development of the young child's ability to distinguish between reality and make-believe.
- Expansion of section on parental gender differences in play.
- New section on the toddler's ability to understand the mental states of other people.

Chapter 4

- Expansion of section on preschoolers' understanding of the difference between fantasy and reality.
- Totally new "Computers in the Preschool" boxed insert.
- Expanded section on play in the natural environment.
- Deletion of the section on play and television.

Chapter 5

- New section on video game playing.

Chapter 6

- Updated throughout.

Chapter 7

- Significantly revised section on children with autism.
- New section titled "The Lack of a Theory of Mind."

- New section titled "Autism and Play."
- New section titled "Intervention Approaches With Autism."
- Expanded section on the special child in the classroom.
- Expanded section on victims of child abuse.

Chapter 8

- New section on blocks and mathematical ability.
- Expanded section on creative movement.
- New section on play and the development of literacy, to replace the section on language play.
- New discussion of the concept of emergent literacy.
- Expanded section on fantasy play and divergent thinking.

Chapter 9

- New section on the impact of attachment on children's development.
- Extensive revision of sections on music and creative movement.
- Expansion of material on social intervention programs for children with social difficulties.

Chapter 10

- Inclusion of new material on filial play therapy.
- Removal of the section on costume play therapy.
- Complete revision of the section of the benefits of play in therapy.

Ancillary Material

Instructors' materials further support and enhance the learning goals of *Children, Play, and Development, Fourth Edition.*

Instructor Resources on CD

This CD offers the instructor a variety of resources that supplement the book material, including PowerPoint lecture slides and a comprehensive test bank with multiple-choice, true or false, short-answer, and essay questions for each chapter. Additional resources include teaching tips, sample syllabi, and Web resources.

To obtain a copy of this CD, please contact SAGE Customer Care at 1-800-818-SAGE (7243), 6am–5pm PT.

Acknowledgments

I would like to thank all those who have adopted my earlier editions for use in their classes, many of whom have offered unsolicited comments and helpful suggestions. There is a sense in which you have made this edition possible.

I would like to thank my reviewers. Reading critical reviews is never easy, but it is made easier if the reviewers are positive and constructive in their approach. My reviewers were constructive and helpful, and I thank them.

Reviewers of the fourth edition were:

Ann Barbour, *California State University–Los Angeles*

Yash Bhagwanji, *Florida Atlantic University*

Darragh Callahan, *Boston University*

Elizabeth Elliott, *Florida Gulf Coast University*

Jill Gelormino, *St. Joseph's College*

Jill M. Raisor, *Southern Illinois University*

Kimberly M. Ray, *Syracuse University*

L. Kathryn Sharp, *University of Memphis*

Ruslan Slutsky, *University of Toledo*

I want to thank my editor at SAGE, Diane McDaniel, who not only encouraged and supported me in this project but also made a number of suggestions that will substantially improve the book. I was planning my retirement when Diane first contacted me, and I have since retired. I was by no means certain that I wanted to continue any form of work, even a book that has always been a labor of love for me. It was Diane's enthusiasm for this project that persuaded me to do it, and I'm very glad I did. It has been exciting for me to see how the field has changed in the past number of years, and it has been rewarding to return to the world of scholarship, since for the 3 years prior to my retirement I was a full-time academic dean. Finally, I would like to thank Leah Mori and Ashley Conlon, Diane's editorial assistants at SAGE, for the careful attention they have given to this project and for their much appreciated help and encouragement.

PART I

The Context of Play

This section sets the stage for a discussion of the topic of play by defining it and differentiating it from other childhood activities such as exploration and work. The significance of play and the reasons for its occurrence are then explored in a section on traditional and contemporary theories. Play is then placed in its historical context by examining the ways in which past cultures viewed the activity and illustrating how the historical threads interweave to form our modern perspective on play. The context of play is further examined by comparing human play to the play of other animals and finally by reviewing the most often observed differences in play across human cultures.

1

Chapter 1

HISTORICAL AND THEORETICAL VIEWPOINTS

Scott, a first grader with little interest in competitive sports, agreed to join a school soccer team only because his parents insisted on it. However, playing soccer frightens Scott, and on the evening of each game he is so overcome by anxiety that he can scarcely eat his dinner. Six-month-old Michelle can spend extensive amounts of time exploring the contents of her mother's purse; she seriously and methodically inspects every item she discovers before moving on to the next one. Jennifer loves her job as a copyeditor for the local newspaper; she often comments to friends that she feels almost guilty to be drawing a salary for doing something that she enjoys so much.

When Scott is on the soccer field, is it accurate to describe him as a child at play? Is Michelle playing when she examines the contents of her mother's purse? And what about Jennifer? When she is at the office, is she working, or is there a sense that her work is really a playful activity?

A DEFINITION OF PLAY

What exactly is *play?* What is the dividing line between *play* and *work?* Can an activity be both play and work at the same time? Can an activity begin as one and gradually evolve into the other? Actually, there is no simple definition of play, and the borderlines between play and other activities, such as work, exploration, and learning, are not always clear. Nevertheless, social scientists have identified a number of elements that are typical of play, so we will now try to arrive at a definition of play by examining some of these generally agreed-upon essential characteristics.

Learning Objectives

After reading Chapter 1, a student should be able to:

✦ Understand the essential characteristics of a definition of play and recognize the difference between play and work according to these criteria.

✦ Identify different beliefs about the relative values of play and work in the early childhood education curriculum.

✦ List and describe the central characteristics of the "developmentally appropriate curriculum" as outlined by the National Association for the Education of Young Children.

✦ Trace the history of attitudes toward children's play from the Mediterranean world before the birth of Christ to the present day.

✦ Compare and contrast the French naturalistic view of child development with that of British empiricism and recognize how both of these philosophical positions are reflected in modern American attitudes toward children's play.

✦ Recognize the similarities and the differences between the psychoanalytic, cognitive, contextual, and arousal modulation theories of children's play.

Essential Characteristics of Play

Before an activity can be described as play, it must contain five essential characteristics (Rubin, Fein, & Vandenberg, 1983). First, play is *intrinsically motivated*. It is an end in itself, done only for the satisfaction of doing it. A second, related characteristic of play is that it must be *freely chosen* by the participants.

As Vandenberg (1998) observed, "the excitement of play results from the sheer exercise of freedom over necessity" (p. 303). If children are forced into play, they may not regard the assigned activity as play at all. In one study (King, 1979), for example, it was found that if a kindergarten teacher assigned a play activity to her pupils, they tended to regard it as work, even though they described the identical activity as play if they were allowed to choose it themselves.

A third essential characteristic of play is that it must be *pleasurable*. In fact, adults observing children's play episodes identify "positive affect" as the most typical behavioral criterion of play (Jenvey & Jenvey, 2002). If we think of Scott, the first grader who reluctantly agreed to play soccer only because his

PUTTING THEORY INTO PRACTICE 1.1

Allowing Freedom of Expression in Play

Do not discourage children from exploring in play such "unacceptable" feelings as anger, fear, and sexual curiosity. Such play can help reduce their anxiety and can teach adults a good deal about the children's psychological needs.

Fluid materials such as clay and finger paints are excellent media through which children can express anger as well as curiosity about body parts and functions. With clay, children can tear and pound harmlessly, and they can also create human figures that often have anatomically correct parts. With clay, sand, or blocks, they can be safely destructive and will learn that their own destructive impulses are not necessarily harmful and should not frighten them. Sometimes the pleasure of creating is enhanced by the anticipation of destroying what one has created. With dolls children can create family scenes and explore family-related anxieties. If they are allowed to communicate freely when using hand puppets, children can reveal some of their innermost feelings, in actions or words, since it is not they but the puppets who are communicating.

Adults need to exert control over the behavior of young children, so they must place restrictions on free expression with materials. For example, clay can be pounded, pulled apart, or squashed but should not be thrown at the wall or at other children. However, adults should try to remember that if they are overly restrictive, the play will lose some of its emotional value for children. They should also realize that even a young child can make a distinction between knocking over a block structure that he or she has created and knocking over the furniture in the classroom.

parents wanted him to, it becomes apparent that his activity on the soccer field fails to satisfy any of the characteristics of play that have been mentioned thus far. Soccer is certainly not intrinsically motivating for Scott; his motivation for doing it is to please his parents. It is not a freely chosen activity because it was chosen for him by his parents. Finally, an activity that engenders so much stress in the participant can hardly be described as pleasurable!

A fourth characteristic of play is that it is *nonliteral*. That is, it involves a certain element of make-believe, a distortion of reality to accommodate the interests of the player. This is particularly true of the symbolic play that is so characteristic of the preschool years, when children spend much of their time experimenting with new roles and playing out imaginary scenes. Finally, play is *actively engaged* in by the player. The child must be involved—physically, psychologically, or both—rather than passive or indifferent to what is going on.

Play, Work, and the Education of Young Children

Play differs in a number of ways from what is usually regarded as work. The major difference is that, even when work is enjoyable, it is still extrinsically motivated. It has a goal, such as to earn money, enhance status, feel useful, or attain success in a chosen field. Like play, work is sometimes freely chosen, but the option to avoid work is rarely available in our society. A person who regards work as pleasurable is fortunate; for most workers, it is not. The non-literal element that typifies play is not usually found in work activities. Finally, work resembles play in the last characteristic: Both are actively engaged in, to some extent at least, by the participants.

Psychologists and educators agree that spontaneous, goal-free play facilitates children's development, but what is the value of work? Is play a valuable activity for children's development while work is not? Is there a role for work in children's lives? As a matter of fact, work has its place along with play, and this is particularly apparent when we address issues concerning the education of children.

How much work and how much play should be involved in the education of a young child? Few would suggest that all learning occurs through spontaneous play while teachers assume only minor and passive roles, and perhaps no one maintains that play is completely unrelated to learning. Instead, there is a range of opinion as to the relative importance of work and play. Toward the play end of the play-work continuum, the National Association for the Education of Young Children (NAEYC) suggests in a listing of developmentally appropriate practices that children should be allowed to direct their own play activities, that they are more likely to "feel successful when they engage in a task that they have defined for themselves," and that learning should not be influenced by "adult-established concepts of completion, achievement and failure" (Bredekamp, 1987, p. 3). (See Table 1.1.) The teacher's role, therefore, is to be supportive but not overly directive. It would be inappropriate for teachers to "use highly-structured, teacher-directed lessons almost exclusively," to "direct all the activity," or to "decide what the children will do and when" while expecting the children to listen passively or do pencil and paper tasks for long periods of time (Bredekamp, p. 3).

On the other hand, the NAEYC position is that while a curriculum that emphasizes spontaneous play but ignores the role of work might be beneficial to children's overall development, it would be insufficient from an educational standpoint. After all, teaching is intended to encourage learning, and if children's activities are totally unstructured, the children may be bored and will need a teacher-directed activity to help them focus their attention (Hatch et al., 2002). "Child-initiated learning does not occur in the absence of teacher guidance or input" (Bredekamp, 1993, p. 118).

TABLE 1.1   The Developmentally Appropriate Curriculum

Curriculum goals should address all areas of children's development in age-appropriate ways. This includes physical, social, emotional, and cognitive development in an integrated approach, since development in one area inevitably affects development in the other three.

Goals and plans should be based on the needs, strengths, and interests of the individual child. Information about family and cultural background should be considered in order to broaden the curriculum to include all children.

Children should be active participants in their own education and should be encouraged to freely explore materials, adults, and other children. Unstructured free play is an essential part of this process.

Learning materials should be concrete, real, and relevant to the lives of young children. Children should be allowed to manipulate materials before they are expected to deal with symbols such as letters and numbers.

Adults must be aware that chronological age is not the best predictor of developmental level. Available materials should reflect the entire range of the age span, and provisions must be made for the child whose interests and skills are beyond the normal developmental range.

Teachers should provide a variety of activities and materials for children and should increase the level of complexity as children develop their understanding and skills.

The teacher's role is to prepare the child's environment with a variety of interesting and challenging activity choices and then to encourage children to initiate and direct their own activities.

Children of all ages should be exposed to a multicultural and nonsexist experience in terms of activities and educational materials. Such exposure not only enhances a child's self-esteem but also encourages children to be appreciative of and respectful of individual differences.

Source: Adapted from S. Bredekamp (Ed.) (1987).

Is there some ideal balance of work and play in early childhood education settings? Joan Goodman (1994) of the University of Pennsylvania suggested that educators and psychologists too often have limited themselves by making an artificial either/or distinction between the two. Play, she argued, may be different from work but is not its direct opposite. To be sure, there are purely work-related activities, such as when a child is struggling with a difficult arithmetic assignment and cannot wait to complete it. There is also pure play, such as when a child frolics in the waves at the beach. Somewhere between the two, however, is a type of activity that Goodman called play/work. For example, a child, with a teacher's direction and encouragement, is struggling with a block-building project. This is a goal-directed activity—and one that is occasionally frustrating. At the same time, however, the child is completely absorbed and self-motivated. It is here at what Goodman saw as the midpoint between play and work that the best teaching occurs. The child enjoys the project for the sake of itself and considers it his or her own and not the teacher's. The teacher, however, provides the underlying skills necessary to solve the problem, determines that certain problems are more appropriate than others, and offers continuing support and encouragement throughout the problem-solving process.

THE HISTORY OF PLAY IN THE WESTERN WORLD

In order to understand the various theoretical perspectives on the significance of play to child development and to appreciate current attitudes in the United States toward play, it is important to know something about the history of conceptions of childhood, not only in this country but in the entire Western world. Let us now look briefly at childhood in its historical context, with particular reference to the attitudes of adults toward children's play.

From Ancient Times to the Middle Ages

For a thousand years before the birth of Christ, the recorded history of all the major cultures in the eastern Mediterranean world indicates a fairly similar view of childhood. Children were never romanticized, as they often are today; they were not seen as naturally innocent and pure. However, they were thought of as helpless, incapable of directing their own affairs, and having special needs, including the desire and the need to play. Play was an understandable and an acceptable part of children's lives. In ancient Egyptian wall paintings, for example, children can be seen playing with balls and dolls, as well as jumping rope (French, 1977).

Children in ancient Greece were seen as naturally playful, and play was allowed and even encouraged. Children also were seen as naturally more unformed, unruly, helpless, fearful, cheerful, and affectionate than adults. Even though childhood and children's activities were appreciated, the role of the adult was to guide the child gently into becoming a useful and responsible citizen (French, 1977). The gentle and respectful nature of this guidance is illustrated by the writings of the philosopher Plato. Although he described the young boy as "the craftiest, most mischievous, and unruliest of brutes" (*Laws*, Book 7, 360 BC/1961, p. 808), Plato was also concerned that excessive adult supervision could be harmful. Spoiling children can make them "fretful, peevish, and easily upset by mere trifles," he wrote, but harsh childrearing approaches can make them "sullen, spiritless, servile, and unfit for the intercourse of domestic and civic life" (*Laws*, Book 7, 360 BC/1961, p. 91). Although perhaps less gentle in their approaches to child guidance, the ancient Romans shared the Greek view of children as affectionate, cheerful, and playful, but they saw children as being in need of discipline tempered with affection (French, 1977).

The special nature of childhood continued to be recognized in the Western world from the early Christian era to the Middle Ages, approximately 12 centuries after the birth of Christ. The early Christian view was that a child is important to God, has a soul, and therefore is not to be abused by adults. Indeed, the Church had a special role in promoting the welfare of children. Although children in the Middle Ages were not sheltered from the hardships and realities of life (as is often the case today), neither were they seen as miniature versions of adults, and special childhood activities, including play, continued to be thought of as both acceptable and appropriate (Borstelmann, 1983).

The Renaissance Perspective

Negative attitudes about children—and about the need for them to have special activities—began to surface in Europe during the period known as the Renaissance (1300–1600 AD). While the Renaissance is generally recognized as one of the most creative periods in European history, a time of openness to new ideas in all areas of the arts and sciences, children apparently did not benefit from this open-mindedness. For example, it was common practice to place children in the custody of a nurse or a succession of nurses, who usually saw their caretaking roles in purely monetary terms. Children were believed to be of little importance compared with adults and were said to lack strength, wit, and cunning. Often they were the subject of jokes and were placed in the category of fools and senile old people (Tucker, 1974). A commonly heard phrase was "Who sees a child sees nothing" (Whiting & Whiting, 1968, p. 83).

All distinctions between the world of childhood and that of adulthood vanished, it seems, during the Renaissance. Children were put to work as soon as was reasonable because idleness was considered both sinful and unprofitable (Tucker, 1974). It was only in elite families that children were sent to school, and that was not a pleasant prospect for them; there, they would spend long hours in the care of stern, unfeeling teachers. Nevertheless, there seems to have been time enough for play as well, and many of what we would call children's play activities can be observed in paintings depicting scenes from everyday life in Renaissance Europe.

However, it is not only children who can be seen playing. Since there was no distinction between the world of children and that of adults, people of all ages played the same games and chanted the same nursery rhymes. In fact, the only real nursery rhymes were those composed specifically for the nursery, and the only chants that truly belonged to the world of childhood were lullabies (Tucker, 1974). Riddles were typically made up by adults and for adults, and many popular chants that have come down to us from that period were originally sung by adults and often contained interesting political or social messages. For example, the children's rhyme "Sing-a-Song-of-Sixpence" was an adult song telling of King Henry VIII's love for Anne Boleyn and other events at the beginning of the Protestant Reformation (Opie & Opie, 1957; Borstelmann, 1983).

Interestingly, it was during the Renaissance that, in southern Germany, the toy-manufacturing industry was born. Along with such homemade toys as kites and tops that had been seen during the Middle Ages, now there were also lead soldiers, elaborate wooden dolls, and glass animals. We should not presume, however, that these toys were made for children. The lack of a distinction between the child's world and that of adults is nicely illustrated by the fact that the Renaissance toys were intended not only for children but for adults, too. In fact, many toys of this era—and of the 17th and 18th centuries, as well—were so elaborate and so delicate (e.g., tea sets, dolls, dollhouses) that it is likely that children were not allowed even to touch them (Somerville, 1982).

In the 17th century, as the Renaissance era was coming to an end, European attitudes about children and about play were beginning to change. There arose what has been described as a "new consciousness of childhood" (Pinchbeck & Hewitt, 2005, p. 197); children began to be seen as worthy of attention and having developmental needs and problems that were different from those of adults. The 17th century was also a period of enthusiastic colonization of the New World, and because of colonization patterns, the major European influences on American attitudes toward work and play came from the countries of France and England.

French Influences

As Europe emerged from the Renaissance at the dawn of the 17th century, the French attitude toward play could be characterized as one of acceptance, and this acceptance has continued to one degree or another until the present day. Even though the Catholic clergy took a dim view of play without the redeeming social value of work, they were apparently powerless to prevent its occurrence (Aries, 1962).

Perhaps the most complete record of children's play in 17th-century France can be found in a diary kept by Jean Heroard, the physician who attended young King Louis XIII. Louis was hardly a typical French child of the time.

What is more, the diary seems to contain a number of exaggerations and distortions intended to put the child in the best possible light (Marvick, 1974). Heroard claimed, for example, that Louis understood human speech when he was only 5 weeks old; on being told that God placed him in the world for a purpose and therefore he must be good and just, the infant responded with a knowing smile!

If we disregard Heroard's self-serving suggestions about Louis's remarkable precocity, the diary tells us much about the 17th-century attitude toward children in general and toward play in particular. Louis had windmills to play with, hobbyhorses, and whipping toys resembling modern tops. By the age of 17 months, the future king was able to play the violin and sing at the same time. (Perhaps this is another bit of exaggeration.) As a toddler, he played ball exactly as did the adults of his time, and by the age of 2, he had a little drum to bang on and was already becoming a skillful dancer. At 4, he liked to play cards and to shoot with a bow and arrow, and by the age of 6, he was beginning to play chess and to enjoy parlor games (Aries, 1962).

The most revealing feature of Louis's play is its similarity to that of the adults of his time. As a matter of fact, many of Louis's playmates were adult servants and courtiers. Play that involved music, athletic skills, board games, and parlor games was engaged in by noblemen and noblewomen of all ages because beyond the age of infancy there was no separation between the games of children and those of adults. Indeed, as was true during the Renaissance, virtually no distinction existed in the early 17th century between the world of children and the world of adults; there was as yet no concept of childhood innocence, and there was little separation between work and play.

As the century progressed, however, a separation gradually appeared between the worlds of childhood and adulthood and between the games of children and adults. The games of children (and fools) were physical in nature, whereas adults—at least those of the nobility who aspired to some degree of sophistication—played only games of intellect and wit. Work and play were increasingly thought of as separate activities. Work became the center of adult life, while play came to be seen as an activity reserved for children and for those with childish minds. Nevertheless, play continued to be at least tolerated in France, as it was not to be in England, and the French retained a definite appreciation for the period of childhood.

The French appreciation for childhood—and for children's natural activities—was later embodied in the writings of France's most influential philosopher of the 18th century, Jean-Jacques Rousseau (1712–1778). Rousseau (1762/2007) expressed the philosophy of **naturalism**. "God makes all things good," he wrote. "Man meddles with them and they become evil" (p. 11). Children come into the world not as empty organisms waiting for experience to shape them but as original human beings equipped by nature with an innate plan for their development. The child is more than an incomplete version of an adult, and adults must appreciate children for who they are. "Childhood has its own way of seeing, thinking, and feeling, and nothing is more foolish than to try to substitute ours for them," wrote Rousseau in *Emile* (p. 63), his classic work on education.

Rousseau believed that little harm would come to children if they were allowed to grow without excessive adult supervision. The first 12 years of life should be a time of leisure, during which the only education should be negative. That is, adults should try not to teach virtues to children but only to prevent them from acquiring vices. "Give him no orders at all, absolutely none," wrote Rousseau. "Do not even let him think that you claim authority over him" (1762/2007, p. 63).

The widespread acceptance of Rousseau's ideas tells us as much about the age in which he lived as it does about the character of the French people. Europe in the 18th century witnessed the emergence of the spirit of Romanticism, in which childhood was glorified and childhood innocence celebrated. It is unlikely, of course, that all French people of the time agreed with Rousseau's views on child development or that the average citizen read his books (or anything else for that matter). However, it reveals much about the French view of life that Rousseau should have gained so large an audience in that country. His ideas were not as well received in England, even in the Romantic era; nor was he as widely read in the American Colonies as was John Locke, whose ideas will be discussed in the following section. As we shall see, England lacked the fertile soil in which the radical democratic ideas of naturalism could grow.

British Influences

As in other European countries, there was in 17th-century England a growing awareness of the child as an individual with special needs and a worldview different from that of adults. Nevertheless, this enlightened perspective did not lead to a greater acceptance of children's play. In fact, while the French maintained an appreciation for play, even as they relegated it to the realm of childhood, the emphasis in England in the 17th and 18th centuries was almost completely on the value of work for both children and adults. What was responsible for the overwhelming emphasis on work and the corresponding de-emphasis on play in England? Actually both religious and philosophical reasons contributed to the devaluation of play in English life.

The religious influence most responsible for the devaluation of play in England was the rise of Protestantism. While Catholicism stressed the necessity of faith in achieving salvation, the Protestant view was that faith alone would not suffice. Hard work was also necessary, as was self-discipline; material success was thought to be indicative of good moral character. Play was viewed as the opposite of work and so was both sinful and irresponsible. In the words of the theologian John Wesley (1768, p. 283), "He that plays when he is a boy will play when he is a man." (One can assume that this statement was meant to apply to girls and women as well.)

As Rousseau was later to become the preeminent philosopher of France, the philosopher whose views on the nature of children would be the most widely accepted in England was John Locke (1632–1704). Locke was representative of 17th-century thinking in his belief that each child is a unique and valuable human being whose developmental needs must be recognized by adults. Not surprisingly, he also represented the religious tradition in which he was raised. The son of Puritan parents, Locke held ideas on childrearing that were quite consistent with the Puritan worldview, which will be discussed in the following section. Locke's ideas were also consistent with those of virtually every other Protestant sect in England at the time.

Locke apparently loved children and felt a special empathy with them yet neither romanticized them nor recommended that they be indulged. Instead, he argued that the child needs firm adult direction. A central assumption of Locke's theory was that the human organism is empty at birth—that the mind of the newborn is a **tabula rasa**, or blank slate—and that all knowledge of the world comes through the senses. It follows that the environment is all-important in shaping a person's direction, so beginning in infancy, the foundations of good character must be laid down by parents.

Indulgence must be avoided because children have no natural awareness of what is best for them. Their natural tendency is to seek freedom to do what they want and to exert control over the world around them; but other than satisfying their basic physiological needs, parents must never give children what they cry for. "Children must leave it to the choice and ordering of their parents, what they think properest for them, and how much: and must not be permitted to chuse for themselves," Locke wrote in *Some Thoughts Concerning Education* (1693/1964, p. 41). Parental direction is necessary for the mind to be "made obedient to discipline and pliant to reason when it [is] most tender, most easy to be bowed" (p. 54).

Although he emphasized the value of firm direction for children and even went so far as to suggest that their feet be immersed in cold water every day to harden them against the chilly English climate, Locke's views on childrearing and education were actually quite humane. He advocated gentle and respectful approaches to parenting. For example, he condemned both physical punishment and excessive nagging and argued in favor of methods that would help children develop their own internal controls. Furthermore, it was his hope that as children matured, parents would need to exert their authority less and less so that the parent-child relationship would eventually come to be based on equality. Parental authority, wrote Locke in *Thoughts,* "should be relaxed as fast as their age, discretion, and good behavior could allow it. . . . The sooner you treat him as a man, the sooner he will begin to be one" (1693/1964, p. 88).

Locke's ideas were widely circulated during the late 17th and the 18th centuries, not only in England but also throughout Europe and in the Colonies of the New World. His ideas about the importance of firmness, rationality, discipline, and moral education were enthusiastically received. Although his philosophy was certainly more respectful of children as individuals than was the Renaissance perspective, Locke was no advocate of naturalistic childrearing approaches. Indeed, the "natural" elements of childhood were those that needed correction, and while he did not actually condemn play, Locke made it clear that work, rationality, and discipline were the central ingredients in a child's optimal development.

In summary, the ideas of Protestant reformers had a dramatic impact on British attitudes toward childrearing in general and toward work and play in particular. Locke, influenced by his Protestant upbringing and by a revolutionary 17th-century view of the child as a distinct and original creation of God, came to have a significant influence on British—and later American—beliefs about children. Work and self-discipline were seen as paths to eternal salvation, to material success, and to mature rationality; play was at best a distraction, at worst a sin against God. The result was that play was virtually suppressed by the middle and end of the 18th century. Many English towns even went so far as to enact laws forbidding certain forms of play, such as playing with tops or running races in the public streets.

Childhood in the United States

The Puritan Legacy

The earliest permanent settlers in what would become the American Colonies were the Puritans, a religious reform group who left England in 1630 to seek freedom of expression in a new world. The Puritan influence was widely felt in the Colonies of New England. This group was to have a significant impact on later U.S. attitudes toward work and play, although the Puritans themselves—and their influence on U.S. thought—are often misunderstood.

The Puritans are often stereotyped as a harsh, unfeeling people who treated their children with a sternness bordering on cruelty and had little use for play of any sort. In fact, this was not the case at all. Puritan views on childhood, as exemplified in the writings of John Locke, were considerably more humane and enlightened than were the views of most of the Puritans' contemporaries (Somerville, 1982).

The Puritans were reformers, after all, who envisioned a world that was new and better than their own. Reformers tend to be future-oriented people, and the children of Puritan society were highly valued as representing the hope of the future. They were seen as individuals in their own right instead of mere family replacements, a status that was indicated by the names they were typically given (Somerville, 1982). The European pattern of naming had always been to bestow on a child the name of a parent or another relative. In fact, siblings in the Middle Ages often were given identical names and were referred to not by name but by labels indicating their birth order (Illick, 1974). By contrast, the Puritans gave names that symbolized their hope for a better society under God (Prudence, Thankful, Safe-on-High), and the very fact that Puritan children received original names is an indication that they were perceived as unique and original human beings.

The Puritans believed that children needed a considerable amount of discipline and instruction if they were to live orderly and responsible lives. The child was thought to be born ignorant and sinful but at least capable of being enlightened (Borstelmann, 1983). Proper discipline would make this partially rational but evil-natured creature behave reasonably and thereby reflect credit on its parents in the eyes of God.

In terms of instruction, the Puritans thought it important to provide children with the knowledge—and particularly the religious knowledge—that would enable them to serve God better and increase the chances of their own salvation. To that end, the Puritans were the first Americans to publish books especially intended for children, and until the early 18th century, most books written in English and addressed to a child audience were written by Puritan authors (Somerville, 1982).

Not only were Puritan adults sensitive to the special needs of children and aware of developmental differences between their children and themselves, they also did not despise all forms of playfulness, as is commonly believed. Nevertheless, it is true that play was discouraged in the life of the Puritan child. Play was not seen as evil in itself but as an activity that would distract a child from the study and vocational training that were needed to acquire appropriate self-discipline. From a practical standpoint, it is hard to imagine a Puritan child having much time for play, in any case, since school began as early as 7 a.m., 6 days a week, and did not end until 4 or 5 p.m. and since children were expected to perform their household chores as well (Illick, 1974).

Ultimately, the Puritan experiment in the Colonies was doomed to failure because, by the end of the 17th century, each new generation seemed to lose some of the religious zeal of its predecessor (Walzer, 1974). Nevertheless, the

Puritans had a lasting influence on American attitudes toward children as developmentally different from adults and as symbols of the hope for a better future. They had another type of influence as well, perhaps one that has been less positive. Despite a degree of acceptance that was almost revolutionary for its time, there were also elements of rejection in the Puritan attitude toward children. The reasonable behavior that was the purpose of discipline and instruction was thought to be against a child's basic nature; thus, the goal of childrearing was to make children into something that by nature they were not. Such a view hardly constitutes acceptance of children in their own right and might be described as an effort to subdue the very individuality that the Puritans were among the first to recognize in the child.

In the Puritan attitude toward children, therefore, there was a degree of ambivalence that was to evolve in this country into a feeling of uncertainty about the value of childhood and the relative importance of the seemingly natural activities of children and adults: play and work. As a part of our Puritan legacy, this ambivalence would continue for several centuries. Some would argue that it continues to the present day.

Colonial Times

In the Colonial United States of the 18th century, the Puritan legacy of ambivalence about the value of children was evident, and perhaps as a result, there was a certain ambiguity about the relationship between work and play (Walzer, 1974). On the one hand, Colonial parents were genuinely interested in their children, rejoiced at their births, played with them, gave them presents, wrote letters to them when separated, and grieved considerably when a child died. There seemed to be in the Colonies a greater fondness for children and a closer relationship between parent and child than was found in England at the time.

On the other side, however, early American parents engaged in many activities that distanced them from their children. Infant abandonment, a common occurrence in Europe, was rare in the New World, but very young Colonial children were often "put out." That is, they were given over to the custody of nurses, schools, tutors, or assorted relatives, a practice that modern Americans would certainly see as unusual. As an illustration of this practice, in May 1782 Pamela Sedgewick of western New England wrote of her young daughter to her cousin Betsey Mayhew in Boston: "I have a little prattler, your namesake. If you do not burden yourself with a family before [she] is old enough to leave her mama, I intend to send her to your care. So you see, my dear, you must not expect to get rid of trouble by living single" (Walzer, 1974, p. 353).

The rejection of children in Colonial America also took another form: the complete submission of the child to parental control. It was the parents' role, as it had been in Puritan times, to shape children according to their own strongly held religious convictions. In that sense, children had value only insofar as they served as extensions of and reflected well upon their parents. Again, there was that curious contradiction. How could children be appreciated in their own right and at the same time be seen as creatures in desperate need of shaping and correcting?

Compared with the 17th-century view, the 18th-century American view of childhood was considerably more diversified. There was a blending of Locke's environmentalist views with the new Romanticism typified by Rousseau's naturalistic perspective. The question of the relative influences of nurture and nature on development was now raised in earnest: Are children nothing more than reflections of the sum total of their experiences, or do innate characteristics play a role in determining who and what a person grows to be?

The 19th Century

As the British had established Colonies along the eastern seaboard, there had been extensive French colonization in the American South and Midwest. It is apparent that early American attitudes about play came to reflect the perspectives of both countries. The British emphasis on discipline, hard work, and moral rectitude was definitely reflected in 19th-century American thought, although to a lesser degree than in the mother country. In fact, British visitors to the United States in the early 1800s were horrified by what they considered the irreverent and disrespectful behavior of American children; they typically attributed this state of affairs to overindulgence by American parents, and they expressed surprise at the degree of intimacy and familiarity that characterized parent-child relationships in this country (Borstelmann, 1983). British observers typically described Americans as more relaxed, frivolous, and fun loving than they. Perhaps they still do so, just as we still tend to describe the British as somewhat serious and formal.

As has already been mentioned, the French had always maintained an attitude of greater acceptance toward play and toward the naturalness of childhood than had the British. How, then, would a French visitor have described Americans of the 19th century? While the British saw them as lacking in discipline, French observers characterized Americans as rather serious minded compared with themselves. Typical were the views of Alexis de Tocqueville (1805–1859), who toured the new republic in the early 1800s and described our Colonial ancestors as a sober and serious people, unable to enjoy play unless it was integrated in some way with work (Tocqueville, 1835/1946).

Early American play was, indeed, somewhat work oriented in nature. Supposed play activities, such as raising a barn or making a quilt, were obviously related to the necessary work of an agricultural society. This blend of work and play probably reflected a blend of the early British and French influences on the American Colonies. The net result of these competing perspectives was an American ambivalence about play that carried through the 19th and into the 20th century, compounded by the diverse and continuous immigration pattern that created a multicultural American society.

There are numerous illustrations of the 19th-century ambivalence toward children and play. On the one hand, the mid-19th century is often regarded as a period in which parents exerted considerable psychological rather than physical control over their children (Davis, 1976). That is, the emphasis was on strong parental authority, with little empathy for the child; the repression of personal feelings; and the encouragement of children's practicing self-control motivated by feelings of guilt.

Yet this also was a period in which American children were encouraged through their play to become more mobile and to achieve greater degrees of mastery over the environment. Toys became increasingly complex; for instance, there appeared a variety of miniature vehicles, such as trains, that were made up of many parts and presented a challenge to the player as well as a source of education. Board games appeared at this time, and these required skill and a flair for competition. The first cap pistol was produced in 1859, allowing a child a new means of expressing aggression and mastery over the environment (Davis, 1976). The message to children was that they must look inward to control themselves and also turn outward to attain a degree of mobility and control over their surroundings.

It was in the middle of the 19th century that educators began to emphasize the importance of children's play, although, consistent with 19th-century attitudes, play was seen as purposeful rather than a desirable end in itself. The Swiss educator Friedrich Froebel (1782–1852) developed the first kindergarten and introduced play into the early childhood education curriculum. He saw such structured play as the manipulation of balls and blocks, singing, engaging in organized games, and practicing various crafts as means of helping children acquire abstract ideas and spiritual values that would serve them well as adults. In structured play children could learn to be creative, moral, and responsible members of society. They could learn about the unity and harmony in the world around them. The Italian educator Maria Montessori (1870–1952) designed play materials for children and observed how they played with them in her classroom. Based on her observations, she determined what were the essential elements of play and the learning that different forms of play produced. For example, play could teach children about colors, numbers, size, and different shapes of objects. She then went on to use specific materials to teach specific concepts. Neither Froebel nor Montessori supported the use of spontaneous or imaginative play in their curricula. In fact, Montessori believed that free play could actually interfere with learning and make-believe play could hamper a child's understanding of reality (Spodek & Saracho, 2003).

20th-Century Attitudes

In the first 10 years of the 20th century, there were efforts to lessen the repressive internal controls that had previously been fostered in children, with a corresponding increase in willingness to let children—and adults for that matter—express their feelings openly (Davis, 1976). There was also greater parental interest in understanding the perspectives and feelings of their children. The interest, at least temporarily, was not in molding the child into a satisfactory adult but in reaching the child—in understanding children as they were.

This was the era in which the child study movement began to flourish, a movement characterized by efforts to develop a genuine science of child development and typified by the writings of the renowned American psychologist G. Stanley Hall (1844–1924). It was also the era in which early childhood educators moved away from the highly structured use of play in the classroom to a more flexible approach, which allowed for a greater amount of spontaneity and creative expression (Nawrotski, 2006). John Dewey (1859–1952) was the founder of the Progressive kindergarten movement, in which children's spontaneous play was seen as an opportunity for learning. This was the basis of the modern educational concept of play as a vehicle for child development and learning (Saracho & Spodek, 1995).

Even as the trend was beginning to move toward a greater appreciation of the individuality and special developmental characteristics of children, a new force was emerging in American psychology. This was the appearance, between 1910 and 1920, of the theory of **Behaviorism**, as set forth in the writings of the man who would be the most influential of all American psychologists, John B. Watson (1878–1958). Influenced by the ideas of John Locke, Watson also believed that the mind is a blank slate at birth and that people grow to be what they are made to be by the environment (Langer, 1969). "Give me a dozen healthy infants," wrote Watson, "and my own specified world to bring them up in and I'll guarantee to take any one at random and train him to become any kind of specialist I might select—doctor, lawyer, artist, merchant, chief, and yes, even beggarman and thief, regardless of his talents, penchants, tendencies, abilities, vocations, and race of his ancestors" (Watson, 1925, p. 82).

A Behaviorist Speaks About Childrearing
Some Thoughts From John B. Watson

John B. Watson was not only the author of the theory of Behaviorism; he also wrote many articles in popular magazines encouraging American parents to incorporate Behaviorist principles into their childrearing practices. This is an example of his advice:

Even granting that the mother thinks she kisses the child for the perfectly logical reason of implanting the proper amount of affection and kindliness in it, does she succeed? The fact that . . . we rarely see a happy child is proof to the contrary. The fact that our children are always crying and always whining shows the unhappy, unwholesome state they are in. Their digestion is interfered with and probably their whole glandular system is deranged.

There is a sensible way of treating children. Treat them as though they were young adults. Let your behavior always be objective and kindly firm. Never hug and kiss them, never let them sit on your lap. If you must, kiss them once on the forehead when they say good night. Shake hands with them in the morning. Give them a pat on the head if they have made an extraordinarily good job of a difficult task. Try it out. In a week's time you will find how easy it is to be perfectly objective with your child and at the same time kindly. (Watson, 1928, pp. 80–81)

Considering the importance of the environment in setting a person's developmental direction, it follows that parents must take an active—even aggressive—stance when raising their children. They must be firm, logical, and consistent, and they must realize that sentiment has nothing to do with childrearing. Watson even advised parents not to kiss or cuddle their children because cuddled children grow up to expect cuddling as adults; they become chronic complainers, always expecting sympathy from other people. (See the boxed item, which contains some of Watson's advice to parents.)

How did children's play fit into the behaviorist view of the world? Play was seen not as a valuable end in itself but as a means of bringing about social reform. Its value was that it could be a learning experience that allowed children to cultivate socially acceptable behaviors. A reader of the magazine *Parents* in the early 1930s wrote to ask, "Must boys fight?" The magazine's response was that fighting can actually have value in "cultivating strength and skill. . . . As our boys grow older they can be shown how the energy that might be spent in fighting can be utilized in wholesome sports or other worthwhile activities" (Leigh, 1931, p. 25). Perhaps she was responding to the Behaviorist emphasis on reinforcement when cultural anthropologist Margaret Mead wrote in the late 1920s that Americans tend to see play as a reward for work, rather than thinking of work and play as natural separate-but-equal features of everyday life.

In the mid- and later 20th century, there was a growing recognition that the perspectives on childrearing that typified the years through the 1920s were unduly narrow. Most post–World War II parents would consider John Watson's advice on childrearing both bizarre and cruel, for example. The trend in the past 40 years has been toward a degree of autonomy and freedom of expression for children that has no precedent in either ancient or modern history (Davis, 1976). Play has at last been accorded a place of significance in a child's development. Not only are children now *allowed* to play, but also it is believed that they *should* play because play affords the opportunity for intellectual and social development as well as for emotional release. Here we can see the influences of both psychoanalytic and cognitive-developmental theorists.

Before we conclude, however, that we have finally come to a total acceptance of children's play, we should recognize that many psychologists continue to wonder if we are as tolerant of play as we believe. Many (e.g., Hartley, 1971; Logan, 1977; Elkind, 1981, 1987) suggest that our acceptance of play—and of children in general—is highly conditional. Ruth Hartley (1971), one of the pioneer researchers in the area, worried that play is often misunderstood by parents and even by early childhood educators who see it as a natural part of childhood but one that has little developmental value. Cross-cultural psychologist Richard Logan (1977) suggested that even as we argue that children should be allowed to play, we unconsciously resent them for having the opportunity to do so while we adults must work to earn a living. David Elkind (1981, 1987) has expressed repeated concern that children today are being forced to grow up too fast and that childhood activities like play are being replaced at earlier and earlier ages with the "meaningful" life pursuits of educational and occupational success.

THEORIES OF PLAY

What is the value of play in a child's development? Is play necessary? What function does it serve?

In an effort to answer questions of this sort, psychologists have proposed a number of theories of play (see Table 1.2). As these theories are discussed, it is important to keep in mind that no one theory has ever been able to explain completely the significance of play in children's development. In fact, no one theory is adequate to explain any aspect of child development. Theories must be seen as only tentative models, helpful frameworks within which child development and behavior can be better understood.

TABLE 1.2 Theories of Play

Theory	Theorists	Reasons for Play	Greatest Benefits
Surplus Energy	H. Spencer	To discharge the natural energy of the body	Physical
Renewal of Energy	G. T. W. Patrick	To avoid boredom while the natural motor functions of the body are restored	Physical
Recapitulation	G. S. Hall	To relive periods in the evolutionary history of the human species	Physical
Practice for Adulthood	K. Groos	To develop skills and knowledge necessary for functioning as an adult	Physical, intellectual
Psychoanalytic	S. Freud, A. Freud, E. Erikson	To reduce anxiety by giving a child a sense of control over the world and an acceptable way to express forbidden impulses	Emotional, social
Cognitive-Developmental	J. Bruner, J. Piaget, B. Sutton-Smith	To facilitate general cognitive development To consolidate learning that has already taken place while allowing for the possibility of new learning in a relaxed atmosphere	Intellectual, social
Arousal Modulation	D. E. Berlyne, G. Fein, H. Ellis	To keep the body at an optimal state of arousal To relieve boredom To reduce uncertainty	Emotional, physical
Contextual	L. Vygotsky	To reconstruct reality without situational influences or restraints	Intellectual

Classic Theories

Early play theories, those that appeared in the latter part of the 19th century and the early years of the 20th, emphasized the biogenetic significance of play. That is, they described play as an instinctive mechanism that either promoted optimal physical development or reflected the evolutionary history of the human species. These theories were grounded more in philosophical speculation than in the empirical research that is characteristic of modern theories of play (Saracho & Spodek, 2003).

Herbert Spencer (1873), in his **surplus energy theory**, described play as necessary to allow children to discharge pent-up energy. He argued that nature equips human beings with a certain amount of energy to be used in the process of survival. If this energy is not used for that purpose, it must be discharged somehow, and children discharge their excess energy in play. Spencer was right in the sense that play can indeed be used to release energy; parents and teachers often notice that children are more relaxed after vigorous exercise. However, adults also notice the exact opposite phenomenon: A child will often play to the point of sheer exhaustion and appear to be even more energized afterward than before!

A view of play that was almost the opposite of Spencer's was expressed by G. T. W. Patrick (1916). The purpose of play, according to Patrick, was the renewal of energy. When children are tired and relaxed, play keeps them occupied and helps them avoid boredom while they wait for their natural energy supply to be restored. However, while such a theory might explain the sedentary play that children often engage in, how would it account for the rough-and-tumble play that also makes up a part of any healthy child's day?

G. Stanley Hall, one of the leading figures in the early years of American psychology—and one of the first to write extensively about childhood and adolescence—had a unique perspective on the meaning of children's play. In an article titled "The Contents of Children's Minds" (1883), he put forth his **recapitulation theory**, according to which each person's development reflects the evolutionary progression of the entire human species. An infant crawling about at play might be reflecting some unspecified period in human evolution when humans walked on all fours; a first grader playing "cops and robbers" might be reliving the experiences of a prehistoric ancestor whose daily activities included hunting and gathering food. Hall's was certainly an intriguing theory of play (and of human development in general), but it was based on a rather unsophisticated view of physical anthropology. It is a theory that would find little acceptance among developmental psychologists today.

A final biogenetic theory was expressed by Karl Groos (1901), who suggested that play is the body's natural way of preparing itself for the tasks of adult life. Just as a kitten chasing a ball of string is rehearsing skills that will later be used in stalking food, the child who plays "house" may be preparing for the experience of someday running a household. In fact, much of children's play does resemble adult activities, particularly when children begin to explore adult roles in dramatic play. However, many children's play activities bear little real resemblance to activities pursued in adulthood and can be seen as preparation for adult life only in the most general sense.

Contemporary Theories

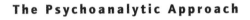

None of the early play theories, with their emphasis on instinctive—and often unspecified—biological mechanisms, has strong advocates among modern psychologists, although each contains at least some element of truth. More typical of the modern view are theories that emphasize the psychological value of play and its significance to a child's intellectual, social, and emotional development. Let us turn now to an examination of some of these contemporary theories.

The Psychoanalytic Approach

© Brand X Pictures

Psychoanalytic theorists believe that an infant playing with a toy derives a sense of power that helps relieve objective anxiety.

According to psychoanalytic theorists, most notably Sigmund Freud (1856–1939) and Anna Freud (1895–1982), play's value is primarily emotional in that it allows children to reduce anxiety (Freud, 1974). But why would a child suffer from anxiety in the first place? There are two types of anxiety that characterize the years of infancy and childhood.

Objective anxiety is fear of the external world. Infants and young children realize their helplessness and know that they must rely on the good will of others to have their basic needs met. The fear of abandonment is particularly strong in early childhood, and this is not surprising since a child, unlike an adult, needs a caretaker for its very survival. Play reduces objective anxiety by giving a child the illusion of power and control. The rattle a baby plays with becomes an extension of the body and provides the child with a greater sense of power. An older child building a tower of blocks or playing with dolls or miniature life toys is reducing the ordinarily large and overwhelming world to a size that he or she can handle. Play provides at least the temporary illusion of being in command. In much the same way, the child who plays at being a monster can, by reversing roles, allay a fear of monsters, and the child who punishes a doll can work through anxiety at being punished by a parent.

A second form of anxiety experienced by children is **instinctual anxiety**. Anna Freud (1974) observed that "the human ego by its very nature is never a promising soil for the unhampered gratification of instinct. . . . Its mistrust of their demands is always present." She added that "the effect of the anxiety experienced by the ego is . . . [that] defense mechanisms are brought into operation against the instincts, with all the familiar results in the formation of neuroses and neurotic characteristics" (pp. 58–59).

Psychoanalytic theorists noted that many of a child's feelings, including anger, unreasonable fear, sexual curiosity, and the wish to be messy or destructive, are frowned on by adult society. Since the powerful adults in his or her world disapprove of these feelings, the child comes to fear expressing them, and soon the very feelings themselves, whether or not they are translated into behaviors, trigger a reaction of anxiety in the child.

Play allows the child to explore unwelcome feelings without the repercussions of adult disapproval. For instance, the desire to break a window, strike a playmate, or wallow in the mud may frighten a child, but in play the child is free to be both destructive and messy, within limits of course. Many timid children become aggressive when squeezing and pounding ceramic clay, destroying a sand castle, or punching a Bobo doll, and the cleanest, neatest children are often the first to be covered to the elbows in finger paint.

The psychoanalytic perspective on play is also reflected in the writings of Erik Erikson (1902–1994). Erikson rejected as unduly narrow Freud's view that the major function of play was anxiety reduction. He suggested that play can also have an ego-building function, since it brings about the development of physical and social skills that enhance a child's self-esteem. During the first year of life, play centers on the exploration of the child's own body. In the gradual recognition of their sensory and motor skills (e.g., looking, listening, talking, walking) and in the exploration of their own bodies (e.g., playing with their hands and feet), children come to have an understanding of themselves as different from other people. Erikson called play with one's own body **autocosmic play**.

Children in the second year of life begin to go beyond their own bodies in play and to acquire mastery over objects, including toys. This form of mastery play further enhances the ego, and Erikson referred to it as **microsphere play**.

PUTTING THEORY INTO PRACTICE 1.2

Making Sure That Play Is Really Play

If a child is not enjoying what is supposed to be a play activity, for that child the activity is not play at all. Find ways to increase the child's enjoyment (e.g., by teaching appropriate skills or offering encouragement), or direct the child to an activity that is more appropriate.

If a child does not find an activity enjoyable, it is not play. However, a lack of enjoyment may not mean that the activity is inherently uninteresting or that it could not become play under the guidance of a sensitive adult. Sometimes a child's inability to enjoy what others see as play may result from social anxiety, lack of self-confidence with the material, or uncertainty about what is expected. In addition, some play materials are more approachable than others. For example, blocks may be the least intimidating of materials because they are clean, relatively indestructible, and familiar to most young children, and they lend themselves easily to the creation of a product. A more fluid material, such as clay or finger paints, may cause discomfort in children who are fearful of making a mess or who tend to be product oriented in their approach to play.

It is not only play materials that vary in their appeal. Some play activities are more approachable than others. A child who has difficulty interacting with peers may find group activities stressful, with the result that activities requiring peer interaction and cooperation will be challenging to the point that they are not play at all. A socially uncomfortable child would be more comfortable in solitary or parallel play.

A sensitive adult will realize that not all play materials and activities are suitable for all children and that one child's play is another child's work. The most effective way to make sure that play is really play is to follow a few basic principles:

- Make sure that a variety of play options are available.

- Be sure that play materials and activities vary in the degree of social interaction that they require, as well as in the extent to which the materials could threaten an inhibited or insecure child.

- Make available play materials that facilitate but do not force social interaction. Blocks are an excellent example of such a material.

- Do not underestimate the need to provide instruction in the use of play materials or activities. Some children are experienced players. Others are not.

- Model play activities for children, and provide instruction in the form of gentle suggestions as the children are playing.

Finally, during the preschool years, children at play move beyond mastery of their own bodies and mastery of objects to mastery in social interactions. Playing with peers, sharing both fantasy and reality with them, and demonstrating skills in a social setting are all elements of **macrosphere play**, which again strengthens children's egos as they realize that they can be successful in the larger social world. Erikson suggested that successful macrosphere play helps children better understand their culture and the social roles that they—and everyone else—are expected to assume.

The Cognitive-Developmental Approach to Play

Rather than emphasizing its emotional value, cognitive theorists typically regard play as a tool for facilitating intellectual growth. Jerome Bruner (1972) and Brian Sutton-Smith (1967), for example, both maintained that play provides a comfortable and relaxed atmosphere in which children can learn to solve a variety of problems. Later, when children are confronted with the more complex problems of the real world, the learning that took place during play is of great benefit to them.

Perhaps the most extensive treatment of play by a cognitive theorist can be found in the writings of the Swiss biologist and philosopher Jean Piaget (1896–1980), the author of what is certainly the most influential of all theories of children's intellectual development. Piaget (1962, 1983) maintained that a primary function of all living organisms is to adapt to the environment. Such adaptation is necessary for survival and can be physical, as when an overheated organism perspires to cool the body down, or psychological, as when people adapt their ways of thinking to incorporate new information presented to them. Physical adaptation is necessary for the survival and growth of the body; psychological adaptation ensures the continued growth of the intellectual structures of the mind.

Assimilation and accommodation. Adaptation involves two processes that usually occur simultaneously: assimilation and accommodation. **Assimilation** means taking new material from the outside world and fitting it into one's already existing structures. In a physical sense, the body assimilates food by digesting it. In an analogous manner, we are able to assimilate new intellectual materials—ideas, concepts, points of view—into the existing structures of our minds so that those new ideas eventually become incorporated into our own worldviews.

Accommodation is the adjusting of the structure in reaction to the newly incorporated material. Thus, the body accommodates food by salivating, by stomach contractions and the flow of gastric juices to break down the foreign substance, and eventually by growing and changing. So, too, the mind accommodates new intellectual material, as when a person adjusts his or her perspective on life, even ever so slightly, after incorporating a new idea. Growth, either physical or intellectual, will not occur unless *both* assimilation and accommodation take place.

Assimilation and accommodation generally occur at the same time, but there are instances in which one occurs to a considerably greater extent than the other. Play, according to Piaget, is the dominance of assimilation over accommodation. That is, it is the incorporation of new intellectual material into already existing cognitive structures without a corresponding alteration of the structures themselves. As a concrete example, 6-year-old Peter finds an empty cardboard box and determines that for his purposes it is not a box at all but a rocket that will take him to the moon. Thus, Peter forces reality to conform to his perspective rather than adjusting his way of thinking to fit reality. Piaget spoke of play as a consolidation of newly learned behaviors: A child first learns something new and then repeats what is learned over and over again until it becomes an established part of his or her repertoire (Rubin et al., 1983; Sutton-Smith, 1985). As an example at the level of motor activity, a child who is learning to use a skateboard must first learn how to stand on it without falling and must rehearse the basic maneuvers involved in balancing until these become firmly established routines. Only after the simpler motor patterns are consolidated can the child move on to more elaborate ones, but such consolidation obviously involves the rehearsal of old learning rather than the learning of something new.

Play and intellectual development. Piaget's primary goal was to create a comprehensive theory of children's intellectual development, and he treated play as a reflection of the development of thought rather than as a stimulus to intellectual growth. It was Piaget's contention that intelligence is sensory and motor in nature in the first year of life; becomes representational, or symbolic, in the second year; and begins to incorporate elements of logic at about the time the child is ready to enter school. These three stages are the sensorimotor stage, the preoperational stage, and the operational stage, and as will be seen in Chapters 3, 4, and 5, the stages are reflected in three very different forms of play—sensorimotor play, symbolic play, and games with rules. In that sense, play could be seen as reflecting intellectual development, and development could be seen as leading play.

While play is not synonymous with intellectual development in Piaget's theory, however, it can certainly facilitate development. For example, an infant's play with a rattle, a sponge, a ball, or a spoon could improve eye-hand coordination, balance, and physical strength and could teach about differences in size, shape, texture, and weight that characterize objects in the physical world. An older child who builds a fortress out of sticks might try to make it as realistic as possible and in the process might learn something about logical classification, part-whole relationships, measurement, balance, and spatial relationships. In that sense, make-believe play can lead to what Piaget called **games of construction**, which he saw as representing an area of transition between symbolic play and "nonplayful activities, or serious adaptation" (Piaget & Inhelder, 1969, p. 59). Finally, the rule-oriented games of the elementary-school child may not be engaged in for the specific purpose of learning and typically involve the consolidation of skills rather than intentional efforts to learn new ones, but they can easily stimulate intellectual growth. In such games, children learn to share, to remember and follow rules, and to acquire new skills as they move from one level of mastery to another.

Arousal Modulation Theories

A distinguishing feature of play is that it is intrinsically motivated. As we have seen, both psychoanalytic theory and that of Jean Piaget accepted the concept of internal motivation, whether it was to reduce anxiety or to consolidate previously learned activities. However, behavioral learning theorists in the United States (e.g., Hull, 1943) maintained that external motivation—and specifically the need to satisfy one's basic physiological needs—is at the root of even the most psychologically sophisticated behaviors.

The motivation for some behaviors, however, cannot be explained in terms of basic physiological needs; these behaviors include play and exploration of the environment. Human beings—and lower animals as well—play with and explore their surroundings simply because they want to; there is no reason for these behaviors that can be understood in terms of physiological need reduction. Learning theorists attempted to explain play, therefore, by referring to the concept of internal rather than external motivation and more specifically to the concept of arousal modulation.

The underlying premise of **arousal modulation theories** of children's play is that there is some optimal level of central nervous system arousal that a human being tries to maintain (Berlyne, 1969). The ideal environment, therefore, affords neither too much nor too little stimulation but just enough to keep a person optimally aroused. What is this optimal level? It falls somewhere between uncertainty and boredom. When there are new or confusing stimuli in the environment, the person feels confused and uncertain, and the level of central nervous system arousal is elevated. To reduce this level, the person must explore the environment in order to reduce its uncertainty. In contrast, when there is a lack of stimulation in the environment, the person is bored and seeks stimulation to maintain the desired arousal level. It is here that play comes in, because children use play to generate environmental stimulation where a sufficient amount does not already exist (Berlyne).

Similar views of play as arousal modulation were offered by Ellis (1973) and Fein (1981), who suggested that children's play provides a variety of forms of stimulation to an organism in need of it. Included are kinesthetic, or physical, stimulation; perceptual stimulation; and intellectual stimulation. Children at play produce novel effects and at first are made apprehensive by the uncertainty of the new situation. Later, however, as the uncertainty of the situation is reduced, the effect of play is generally positive. It is then that children will work to create new uncertainties, which they immediately proceed to reduce, thus perpetuating a cycle of creation and reduction of uncertainty. Indeed, children appear to enjoy activities characterized by degrees of novelty and risk, such as playing with fire, climbing trees, playing monsters, and so forth. Perhaps children include this element of danger, of limits testing, because they are seeking stimulation unavailable in nonplayful activities.

A Contextual Cognitive Approach: Vygotsky's Social-Historical Theory

All of the theories presented thus far have something in common: They are based on an unstated assumption that stages of play and reasons for play are universal, occurring in much the same way in children in every culture. **Contextual theories**, on the other hand, are rooted in the belief that a child's development cannot be fully understood without referring to the social-cultural and historical setting in which it occurs. In other words, child development can be understood only if we look at the overall picture, which might include the child's family history, economic circumstances, and degree of comfort in the current social setting. This global approach, which has become increasingly widespread in recent years among child development professionals, is represented by the writings of the Russian psychologist Lev Vygotsky.

Born in Russia, Vygotsky (1896–1934) was educated in literature and law before earning his doctoral degree in psychology. Perhaps because his education was so broad, he came to believe that psychologists view human beings too narrowly, focusing on the inner workings of the mind while sometimes ignoring the larger social context. For example, he criticized theorists such as Freud and Piaget for paying too little attention to the cultural context of development. As Vygotsky observed, "The developmental uniformities established by Piaget apply to the given milieu, under the conditions of Piaget's study. They are not laws of nature, but are historically and socially determined" (1962, p. 23). He also pointed out that "Piaget observed children at play together in a particular kindergarten, and his (findings) are valid only for this special child milieu" (1962, p. 23–24).

Vygotsky believed that there are two simultaneous lines of development, which continuously interact with one another. The *natural line* describes development from within; the *social-historical line* describes development from without. While the natural line is very important during the first two years of life, the social-historical line becomes increasingly influential after the age of 2. In other words, infant development may be largely explained by internal mechanisms, but development beyond infancy is heavily influenced by the environmental context in which it occurs.

Vygotsky argued that there are a number of acquired and shared tools that aid in human thinking and behavior—skills that allow us to think more clearly than if we did not have them and to better understand our own thinking processes. These include human speech, writing, systems of numbering, and various logical, mathematical, and scientific concepts. These tools are not intuitive but must be provided by formal instruction, and the role of parents and teachers is critical in transmitting their knowledge and beliefs to children (Maratsos, 2007). While the basic tools are found in virtually every society, the more sophisticated tools of scientific reasoning are available in some cultures but not in others; so development cannot be studied apart from its cultural context.

One of Vygotsky's more interesting concepts to those who study child development and education nicely illustrates the importance of the social context. This is his belief in the **zone of proximal development**. If asked to work independently on a problem, such as sorting objects according to shape or function, a child will display a particular level of performance. Vygotsky believed, however, that the child's performance may not reflect his or her true potential. If the same child is allowed to work with other children on the problem or is given direction by an adult, he or she might perform at a higher level than when working alone. The distance between the child's actual performance when working alone and his or her potential ability in a different social context is the zone of proximal development.

Vygotsky's concept of the zone of proximal development has major implications for those who study child development in general and children's play in particular. It seems clear, first of all, that development does not depend only on internal mechanisms but can be enhanced by appropriate social experiences. Educators can observe the child in his or her zone of proximal development, create appropriate learning experiences that build on the child's existing understanding (a process known as "scaffolding"), and actually further the child's development. In that sense, learning leads development rather than simply reflecting the child's developmental level (Levykh, 2008).

It is also clear in Vygotsky's framework that anyone wanting to understand an individual child's behavior must observe that child in more than one social setting. A child may play unimaginatively in the block corner when alone, simply stacking blocks and then returning them to the shelves, but may soar into flights of fantasy and may use the blocks in more complicated ways when provided with gentle direction by an encouraging teacher. This point was illustrated in a study by Gregory, Kim, and Whiren (2003), who trained adults to recognize varying degrees of complexity in block construction and then had them observe children at block play and offer verbal support for creating increasingly complex structures. While the adults didn't interfere in the play and took a supportive rather than a directive role, they engaged in such verbal scaffolding as asking open-ended questions, thinking of possibilities out loud, and occasionally posing problems (e.g., "What would happen if . . . ?").

The result was an increase in the complexity of the children's block structures. One might assume that the next time these children play with blocks, they may reconstruct the experience inspired by the teacher but in their own imagination, without any external influences or constraints. In other words, symbolic play re-creates an experience in which knowledge and skills were transmitted to a child and thus may help him or her better understand reality. In that sense, play leads development (Vygotsky, 1978). It might appear that Vygotsky reduced the symbolic play of the young child to an imitative process, and in fact he did suggest that make-believe play is primarily an imitative process (Lambert & Clyde, 2003).

The necessity of taking a contextual approach seems more apparent in the United States today than ever before, since there is increasing diversity in what Vygotsky would have called the social-historical line. That is, U.S. schools are becoming more and more ethnically diverse, with 4 in 10 children in public schools being members of minority groups. When we study play, therefore, or any other aspect of children's development, we must be careful to look at what has been described as "children in relation" (Lubeck, 1994, p. 153).

Summary

Play has five essential characteristics. It is intrinsically motivated, freely chosen, pleasurable, nonliteral, and actively engaged in by the participants. Early theories of play emphasized its biological and genetic elements, such as its biologically determined role in releasing the body's excess energy or in preparing a child for adult living, while contemporary theories stress the emotional, intellectual, and social benefits of play. For example, the psychoanalytic perspective is that play is a defense against anxiety, cognitive theories emphasize play's intellectual value, and arousal modulation theories suggest that children play in order to provide themselves with an optimal level of stimulation.

From the time of the ancient Egyptians until the end of the Middle Ages in Europe, children were thought of as having special needs and special activities, including that of play. During the period of the Renaissance, however, children came to be thought of as having little importance compared with adults and were fully integrated into the adult world, in the sense that people of all ages worked and played together.

In the 17th century, a new consciousness of children developed. They were now seen as deserving attention and as having developmental needs and problems that were different from those of adults. The French were always more accepting of play than were the British. In France, play came to be seen as suitable only for children, while in England play was seen as a frivolous activity that interfered with a child's development of discipline and time for work. The Puritan legacy in the United States has been ambivalence about children and about the value of play: Compared with the British, Americans have been closer to their children and more indulgent with them, yet unlike the French, they have not fully accepted children's playfulness. Americans today, however, are more accepting of play and more aware of the special developmental characteristics and needs of children. Questions remain, though, about the extent of that acceptance. Some psychologists argue that we try to accept play but do not understand its functions, while others believe that we begrudge children the opportunity to play and make efforts to hurry them into adulthood.

Key Terms

Accommodation	p. 28	Games of Construction	p. 29
Arousal Modulation Theory	p. 29	Instinctual Anxiety	p. 25
Assimilation	p. 27	Macrosphere Play	p. 27
Autocosmic Play	p. 26	Microsphere Play	p. 27
Behaviorism	p. 19	Naturalism	p. 11
Contextual Theory	p. 30	Objective Anxiety	p. 24

Issues for Class Discussion

1. It has been found that young children may regard even a supposedly playful activity as work if it is assigned to them rather than freely chosen. How can a teacher suggest a playful activity to children yet avoid the impression of imposing it on them?

2. Why would practitioners in the field of early childhood special education put less emphasis on play than do those who work with "normal" children? Is this an understandable emphasis, or is it unfair to children with disabilities?

3. What is a theory? How are theories developed? What is their purpose?

4. How do the psychoanalytic and the cognitive theories of play reflect their different conceptions of human nature in general? Is it possible that both the psychoanalytic and the cognitive theorists are correct in their interpretations of children's play?

Chapter 2 ETHOLOGICAL AND CULTURAL PERSPECTIVES

One of the pleasures of owning a young pet comes from sharing in the almost limitless exuberance of its play. A young animal, such as a puppy or a kitten, is often a very appropriate playmate for a child. When we watch a puppy frolicking in an open field, chasing a ball, or engaged in mock fighting, we realize how similar such behaviors are to those of children, and we sense that there is a certain universality to play that cuts across human cultures and even across animal species.

In the first chapter of this book, we took the long view, examining children's play from a historical standpoint. Now we turn to what might be called a wide view, not looking to the past but comparing human and animal play in the present time and then examining the variety of playful activities observed in diverse human cultures. The purpose of these comparisons is not so much to learn about life in other societies or about the habits of lower animal species but to come to a better understanding of our own culture. Understanding the characteristics of animal play may provide us with insights into the significance of children's play; the study of life in other cultures may offer us clues about the values that are reflected in the play of U.S. children.

CHARACTERISTICS OF ANIMAL PLAY

As we begin our discussion of play in lower animals, there are four important points to remember. First, play is not easy to observe in all animal species and is most likely to be seen in those species, such as mammals and some birds, that are higher up the phylogenetic ladder (Reynolds, 1981). Even within categories,

Learning Objectives

After reading Chapter 2, a student should be able to:

✦ Recognize the similarities between human play and the play of lower animal species.

✦ Understand the role of play in the lower animal socialization process.

✦ Differentiate between aggressive play and genuine acts of aggression among animals and understand the functions of "mock aggression" in animal development.

✦ Define competitive games of physical skill, games of chance, and games of strategy and describe the type of culture in which each type of game predominates.

✦ Understand the relationship between competitive and cooperative play and identify the cultural conditions that foster the development of each.

✦ Describe the cultural and the subcultural differences that have been found in the prevalence of symbolic play and explain the possible reasons for these findings.

play is related to overall sophistication. Play among birds, for example, is most typically found in those with the largest brains, the greatest degree of behavioral complexity and fine motor control, and the longest growth period before adulthood (Burghardt, 2005).

Second, play is generally found only among the immature members of a particular species. It is rare among adult mammals, and when adults *do* play, their play occurs in the form of highly organized activities, in contrast with the spontaneous free play of the young (Gandelman, 1992). Human adults have been accused of forgetting how to play, but in fact the human adult is more likely to engage in play of some sort than are the adult members of most other animal species.

Third, the two forms of play on which it is easiest to compare human and lower animal species are (a) solitary manipulation of objects and (b) rough-and-tumble play; the social pretend play of a young child that will be discussed in Chapter 4 involves a huge range of activities, while the make-believe of other animal species is usually restricted to the area of play fighting (Power, 2000).

Finally, even though there are obvious similarities between human and animal play, we must be careful not to carry the comparisons too far. Research on animal play may be used to suggest possible explanations for human play, but a link between human and lower animal behaviors of any sort is far from being clearly established. We must be particularly careful not to impose human feelings or intentions on the behavior of lower animals since animal behavior, including play, is not governed by consciousness, rationality, or free choice.

Play as Simulation

Like human play, the play of animals is characterized by an element of pretense. In fact, the single most distinctive feature of animal play is that it involves taking skills ordinarily displayed in one context and applying them in contexts in which their true functions cannot possibly be achieved (Fagen, 1984). For example, a puppy may engage in playful biting in a variety of situations, such as when it spies the evening newspaper or its favorite old slipper. The "normal" context of biting, however, is in situations that require aggressive behavior, as when the animal is threatened and must defend itself or is in competition with another dog for the same piece of food.

The "pretend" component of animal play resembles the nonliteral component of human play discussed in the previous chapter and may explain why play is found only in the more sophisticated animal species. It takes a certain amount of plasticity, or flexibility, for an animal to display behavior patterns in a variety of out-of-context settings. Play can be thought of as a simulated type of activity. That is, it allows the player—animal or human—to try out behaviors without having to face any serious consequences. Real fighting could result in bodily harm or even death; play fighting is usually harmless, but it gives the animal a

© Photodisc

Children love to play with animals, and like humans, animals are very playful when they are young. Just as human play involves an element of pretense, animal play involves behavior that is out of context.

chance to try out skills that might someday be needed if a real fight should occur (Reynolds, 1981). Do animals who engage in a good deal of play demonstrate greater skills in real-world situations than do animals of the same species who rarely play? It appears that they do. What is not clear, however, is *why* they do. For example, Chalmers and Locke-Hayden (1985) discovered a relationship between amount of play and the possession of various skills (manual dexterity, agility, and the ability to compete for food) in young marmosets. Those who played the most later proved to be the most motorically skilled and the most efficient when it came to seeking food. However, there is more than one possible explanation for this finding. It might indeed be the case that the animals' experiences at play really caused an improvement in motor skills. It is also possible, however, that animals who are naturally the most skillful to begin with are the ones who play most often, either because of their greater innate ability or because they simply have more opportunities for play (Chalmers, 1984).

Play and Aggression

One of the intriguing features of animal play, particularly the play of mammals, is the frequency with which it contains elements of aggressive activity: chasing, pawing, hitting, biting, butting, wrestling, and scratching. It has been found, for example, that 80% of the play of young rats is aggressive in nature (Pellis & Pellis, 1987). Not surprisingly, four out of five articles about animal play deal with play fighting (Pellis & Pellis, 1998).

While prolonged, intense, nonplayful aggression may indeed be an indicator of emotional disturbance, human parents often condemn aggressive activity of *any* sort in their children and consider even playful aggression to be a sign of immaturity. It is interesting, however, to observe that aggressive play in animals actually indicates the maturity of the organism. The pattern of such play resembles an inverted U: It begins during infancy, increases until the animal is mature enough to establish its position within the hierarchy of the group, and then declines (Pellegrini, Dupuis, & Smith, 2007; Power, 2000). In fact, there is a correlation between the appearance of play aggression and the maturity of the frontal lobes of the brain. The frontal lobes are responsible for reflection, imagination, empathy, and play/creativity, and their development allows for greater behavioral flexibility and foresight and for well-focused goal-directed behavior. As the frontal lobes mature, play fighting decreases; frontal lobe damage is related to a higher level of playfulness (Panksepp, Normansell, Coc, & Siviy, 1995). For example, if the frontal lobes of young rats are reduced in size by surgery, the result is an increased level of playfulness and hyperactivity. However, when the rats who have undergone the surgery are given plenty of

PUTTING THEORY INTO PRACTICE 2.1

Dealing With Aggression in Play

Do not discourage children from engaging in aggressive play. It is normal for humans to play aggressively, as it is for lower animals. However, aggressive play needs to be carefully monitored to prevent children from crossing the line between mock and real aggression.

Real aggression should never be accepted, and children who engage in real aggression should be monitored carefully, instructed in appropriate social behavior, and reinforced for prosocial acts. Adults should be particularly careful to ensure that aggressive acts are not the only reason that a child receives attention.

There are several points that a caregiver should attend to when determining if aggression is real or simply a form of play:

- When engaged in fantasy play, most children incorporate aggressive themes at some time or another, but they also incorporate prosocial and nonaggressive elements into their make-believe. However, some children always play aggressively, and this is an indicator that adult intervention is warranted.

- While a child may hurt another child accidentally in normal rough-and-tumble play, some children seem to use aggressive play as an excuse to bully or harm others. If a particular child always seems to be hurting other children and seems to be using play as an opportunity to hurt others, intervention is needed.

- Adults should differentiate between hostile and instrumental aggression. Hostile aggression is intended to hurt another person, while instrumental aggression is used to reach a specific goal such as playing with a toy that another child is using. Both are unacceptable. However, instrumental aggression can often be dealt with by modeling and directly teaching appropriate ways of getting things we want, such as waiting, taking turns, asking permission, or finding another toy to play with.

- The willingness of other children to engage in aggressive play with a particular child should be monitored. If a child usually seems to be pressuring or forcing others into aggressive play, intervention is needed.

opportunity to engage in rough-and-tumble activity, the decline in play with maturity is even more dramatic than the decline that occurs in the normal rat, leading to the speculation that rough-and-tumble play not only is related to frontal lobe development but actually may promote it (Panksepp, Burgdorf, Turner, & Walter, 1997).

Successful acts of aggression may earn for a particular animal a higher position of dominance in relation to its peers. In fact, some animals deprived of the opportunity to play seem to have difficulty becoming successfully aggressive as adults. Research on rats, for example, indicates that those not allowed to play do not seem to know how and when to defend themselves against an attack. Either they perceive a threat when there is none, or they fail to see a threat that is real (Einon & Potegal, 1991). One can imagine the socially disruptive consequences of such misperceptions for any animal—or for any society for that matter!

Although play in lower animals often resembles aggression, it also differs from serious acts of aggression in a number of ways. First, even aggressive play still seems to be a joyful experience; chimpanzees, for example, will fight in play, but at the time they will be displaying a "play face," a facial expression that indicates that their attacks on one another are all in fun. Second, unlike real aggression, aggressive play is altered so that none of the players will get hurt. Animals will put limits on their strength, particularly when playing with a younger partner (Bekoff, 1972). Third, aggressive play is characterized by role changes: A player may decide to go from being the aggressor to the victim and back again (Pellegrini & Smith, 1998). Such role changes would not occur in real fighting. Finally, there are pauses in aggressive play, as there are not in genuine incidents of aggression. Players may stop what they are doing to engage in a bit of exploration before going back to the original activity.

Why is there such a marked similarity between play and aggression in lower animals? Play seems to be a type of fine-tuned aggression—and one that appeared later in the evolutionary development of the species. The sophistication of play is that, at least in the case of playful aggression, the animal is able to inhibit an activity before it is finalized. A playful kitten may bite its owner's hand, but it knows when to relax its jaw pressure so as to avoid inflicting serious damage.

Play and Socialization

Even when play involves a high degree of mock aggression, it still provides opportunities for intense, prolonged intimate contact with peers. In fact, a relationship between animal play and socialization has been fairly well established in the research. Play in animals is related not only to their phylogenetic position but also to the extent to which they must adapt to their peer groups. Animals who must assume specific positions within a social order established by their peers are the most likely to engage in play, and this suggests that play is an adaptive behavior that can teach about communication, cooperation, and intention (Bekoff & Allen, 1998). Stable socialization patterns, or "social meanings," seem to be learned in the specific forms of play that are found in a variety of animal species (Brown, 1998, p. 255).

Among the earliest and most influential studies of social play was that of Harlow and Harlow in 1962 at the University of Wisconsin. The Harlows manipulated the amount of peer play that young rhesus monkeys could engage in. In one condition, monkeys were raised by their natural mothers but were allowed no contact with peers at all; in a second condition, monkeys were given a cloth mother substitute to attach themselves to as they would their real mothers but were allowed to play extensively with peers. The Harlows found that the monkeys raised by their natural mothers but prevented from playing with peers later appeared to be somewhat retarded in their social and sexual development. As a result, their age mates rejected them and even displayed aggressive behaviors toward them (Harlow & Suomi, 1971; Novak & Harlow, 1975). On the other hand, those allowed to engage in social play with peers later appeared to be socially and sexually normal, suggesting that social play provides important and necessary socialization experiences for rhesus monkeys and protects them from social failure in maturity (Suomi, 1991, 2005).

Can rhesus monkeys deprived of peer play ever recover as adults? It appears that they can. Although their age mates reject them, younger monkeys are apparently willing to play with them (Novak & Harlow, 1975). Thus it seems that the nature of monkeys' social play changes with age and that the type of play they engage in may serve one particular stage of development but not others; in other words, social play seems to serve different developmental functions at different ages (Vandenberg, 1978). Perhaps in social play the animal can try out certain behaviors in a safe setting; social blunders, if developmentally appropriate, will be forgiven by one's age mates. Such blunders will not be forgiven, however, if, as in the case of the Harlows' play-deprived monkeys, they are seen by peers as below their appropriate level of development.

As a closing comment about the role of play in the socialization process, it was mentioned earlier that play is rare among adults in nonhuman species. There are exceptions, however. These usually take the form of playfulness with a prospective mate or play between a parent and its offspring. In other words, play often takes on "the shape of love" and is involved in the most intimate of relationships at all points in the life span (Fagen, 1995, p. 36). Even in a purely sexual sense, play is related to socialization. For example, Fagen (1993) discovered that playfulness during childhood is a predictor of later reproductive success in baboons, probably because a well-nourished baboon is more likely to play and also more likely to reproduce successfully later on. In summary, play is intimately connected with the socialization process, particularly in primates, and may actually help some animals develop close relationships with peers when they enter adulthood, as well as help develop close relationships between parents and their offspring (Fagen, 1995).

Animal and Human Play

Now that we have discussed some of the general characteristics of animal play, we come to the ultimate question. What, if anything, can research on the play of lower animals tell us about the play of the human child? As was mentioned earlier, great care must be taken to avoid easy generalizations across animal species. However, there are some obvious similarities between the play of human beings and that of other mammals:

1. In all mammalian species, including humans, play is characteristic of the immature organism and is found in adults to a considerably lesser degree.

2. Play in all mammalian species involves an element of pretense, of the application of behaviors in out-of-context situations. In a sense, the organism at play is flexible enough to make reality conform to its own needs, rather than adapting its behaviors to the environment.

3. Play provides, for human beings and lower animals alike, an opportunity to practice, in a safe setting and without consequences, many of the skills that are needed for success in the real world. In that sense, play allows the imma- ture animal to prepare for adulthood, although this should not be taken as evidence that such practice is the sole—or even the major—purpose of play.

4. Play allows for opportunities for intimate physical contact and intense social interaction, including the chance to experiment with social roles and role reversals. Play experience is related to successful social and sexual functioning in monkeys, and it certainly can be said that some forms of play promote social development in the human child.

5. Both human and animal play contains substantial components of aggres- sion, and this is particularly true of the play of males of all species that have been investigated (Pellis & Pellis, 1998).

An examination of the similarities in the play of the various mammalian species leads us to a number of tentative conclusions. First, play is a normal activity for mammals, particularly for those who are young. It is not an aberration. It is not something that animals do only because they have no more serious business to keep them occupied. Perhaps the animal research might be useful for those who sometimes find it necessary to argue that play is a normal activity for a human child. Unfortunately it is not so unusual to have to make such an argument in an age in which children are encouraged too early to take up the mantle of adulthood (Elkind, 1981, 1987) and in which nursery schools are often designed to start their pupils on the path toward Ivy League universities.

Second, children's play is a reflection of their flexibility, their adaptability, and their creativity. In play, they are distorting reality to suit their purposes, a phenomenon Jean Piaget (1962) described as the dominance of intellectual assimilation over accommodation. Such distortions of reality constitute a valuable intellectual exercise and one that demonstrates the intellectual sophistication of the human organism. Third, while this is not its sole purpose, play clearly seems to provide opportunities for the practice of skills that may be of use in other areas of life. Fourth, play in mammals is obviously related to socialization; in children, play promotes social development and may have an important role in teaching developmentally appropriate social skills (Athey, 1984). Finally, play allows children to display aggressive behaviors in a safe setting. Are such aggressive behaviors normal for human beings? Should they be encouraged, discouraged, or simply accepted for what they are? No one knows for certain, but aggressive behaviors are typical in young children, and if nothing else, play may provide a socially acceptable arena in which these behaviors can be demonstrated. It seems inappropriate to label a child as "aggressive" simply because he or she has a fondness for aggressive play (Power, 2000).

CULTURAL DIFFERENCES IN PLAY

Play has been observed in virtually every human culture, past and present. It is a true cultural universal. Even in societies in which there is little time for play, children somehow manage to make the time by integrating play into their work routines. For example, in the Kipsigis community in Kenya, children have numerous chores, yet they discover ingenious ways to make play of their work. Harkness and Super (1983) described the practice common among Kipsigis children of playing tag while they watched the cows or of climbing trees while they supervised their younger siblings.

PUTTING THEORY INTO PRACTICE 2.2

Helping Children Engage in Make-Believe

When working with a group of children, recognize that they may differ in the ability to engage in pretend play. Some may have had limited opportunities to pretend in the home and then have difficulty doing so in school.

While it isn't advisable for an adult to be overly intrusive in children's fantasy play, it is appropriate for the adult to observe, make suggestions about themes if the children seem to be running out of ideas, and even occasionally assume a role that can then be handed off to one of the children. One strategy that works very well is to provide a script on which fantasy play can be based by reading a story and then having children act out the roles of the characters. At first the roles and themes may be based very literally on the story, but then they will become increasingly improvisational, particularly if an adult offers subtle guidance.

Children who are particularly low in fantasy predisposition can be recognized because:

- They often just observe fantasy play from the sidelines.
- They can't sustain fantasy play for very long when they do participate.
- They seem to fail to understand the roles assigned to them by other children.
- They need elaborate and realistic props, unlike a child with a rich imagination, who can play with minimal props.

For such children, realistic props should be available, suggested themes (e.g., stories on which to base the play) are especially helpful, and modeling of roles by an adult may be necessary. Children low in fantasy disposition may benefit if assigned to small play groups of three or five children. Included in such a group should be at least one child who is particularly imaginative and particularly supportive of others, as well as children who are average in fantasy predisposition.

On the other hand, vast differences in both the amount and types of human play have been observed both cross-culturally and within cultures. These differences have been found in object play and even more strikingly in symbolic play and in children's rule games. In addition, researchers who focus on human culture point out that the motivation for play may vary from one society to another, and it would be a mistake to assume that play in all cultures is similarly motivated (Gaskins, 1996; Keller, 2003). Clearly we cannot understand children's play unless we are familiar with the social and cultural context in which it occurs.

The Influence of Culture on Object Play

As will be discussed in Chapter 3, toddlers in the United States typically play in elaborate ways with objects, manipulating them, relating them to one another, and examining them as if to understand their properties. In some cultures, however, toddlers of the same age may simply pick up and drop objects, mouth them, or bang them. This was illustrated in studies by Suzanne Gaskins (1996, 1999) of play in the Mayan culture in the Yucatán Peninsula in Mexico. How might these cultural differences be explained? Gaskins (1996) observed that Mayan children have few objects to play with and none that we call toys in that they are designed specifically to encourage play. Mayan adults value play in young children only because it distracts the child and allows the mother the opportunity to get her work done. When adults engaged in object "play" with children, it was only to offer objects or take them away. Rarely did an adult talk about or suggest uses for the object. The motivation for the play was obviously not for the child to learn about the properties of objects or to engage in a social interaction, as it frequently is in the United States (Gaskins, 1996).

An interesting study of the influence of culture on object play was carried out by Keller (2003), who compared parenting approaches of German mothers with those of the Nso tribe in western Africa. Parents in each culture were videotaped while interacting with their infants and then were shown the videotape of the other group. In the Nso culture, the primary goal of parenting is to raise physically healthy children, and the emphasis is on breastfeeding, close body contact, and stimulation of the child's motor development. It is thought that a healthy child with accelerated motor development can earlier assume responsibility for successful family functioning. Object play—and play of any sort—was rarely observed; nor was there much in the way of mother-child eye contact. German mothers commented negatively on the lack of eye contact between Nso mothers and their babies, on the tendency of Nso mothers to pay little attention to their children unless they were distressed, and on the shaking engaged in by Nso mothers to stimulate their children's motor development.

German mothers on the videotape played with their babies, talked to them quite a bit, responded to signs of positive affect, and made a good deal of eye contact but were not overly interested in stimulating motor development. While the Nso mothers observing the German mothers often complimented them on talking to their babies, they were not critical of the episodes in which little talking occurred. The Nso mothers were critical, however, of the extent to which German mothers allowed their babies to lie quietly rather than stimulating their limbs.

If we applied our own standards and simply ignored the cultural context, we might conclude that the Mayan and the Nso children are developmentally less sophisticated in their object play than are the Americans and the Germans. This would be an erroneous conclusion. In fact, what the research indicates is that differences in object play suggest that different cultures place different values on the activity. They see it as serving different functions.

The Influence of Culture on Symbolic Play

If the object play seen in a particular culture reflects that culture's values and expectations for its children, can the same be said of other forms of play? For example, can the pretend play of preschool children tell us anything about the values of their elders? Apparently it can. There are significant cultural variations in the content of symbolic play, in its perceived functions, and in the overall amount that can be observed.

In terms of *content*, it is not surprising that children's make-believe reflects their life experiences. It has been suggested that children involved in dramatic play "work out the scripts of everyday life—adult skills and roles, values and beliefs" (Rogoff, 2003, p. 298). Children enact the roles that they have been exposed to. In cultures in which they participate regularly in the life of the community, children play out realistic adult social and work roles. In cultures in which they are separated from the world of adults, children are more likely to play out the roles of fantasy characters, such as those they have seen on television or in video games (Farver & Shin, 1997; Haight, Wang, Fung, Williams, & Mintz, 1999). Such role-playing may represent more than simple imitation. It may be preparation for the adult roles that the child will eventually play. For example, children in Botswana play what is called the "cow game," in which some children play oxen yoked with twine to a toy sled on which they pull dirt or other materials. Other children are the drivers who control the oxen, a skill that is actually required in adult life. As the children grow up and assume their work responsibilities, the game is played less and less, which indicates perhaps that it has served its function (Bock, 2002; Bock & Johnson, 2004).

As evidence of cultural differences in the perceived *functions* of symbolic play, consider the findings of Tamis-LeMonda, Bornstein, Cyphers, Toda, and Ogino (1992), who compared mother-toddler play in the United States and Japan, countries that differ considerably in their histories, cultures, and childrearing beliefs but resemble one another in degree of technological sophistication. The researchers studied the behavior of 38 American and 40 Japanese toddlers (average age: 13 months) and their mothers in a free-play situation in which a set of toys was provided but no specific instructions were given. It was found that the Japanese mothers encouraged their children to engage in interactive or other directed kinds of pretense. For example, they would prompt their children to kiss a doll or to offer the doll some food. The Japanese mothers seemed to view the play activity as an opportunity to teach their children to communicate and to interact with others. American mothers, on the other hand, emphasized the functional uses of toys ("Push the bus") and spoke more than did the Japanese about the characteristics of the toys themselves. The Americans seemed to be using play to teach their children about the world and to encourage them to explore it on their own.

The observed play differences mirrored the findings that emerge consistently from comparisons of Japanese and American mothering patterns (Stevenson, Azuma, & Hakuta, 1986). American mothers typically emphasize independence in their toddlers and encourage them to assert themselves both physically and verbally. Americans also direct their children's attention to the features of the environment and encourage them to explore. Japanese mothers put greater emphasis on drawing their children close to them and encouraging them to be dependent. Adapting to the needs of and maintaining good relationships with other people seem to be a higher priority in Japanese than in U.S. society. Not surprisingly, these values seem to be reflected in the make-believe play of American and Japanese children. American caregivers tend to be more directive than those who are Japanese. For example, they try to move the play forward by offering clear suggestions, while Japanese mothers rely less on their authority role and instead let the children initiate play activities (Shapiro, Ho, & Fernald, 1997).

Cultural variations in the *amount* of symbolic play were illustrated by Gaskins (1999) in her previously mentioned study of play among Mayan Indian children. In the United States, symbolic play is the dominant play activity during the preschool years, it is highly valued by adults, and it is even seen as necessary for optimal development. Among the Mayan children, however, symbolic play is extremely rare. Gaskins (1999) observed a 5-year-old Mayan boy for a total of 9 hours and observed not a single episode of make-believe play. She observed two little girls, one of whom was 20 months old and the other 3.5 years, and observed only three episodes of make-believe play. Unlike parents and teachers in the United States, Mayan parents do not see play of any sort as essential for development. Mothers tolerate it because it keeps children occupied; fathers actively discourage it because it keeps children from their work. It is hardly surprising that Mayan children refrain from make-believe play, and it doesn't suggest that they are unable to play imaginatively. In addition, there is no evidence that children in cultures in which there is little fantasy play are at a disadvantage later on either socially or cognitively (Chen & Kaspar, 2004).

To observe cultural variations in symbolic play, one does not need to make cross-cultural comparisons. Even within the United States, a society characterized by an increasing amount of ethnic diversity, cultural groups vary considerably in their appreciation of symbolic play. Needless to say, if make-believe is less apparent in one particular ethnic group than in another, this difference is more likely to reflect cultural expectations than basic play deficiencies.

An example of ethnic diversity in play within the United States can be seen in several studies of the social pretend play of Korean-American preschool children (Farver, Kim, & Lee, 1995; Farver & Shin, 1997). Psychologist Jo Ann Farver of the University of Southern California and her associates found consistently that social pretend play occurred less often in all-Korean preschools than in schools attended primarily by Anglo-American children. Even though the teachers in the Korean schools were Korean Americans educated in universities in the United States, they still emphasized traditional Korean values. They saw the purpose of nursery school as teaching academic skills and encouraging task perseverance and passive involvement in learning. The school day was highly structured, creative play materials were not available to the children, and play of any sort was rarely seen. By contrast, teachers in the Anglo-American schools typically encouraged independent thinking and problem solving, engaged the children actively in learning, and provided numerous opportunities for social interaction and play. Not surprisingly, social play—and social interaction in general—occurred more often in those environments in which it was encouraged.

Perhaps the most frequently cited study of cultural differences in sociodramatic play is Smilansky's (1968) analysis of two groups of Israeli children aged 3 to 6. One group was of European descent and was identified as middle class; the second group, of North African parentage, was categorized as lower class. Smilansky found that among the lower-class children there was significantly less sociodramatic play, defined as imitative role play, make-believe play with objects, social interaction, and verbal communication. She suggested in explanation that lower-class parents may provide less direct training in and offer less encouragement for pretend play and that lower-class childrearing techniques may inhibit the verbal, social, and cognitive skills that promote the development of fantasy in children.

Results similar to Smilansky's were found in studies of children within specific cultures in a variety of areas throughout the world (Gaskins, 2000; Gosso, Morais, & Otta, 2007; Gosso, Otta, Morais, Ribeiro, & Bussab, 2005; Haight et al., 1999). To be sure, there have been studies (e.g., Dyer & Moneta, 2006; Taylor, Wiley, Kuo, & Sullivan, 1997; Weinberger & Starkey, 1994) that arrived at the opposite conclusion that there were no measurable social class differences in pretend play, but these results constituted a minority opinion.

In summary, the research to date is characterized by a fairly consistent pattern of social class differences in make-believe play. What is not known, however, is why these differences exist, and there is much disagreement as to whether these differences should be thought of as deficits in need of correction. Might the socioeconomic status differences reflect differences in basic cognitive ability, in stress levels, or in the closeness of parent-child attachment, all of which could affect the quality of make-believe play?

There are indicators that pretend play differences cannot be attributed simply to basic intellectual deficits. For example, Doyle, Ceschin, Tessier, and Doehring (1991) studied the group pretend play of kindergarten and first-grade children identified as having either lower or middle socioeconomic status. They found, as expected, that children in the lower-socioeconomic-status group spent less time at such play, but there was *no* relationship between the quality of pretend play and measures of children's cognitive abilities.

One major criticism of many of the studies in this area is that the situational effects of testing were not properly considered. Schwartzman (1984) pointed out, for example, that children's imaginative skills are usually tested in a school or laboratory setting and are rarely if ever looked at in children's natural surroundings. School may be a more natural and comfortable environment for a middle-class than for a lower-class child, however, and one in which a middle-class child will more easily display his or her imaginative skills. In fact, it has been found that lower-class children display a larger variety of verbal and social skills outside school than within it.

There are other aspects of the conditions of testing that need to be considered as well. A child from a poor family probably has fewer toys and, when asked to use toys as props in pretend play, may not know what to do with them (McLoyd, 1983). Perhaps, as Smith (1983) suggested, teachers should familiarize their pupils of low socioeconomic status with a variety of toys and play materials before testing their proficiency at symbolic play. In other words, the competence may actually be there, but children may not perform as well as they would be able to if the testing materials were not strange to them.

Since all the specific causal variables have not yet been identified, psychologist Vonnie McLoyd (1983, 1986) has argued that the evidence pertaining to cultural differences in symbolic play is still inconclusive. She further suggested that in much of the research on socioeconomic status differences in pretend play, no clear and consistent definition of social class was established. In some cases, several factors, including occupational status, family income, and educational attainment, were used to determine a child's social class, but in others, class was determined simply by asking the parents of the children involved to categorize themselves. Until there can be consistent definitions of the concept of social class, it will be difficult to arrive at any firm conclusions about the effects of culture on children's symbolic play.

The Influence of Culture on Competitive Games

The competitive game is a form of play in which participants follow established rules as they compete against one another with the intent of winning. Before discussing cultural variations in competitive games, it should be noted that there are many cultures that seem to have no competitive games of any sort. What types of societies are these? Bonta (1996) summarized the research on a variety of what he called "peaceful societies" (p. 406), in which violence and aggression were seen as unacceptable, and observed that children in such societies did not engage in competitive games. Children are intentionally raised to avoid competition, which is equated with violence and aggression. An approach that parents use is to devote a great deal of attention to their children until they are 2 or 3 years old and then to virtually ignore them. The intent is that the children do not feel special but feel instead like minor members of the social group. In those cultures, the parents model nonviolent and noncompetitive behaviors, and parents and teachers talk explicitly to their children about the value of cooperation over competition. The apparent result of such practices is that children engage only in cooperative play, such as showing off their physical skills, telling stories, or playing out adult roles.

Despite the absence of competitive play in some cultures, competitive games have been observed in most cultures. However, these games vary considerably

© Photodisc

Basketball is a game that involves physical skill, an element of chance, and intellectual planning. In that sense, it could be described as a game of strategy.

in type. The outcome of some competitive games depends solely on the physical skills of the players; in others, the outcome is influenced by chance factors over which the players have little control; and in a third group, the ability to make rational decisions determines who will win and who will lose.

In **games of physical skill,** the outcome is determined only by the physical skills of the players (Sutton-Smith & Roberts, 1981). A foot race is an example, as is a weightlifting competition. The outcome in both cases depends not on chance or on mental strategy but totally on the physical prowess of the competitors.

Games of physical skill are generally the only forms of competition found in simple cultures of limited technological sophistication, in which day-to-day survival depends on the possession of specific motor skills. In hunting-and-gathering societies, for example, the ability to use weapons effectively is essential, as is among jungle-dwelling peoples a certain proficiency at using sharp instruments to cut through the dense undergrowth. The element of play comes in when the same skills used in work are demonstrated in playful competition. For example, the games of hunting societies include foot races, competitive tracking, and spear-throwing contests. The play of tropical jungle dwellers often involves demonstrations of speed and skill in the use of a machete or similar instrument. In other words, it appears that the games rely on the same physical skills, with minor variations, that are needed in work; the difference is that in play the skills are exhibited in an atmosphere of enjoyment and relaxation.

The outcome of **games of chance** is determined by sheer blind luck. Whether a player wins or loses may depend on the roll of a die or the spin of a wheel. As could be expected, such games are typical of societies in which fate plays a large role in everyday life. These are highly diverse and geographically widespread peoples whose common characteristic is that their fortunes depend on factors they cannot control (Sutton-Smith & Roberts, 1981). Thus, they learn to live with a high degree of individual, social, and environmental uncertainty.

Cultures that emphasize in play the element of chance that dominates their lives include nomadic peoples who wander in search of an uncertain livelihood and whose very existence is determined by uncontrollable variables, such as weather conditions. Since rationality seems to be of little use, such peoples often turn to religious rituals and divination in making decisions about the future; prophecies based on a "reading" of the entrails of an animal may be as valid a method of decision making as any other.

Games of strategy are those whose outcomes are determined by the rational choices made by the players and are found in cultures that are technologically advanced and highly complex. Survival—or perhaps we should say success—depends on a person's ability to make correct rational choices and not to any considerable degree on physical skills or on the whims of fate.

Included in the category of games of strategy are board games (e.g., Monopoly, checkers, or chess), card games, computer games, and a wide variety of games that involve guesswork or memory (e.g., 20 Questions, Charades, Concentration). Included also are highly organized sports that, although obviously dependent on the physical skills of the participants, also require creativity, planning, strategy, and the ability to imagine oneself in the role of one's opponent.

The three types of games can be arranged in a hierarchy that is reflective of cultural complexity, with games of physical skill at the bottom and games of strategy at the top. That is not to say, however, that one type of competitive game is better than another in an absolute sense or that people who engage only in games of physical skill are less intelligent than those who play games of strategy. The hierarchy is based only on cultural complexity and tells us more about environmental conditions in which a society finds itself than about the basic abilities of individual society members. As Sutton-Smith and Roberts (1971) concluded, "In games, children learn all those necessary arts of trickery, deception, harassment, divination, and foul play that their teachers won't teach them, but that are most important in successful human relationships, in marriage, business, and war" (p. 86).

The Competition-Cooperation Balance

In the United States, parents often complain that their children are encouraged at too early an age to become involved in competitive play. If we could just eliminate competition, these parents argue, children would instead play cooperatively. The assumptions of such a point of view are that (a) competition and cooperation are mutually exclusive categories of play, (b) competitive play is inherently psychologically damaging to children, and (c) if competitive play did not exist, it would automatically be replaced by cooperation. In fact, all of these assumptions are incorrect.

In the first place, it is inaccurate to think of competition and cooperation as mutually exclusive categories. Few cultures are exclusively cooperative or exclusively competitive in their play, and perhaps it could be argued that most social interactions among children involve elements of both cooperation and competition (Richard et al., 2002). Indeed, most children in most cultural settings play *both* competitively and cooperatively, often within the same game, and in some societies group competition is encouraged precisely because it encourages cooperation and group loyalty. To understand this apparent contradiction, consider the example of a baseball player who is competing with members of the opposing team to win the game but is at the same time intensely involved in cooperation with his or her teammates. The perception of a common enemy can foster cooperation, and as games become increasingly complex, the players' willingness to cooperate in fulfilling their interdependent roles becomes increasingly essential (Parker, 1984).

Another factor to consider when examining competition in the play of children is that it is probably the case that there are different types of competition. It has been suggested, for example, that there is a vast difference between competition to show that one is better than others and competition that reflects a personal desire to be successful; the former is referred to as *other-referenced competition* while the latter is called *task-oriented competition* (Schneider et al., 2006). Children themselves certainly know the difference between the two forms of competition. Those who compete simply to show their superiority to others are likely to be seen as aggressive and to be socially rejected. On the other hand, children who compete to achieve their own personal goals are likely to be socially accepted (Tassi & Schneider, 1997).

Is competitive play psychologically damaging to children? Apparently it need not be since children who compete do not usually forget how to cooperate. What is more, since children's play to some degree reflects the values of their culture, it is likely that when children are highly competitive in their play, their elders are highly competitive as well. Indeed, one could argue that competitive play can help prepare a child for the necessary competition of the adult world. In the United States, children, as we shall see, engage in a considerable amount of competitive play, but they also live in a society in which individual self-determination and individual achievement are valued adult characteristics and in which the ability to compete for success is a necessity.

Cultural Predictors of Competition

Cultures that are affluent, technologically advanced, and highly complex are likely to have the highest levels of competition in the play of their children. Those that are dependent on a subsistence economy in which people seem to live from hand to mouth are the least likely to tolerate competition in play (Kagan & Madsen, 1972; Knight & Kagan, 1977; Shapira, 1976; Sutton-Smith, 1980). It seems that in simpler cultures people must cooperate within their family units in order to guarantee their very survival. When resources are scarce, it is adaptive to share. If a child in such a culture were to compete for a larger portion of food, he or she would be criticized by adults on the grounds that if one person earns more, other family members must receive less. Thus, competition is selfish, has little adaptive significance, and is tolerated neither in play nor in any of the other activities of daily life. In more complex cultures, however, there is less sense of community, and individuals are expected to compete to ensure the economic survival of their families. Competition is valued among adults, therefore, and is also valued—or tolerated at least—in the child's world of play (Madsen, 1971).

Not surprisingly, cultures in which survival is a day-to-day affair are likely to emphasize **collectivism**, stressing the importance of group goals, group loyalty, and group identification. They also encourage communal labor and communal property and discourage the formation of potentially divisive allegiances to subgroups like the family. An emphasis on **individualism**, on the other hand, is characterized by a belief that loyalty to self comes before group loyalty, that people should develop their own individual identities rather than identifying with the group, that the purpose of work is more to benefit individual workers and their families than it is to benefit the state, and that individuals have a right to own property (Smith, Bond, & Kagitcibasi, 2006). It should be pointed out that individualism and collectivism are matters of degree. They should be thought of as points on a continuum rather than mutually exclusive categories. Most cultures have aspects of both collectivism and individualism (Tietjen, 2006).

In the United States, the emphasis is on individualism rather than collectivism. Our goal is to raise human beings who have a sense of individual autonomy and individual initiative. Our children have their own possessions; sharing may be encouraged, but there is no question that it is *their* property that they are being asked to share. Cooperation is valued, but so is competition, and it is through their competitive efforts that children can demonstrate their individual accomplishments and enhance their personal status (Sutton-Smith & Roberts, 1981). Children in the United States—and particularly those of northern European extraction—seem drawn to competitive approaches that draw attention to their own uniqueness and individuality (Lehman, Chiu, & Schaller, 2004).

Is the U.S. sense of individualism represented in the play of U.S. children? To answer that question, Madsen (1971) developed an interesting technique to measure cooperative and competitive efforts in children's play: the Madsen Cooperation Board (see Figure 2.1). Four children sit at a table around an 18-in. square board, one child at each corner. The board is covered with paper, on which four target circles are drawn; at its center is a weight, attached to which is a pen with the point facing down and touching the board. Four strings are connected to the weight, each running to a separate corner of the board, through an eyelet hook, and into the hands of one of the players. The children are able, therefore, to draw on the paper with the pen by simply pulling on the strings. Actually it is not so simple a task at all, depending on the extent to which the players are willing to cooperate with one another.

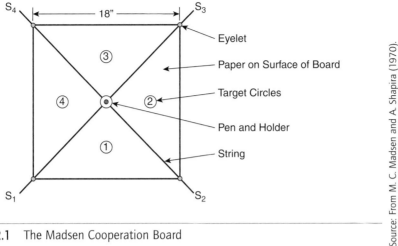

Source: From M. C. Madsen and A. Shapira (1970).

FIGURE 2.1   The Madsen Cooperation Board

In a cooperation condition, the four children are told to work together to draw lines across each of the four circles in numerical order. They are promised that every time a circle is crossed, each of them will receive a piece of candy, but they are warned that no one will receive a reward unless everybody else does. Children typically have little difficulty earning their rewards after being given this set of instructions. In the competition condition, some groups of players have a much more difficult time of it. The children are told that a circle has been designated for each of them, with his or her own name on it, and that a child will get a reward only if the pen crosses his or her circle.

It is obvious that, even in the competition condition, the strategy that will earn the greatest rewards on the Madsen Cooperation Board is cooperation. If all the children pull their strings at the same time, no player will be able to move the pen in the direction of his or her circle. If, on the other hand, the children decide to cooperate, each of them can easily earn a reward; they can simply agree to take turns at winning, with one child at a time being allowed to pull the pen in his or her direction while the other three willingly release their strings.

A vast amount of cross-cultural research using the Madsen Cooperation Board or similar devices suggests that there are dramatic cultural differences in children's ability to cooperate when they play. For example, rural children seem to cooperate better than children who live in cities; children from cultures that are less technologically advanced cooperate better than those from more sophisticated Westernized cultures; Mexicans—and even Mexican Americans—display a greater amount of cooperation than do Anglo Americans (Kagan & Madsen, 1972; Shapira & Madsen, 1974).

Children in the United States tend to be extremely competitive as a group compared with children in other cultures, even when such competition is clearly counterproductive. To understand why, let us look at differences in the attitudes of U.S. and Mexican mothers toward the performance of their children. Mexican mothers appear to be more likely than U.S. mothers to reward their children even for failure, to praise them because at least they tried. They are also more likely to actively discourage aggression toward peers. Mothers in the United States choose more difficult goals for their children and are less willing to lower their expectations if their children fail to meet those goals; they tend to encourage their children to keep trying rather than admit defeat. It seems that the Mexican mothers responded more to how their children were feeling than to the child's level of accomplishment, whereas for the U.S. mothers the pattern was reversed (Kagan & Madsen, 1972; Knight & Kagan, 1977).

Before leaving the subject of cultural differences in competitive games, we should point out that culture is a complex concept, and there is a danger in making comparisons that could be too simplistic. Easy generalizations often result in unfortunate stereotypes. The Madsen Cooperation Board represents an experimental approach to examining cultural differences in competition and cooperation, and many researchers argue that experimental approaches give an incomplete picture of cultural variations. Therefore, the results of the studies discussed above are certainly suggestive of differences, but they should be interpreted with caution.

Experimental approaches have been criticized in recent years for many reasons. First, it is argued that the conditions of the Madsen Cooperation Board game—or any task of that sort—do not reflect children's everyday reality; in other words, such tests are artificial measures of cultural differences. Second, it has been suggested that the amount of competitive behavior displayed may depend on what the children think is appropriate. For example, children might be competitive in other aspects of their play but might not see the Madsen Cooperation Board as an appropriate time to act competitively. Finally, there have been criticisms that the samples used by Madsen and other researchers were not representative of children in general. For example, the differences in competition between Mexicans and Americans were based on the performance of children from the same area of Mexico and from the same areas of Los Angeles. These children may not have been typical of children even in their own countries (Schneider et al., 2006).

The relationship between levels of competition in the play of U.S. children and the individualistic rather than collectivistic attitude that characterizes the

U.S. worldview is only that: a relationship. It would be unfair to say that we specifically train our children to be competitive since many U.S. parents and teachers work very hard to discourage childhood competition. In addition, typical general societal attitudes are not always reflected in the thinking or the behaviors of individual society members. It may be reasonable to speak of a "United States" perspective on the relationship between individuals and groups, but in a culture as diverse as ours, we would expect a substantial amount of diversity in individual points of view.

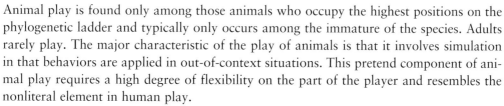

Summary

Animal play is found only among those animals who occupy the highest positions on the phylogenetic ladder and typically only occurs among the immature of the species. Adults rarely play. The major characteristic of the play of animals is that it involves simulation in that behaviors are applied in out-of-context situations. This pretend component of animal play requires a high degree of flexibility on the part of the player and resembles the nonliteral element in human play.

Play in animals resembles but differs from aggression in a number of ways. It is, first of all, a joyful experience, which aggression typically is not. Play also involves a withholding of strength in order to protect the players from harm. Finally, play differs from aggression in that there are pauses and even complete role changes in play, which are not found in acts of aggression. Play is also related to animal socialization; the most socially oriented animals are also the most likely to play. Play appears at just about the time that the animal is beginning to establish its position within the social hierarchy and may have a function in providing valuable social experience and defining social roles within the peer group.

Play has been observed in virtually every culture studied, although there is considerable variation in the amount of play and in the extent to which it involves competition or cooperation. Cross-cultural—and particularly subcultural—differences have been found repeatedly in research on children's symbolic, or make-believe, play. Lower-class children typically engage in less of this type of play than do middle-class children. It is still not known, however, which particular variables associated with socioeconomic status are responsible for the observed differences in the children's performance. Do they stem from differences in education, ethnic background, approaches to parenting, or familiarity with the props that are used to stimulate imaginative play? In fact, the research is characterized by a failure even to provide clear and consistent definitions of social class.

The greatest amount of competitive play is found in technologically advanced and affluent cultures, while competition is rare in underdeveloped societies, in which survival is a day-to-day affair. The type of competitive game that is played reflects the values of the particular culture, and the skills required in play resemble the skills that are necessary for success in life. Games of physical skill are most evident in societies in which physical prowess is necessary for work and survival. Games of chance depend on luck or fate and are emphasized in a variety of cultures that have in common a high degree of individual, social, and environmental uncertainty. The outcome of games of strategy depends on the ability of the players to make rational choices. These games are found in complex and sophisticated cultures in which intellectual strategies are required to achieve success.

Cooperation and competition are not mutually exclusive categories of games. Most children play both competitively and cooperatively, even within the same game. Nevertheless, competition is emphasized over cooperation in some cultures: those that are well-to-do and in which individual identity and achievement are valued more than group identity, loyalty, and dependence. Cultures that emphasize cooperation are either poor and underdeveloped or proponents of a collectivist philosophy, placing responsibility to the group ahead of individual identity and achievement.

Key Terms

Collectivism	p. 54	Games of Strategy	p. 51
Games of Chance	p. 51	Individualism	p. 54
Games of Physical Skill	p. 51		

Issues for Class Discussion

1. What, if anything, does the research on lower animals suggest about reasons for play in the human child? For example, does the research support the argument that human play in childhood is a form of preparation for adult life?

2. If the games of children reflect the values of a particular culture, what do the games of our children tell us about American society?

3. American children appear to be quite competitive in their play compared with children from other cultures. Why are our children so competitive? Is this a problem that we should correct or a condition that should be encouraged?

4. Choose a popular American game, such as football, baseball, tennis, or soccer, and discuss the extent to which the values of that game reflect the values of American society. For example, what is important for success in football that is also important for success in other areas of life?

PART II

The Development of Play

This section highlights the developmental emphasis of the book by describing play at different ages and, more important, by relating play to normal physical, social, intellectual, and emotional development. It is not sufficient for students of play to know what children do at particular ages. They must also realize that play both reflects and enhances development. In this section, play is discussed within the framework of developmental theories, such as those of Piaget and Erikson, as well as the major trends in developmental research, such as research on the development of social relationships.

Chapter 3

THE FIRST
TWO YEARS OF LIFE

At 5 months of age, Lauren seemed to have a great deal of curiosity about the world around her, so her father decided to see if she had any interest in play. He held a piece of paper in front of her, crumpled it noisily, and then offered it to her to see what she would do with it. She immediately reached out and grasped the paper and brought it to her mouth. Is this an example of infant play? The next day, Lauren's father tried the same experiment, and this time the child reacted not by reaching for the paper but simply by staring at it. Is this play?

Answers to our questions should become obvious as we proceed through this chapter, which deals with the play of infants and toddlers. There are several important points to be made here. The first is the rather obvious one that infants really do play, even during the first half-year of life. A second point is that a degree of interpretation is often required to know exactly when a baby is playing and when it is not, because play is defined not by specific behaviors but by the purposes that they serve. It is easy to know what an infant is doing at a given moment but more difficult to understand why. As an illustration of this point, when we attempt to distinguish between play and exploration, it will be seen that the behaviors involved in these theoretically distinguishable activities are often remarkably similar.

A third emphasis of this chapter will be an examination of the various, often related types of play that occur during infancy; these include motor play involving one's own body, play with objects, and representational, or symbolic, play. We shall describe the many forms of play, chart the progression of their development, and discuss the implications of their appearance for the process of child development in general.

Learning Objectives

After reading Chapter 3, a student should be able to:

✦ Understand the behavioral differences between play and exploration of the environment.

✦ Define sensorimotor play and describe the six developmental stages of such play during infancy.

✦ Identify developmentally appropriate play materials for children throughout the first two years of life.

✦ Understand that there are developmentally related qualitative changes in object play during a child's first two years and identify these changes.

✦ Be able to define symbolic play and describe its course of development throughout the second year in terms of increasing decentration, decontextualization, and integration.

✦ Identify the benefits of parent-infant play, understand how such play differs in quality from infant play with siblings or peers, and describe the characteristics of sensitive adult play partners.

✦ Describe the similarities and the differences that are found when mother-infant and father-infant play are examined.

✦ Understand the developmental progression of peer play during the second year of life and identify its benefits.

EXPLORATION AND PLAY

Much has been written about the relationship of play to exploration during infancy. In actuality, the behavior of young children cannot be fragmented into isolated segments since play, exploration, and a variety of other activities continuously flow from one to the other. An adult watching a preschool child might be hard-pressed to determine exactly when one type of activity ends and another begins. Exploration quickly evolves into play, and play often leads to further exploration of the world.

There are ways in which play and exploration can be said to differ, however, just as there are ways in which they are similar. In particular, the differences have most often been described in three areas: children's affective state, the amount of stereotypy in their behavior, and the focus of their attention (Wohlwill, 1984).

In terms of a child's affective state, exploration is often characterized as either a neutral or a mildly negative emotional experience, while play is seen as joyful and highly positive. When children are exploring their surroundings, they are cautious and serious. The mildly negative affect is said to result from the uncertainty they are feeling or the tension that goes with directing their undivided attention to a phenomenon (Hughes & Hutt, 1979).

When children are exploring, they behave in stereotypical ways (Hughes & Hutt, 1979). A child exploring the contents of her mother's purse, for example, might examine each item she finds by smelling it, tasting it, and rubbing it against her cheek in an almost ritualistic manner. In play, however, children are more flexible and more relaxed. They easily jump from one idea or activity to another, and play activities seem to be almost totally devoid of rigidity and stereotypy.

Finally, when children explore, they devote their attention wholeheartedly to the object of their exploration. They appear to be intense, their heart rates are steady, and they are unwilling to be interrupted. In play, however, children's heart rates are variable, and they are less intensely concentrated on what they are doing (Hughes & Hutt, 1979). Exploration comes before play. In unfamiliar surroundings a child first explores, but gradually, as the setting becomes familiar, exploration gives way to play. It seems that the child's attention is dominated by external stimuli that are unfamiliar and complex, but as the surroundings become familiar, the child increasingly dominates: The environment is increasingly likely to be mastered in play (Rubin, Fein, & Vandenberg, 1983).

TYPES OF INFANT PLAY

Turning now to a discussion of the various types of play that occur during infancy, we shall highlight three forms of infant play. *Sensorimotor,* or *practice, play* begins with the infant's accidental discovery of an activity that is inherently satisfying and consists of the continuous repetition of that activity for the sheer joy of doing it. *Play with objects* involves the intentional manipulation of objects, with a definite interest on the part of the player in the results of the manipulation. *Symbolic,* or *make-believe, play* is characterized by the use of mental representation, in which one object is allowed to stand for, or represent, another.

Sensorimotor play and symbolic play are different in terms of their developmental levels; the former is limited to activities of a physical nature, while the latter involves the use of mental representation (Piaget, 1962). Object play, on the other hand, is described in terms of the materials used by the players rather than as a particular stage of cognitive sophistication. In fact, objects are used in both sensorimotor and symbolic play, although in different ways, of course, and the developmental significance of object play is that within a given culture it tells much about the player's level of intellectual, physical, social, and emotional sophistication.

Sensorimotor Play

Much of a child's play in the first year of life consists of what cognitive theorist Jean Piaget called **sensorimotor play** or practice play (Piaget, 1962), the repetition of already assimilated sensory or motor activities for the sheer pleasure of repeating them. As can be seen in Table 3.1, Piaget (1962) suggested that such

TABLE 3.1 Piaget's Substages of Sensorimotor Development and the Types of Play Associated With Each

Stage	Intellectual Characteristics	Type of Play
1. Birth to 1 month	The dominant activity is the simple exercise of reflexes.	There is little in the way of play that can be said to occur during this substage.
2. 1–4 months	Primary circular reactions appear. Individual action sequences, such as sucking or grasping, begin to be coordinated.	Play occurs as the child repeats, for the sheer enjoyment of doing so, an activity that is oriented toward its own body.
3. 4–8 months	Secondary circular reactions appear, involving the repetition of activities not specifically oriented toward one's own body. There is a definite interest in the effects of one's actions on the external world.	In play the child repeats behaviors, such as crumpling a piece of paper or banging on a table, that have a pleasing or satisfying effect on the environment.
4. 8–12 months	There is the appearance of intentional, goal-directed activity, as when a child pushes aside a pillow in order to obtain a toy that is behind it.	The goal-directed infant often abandons the end in order simply to play with the means itself. For example, the very act of pushing aside the pillow becomes a joyful game, and the child seems to forget about the hidden toy.
5. 12–18 months	Rather than precisely repeating interesting events, the child now intentionally varies them to make them more exciting. This behavior is known as a tertiary circular reaction.	There is considerable variation in the action sequences of sensorimotor play, as the child immediately and intentionally complicates play experiences to make them more interesting.
6. Over 18 months	Symbolization—the child's ability to let one thing stand for, or represent, something else—emerges.	Sensorimotor play is increasingly replaced by symbolic, or make-believe, play, which will dominate the preschool years.

Source: Adapted from J. Piaget (1962).

play reflects the child's gradual intellectual progress through a variety of substages of sensorimotor development and thus develops gradually during the first 18 months before giving way to more sophisticated play involving make-believe. The developmental transitions in sensorimotor play are nicely illustrated by the behaviors that Piaget called circular reactions, which appear in three increasingly sophisticated forms.

Primary Circular Reactions

Among the earliest forms of sensorimotor play to appear is the **primary circular reaction**: A baby accidentally discovers an interesting sensory or motor experience related to its own body, apparently enjoys it, and later continues to repeat it. The primary circular reaction, a typical occurrence in babies between the ages of 1 and 4 months, is illustrated in Piaget's description of the behavior of his own 8-week-old son: Laurent "scratches and tries to grasp, lets go, scratches and grasps again, etc. . . . At first, this can only be observed during feeding. Laurent gently scratches his mother's bare shoulder. [The next day] . . . Laurent scratches the sheet which is folded over the blankets, then grasps and holds it for a moment, then lets it go, scratches it again, and recommences without interruption" (Piaget, 1963, p. 191).

Laurent's actions may appear at first to be play with objects rather than play centered on the child's own body, but actually this is not the case. The play is the physical action: the grasping, scratching, and letting go. Laurent appears to be fascinated by the actions themselves but has little interest in the objects he is performing the actions on. In fact, he will initiate the same scratching routine with any object that happens to be placed in his hand. This is the sense in which, even early in the first year of life, babies will manipulate objects; however, they will do so only if those objects are placed directly in their hands. Put a rattle in the hand of a 3-month-old, and the child will "play" with it by shaking, chewing, or simply looking at this interesting thing it has been given (Bayley, 2005). As will soon be apparent, however, such behaviors lack the elements of intellectual awareness and intentionality that characterize genuine object play.

Secondary Circular Reactions

After the age of 4 months, children continue to engage in circular reactions but of a noticeably different type (Piaget, 1962). Now they become interested in the external results that their actions produce. They perform what Piaget called **secondary circular reactions**, the repetition of behaviors that bring about pleasing effects on their surrounding world. Notice the difference between the following circular reaction performed by Laurent Piaget at 4 months and his behavior at 2 months described above. Lying in his crib, the child is looking up at some rattles tied to a string stretched above him. His father then attaches a watch chain to the rattles. "Laurent pulls . . . the chain or the string in order to shake the rattle and make it sound: the intention is clear. . . . The same day I attach a new toy half as high as the string. . . . Laurent begins by shaking himself while looking at it, then waves his arms in the air and finally takes hold of the rubber doll which he shakes while looking at the toy" (Piaget, 1963, p. 164). Thus, we can see that Laurent's interest has now shifted, at least slightly, from his own actions to their environmental consequences.

Tertiary Circular Reactions

While the infant between 8 and 12 months would have repeated an action in an attempt to prolong an interesting environmental result, the young 1-year-old goes a step further. Now the repetition of the previous stage is accompanied by an attempt to vary the activity instead of repeating it precisely, a new behavior referred to as a **tertiary circular reaction.** The playful element in this type of circular reaction is very clear, as the child appears to enjoy novelty and actively looks for new ways of producing interesting experiences. Consider the experimental approach of Piaget's 13-month-old daughter Jacqueline in her bath: "Jacqueline engages in many experiments with celluloid toys floating on the water. . . . Not only does she drop her toys from a height to see the water splash or displace them with her hand in order to make them swim, but she pushes them halfway down in order to see them rise to the surface. Between the ages of a year and a year and a half, she amuses herself by filling with water pails, flasks, watering cans, etc. . . . by filling her sponge with water and pressing it against her chest, by running water from the faucet . . . along her arm, etc." (Piaget, 1963, p. 273).

A good toy for an infant should stimulate as many of the senses as possible. A toy should have variety in color, shape, texture, and sound.

Play With Objects

Once the focus of a child's attention moves from the activities of its own body to the events of the outside world, the stage is set for the

PUTTING THEORY INTO PRACTICE 3.1

Selecting Infant Toys That React

When selecting toys for an infant, make efforts to find those that react when the child acts upon them.

Infants do not have many opportunities to make things happen in the world around them, yet they seem to be particularly interested in having an impact. Personality theorists talk about the need that infants have to develop confidence in their surroundings, and this comes when their behavior, such as crying, results in a predictable outcome, such as a positive response from a parent. Cognitive theorists talk about the motivation to display competence, or to be effective, which is enhanced when babies can literally make something happen in the external world. For example, Jean Piaget (1962, p. 91) talked about the "pleasure in being the cause" that is typical of infants.

The fact that babies enjoy making things happen in their surroundings is demonstrated by their interest in toys that react to their actions. They will actually spend more time playing with reactive than with nonreactive toys. What is a reactive toy? Put simply, it is one that responds to a child's action upon it. A wooden or plastic block may be interesting for grasping but is not reactive. However, a foam block is reactive because it will compress when a child squeezes it and then return to its original shape. If the child presses a button to release a toy from a box or turns a dial to make an interesting sound, the toy is reacting, and the baby discovers that what he or she does actually makes a difference. When selecting toys for babies, it is obvious that adults should ask if a toy is safe, if it stimulates a variety of the child's senses, and if it is age appropriate. A less obvious but equally important question is "Does the toy react to the child?"

appearance of play with objects. In addition to the player's interest in its surroundings, however, there is another obvious requirement for object play: the motor skills needed to grasp and handle play materials. This ability will also appear in the second trimester of the child's first year. Since toys are often the objects that infants are given to play with, and since the most successful toys for a child of any age are those that are developmentally appropriate, our discussion of object play will incorporate information about the preferred and most appropriate toys for the first two years of a child's life (see Table 3.2).

Birth to 3 Months

There is little to say about intentional object play during the first 3 months since the young infant spends much of its time lying on its back and cannot sit erect,

TABLE 3.2   Appropriate Toys for the First Two Years of Life

Age	Play Materials
Birth to 3 months	Toys that are primarily for sensory stimulation, since the infant is not yet ready to grasp objects: rattles, bells, colorful pictures and wallpaper, crib ornaments, mobiles, music boxes, and other musical toys.
3–6 months	Now that a primitive grasp has been acquired, toys for grasping, squeezing, feeling, and mouthing: cloth balls, soft blocks, and teething toys.
6–12 months	Colorful picture books, stacking toys, nesting toys, sponges for water play, mirrors, toy telephones with dials that move, toys that react to the child's activity.
12–18 months	Push toys; pull toys; balls to throw; plain and interlocking blocks; simple puzzles with large, easy-to-handle pieces; form boards, pegboards; stacking toys; and riding toys with wheels low to the ground.
18–24 months	Toys for the sandbox and for water play: spoons, shovels, and pails of various sizes. Storybooks, blocks in a variety of sizes, dolls, stuffed animals, puppets, and miniature life toys.

even with full support, until the age of 9 or 10 weeks and does not yet have even a primitive grasp (Bayley, 2005). While these developmental limitations do not preclude a discussion of appropriate toys for this age period, they do indicate that the primary value of toys for young infants is to stimulate the senses. Toys are for looking at, hearing, and feeling but not yet for physically manipulating.

Parents might wish to string colorful objects across an infant's crib, to surround the child with eye-catching pictures, and to provide bells and rattles for sound production. Intentional, premeditated sound production will not be observed until the age of 6 months, but the younger infant will ring a bell or shake a rattle if the object is placed in its hand, or by its movements in the crib it will cause a dangling object to sound. At first these actions will be accidental, but because of their pleasing consequences the child will make efforts to repeat them (a circular reaction).

3 to 6 Months

By the time they are 4.5 months old, infants begin to show signs of eye-hand coordination when reaching. It is also at about this time that, if seated at a table on the lap of an adult, they will begin to manipulate the table edge with their hands. Play with objects begins in earnest at 5 months, however. Now infants are able to reach out and pick up a block that is set in front of them, and they will soon begin to pass objects back and forth from one hand to the other. The 5-month-old will play with a piece of string or a piece of paper (by crumpling it) and will, sometimes to the annoyance of its parents, playfully bang a spoon or another object on a table.

The functions of play materials change as the infant begins to manipulate objects actively. Toys are now to be grasped and manipulated, as well as merely listened to or looked at. Is there such a thing as an ideal toy for a 3- to 6-month-old? A good toy obviously must be safe and have no sharp edges or small parts that can fit into the child's mouth. It must be sturdy and small enough to be grasped in one hand but large enough not to be swallowed. A good toy will also stimulate as many of the child's senses as possible. Adults are quick to recognize the value of visual stimulation but often fail to take account of the sound or the feel of a toy. Variety is a key element in the selection of a toy. Does the toy itself have much variety, and to what extent does it add variety in color, size, shape, sound, and texture to the child's existing toy collection?

6 Months to 1 Year

Children in the second half of the first year become quite mobile. By 6.5 months they will sit alone, and by 8 months they will creep or crawl a distance of 9 in. or more. They will pull themselves to a standing position by holding onto furniture by 9.5 months and will walk with help as they approach 10 months of age (Bayley, 2005).

Grasping skills continue to improve, and by the age of 9 months children are able to pick up objects using only the thumb and forefinger. In addition, they are able to bring objects together in play. If an adult holds a block in each hand and bangs them together in front of his or her body, the 8-month-old infant will attempt to imitate this behavior—a forerunner of the "pat-a-cake" game that will make its appearance a month later (Bayley, 2005).

Infants from 5 to 8 months appear to be less interested in the objects themselves than in the actions they perform upon them. This focus on one's own actions over objects is suggested by the fact that 6-month-olds seem to treat all objects the same way; they bang them in play, for example, or shake them or put them in their mouths. However, appearances may be deceiving. A more careful analysis of object play at 6 months suggests that these babies may be more discriminating than was first believed. For example, while it is true that younger babies spend more time mouthing objects than older babies do, this may occur because mouthing is their primary way of examining things around them. In fact, younger babies actually mouth more differentially than older babies do. Everything may go into the mouth, but not everything will stay in the mouth as long. Researcher Carolyn Palmer (1989) suggested that as they develop babies have increasingly sophisticated means for exploring objects (e.g., fingering, passing objects from hand to hand) and improve in their ability to differentiate among objects in the world around them. However, they are certainly interested in objects and in differentiating among them even at the age of 6 months.

By the age of 8 or 9 months, infants have the skills needed to allow them to attend carefully to the properties of objects. Now a baby takes note when a plaything is unfamiliar; there is more initial interest in a new object than in a familiar one, and an unfamiliar toy will hold the child's interest for a longer time. In addition, it is increasingly obvious that the child is attending to the specific features of objects when handling them and no longer seems to behave as if all objects are the same (Bourgeois, Khawar, Neal, & Lockman, 2005; Fontenelle, Kahrs, Neal, Newton, & Lockman, 2007). Soft objects are more likely to be squeezed, while hard objects are more likely to be mouthed and scratched, and this trend in differentiation is seen more often at 10 months than at 8 months of age.

Not only do babies handle objects differently in the second half of the first year, but they manipulate surfaces differently as well. This might not be noticed in the home since most surfaces available to manipulate, such as tabletops and highchair tops, are similarly rigid. However, researcher Sarah Fontenelle and her associates at Tulane University (2007) varied surface rigidity by observing babies in a highchair with a tray that was divided in half. One half of the surface was Formica-covered particleboard, and the other half of the surface was made of sponge. Babies at 8 and 10 months were more likely to pick at and press the sponge surface than they were to do the same to the hard surface. They were also more likely to rub an object on the hard surface and to press an object into the soft surface.

When babies aged 6 to 12 months are presented with a series of objects one at a time, younger babies engage in a lot of mouthing, looking, and passing things from one hand to the other, and all three of these activities decrease with age. Older babies tend to run their fingers across the surfaces of objects and change their patterns of manipulation to accommodate the article in hand. When an object is followed by another that differs in texture, babies do a lot of fingering; if successive objects differ in shape, babies will rotate them in their hands and pass them from hand to hand, looking at them from different angles (Ruff, 1984). The older baby appears more sensitive to the features of specific objects and handles them in ways that are appropriate for learning as much about them as possible. Fingering seems to inform the child about texture differences, while rotating objects to view them from different angles offers information about shape. Thus, exploratory play increases with age while non-exploratory play declines (Ruff & Saltarelli, 1993).

Babies in the latter part of their first year love banging and manipulating objects. They seem to particularly enjoy putting things into one another and taking them out again. Stacking or nesting toys appeal to them, as do plastic pop beads, sponges for play in the tub, and "toys" like pots and pans of different sizes or spoons to stir in plastic cups.

By 10 months, a child will look at the individual pictures in a book rather than simply regarding the book in its entirety as a thing to be played with; the child will know, 2 months later, how to turn the pages of a book. It seems clear that the first year of life is a suitable time to begin reading storybooks to children and drawing their attention to the individual pictures within them. Such activities can increase children's attention span, inform them at a very young age of the wonders that books contain, and provide opportunities for quiet, intimate contact between parent and child.

By the end of their first year, children appreciate picture books with colorful illustrations, and they can turn the pages by themselves early in their second year.

© Brand X Pictures

Children in the second half of their first year are likely to play longer with a toy that reacts to their own actions (Fenson, 1986). A relevant question to ask when making a purchase, therefore, is "What kind of a response will the child get from this toy?" For example, a toy that can be squeezed and recover its shape is more interesting than one that is rigid. A toy that produces an interesting sound or visual display *in response to* the child's pushing a button or turning a dial is more appealing than one that either does not respond at all or provides an interesting sensory display regardless of how the child plays with it. It seems that even at this young age, children derive satisfaction from having an effect on the world around them.

Object Play in the Second Year

During the second year of life, object play changes in three ways. First, there is a decline in behaviors involving only one object at a time. Ninety percent of the object play of infants between the ages of 7 and 9 months involves the use of only one object at a time; by the age of 18 months, single-object play activities are relatively rare. At that age, only 1 in 5 episodes of object play involves a single plaything; the rest are characterized by the bringing together of two or more objects in play (Rubin et al., 1983). Even by the age of 12 or 13 months, parents will notice the combining of objects in play. Children will begin, for example, to put beads into a cup, to put a cup on a saucer, to place a shape into a form board, or to build a tower of two blocks (Bayley, 2005).

A second trend in object play in the second year of life has to do with the appropriate uses of playthings. Children now begin to realize the functions of objects. They know, for example, that a ball is to be thrown or that blocks are to be stacked, and this realization makes playthings all the more interesting to them (Fenson, 1986).

In distinguishing between appropriate and inappropriate uses of objects, Rosenblatt (1977) described three types of behaviors that are found in infant object play, the first two of which we have already discussed. *Indiscriminate* behaviors are those in which the child reacts to all objects in the same way, regardless of their individual properties: Steven is given a toy telephone and immediately puts the receiver into his mouth and begins to suck on it. *Investigative* behaviors involve the exploration of the specific features of objects: Stephanie is given a toy telephone and examines it carefully, looking at it from different angles and fingering its various parts. Finally, *appropriate* behaviors involve the use of objects in the ways they were intended to be used: Todd is given a toy telephone, holds the receiver to his ear, and begins to dial with his finger. Indiscriminate and investigative behaviors in object play decline throughout the second year while appropriate behaviors increase in frequency (Rosenblatt).

The third change in object play that occurs between the ages of 1 and 2 years is a dramatic increase in the representational use of objects, which is characterized by the mental substitution of one object for another (Fenson, 1986). For example, when Sean was just a year old, he loved to play with old magazines, looking at the pictures and tearing out the pages; when he was 20 months old, he still liked to play with magazines, but now he used them in a representational way: He rolled up the torn pages and offered them as "meatballs" to his stuffed animals. Thus, the representational use of objects refers to their use by children in make-believe, or symbolic, play, about which we shall have considerably more to say later in this chapter.

Refinements in object play during the second year of life provide useful information about developmentally appropriate toys. For example, early in the second year, the child is motorically sophisticated enough to easily combine objects in play. Even by the age of 13 months, children on the average can place a peg in a pegboard, and by 14 months they are able to place pieces in form boards; they can build a tower of two blocks by the age of 14 months, and by 17 months they are able to balance a third block on the tower.

Appropriate toys for the 12- to 18-month-old are those that capitalize on the development of children's large muscles, allow children to manipulate combinations of small objects, promote interaction between parent and toddler, and do these things in such a way as to help children develop a sense of competence. Children might appreciate balls to throw (which they can do even at 13 months of age); pull toys that can be used when walking; pegboards (and later in the year, hammers to go with them); plain and interlocking blocks; puzzles with large, easy-to-handle pieces; musical toys; stuffed animals; and books with colorful illustrations.

In the latter half of their second year, children often become negative and stubborn as they strive to develop a sense of self that is different from that of their caretakers. They often insist on doing things for themselves, but unfortunately they have a difficult time coping with delay or failure.

Motor skills continue to improve, but the major development in this period is in the use of language. By 18 months, toddlers can use words instead of gestures to make their wishes known. By 20 or 21 months, they can name objects that an adult points to, and they are beginning to put together original two-word phrases, a major turning point in the acquisition of language (Bayley, 2005).

The sandbox becomes an extremely popular place to play, especially if it is equipped with various utensils for shoveling, scooping, sifting, pouring, and molding the sand. The primary interest of sandbox play is sensory exploration, however, and children under the age of 2 years are far from being ready to intentionally create products. A child's block collection should now be added to, with an increase in both the number of blocks and the variety of shapes. Books continue to be favorite playthings, and they capitalize on children's developing linguistic skills. Dolls and stuffed animals become objects of attachment, as well as affording children the opportunity to engage in simple forms of make-believe play. Crayons and paper might be added at this time because even by the age of 18 months, children can imitate a crayon stroke, and by 20 months they can differentiate between scribbles and strokes.

Symbolic Play

Peter was 16 months old, and his father was accustomed to seeing him engaged in a variety of rough-and-tumble play activities. One day, however, a new element appeared in Peter's play. As his father sat reading the newspaper, Peter stood in the room, one hand cupped, and repeatedly dipped his free hand into the cupped one, retrieved something, and brought it to his mouth. "What are you eating?" Peter's father asked. Peter approached, reached into his cupped hand, and held something up for his father to taste. What was it? Both of Peter's hands were empty.

Peter's behavior illustrates the fact that in the second year of life a new type of play is emerging. Children are beginning to represent reality to themselves through the use of symbols to let one thing stand for another. This can be seen in the child's use of language, which involves the representation of objects and people through the use of words. It can also be seen in children's **symbolic play**. In fact, a growing body of evidence indicates a relationship between pretend play competence and the comprehension of language during the second year, perhaps because both involve the ability to work with symbols (Fewell, Glick, & Spiker, 1994; Lewis, Boucher, Lupton, & Watson, 2000; Tamis-LeMonda & Bornstein, 1989, 1990; Vibbert & Bornstein, 1989).

Let us now turn to an in-depth examination of symbolic play, looking first at the development of the individual cognitive elements that it is composed of and then at its intellectual, social, and emotional benefits for the child.

The Developmental Progression of Pretend Play

Symbolic play first appears early in the second year of a child's life, usually at around the age of 12 or 13 months; its appearance is rather sudden, as indicated by month-to-month percentage increases of such play observed in children from 10 to 14 months of age (Rubin et al., 1983). However, although its earliest signs seem to appear quite suddenly, the development of symbolic play follows a gradual and fairly predictable path, often characterized by a series of increasingly sophisticated levels (Fenson, 1986; Piaget, 1962; Tamis-LeMonda & Bornstein, 1991). Perhaps the best way to describe the developmental progression of symbolic play is to examine the development of the three underlying elements (see Table 3.3) on which it is based: decentration, decontextualization, and integration (Fenson; McCune-Nicolich & Fenson, 1984; Piaget).

© Brand X Pictures

Pretending to talk on the telephone illustrates the representation skills that develop in the second year of life and usher in the golden age of make-believe that describes the preschool years.

TABLE 3.3 Developmental Trends in Symbolic Play During the Second Year of Life

Stage	Decentration	Decontextualization	Integration
12 months	Make-believe actions are centered on the self, usually occur when the child is alone, and involve familiar rituals from everyday life.	Realistic substitute objects are used in a realistic manner.	Little evidence of a connection among the various symbolic play activities.
18 months	Pretense involves inanimate objects as recipients of make-believe actions initiated by the child.	Substitute objects are less realistic in terms of appearance and function.	Pairing up of related activities in single-scheme combinations.
24 months	Inanimate objects are now the initiators as well as the recipients of make-believe actions.	Substitute objects may bear no physical resemblance to what they represent and are used in a way that is far removed from their original function.	Multischeme combinations. Two or more activities, each of which involves a different theme.

Source: Adapted from I. Bretherton (1984), L. Fenson (1986), L. McCune-Nicolich and L. Fenson (1984), J. Piaget (1962), H. Werner and B. Kaplan (1983).

Decentration

When we speak of centration and **decentration**, we refer to the degree to which children focus, or center, on themselves in pretend play; the normal developmental progression is from self- to other-centeredness. The earliest pretend play, which appears at about the age of 12 months, consists of make-believe acts that are directed toward the self (Piaget, 1962). Children, usually when alone, will act out familiar rituals from their everyday life experiences, as when they pretend to eat, drink, or go to sleep. When Piaget's daughter Jacqueline was just a year old, she would often pick up a piece of cloth and pretend it was her pillow. She would lie down with it and act as if she were sleeping, although she wasn't tired at the time and didn't actually fall asleep. Such play illustrates the concept of centration in the sense that it is totally self-focused. The child both initiates and is the object of the make-believe action.

Within a few months after the earliest pretend play has appeared, children begin to show signs of decentering. They now incorporate inanimate objects into their pretend play, and they initiate make-believe actions directed not at themselves but at other objects (Fenson, 1986). For example, instead of pretending to wash his own face as he often did when he was younger, Joshua began at 16 months to pretend he was washing the face of his teddy bear. Although he was still the initiator of the make-believe action, the object of the action was no longer Joshua himself but was now his teddy bear.

Toward the end of the second year of life, decentration reaches a new level of maturity. Now the dolls or teddy bears or other inanimate objects, which have for several months been an integral part of the child's pretend play, begin to assume new roles. They—and not the children who play with them—become the initiators as well as the recipients of make-believe actions (Fenson, 1986). The sophistication of children's pretend activities is that now they are able to inject make-believe actors into their own make-believe action sequences. For example, 2-year-old Kristen would arrange her stuffed animals around a table, put empty plates and spoons in front of them, and allow them to enjoy their meal. In other words, Kristen's make-believe characters were expected to initiate the make-believe activity of eating make-believe food!

Decontextualization

The second element of make-believe play, **decontextualization**, refers to the substitution of one object for another (Fenson, 1986). The earliest, least sophisticated form of decontextualization occurs at about 12 months of age when children use realistic, substitute objects in a realistic, appropriate manner. A piece of cloth, for example, might represent a sheet when a child pretends to go to bed. The point is that the cloth actually *does* resemble a sheet, so the child's play with it is quite realistic.

As children mature, however, their substitutions become further and further removed from reality. A substitute play object for a 3-year-old may in no way resemble the real thing, and the manner of play with the make-believe object may be far different from the appropriate use of the object being represented. Pederson, Rook-Green, and Elder (1981) found, for example, that 3-year-olds were able to pretend that a ball was a comb and would go through the motions of combing their hair with it, whereas younger children could not easily do so. Younger children would often simply bounce the ball and, when asked to pretend that it was a comb, respond, "I can't. It's a ball."

Integration

The third element in symbolic play is referred to as **integration** (Fenson, 1986). This means that as children develop, their play becomes increasingly organized into patterns. Fenson pointed out that during most of the first two years of life there is a "piecemeal" quality to children's play. They drift from one activity to another, with little in the way of any connection between activities. Then, late in the second year, there is evidence of linkages between successive actions. First, there is the simple pairing up of related activities, initially seen at around the age of 18 or 19 months (Fenson & Ramsay, 1980). For example, Jonathan has his teddy bear "climb" to the top of a tower of blocks and jump off the other side; the teddy bear is followed in this same activity by several of Jonathan's other stuffed animals. Thus, a single theme—jumping off—unites a succession of activities in single-scheme combinations (Fenson, 1986; Howes, Unger, & Matheson, 1992).

The Effects of Drug Abuse on Toddlers' Play

The changes normally seen in play during children's second year—increases in the likelihood of combining objects, using them appropriately, and using them in representational acts—are so predictable that they can serve as indicators of normal development. What can be said, however, of the toddler who does not play in the expected ways? Might the failure to play appropriately be a sign of more general developmental problems?

One possible cause of developmental delays in young children is the taking of abusive drugs by their mothers during pregnancy, which is almost certainly related to impaired fetal growth and behavioral abnormalities during infancy. However, such abuse may be linked to developmental problems in toddlers as well and to abnormalities in their play. This was the finding of a group of researchers at the University of California–Los Angeles School of Medicine (Beckwith et al., 1994), who examined the play of 31 2-year-olds in inner-city Los Angeles whose mothers had used the drug PCP during pregnancy. Not only did these infants have PCP in their urine at birth, most had crack cocaine as well. Also examined was a comparison group of children who were born in the same or nearby hospitals and shared the same ethnic background and socioeconomic status but were drug-free at birth.

The children in both groups were videotaped with age-appropriate toys (e.g., dolls of different sizes, doll furniture, cars, a truck, a telephone, a comb, a brush, and a mirror). The researchers looked at the children's (a) *manipulative acts* (banging, mouthing, throwing objects), (b) *relational play* (stacking, placing one object inside another), (c) *functional acts* (brushing one's hair, driving the car into the garage), and (d) *symbolic acts* (letting a doll listen to the phone, pouring imaginary tea into a cup). The children's ability to combine acts into sequences, as opposed to simply repeating the same act over and over again, a less mature behavior, was observed.

A knowledge of toddlers' play would lead to a realization that manipulative acts are less mature than symbolic ones and that play with a single theme is less mature than play in which themes are combined and integrated. In addition, make-believe acts directed toward the self (e.g., combing one's own hair) are less mature than similar acts directed toward others (e.g., combing a doll's hair).

(Continued)

(Continued)

The researchers found that the play of the toddlers exposed prenatally to drugs was less mature than that observed in the drug-free group. The drug-exposed children displayed more manipulative acts, such as banging, mouthing, and throwing toys. They were more likely to repeat the same acts again and again rather than combining them into novel sequences. They were more likely to direct their activities toward themselves than toward others. In addition, they were less attentive than the drug-free children, less purposeful in selecting toys to play with, and more likely to jump abruptly from one activity to another.

The play of young children, as of children of any age, can tell us much about their developmental progress. Play is more than just a pleasurable activity for children; it is also a diagnostic tool that offers valuable clues about each child's psychological world.

By the time a child is approaching his or her second birthday, integration is becoming increasingly complex (Fenson & Ramsay, 1980). Now there is the appearance of multischeme combinations (Fenson, 1986; Howes et al., 1992), which are made up of two or more activities, each involving a different theme. Jonathan, now going on 2 years, involves his stuffed animals in a game of (a) jumping off a tower, followed by (b) crawling through a tunnel. Play is moving from being an uncoordinated collection of activities to one that is coordinated and schematic, a trend that parallels the transition at the end of the second year of life from one-word utterances to original, two-word combinations in speech.

SOCIAL ASPECTS OF INFANT AND TODDLER PLAY

Children's play, even in the first year of life, cannot help but involve the other people in their environment, and those playmates most typically are parents and siblings. In recent years, it has become increasingly probable for a young child's playmates to come from outside the family as well; included in this group are teachers, child care workers, and peers. Let us look first at the ways in which adults influence the play of infants and toddlers and then at the play of very young children with their peers, which is surprising both in its extent and in its level of sophistication.

Play With Adults

Symbolic play reflects children's progress in their ability to engage in representational thought. It also has major social functions, however, as can be seen from an examination of the parent's role in a young child's acts of pretending.

PUTTING THEORY INTO PRACTICE 3.2

Using Approaches That Optimize Adult-Infant Play

Playing with an infant or a toddler may seem like common sense, but many adults are not very skilled at doing it and may overstimulate, understimulate, or even frighten a child.

For play to be the most beneficial for a very young child, an adult play partner should have a number of characteristics, many of which have been successfully incorporated into parent education programs. The following are characteristics of successful approaches to adult-infant play:

- Being sensitive to children's cues:
  - Being able to correctly assess a child's intentions and abilities
  - Correctly reading a child's responses
  - Knowing how and when a child needs direction and an adult should intervene
  - Simply imitating the child's behavior and then expanding on it

- Maintaining a playful and available attitude:
  - Showing an enthusiastic approach to play
  - Smiling and laughing during play
  - Making frequent eye contact
  - Using infant-directed speech (raising the pitch of one's voice, using exaggerated pronunciations, repeating phrases again and again)
  - Making playful facial gestures

- Making an effort to keep children at an optimal arousal level:
  - Keeping a child from being bored or overly excited
  - Offering a new toy when a child is tiring of the current one
  - Initiating rousing physical play
  - Calming and soothing an overly excited child by reducing the intensity of play and simply holding and caressing the child

- Being willing to engage in social games with infants and toddlers:
  - Playing games, such as peek-a-boo, that involve sharing, playing complementary roles, and taking turns

In fact, from its earliest appearance, pretend play is an intensely social activity (Haight, Masiello, Dickson, Huckeby, & Black, 1993; Haight & Miller, 1992, 1993). For example, mothers typically prompt their children to engage in acts of make-believe, particularly when, early in their second year, the children are less likely to pretend spontaneously (Damast, Tamis-LeMonda, & Bornstein, 1993; Tamis-LeMonda & Bornstein, 1991; Tamis-LeMonda & Damast, 1993).

Mothers will often demonstrate an activity, such as pretending to talk on a toy telephone, and then offer it to a child with encouragement to do the same thing. As the child matures, such mother-generated acts of make-believe decrease and are replaced by spontaneous "child-generated" pretense, suggesting that sensitive mothers match their play to the child's level of sophistication (Fein & Fryer, 1995; Tamis-LeMonda & Bornstein). Mothers move from initiating pretend play at the beginning to responding to their children's initiatives later (Kavanaugh & Cinquegrana, 1997). While mothers in general are fairly sensitive to developmental progressions—realizing, for example, that simple exploration precedes functional play, which precedes symbolic play—some are undoubtedly better than others at matching their play to the level of sophistication of their child (Tamis-LeMonda & Damast; Tamis-LeMonda, Damast, & Bornstein, 1994).

Since children in their second year are just beginning to form impressions of the real world, might they be confused when their parents engage in acts of pretense? Perhaps because, when pretending, parents signal to their children that what they are doing is only make-believe, it seems that engaging in pretense with toddlers will not confuse them, and they still manage to separate the real from the make-believe. Lillard and Witherington (2004) observed a group of mothers eating some cereal and drinking some juice in the presence of their 18-month-olds and, at another time, observed the same parents pretending to eat the cereal and drink the juice. When pretending, the parents behaved differently than they did when actually eating and drinking. They looked at their children more, spoke more, and smiled and laughed more. They engaged in exaggerated behaviors, such as keeping the hand with the make-believe food at their mouths longer than they would when eating real food. Whether they realized it or not, they were communicating to their children that there is a difference between reality and make-believe. The children may have been amused but were not confused. However, it should be pointed out that a clear understanding of the difference between pretense and reality is not attained until the age of 3 years, and even then the line between fantasy and reality is often crossed, particularly in emotionally charged situations such as fearing imaginary monsters (Ma & Lillard, 2006).

Even though parents generally see the value of pretending as a source of enjoyment for the child and as an opportunity to observe their child's development, they see it as having important socialization functions as well (Haight, Parke, Black, & Trousdale, 1993). When parents initiate episodes of make-believe with their toddlers, they do not always do so simply because the child enjoys it. One recent study (Haight, Masiello, et al., 1993) found that one third of all symbolic play episodes initiated by mothers had instrumental functions.

That is, the play was intended to educate the child in some way or to control the child's behavior. For example, one mother encouraged her children to come to the breakfast table by pretending pancakes were bunnies and proceeding to eat them. What parent hasn't at some time played the airplane game when trying to feed a frisky toddler? Another mother played shoe store with her 2-year-old to prepare her for a trip to a real shoe store later in the day.

Benefits of Infant-Parent Play

More than 40 years ago, psychologist Sibylle Escalona (1968) carried out what has become a classic study of the play behaviors of 128 infants and their mothers. Her main interest was to find out if infants played differently when left alone than when they had their mothers as social partners and playmates. Escalona's major finding was that, even if they had a large variety of toys to play with, the sensorimotor play of babies playing alone was less complex and less sustained than that of babies who had an adult to interact with. The mothers seemed to be skilled social directors. They tended to adapt the play activities to the immediate needs of the children by varying their own activities in response to what the children were doing. For example, mothers would vary the rate at which they offered new play materials, introduce variations or increase the intensity of play when the children seemed to be losing interest, reduce their own level of activity if the children became overly excited, offer reassurance if the children were having a difficult time, and reinforce their behavior when they did something well. As a result, the mothers were able to sustain their children's interest in the various play activities and thereby increase the length of their attention spans.

Later research offered support for Escalona's (1968) conclusion that infant and toddler play is facilitated and encouraged by the parent's structuring role and that the play that results is more sophisticated than would be found in children with limited access to adult play partners (Bigelow, MacLean, & Proctor, 2004; Stevenson, Leavitt, Thompson, & Roach, 1988). The value of such play includes the following:

- It provides the infant with a feeling of control over its environment, thereby fostering self-confidence and promoting intellectual growth.

- It exposes the infant to intense social interaction with its parents and so facilitates the process of parent-infant attachment.

- It encourages the infant to explore its surroundings.

- It causes the infant to attend more closely to the social aspects of language.

Because the pace of the play is regulated by the parent and depends on the child's level of interest, parent-infant play also keeps the baby at an ideal level of arousal, preventing boredom or overexcitement. There is no ideal play tempo, and there is much variation across cultures. American parents play at a fast tempo with their children, changing toys and activities often; Swedish parents have been found to play at a slower tempo, spending larger amounts of time on fewer activities. However, Swedish babies don't become bored with play, and American babies don't become overexcited (Hedenbro, Shapiro, & Gottman, 2006).

Not all parents are equally successful play partners, and psychologists have tried to discover which parental characteristics predict the amount and quality of play seen in an infant or a toddler. Among the many variables that could be predictors of play, two appear to stand out: maternal education and maternal responsiveness. In terms of education, the children of mothers who did not complete high school tend to be less sophisticated in their play than do the children of high school graduates, and, in general, the better educated a mother is, the more likely it is that the play of her child will be developmentally appropriate (Fewell, Casal, Glick, Wheeden, & Spiker, 1996). If one is interested in enriching the play of young children, one can do little about the level of maternal education, of course. However, the other variable, maternal responsiveness, can be influenced by intervention programs (Glick & Fewell, 1995). First of all, what is maternal responsiveness? A highly responsive mother is sensitive to the social signals emitted by her child and responds promptly and consistently to even those very subtle behaviors that other people might not detect. She seems to know what her baby wants and when he or she wants it! A highly unresponsive mother, on the other hand, is more interested in her own needs, wishes, and moods than in those of her baby, and when she interacts with the child, it is not because the child has signaled a need but because the interaction meets her own needs. Sensitive play partners, whose children are most likely to play in a developmentally appropriate manner, can engage their children in play and are successful at getting them to participate in social games that involve taking turns. And in those games, effective adult play partners are not overly directive. They avoid constantly asking questions, giving commands, or offering hints as to how the child should play a game (Glick, Wheeden, & Spiker, 1997).

Mother-Father Differences in Play With Infants and Toddlers

A considerable amount of research indicates that there are gender differences in parent-infant play. However, before we describe those differences, we should point out that, on balance, mothers and fathers are more alike than different when they play with their babies. Mothers and fathers play multiple roles; both are teachers, both are sensitive communicators, and both enjoy rousing physical play with their babies (Roggman, Boyce, Cook, Christiansen, & Jones, 2004; Shannon, Tamis-LeMonda, London, & Cabrera, 2002; Tamis-LeMonda, 2004). Mothers and fathers are equally sensitive to their babies' developmental changes; they both make the appropriate adjustments in play as their babies develop (Lamb, 2004). For example, during the first year of life, there is much physical play, but as children move into their second year, the emphasis of the parents changes from physical to make-believe play, which, in keeping with what we discussed earlier in this chapter, is an appropriate developmental transition (Power, 1985; Stevenson et al., 1988). There is also a developmentally appropriate expectation in the second year that parent and infant can take turns in play, as well as an attempt, again quite reasonable, to get the infant to coordinate play materials in a complex manner (Power & Parke, 1986).

Despite the overall similarity, however, there are some fairly consistent mother-father differences in play with their babies. One is that fathers engage in more rousing physical play, defined as rough-and-tumble activities and run-and-chase types of games, than mothers do (Hewlett, 2003; MacDonald & Parke, 1986; Parke & Tinsley, 1987; Stevenson et al., 1988; Tamis-LeMonda, 2004). Fathers are more likely to lift their babies, bounce them, and move their arms and legs, while mothers are more likely to offer toys or to play conventional games such as pat-a-cake or peek-a-boo (Power & Parke, 1982; Yogman, 1980). The rough-and-tumble quality of father-infant play is more evident with a male than with a female child (Power & Parke). It isn't clear why fathers are rougher when playing with young children. Some researchers (e.g., Paquette, 1994) believe there is a biological explanation, while others argue in favor of social and cultural factors. For example, Hewlett suggests that fathers typically have less time than mothers to play with their babies and so their play must be strongly arousing and attention getting. For an examination of some possible benefits of parent-child physical play, refer to the section in Chapter 9 titled "Physical Play and Social Competence."

Mothers seem more closely attuned to their infants' interests and are more likely than fathers to follow a child's lead; for example, mothers typically allow their babies to explore as they wish and to choose their own activities. Fathers, on the other hand, seem to be more intrusive social directors. They are likely to disregard their babies' interests and to steer the play activity in the direction they would prefer it to go (Lamb, 2004). They are also more likely than mothers to suggest new ways of using objects by incorporating them into nonconventional games (Labrell, 1996). It is not known why this parental sex difference in directiveness appears. Perhaps fathers are less sensitive than mothers to their children's interests or more likely than mothers to see actively directing their babies' play as their responsibility (Power & Parke, 1986).

A final major parental difference is that mothers engage in more instructive play with infants than fathers do (Stevenson et al., 1988). In other words, the play of mothers is more likely than the play of fathers to contain a teaching emphasis. Mothers will make a point, for example, of naming objects, colors, or numbers and then asking the infant to demonstrate that he or she has learned the label by looking directly at the object as the mother names it, by pointing to it when asked, or, in the case of an older child, by responding correctly when the mother says, "What do we call this?" Fathers are more tactile in play, relying heavily on the sense of touch, while mothers are more verbal in their interactions with their infants (Parke & Tinsley, 1987).

No human interaction is one-directional, of course, so it is difficult to speak of how mothers and fathers behave without also looking at the characteristics of the infant they are playing with. It has been found, for example, that mothers behave differently when playing with an infant son than with a daughter (Clearfield & Nelson, 2006). They engage in more conversation with their daughters and make more statements about the baby's feelings, needs, or wishes. With sons, on the other hand, mothers converse less but make more directive comments (e.g., "Come here") and more comments intended to call the baby's attention to his surroundings (e.g., "Joey, look at that!").

The pattern of parental gender differences in play with infants and toddlers is not a universal one. For example, mother-father comparisons in Sweden (Lamb, Frodi, Hwang, Frodi, & Steinberg, 1982) and in the Israeli kibbutz (Sagi, Lamb, Shoham, Dvir, & Lewkowicz, 1985) reveal no gender differences in parental play with infants. It has been suggested that both Swedish culture and that of the Israeli kibbutz are characterized by more egalitarian attitudes toward gender roles than are found in the United States; differences in mothers' and fathers' styles of play with infants may reflect general cultural attitudes about the appropriate roles of male and female parents in a child's upbringing (Parke & Tinsley, 1987; Sagi et al., 1985).

Parents Versus Siblings as Playmates

Except in the case of a first-born child, an infant will have older siblings with whom to share its play activities. Research on play with older siblings, however, serves primarily to highlight the importance of parent-infant play. This is because the unique and very special quality of parent-infant play is lacking in sibling play, in the sense that the structure or direction that a parent provides is rarely provided by a sibling (Stevenson et al., 1988). In fact, when infants are playing with their siblings, they are not likely to be involved in the types of activities that require social partners but instead will play with their toys or simply watch their older brothers and sisters. For their part, the older siblings tend to ignore their infant brothers and sisters in play situations (Lamb, 1978; Stevenson et al.). On the other hand, simply watching an older sibling seems to bring about imitation of certain forms of play. It has been found that infants with older siblings engage in more rough-and-tumble play and in more joint pretend activities than do infants without siblings (Barr & Hayne, 2003). Parent-infant and sibling-infant play may serve different purposes; it appears that parents stimulate their babies to develop new skills while siblings help them consolidate those skills that have already been learned (Dunn, 1983). If this is true, there is an obvious value in having multiple play partners available, each of whom might take on a slightly different role in promoting optimal infant development (Stevenson et al., 1988).

Finally, the differences we have described between parent and older sibling play with young children are not universal patterns. In many East African cultures, for example, the sibling is the primary playmate for the infant and toddler, while the mother's role is to watch, to nurture and protect, and to teach but to intervene in play only if necessary (Edwards & Whiting, 1993). While American older siblings typically do not assume a structuring role, Mexican siblings engage in a good deal of teaching behavior. In fact, in terms of making suggestions to younger siblings, commenting on their play, and actually joining in the play with them, Mexican siblings closely resemble American mothers (Farver, 1993). Mayan children in central Mexico typically play with their younger siblings and use play as an opportunity to teach their brothers and sisters how to perform tasks that are required in everyday life (Maynard, 2002). In Indonesia, where close and harmonious sibling relationships are highly valued, older brothers and sisters are sophisticated play partners, assuming many of the scaffolding roles that American mothers do (Farver & Wimbarti, 1995). They freely join in play with little brothers and sisters, make suggestions for pretending, and keep their siblings informed by commenting on the play activities and materials. Indonesian mothers, on the other hand, tend to be reserved and not very playful, seeing play not as a valuable end in itself but as an opportunity to develop children's minds and bodies and to help them learn to cooperate (Farver & Wimbarti).

Infant Social Games

Between the ages of 9 and 24 months, infants acquire the skills needed to play simple cooperative games (Ross & Lollis, 1987). At first, these games are played only with adults, since peers are not able to provide the scaffolding for one another that cooperative play requires. Adults—but not peers—can determine the baby's intentions and goals and can adjust their own behavior accordingly (Brownell, Ramani, & Zerwas, 2006; Callanan & Sabbagh, 2004; Lillard & Witherington, 2004). As early as 9 months, infants begin to coordinate their activities to a sufficient extent that they can engage and even take an active role in games that are initiated by adults (Gustafson, Green, & West, 1979). By 18 months, they are beginning to play games without any adult structuring at all, as evidenced by the fact that in the middle of the second year of life, simple cooperative games with peers make their appearance and that as toddlers approach the end of their second year, there are noticeable increases in the amount of imitative peer play and peer play that includes an element of give and take (Brownell et al.).

What is involved in the early social games between parents and their children? There are several elements, but, as might be expected, the rules are fairly simple. One element is the taking of turns; the parent engages in an action and then stops and waits for the baby to act. There is repetition of roles at the end of each understood round of activity. For example, the parent builds a tower of three blocks; the baby waits until it is completed and then knocks it over; the parent builds again while the baby waits, the baby knocks the tower over again, and so forth. These games are also characterized by the offering of toys to one's partner, by careful observation of one's partner while awaiting one's turn, and by signaling to one's partner that his or her involvement is required (Ross & Lollis, 1987).

As might be expected, the infant's involvement in social games becomes increasingly apparent with age. In a study by Roggman (1989), groups of babies aged 10 and 15 months were observed while seated in a highchair with two toys on the tray. Their mothers, who were seated near them, were told not to interfere in the child's play with the toys and to wait 2 minutes before picking up toys that were dropped. Roggman predicted that after dropping a toy the 15-month-olds would be more likely than the younger babies to look over at their mother to see if she was ready to participate in the dropping game. The younger babies, less interested in the social possibilities of this game, would be more likely to look at the toys. The findings were as expected, indicating the older child's increasing attention to opportunities for social play. In other words, the goals of infant play become increasingly social as the child matures.

The benefits of parent-infant games are readily apparent. The baby learns how to wait for its turn and how to adapt to the schedule of another person. Awareness of others is reinforced in such games because careful attention to a partner's actions is a necessity. Parent-infant play is often so delightful an experience for both parties that it can facilitate the process of attachment between parent and child. And finally, since these early social games involve a considerable amount of verbalization, it has been suggested that such play encourages the development of language in children (Bruner, 1983). Although the direction of cause and effect is difficult to establish, a positive relationship has been found between the frequency of mother-infant games and the sophistication of the child's speech production.

Peer Play

More than two thirds of mothers of preschool children in the United States hold jobs outside the home, and nearly half of their children have had the experience of being in a day care center or another group care facility (U.S. Census Bureau, 2008). Therefore, it seems likely that early peer interaction is the norm for a considerable percentage of our children, and many infants and toddlers have peers available to them as playmates. How well do young children communicate with their peers, and how early can we expect to see signs of cooperative peer play?

Communication With Peers

One of the more interesting studies of infant-peer interaction was carried out by psychologist Alan Fogel (1979), who observed babies ranging in age from 5 to 14 weeks in three social settings. In one condition, the children were alone; in another, they were observed while they watched their mothers; and in a third, the children were seated on their mothers' laps and facing another infant of the same age. When they were alone for a brief period of time, the infants seemed to be relaxed and content. When they saw their mothers, they would smile, sometimes stick out their tongues, and gesture with their arms and legs. The sight of another infant, however, produced reactions that were qualitatively different: The babies would stare intently, often leaning forward as if to get a closer look. They would also make jerky head and arm movements, almost as if they were very excited. There can be little doubt, therefore, that infants are interested in one another even as early as the second month after birth.

The social gestures of the infant in its first year are limited in two important ways. First, they are of very short duration, although the time spent on social gestures will increase throughout the first two years of life. Second, they are relatively simple at first, in the sense that they consist of only one or two behaviors at a time (e.g., waving arms and vocalizing, smiling and leaning forward). Such simple behaviors are eventually combined into more complex patterns in the second year, with the result that social interaction becomes more controlled and more predictable (Brownell, 1986; Hay, Pederson, & Nash, 1982).

By the early months of their second year, children seem to pay attention to—and possibly understand—the wishes, intentions, and perceptions of other people. They can even take account of the intentions and goals of others in governing their own behaviors (Brooks & Meltzoff, 2002; Brownell et al., 2006; Carpenter, Call, & Tomasello, 2005; Dunphy-Lelii & Wellman, 2004; Wellman, Phillips, & Spelke, 2002). These understandings are quite limited at first but will continue to develop throughout their second year. For example, a 1-year-old can infer a person's intentions from his or her specific actions, while a 2- or 3-year-old will be able to understand that a person has prior intentions, mental states that precede actions (Meltzoff, 1995). A 1-year-old will infer the intentions of another person from a limited number of very obvious actions, while a 2-year-old will infer intention from a broader and more subtle range of actions (Poulin-Dubois & Forbes, 2002).

How are the social understandings of a 1-year-old revealed in his or her play with others? One-year-old children at play will show their toys to one another, offer and give one another toys, invite peers to play with them, protest a playmate's actions, and in general communicate their feelings effectively to one another. They will show signs of altruism, such as by handing someone an object that is beyond his or her reach (Warneken & Tomasello, 2007). As discussed earlier in this chapter, they are now capable of initiating very simple social games of their own without the necessity of adult structuring.

Early Forms of Cooperation

In order for cooperative play to occur, a child must understand the goals and intentions of another person and must share those goals and intentions in a coordinated play activity. As mentioned earlier, children play cooperatively with an adult play partner by the end of their first year because the adult scaffolds, or structures, the interaction. However, cooperative play with a peer is far more difficult since neither child is able to take the major role in structuring the game.

By the age of 18 months, toddlers begin to engage in complementary and reciprocal play (Howes, 1988). Complementary activities are those in which each child does something different but the two roles complement one another, and reciprocal play refers to the ability to take turns. Howes also discovered that such activities increase significantly from the ages of 1 to 3 years and that 1-year-olds who are skilled at reciprocal and complementary play grow into 2-year-olds who are skilled at social pretend play.

In an interesting recent study designed to see how well children can coordinate their activities in a cooperative way, Brownell and colleagues (2006) observed children in three age groups—19 months, 23 months, and 27 months—as they played a game. The children were shown a colorful wooden box with two plastic handles on one side and a musical toy on the top. The toy could be activated only if both handles were pulled at the same time, but the handles were placed far enough apart that a child could not reach both of them at once. An adult demonstrated the task and then asked the children to do it, even prompting them to help each other. Clearly this activity required cooperation. The researchers found that there were age differences in the amount of coordinated pulling on the handles. The youngest children were the least successful, and many of them produced no coordinated pulls at all. The amount of coordinated pulling actually doubled from 19 to 27 months, suggesting that while cooperative play with peers can be found in the second year of life, it is rare. However, it increases dramatically as children mature.

Summary

Play and exploration often resemble one another, but they also differ in three areas: the affective state of the child, the amount of stereotypy in the child's behavior, and the focus of the child's attention. In exploring, children appear to be serious, attend very closely to what they are doing, and engage in stereotypical, almost ritualistic behaviors. Children at play are more joyful, more willing to be distracted, and more diverse in their behavior.

Throughout the first year of life, children engage in a good deal of sensorimotor play: the repetition of an already learned sensory or motor activity for the sheer pleasure of repeating it. At about the age of 5 months, infants begin to play with objects, but early object play is somewhat unsophisticated in the sense that infants are less interested in the properties of objects themselves than they are in their own actions upon them. By the age of 9 or 10 months, however, they begin to differentiate among objects; they prefer new rather than familiar objects, and they handle different objects differently, in such a way as to extract as much information from them as possible. Finally, object play in the second year of life is even more mature in that the child now combines objects in play, uses objects appropriately, and begins to incorporate objects into symbolic, or make-believe, play.

Symbolic play appears rather suddenly early in the child's second year, and its further development is characterized by a series of increasingly sophisticated levels. Development can be seen in each of the underlying elements of symbolic play: decentration, the degree to which the child is able to shift the focus of its interest from self to external objects; decontextualization, the use of one object as a substitute for another; and integration, the organization of play into increasingly complex patterns.

The major function of adults in the play of infants is to be skilled social directors, initiating play routines, controlling the frequency with which new playthings are introduced, varying the intensity of play in response to the child's behavior, and providing support and encouragement. Compared with fathers, mothers are less directive, engage in more verbal and more instructive play, and engage in less rousing physical play with their infants. Parent-infant play is more sustained and more active than is solitary play or play with siblings, and it is more likely to teach the infant new skills.

Babies have a definite interest in peers, even during the first few months of life. Not until the middle of their second year, however, is there an extensive amount and variety of infant communication and do the first signs of cooperative peer play make their appearance. Social games with adults precede social games with peers because the adult is the initiator who provides the structure for the game. By the middle of their second year, however, infants are able to provide their own structure, so peer games become possible.

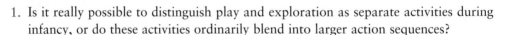

Key Terms

Issues for Class Discussion

1. Is it really possible to distinguish play and exploration as separate activities during infancy, or do these activities ordinarily blend into larger action sequences?

2. Provide some specific examples of developmentally inappropriate toys for infants and toddlers. How would an infant or a toddler react to a developmentally inappropriate toy?

3. Why does symbolic play make its appearance during the second year of life rather than during the first? What are an infant's cognitive limitations during its first year in terms of representational skills? (This discussion might provide an opportunity to highlight the connection between play and level of intellectual development.)

4. As we recognize the benefits of parent-infant play, we might want to examine the implications for play of infant child care arrangements in our society. How might our knowledge of parent-infant play affect our decisions about the qualifications of child care providers?

Chapter 4

THE PRESCHOOL YEARS

From 2 to 5

Every year in a young child's life brings substantial change. This chapter will examine the processes of development that occur in children between the ages of 2 and 5 years. The more typically observed attributes of children at each of the different ages will be presented, but it is important to keep in mind, of course, that human development at any age is characterized by a high degree of diversity.

Appropriate toys and play activities for children at each age will be discussed, because play and development are inseparably connected and because age appropriateness is perhaps the most essential feature of any toy (see Table 4.1).

The second section of this chapter will consist of a description of the general developmental trends in play from age 2 to age 5. Specifically there will be an examination of the ways in which changes in play mirror the changes in the child's level of intellectual, social, and emotional maturity, and much will be said about the type of play that is clearly predominant during the preschool years: symbolic, or make-believe, play.

Finally, this chapter will include discussion of a variety of environmental factors that influence preschool play: childrearing patterns, peer interactions, exposure to day care settings, physical characteristics of the play environment, and the effects of electronic media—specifically television—on play.

Learning Objectives

After reading Chapter 4, a student should be able to:

✦ Provide normative descriptions of the physical, intellectual, linguistic, social, and emotional characteristics of children ranging in age from 2 to 5 years.

✦ Describe appropriate play materials for children at each age from 2 to 5 years and explain why these materials are suitable for each age.

✦ Understand the five categories of social play identified by Mildred Parten and provide concrete examples of each.

✦ Identify the developmental trends in social play that occur during the preschool years.

✦ Describe the significance of the different types of roles that children assume when engaged in sociodramatic play.

✦ Identify the various functions of sociodramatic play in the life of the young child and describe its affective, intellectual, and social benefits.

✦ Understand the relationship between play and the quality of attachment between parent and child.

✦ Describe the influence of peers on preschoolers' sociodramatic play in terms of the variables of peer familiarity, sex of playmate, and age of playmate.

✦ Describe both the positive and the negative effects of exposure to a group child care setting on preschoolers' play and reconcile the apparent contradictions suggested by the research findings.

THE 2-YEAR-OLD

General Characteristics

As children enter their third year of life, a number of developments directly influence the quality of their play. In terms of sensory and motor development, the 2-year-old can get around easily. Not only can 2-year-olds walk and run; they also can easily climb up and down stairs. In addition, they can work with simple puzzles that have large pieces, string beads, and manipulate clay. They are still limited, however, in the development of fine motor skills, such as those required for cutting, pasting, or using a pencil or paintbrush effectively. Large muscle play activities are definitely preferred.

TABLE 4.1   Characteristics of Preschool Children and Appropriate Play Materials

Age	General Characteristics	Appropriate Play Materials
2	Uses language effectively. Large muscle skills developing but limited in the use of small muscle skills. Energetic, vigorous, and enthusiastic, with a strong need to demonstrate independence and self-control.	*Large Muscle Play Materials:* Swing sets, outdoor blocks, toys to ride on, pull toys, push toys. *Sensory Play Materials:* Clay, finger paints, water play. Blocks, books, dolls and stuffed animals.
3	Expanded fantasy life, with unrealistic fears. Fascination with adult roles. Still stubborn and negative but better able to adapt to peers than at age 2. Early signs of product orientation in play.	Props for imaginative play (old clothes, etc.). Miniature life toys. Puzzles, simple board games, and art materials, such as paintbrushes, easels, marker pens, and crayons, which allow for a sense of accomplishment.
4	Secure, self-confident. Need for adult attention and approval—showing off, clowning around, taking risks. More planful than 3-year-olds, but products often accidental. Sophisticated small muscle control allows for cutting, pasting, sewing, and imaginative block building with smaller blocks.	Vehicles such as tricycles and Big Wheels. Materials for painting, coloring, drawing, woodworking, sewing, and stringing beads. Books with themes that extend well beyond the child's real world.
5	Early signs of logical thinking. Stable, predictable, reliable. Less self-centered than at 4. Relaxed, friendly, willing to share and cooperate with peers. Realistic, practical, responsible.	Cut-and-paste and artistic activities with models to work from. Simple card games (e.g., "Old Maid"), table games (e.g., Bingo), and board games (e.g., Lotto), in which there are few rules and the outcomes are based more on chance than on strategy. Elaborate props for dramatic play.

The child of 2 years is interested in sensory exploration; the feel of play materials like paints, clay, or sand is more important for a 2-year-old than is the possibility of creating a product.

Two-year-olds are also beginning to use language effectively. For example, they combine two words into phrases by the age of 21 to 24 months (e.g., "Want milk," "Push car"), and they are increasingly likely to become frustrated if an adult fails to understand what they are trying to say; at 18 months they showed no such frustration. During their third year, they typically speak in simple three-word sentences, and their vocabulary expands dramatically. They can tell you their names and whether they are a boy or a girl. They enjoy having someone read to them.

The increasing linguistic proficiency of the 2-year-old has a decidedly positive effect on the child's social maturity because it makes communication more efficient. The young 2-year-old is likely to give affection to adults and other children and in general to do things to please people. And because of their greater ability to communicate, they are more likely than a younger child to make attempts to play cooperatively with peers. Social contact among 2-year-olds is brief and fleeting, however. They enjoy being near other children but are still quite limited in their ability to share and to cooperate.

Two-year-olds are energetic, vigorous, and enthusiastic. The need is strong to demonstrate independence, to show that they are capable of doing things for themselves—what psychoanalytic theorist Erik Erikson (1963) referred to as the crisis of autonomy versus doubt. In effect, children of this age are saying to their caretakers, "I am myself. I am separate from and different from you." The ability to demonstrate control over their own bodies is all important, and 2-year-olds take great pride in physical accomplishments like climbing up a jungle gym, turning a light on or off, sliding down a slide, or developing a measure of bowel or bladder control.

The need of 2-year-olds to assert their independence can be manifested in stubbornness, rigidity, and negativism. There is often an unwillingness to make any sort of compromise. Parents will comment, for example, that their 2-year-old likes to have the same story read over and over again in exactly the same way. If a page is skipped or the reader introduces variations of any sort, the child may protest. Another frequently heard adult complaint is that children of this age refuse on principle to do what is asked of them. Tell them to stay outside, and they will want to come in; tell them to come indoors, and they will insist on staying outside. Such negative attitudes are not necessarily indicators of impending juvenile delinquency. Instead they serve to indicate the extent of the 2-year-old's need for autonomy.

Play Materials

The best play materials for a 2-year-old, as for a child of any age, capitalize on the child's developmental needs. For example, play materials that develop large muscle skills are most appropriate. For outdoor play, a 2-year-old could benefit from parallel bars to hang on, ladders to climb, wagons to pull and toy lawn mowers to push, outdoor blocks to drag around and to stack, and small spaces to crawl in and out of. Toys on which the child can ride are also favorites and help develop strength and large muscle coordination. For sensory exploration, clay and its many variations provide wonderful opportunities for squeezing, squishing, and molding (but not for product creation at this age). Finger paints serve much the same purpose, and water play (e.g., squeezing and dipping sponges, pouring water from one container to another, blowing bubbles, sailing boats in the bathtub) becomes a highly enjoyable activity.

Two-year-olds are now stacking blocks, and they enjoy playing with things that can be put together and taken apart, so the block collection that was begun in the second year can be added to. Blocks in basic shapes (squares, rectangles, triangles) are the most appropriate since 2-year-olds are more interested in manipulating and combining the blocks in different ways than in making things with them. Similarly, additions might be made to the library since children of this age enjoy books and love being read to—even if it is the same story read over and over again in exactly the same way. Finally, 2-year-olds often develop the habit of clinging to a favorite doll or stuffed animal, and such toys are now considerably more appreciated than they were the year before.

THE 3-YEAR-OLD

General Characteristics

The average child of 3 years is highly imaginative. There is significant expansion in 3-year-olds' fantasy lives, which sets the stage for great strides in imaginative play and, on the negative side, explains the appearance of such unrealistic fears as fear of the dark, monsters, or loud noises.

There are clear indications that 3-year-olds, unlike 2-year-olds, begin to identify strongly with adults—to become increasingly interested in what adults do and to imagine themselves doing the same things. Perhaps as a result, 3-year-olds become interested in dramatic play in which they have an opportunity to act out adult roles for themselves.

Dramatic play reflects the social maturity of the 3-year-old as compared with that of the 2-year-old, not only because such play requires an appreciation of the roles of others but also because the success of role-playing games depends on the cooperation of the players: Each child must act out his or her individual part, or the play will not work. The social component of dramatic play becomes evident when one realizes that 70% of all such play among 3-year-olds occurs in a group setting (Johnson & Ershler, 1981).

Like the 2-year-old, the child of 3 years can still be very stubborn and negative. However, at 3 there is at least a slightly greater willingness to conform to the expectations of others. It is obvious that the child of 3 is moving into a world of increasing social interaction, because 3-year-olds are better able to share, to await their turn, and to cooperate with adults and with peers. People are more important to a 3-year-old than they are to a child of 2, and the 3-year-old seeks out social interaction and recognizes the value of membership in a group.

Finally, compared with 2-year-olds, 3-year-olds are more interested in the effects of their behaviors on the surrounding world. In their orientation, they are beginning to move from process to product, from actions to their end results. Unlike the 2-year-old, the 3-year-old is able to draw satisfaction from making things that he or she can show to others. We should point out, however, that the 3-year-old is not a planner in the sense of deciding on goals and following through; such abilities will not appear until the age of 4 or 5 (Hartley, Frank, & Goldenson, 1952). Many of the products that 3-year-olds are proud of are accidental rather than intentional creations.

Play Materials

Play materials for 3-year-olds should reflect their increasing social maturity, their emerging interest in adult roles, and the expansion of their imagination compared with that of 2-year-olds. A major addition to the supply of playthings, therefore, would be props for imaginative play: articles of adult clothing no longer used, eyeglasses, a plastic or wooden shaving kit, a doctor kit, makeup, and other props that allow children to be just like Mom or Dad or other adult figures. For the same purposes, 3-year-olds appreciate miniature toys that represent adult models: toy trucks, gas stations, dolls, dollhouses, spaceships, and so forth.

The expansion of the child's imagination affects the ways in which children use play materials that are already familiar to them. For example, 3-year-olds, like 2-year-olds, continue to enjoy block play, but blocks can be used differently now. At 3, children will incorporate blocks into fantasy play rather than simply stacking or arranging them in interesting combinations. Three-year-olds will use blocks to further their interest in the world of adults. They will create structures, such as buildings, streets, and tunnels, that represent the adult world in miniature, and they will use these structures to play imaginatively. The time is right, therefore, for the adult to increase the supply of available blocks, both of the indoor and the outdoor variety, and in doing so make certain that the blocks are varied enough to facilitate make-believe play; square blocks may make fine small buildings, but long rectangular blocks and ramps will suggest the building of roads; arches raise the possibility of bridge building; and large outdoor blocks can be transformed into habitable structures, such as forts, houses, or boats.

Finally, the preliminary signs of product orientation in some 3-year-olds should be taken into account when play materials are selected. Adults should certainly not demand or even expect a product from such a young child. Nevertheless, whether they are puzzles, simple games, interlocking blocks, or art materials, toys should be selected with the possibility of a child's accomplishment in mind. Let us look at art materials as an example. Whereas 2-year-olds are process oriented and enjoy art materials like finger paints and clay primarily for their sensory appeal, 3-year-olds are interested as well in the results, however unintentional, that their efforts produce. Now there is a joy in accomplishment and an interest in showing off one's creations, and finger paints may be too formless to capitalize on that interest. Art materials should be provided, therefore, that allow children to demonstrate their skills and to produce something, even if accidentally, that can be shown to others. Included might be paintbrushes, easels, marker pens, and crayons.

THE 4-YEAR-OLD

General Characteristics

Compared with 3-year-olds, 4-year-olds appear to be more secure and self-confident. Their bodies are considerably more efficient than they were a year ago. They can balance themselves by standing on one foot, can roller-skate, and can ride a small bicycle with training wheels.

Four-year-olds' small muscle control is also more sophisticated, so they can button large buttons and even tie their shoelaces. In addition, they are able to engage in many play activities that were difficult and frustrating the year before. They enjoy drawing, cutting things out of paper, painting, coloring, woodworking, and imaginative block building with smaller blocks of various shapes. When working with such materials, the 4-year-old is more product oriented than the 3-year-old; still, the products are often unintentional in that they evolve as the project develops. In other words, 4-year-olds are more likely than 3-year-olds to make plans at the outset, but the plans may change continuously as the play material changes in appearance.

Four-year-olds are more thoroughly involved than 3-year-olds in the process of identification with adults. They are becoming keenly aware of their own masculinity or femininity and may go to great efforts to demonstrate their similarity

© Eyewire

Children of 4 and 5 years have successfully used instructional technology to count, to learn the alphabet, and to develop language skills and skills in the areas of art, mathematics, and science.

to the same-sex parent. Nevertheless, gender lines are still somewhat indistinct at this age; children do not yet see gender as a fixed and unchanging characteristic of a person's being and may ascribe gender differences to such surface features as hair length or type of clothing (Kohlberg, 1966).

The focus on adults may cause the 4-year-old to engage in many socially immature behaviors designed to elicit adult attention and approval: for example, showing off, clowning around, or bragging (Hartley et al., 1952; Hartley & Goldenson, 1963). Parents may find themselves constantly enjoined to "Watch me" or "See what I can do." Parents also discover that their children's new-found self-confidence can lead them into risky and dangerous behaviors.

Play Materials

Play materials for 4-year-olds should reflect their increasing sociability and the fact that they simply cover a lot more territory in their daily wanderings. It is appropriate, therefore, to provide them with vehicles, such as tricycles, Big Wheels, or wagons, which will facilitate social interaction and allow them to demonstrate their large muscle skills both for peers and for adults. In addition, children of 4 years need play materials that help them develop their small muscle skills, and these might include materials for sewing, woodworking, stringing beads, coloring, painting, and drawing. A question to keep in mind when selecting materials is whether an activity allows children to extend the range of implements they use in play—beyond the ordinary pencils, brushes, and scissors to include items like pickup sticks, jacks, and even computer keyboards. Finally, books continue to have high interest value, and now an adult might look for those that capitalize on the child's sense of adventure, with themes and locales that extend far beyond the child's everyday world.

THE 5-YEAR-OLD

General Characteristics

From an intellectual standpoint, 5-year-olds are already showing signs of logical thinking as they begin the transition to what cognitive psychologist Jean Piaget (1962) referred to as concrete operations. Their thinking is better organized than before; as a result, they tend to see the world as a rational and orderly place. They are more stable, predictable, and reliable than they were when younger, and they are less self-centered. As a result, they are often perceived by adults as relaxed and friendly, and when they play with peers, there is usually a willingness to share, take turns, and cooperate.

This same spirit of reliability and cooperation is seen in the home. The parents, particularly the mother, occupy a central place in the child's life. Five-year-olds like to please their parents, and they demonstrate a willingness to take on new responsibilities in caring for themselves and their belongings. They are often willing to help care for their younger siblings, even though they typically get along better with children outside the home.

Remember that the 3-year-old is entering a world in which there is a significant expansion of fantasy and a blurring of the distinction between fantasy and reality. By the age of 5, however, children are considerably more realistic. Their fears, for example, are based more in reality (e.g., fear of physical dangers, accidents, illnesses, war, death) than are the fantasy-world fears of the younger child, who may really believe there is a monster in the closet! The realism of 5-year-olds can also be seen in their dramatic play. No longer satisfied with the minimal props used by 3- and 4-year-olds (e.g., sticks for swords or a red paper hat to indicate that one is a firefighter), they want the entire costume, or they argue the need for realistic store-bought props instead of miscellaneous items found around the home.

Play Materials

Like the 4-year-old, the child of 5 years enjoys activities like drawing, painting, coloring, and working with scissors, but the 5-year-old is more interested in precision and realism. The child now seeks direction from adults and often appreciates having a model to work from. Unfortunately, at 5 there is often an excessive concern with making things correctly and a tendency to compare one's work with that of others. The child may be extremely judgmental about the quality of his or her own work, even if adults go to great efforts to discourage such self-criticism.

Skill-oriented play materials that allow the child to plan an activity and to work it through should contain appropriate directions and allow for the possibility for children and adults to work together, at least occasionally. Art materials continue to be valued playthings and should be either structured in terms of an expected product (e.g., coloring books, a paint- or color-by-numbers set) or unstructured (e.g., paints and brushes, crayons, marker pens, glue, scissors, stencils, sequins and glitter, clay, play dough). Some adults may complain that such "structured" art materials may inhibit the development of a child's creative expression, but they should realize that artistic production involves skill as well as creative expression, and children of 5 years are particularly interested in developing and displaying their skills. For these reasons, a 5-year-old might also appreciate receiving toys like a workbench with realistic tools, playing cards, table games, and board games with dice. A necessary feature of games for this age group is an emphasis on the element of chance, rather than on a high degree of strategy for success.

GENERAL PATTERNS OF PLAY

Increasing Social Play

More than 75 years ago, psychologist Mildred Parten (1932) recorded the changing nature of children's play between the ages of 2 and 5 years. Her observations were so perceptive that her categories of play are still seen as a meaningful framework within which to examine the increasing social maturity of the child.

Parten (1932) described the transition from the solitary play that is so typical of 1- and 2-year-olds to the highly interactive cooperative play of the average 4-year-old. In doing so, she outlined a series of stages of play that increase in level of social sophistication. Let us now describe those stages and their implications for children's development.

The children in this photograph are engaged in parallel play. Each is involved in his or her own play activity, but all are together in terms of the materials they are using and the space they are playing in. Each is interested in what the others are doing.

Categories of Social Play

Typical of 2-year-olds, **solitary play** is the lowest level of social play. The child is playing while totally alone in his or her own world, even if surrounded by other children. Approximately half of the separate observations of 2-year-olds in Parten's (1932) study found them engaged in solitary play. Two-year-olds also engaged in a considerable amount of **onlooker play**, which occurs when a child watches another child or other children at play and is definitely involved as a spectator, even to the point of asking questions or offering suggestions, but does not become an active participant.

Next comes the form of play most commonly observed in all age groups in the Parten (1932) study: **parallel play**, in which children play separately at the same activity at the same time and in the same place. They are aware of the presence of peers—in fact, the presence of others obviously has some meaning for them—but each child is still playing separately. Parallel play seems to represent a point of transition between the socially immature level of solitary play and the socially sophisticated level of genuine cooperation. Interestingly enough, parallel play often draws children into cooperative activities but is rarely followed by the less mature solitary play, leading some psychologists to suggest that playing in parallel is a safe way to set the stage for more intense group interaction (Damon, 1983).

Associative play, common among 3- and particularly 4-year-olds, resembles parallel play in that each child is still focused on a separate activity, but now there is a considerable amount of sharing, lending, taking turns, attending to the activities of one's peers, and expansive communication. Two children may be painting at adjacent easels, for example, and while each is producing a separate work of art, there is discussion about their paintings (or about anything else), sharing of materials ("I'll lend you some of my red if you lend me your blue"), and a genuine interest in socializing that may be more compelling than the act of painting a picture. Children from poor families with limited play materials seem to engage in greater amounts of associative play than do middle-class children, perhaps because children with limited resources are more likely to have to share and wait their turns (Dyer & Moneta, 2006).

Four-year-olds engage in a good deal of **cooperative play**, which represents the highest level of social maturity. Cooperative play occurs when two or more children are engaged in a play activity that has a common goal, one that can be realized only if all of the participants carry out their individual assigned roles. Several children in the sandbox decide, for example, that they will build a city; one child works on the road, two children work on a bridge, and others dig a tunnel.

Developmental Trends in Social Play

Parten (1932) noticed that as children developed from age 2 to 4 years, there was a significant decline in solitary activities, as well as in passive watching while others played. She also noticed that the size of children's play groups was related to age; in all age groups except the oldest (4.5 to 5-year-olds), the most popular group size was two, but in the oldest group, the most popular size was in the range of three to five children. The tendency to play in groups of five or more definitely increased with age.

In analyzing the preferred play materials and activities of the children in her sample, Parten (1932) found that children between the ages of 2 and 2.5 years seemed to prefer, in order, the following activities: sandbox play, trains, "kiddy" cars, idly looking, and idly sitting. The preferred activities— again, in rank order—of the 4-year-olds were paper cutting, clay, family (house, dolls), sandbox, and swings. The preferences of Parten's children make some interesting points about child development. The preference for solitary activities among the younger children, compared with the older ones, is striking. The older children were more likely to be involved in social play (family) and small muscle activities (paper cutting). Even when the same activity appeared in both preference lists, the form of the play often differed. For example, when younger children played in the sandbox, they typically played by themselves, feeling the sand, pouring it back and forth from one container to another, or making molds of it. The older children showed signs of cooperative play in the sandbox, working in groups to construct roads, tunnels, or bridges. These differences attest to the increasing social maturity of the child throughout the preschool years; cooperation becomes increasingly common, as does the tendency in play to identify with the world of adults, as children are doing when they try out the roles of mother or father, construction worker, or train engineer.

Parten's Work in Perspective

Mildred Parten's (1932) work was extremely valuable in helping us understand the various degrees of social involvement that categorize young children's play. However, modern psychologists question whether her categories are really developmental stages, which would mean that each represents a qualitative advance over those that precede it and that developing children should move through them in a predictable sequence. The more typical view today is that preschool children of all ages engage in all types of play, depending on the circumstances they are in (Howes & Matheson, 1992; Howes & Tonyan, 2003; Hughes & Dunn, 2007). Therefore, it would not be correct to assert that toddlers are unable to play cooperatively or that solitary play in an older child is always a sign of social immaturity.

Parten (1932) underestimated the abilities of young children to play cooperatively. It is now widely believed that children as young as 18 months will sometimes cooperate in play with age mates, as when they play peek-a-boo or run-and-chase, in which they take turns running after each other (Brenner & Mueller, 1982). Perhaps the toddlers observed by Parten didn't cooperate because she observed their behavior in the context of nursery school groups that ranged in size from 2 to 15 children; many of the children in these groups, particularly among the 2-year-olds, were not well known to one another. We now know that children are most likely to communicate effectively and to cooperate in play when interacting with children they are familiar with.

Parten's (1932) implication that solitary play is a sign of social immaturity has also been challenged. A child who plays alone may not be incapable of relating to peers but may instead simply seek solitude to explore play materials or to work quietly on a play project. Preschool children who engage in a lot of solitary play are not necessarily seen as less popular than their peers (Steinkamp, 1989).

The Expansion of Make-Believe

Developmental Trends in Pretend Play

As discussed in Chapter 3, even in their second year of life children engage in make-believe play. However, one of the most significant advances during the third year is in the child's ability to share symbolic meaning while engaged in activities of pretense. Children seem to spontaneously take on complementary roles, so the solitary pretense of the toddler becomes the social pretense of the preschool child (Rubin, Coplan, Nelson, Cheah, & Lagace-Seguin, 1999). The years from age 3 to age 6 are generally recognized as the golden years of make-believe. At no other time in life is a human being so thoroughly involved in the world of fantasy.

Adults may wonder if such young children know the difference between fantasy and reality, but you will recall from Chapter 3 that a 1-year-old does not seem confused by the fantasy-reality distinction, although the distinction is easily blurred in emotionally charged situations (Lillard & Witherington, 2004; Ma & Lillard, 2006). However, it is not until the age of 3 years that children clearly know the difference between reality and make-believe (Custer, 1996, 1997; Golomb & Kuersten, 1996; Harris & Kavanaugh, 1993; Howes & Tonyan, 2003). Illustrating this point is the work of Golomb and Kuersten, who deliberately interrupted children's make-believe activities (e.g., by walking across a blanket that the children were pretending was a river). The children would stop their play, stepping out of the pretense mode, and then, when the adult had gone, would move effortlessly into pretending again. In other words, they realized that the blanket was really a blanket and that they were mentally representing it to themselves as a river.

Although psychologists agree that young children distinguish between reality and make-believe, there has been disagreement over whether preschoolers know that pretense involves a mental representation of reality. If Dad pretends to be a bear chasing her around the room, can 3-year-old Jody look into his mind and attribute to him the mental act of pretending? Or is her understanding limited to knowing that Dad is acting like a bear? Some researchers (e.g., Custer, 1996, 1997; Davis, Wooley, & Bruell, 2002; Joseph, 1998) provide evidence that young children know that pretending requires mental activity, including planning and intention. However, the findings from other studies (e.g., Lillard, 1996, 1997) support the view that children see pretense only in terms of behavior.

How is the question to be resolved? It appears that 3- and 4-year-olds can sometimes understand the difference between pretending as an act of the

PUTTING THEORY INTO PRACTICE 4.1

Attending to Unexpected Trends in a Child's Play

Watch for signs of stress indicated when a preschooler regresses in play, such as by moving from cooperative to parallel or solitary play or from more to less imaginative dramatic play.

The play of a child observed over a short period of time tells us little about that child's over-all intellectual, social, or emotional development. This is because a snapshot of play at a par-ticular time can be interpreted in a number of ways. For example, a teacher observes that for the past week 5-year-old Paul has spent most of his free playtime playing alone. When he did interact with other children in group make-believe, his play was neither sustained nor partic-ularly imaginative. For example, he wanted to play the same role all the time, and the themes of his dramatic play involved performing the same action sequences over and over again. The teacher knows that Paul's play is immature for a 5-year-old, but there could be many rea-sons why. Is the play immature because Paul lacks the necessary skills for social interac-tion? Does Paul have a limited amount of creative imagination compared with other children of his age? Is the play immature because Paul's mother left on a business trip that morning and he will be picked up from school by a sitter? Is it because Paul is tired? Is it because he is new to the classroom and knows very few of the other children? Is it because he is sick? Does his solitary and unimaginative play result from a combination of all of these factors?

  While snapshots tell us little, trends over time in play can be very revealing. Let us say that at the beginning of the school year Paul was one of the most socially perceptive children in the classroom. He made friends easily, rarely engaged in solitary or parallel play, and demonstrated sophisticated cooperation skills. In addition, teachers described him as an imaginative child, and he often took the lead in suggesting fantasy themes to the other children. The teacher knows, therefore, that Paul does not have basic social interaction difficulties; nor does he lack creative imagination, so his regressive behavior in the past 2 weeks takes on new meaning. While the teacher cannot determine exactly why his play regressed, she at least can rule out a number of hypotheses. In all likelihood she will look at stressors in his life as potential causes of regression in Paul's play.

mind and pretending as a simple behavioral act, but whether they do or do not depends on the circumstances or the context of the fantasy (Sobel, 2006). Illustrating this point, Ganea, Lillard, and Turkheimer (2004) had preschool children watch an adult announce her intention to act like a kangaroo and then proceed to behave in a way that was totally unlike a kangaroo, while another adult said she wanted to act like a kangaroo and then produced a close imitation of kangaroo behavior (hopping). The children agreed that even the "bad pretender" was pretending because she had announced this as her intention. In other words, they knew that pretending is an act of the mind and not just a behavior when an intention to pretend is openly stated in advance. The researchers suggested that an understanding of pretense as a mental activity was present but that it is fragile in the mind of a preschool child.

Pretend play can be a solitary activity, as when a child shares a personal fantasy world with dolls, other miniature life toys, or imaginary companions. Jean Piaget (1962) described solitary pretend play as the first and least mature stage of symbolic play, although it should not be forgotten that a good deal of highly creative activity can result from solitary make-believe. Pretend play can occur in parallel, when two or more children are ostensibly playing together but each is under the spell of a separate fantasy. Finally, pretend play can involve intense group interaction, with each group member taking a role that complements the roles played by all others in the group. Group pretend play, which is also referred to as dramatic or **sociodramatic play**, comprises approximately two thirds of all the pretend play of preschool children (Rubin, 1986).

The ratio of activities involving make-believe to all episodes of free play increases significantly from the age of 3 to the age of 6 (Hetherington, Cox, & Cox, 1979; Johnson & Ershler, 1981; Rubin, Fein, & Vandenberg, 1983), and this increase is due primarily to increases in the number of episodes of group-oriented sociodramatic play (Connolly, 1980; Hetherington et al.; Rubin et al.). Solitary and parallel pretend play episodes remain fairly stable throughout the preschool years. Is it fair to characterize solitary pretense as inherently less sophisticated than group pretense requiring cooperation and the assumption of complementary roles? From a practical standpoint, should a parent or teacher be concerned if an older preschooler still enjoys solitary pretend play? There is a sense that solitary pretense is less mature than social pretense, but judgments about children's social maturity should never be made on the basis of individual make-believe play episodes. Instances of solitary pretend play occur throughout the preschool years and even beyond and should not be a cause for concern.

On the other hand, solitary and parallel pretend play activities constitute a distinct minority—approximately 13% and 17%, respectively—of the pretend play activities of preschoolers; as pointed out earlier, most of the pretend

Computers in the Preschool: What Is the Effect on Play?

In recent years there has been a dramatic increase in the availability of computers and other forms of instructional technology, and materials of this type are finding their way into preschool classrooms (Clements & Sarama, 2002; Fein, Campbell, & Schwartz, 1987; Henninger, 1994; Nikolopoulou, 2007). The educational benefits of instructional technology in the preschool classroom have been well documented. Children of 4 and 5 years have successfully used instructional technology to count, to learn the alphabet, and to develop language skills, as well as skills in the areas of art, mathematics, and science (Chera & Wood, 2003; Din & Calao, 2001; Fletcher-Flinn & Gravatt, 1995; Segers & Verhoeven, 2002; Spencer & Baskin, 1997; Vernadakis, Avgerinos, Tsitskari, & Zachopoulou, 2005).

In terms of the impact on social interaction, some researchers have discovered that the arrival of a new computer has little effect on peer play (Fein et al., 1987; Strein & Kachman, 1984), while others have offered evidence that social encounters actually increase when a computer is present (Borgh & Dickson, 1986; Hawkins, Sheingold, Gearhart, & Berger, 1982; Wright & Samaras, 1986; Zaijka, 1983). A typical pattern is that children become obsessed with a computer only in the beginning, but once the novelty wears off, they become quite willing to share and take turns at the keyboard, and life in the preschool soon returns to normal (Simon, 1985). Young children typically do not fight for their turns on a computer but instead assume complementary roles (e.g., "owner," "participant," "spectator"), each with its own duties, rights, and obligations and each of which children rotate in and out of (Ljung-Djärf, 2008).

The arrival of instructional technology in the preschool has not been greeted with total enthusiasm, however. The Alliance for Childhood expresses concern about the use of computers, suggesting that they are injurious to health and safety (repetitive motion injuries, vision problems), promote social isolation, and limit the child's creative imagination. The alliance argues that "the high-tech agenda pushes children to become skilled little technicians . . . [and] . . . interrupts . . . the playful generation of images from one's own imagination" (Cordes & Miller, 2000, p. 96).

Some teachers fear that children in the presence of computers will emphasize symbolic activities and neglect those that require hands-on work with concrete objects or that teachers will overly structure the young child's activities to the point that child-organized activities will all but disappear. Others are concerned that the presence of the microcomputer in the preschool reflects society's emphasis on computer literacy as a goal of education; the computer is seen as a tool for work, and its presence represents an erosion of the principle that young children should be allowed to play.

What can be concluded about the impact of computer technology on the preschool classroom? Is it positive, negative, or both? Perhaps the answer has to do less with the technology itself than with the ways in which it is used. For example, if technology is allowed to substitute for rather than supplement other forms of preschool learning and play, this could be seen as misuse. In addition, the value of instructional technology may be minimal if preschool children are not provided with adult direction and supervision. In a study of educational technology in Scottish preschools, it was found that children actually received little adult supervision or guidance when playing at the computer. Adults typically intervened only when children exceeded their allotted time or complained that other children were dominating the computers. Without adult guidance, the experience for children was limited both in terms of learning and in terms of play (Plowman & Stephen, 2005, 2007). If a computer is in an isolated area of the playroom and if the teacher offers limited guidance and support, this expensive piece of equipment will be of little value for children's learning or the enhancement of children's play.

activities of preschoolers occur in the context of group interaction. Children who engage in a disproportionate amount of solitary and parallel pretense—and thereby deviate significantly from the observed norms—may indeed be displaying signs of social immaturity. Young children who engage in abnormally high percentages of solitary and parallel pretense, compared with social pretense, tend to be rejected by their peers, have difficulty solving social problems, and be rated by their teachers as socially maladjusted (Rubin, Bukowski, & Parker, 2006).

Dramatic Play Roles

Dramatic play roles have been extensively analyzed, and it has been found that most roles fall into three categories, depending on the extent to which the role-playing involves simply being a character of one's choice or is defined by the performance of a specific action sequence. There are family roles, character roles, and functional roles.

Family roles, which are those most likely to be played out by the preschool child, are the roles of mother, father, brother, sister, baby, and even family pet. The youngest preschool children limit themselves to the roles of mother, father, and baby, while older children are more likely to include siblings, grandparents, and other relatives. Not surprisingly, family roles tend to come in pairs; that is, when a mother character appears in sociodramatic play, it is likely that a father character will appear as well (Garvey, 1977).

Character roles are based on characters that are either stereotyped or fictional. Stereotyped characters are defined by their occupations or by their habitual actions, mannerisms, or personality characteristics. Fictional character roles, on the other hand, are based on specific individuals from the various media—such as books, television programs, and movies. Character roles, which tend to be somewhat flat and one-dimensional in nature, are like family roles in the sense that they need not be expressed in terms of specific action plans. A child may play at simply being an alien from outer space, a wicked witch, a cowboy, or a princess, without following any predetermined course of action.

Unlike family and character roles, which are possible to play simply by *being* a particular character, **functional roles** are always defined in terms of a specific plan of action—preparer of dinner, firefighter, monster, victim, train conductor, passenger on the train. The functional role defines the behavior but not the permanent identity of the character (Bretherton, 1986). A family or character role can become functional at times, as when a father protects his children by chasing away a monster or a cowboy circles his wagons in preparation for an Indian attack. However, family and character roles require no specific action plans because they can be defined by who the character is as well as by what the character does.

The family role is the most central of all roles and the most complex, perhaps because it is the one that children are the most familiar with. The centrality of family roles is illustrated by the pattern of role transformation that is seen in sociodramatic play. Children will typically use the family role as a base out of which one or more functional roles will evolve, but the base will be returned to periodically during the play episode. For example, a father in a dramatic play situation may be transformed into a firefighter, a monster chaser, a chauffeur, or a carpenter, but between transformations he returns regularly to his original father role.

The degree and type of fantasy that children incorporate into their play depend on a variety of factors. Older preschoolers, aged 3 to 5 years, are more likely than 2-year-olds to engage in exotic (e.g., cowboys, pirates) and unrealistic (e.g., space creatures) fantasy play; younger children play more realistically and act out such familiar roles as those of family members or familiar occupations (e.g., mail carrier, police officer). Older preschoolers have an easier time than younger ones using objects for make-believe that differ in form and function from what they are intended to represent (Bigham & Bourchier-Sutton, 2007). This developmental trend, which begins in the second year of life and is known as decontextualization, was discussed in Chapter 3. Boys are less realistic than girls in their choice of roles and themes, a finding that will be discussed at greater length in Chapter 6. The amount of exposure to television, movies, and reading is also related to the degree of fantasy in children's play: Those who see more movies, have more books read to them, watch more weekend television, and prefer unrealistic fantasy TV programs engage in less realistic and more exotic fantasy episodes in their play (Boyatzis & Watson, 1993). Finally, children who have personified objects, such as dolls or stuffed animals to which they ascribe human qualities, to which they regularly talk, and which they take care of, seem to engage in a greater amount of role-playing than children who do not have such special friends (Gleason, Sebanc, McGinley, & Hartup, 1997).

Props for Dramatic Play

Children's dramatic play is obviously facilitated by the availability of props to stimulate them in one direction or another, and one of the questions adults most frequently ask is "How realistic should props for dramatic play be?" There is research to suggest that the child will play more imaginatively with the toy that is less realistic. In an early study, Pulaski (1973) found that kindergarten, first-grade, and second-grade children played more inventively with toys that were less structured in terms of an obvious intended purpose (rag dolls, empty cartons, bolts of fabric) than with those that were highly realistic.

PUTTING THEORY INTO PRACTICE 4.2

Choosing Props for Make-Believe Play

Props for make-believe play should be selected carefully. In some cases, they should not have intended uses that are too specific or too obvious. In other situations, props need to be very specific in what they suggest. It is usually best to choose materials that are familiar to the child but may be used in a variety of ways.

When a child engages in imaginative play with any material, the richness of the fantasy results from a combination of the material itself and the mind of the child who is using it. Materials that are too specific can suggest to the child how they "should" be played with. Offering a child a firefighter's hat to play with suggests that the child should pretend to be a firefighter. On the other hand, if the child is given a plain felt hat, he or she can assume any number of roles—a mother or father, a teacher, a neighbor, or a grandparent, for example. When supplying play materials to children, keep in mind how much of the imagination the child is expected to supply and how much is provided by the material itself.

Are there times when specific props are more appropriate than nonspecific ones? There are at least two situations in which specific props should be used. The first is when the child has a limited range of fantasy. Children low in fantasy predisposition, perhaps because they are not used to engaging in make-believe play, need specific props to get them started. In fact, they may also need direct suggestions from an adult. The second is when it is determined that a child needs to address a particular emotional issue that can be suggested by specific props. Therapists will often use materials (e.g., baby dolls, toy weapons) designed to address a child's individual psychological problems, and parents and teachers often provide props (e.g., medical toys) that relate to a particular issue a child is worried about.

Sometimes an adult will think that imaginative play is encouraged if children are given totally unfamiliar materials to play with. However, if this occurs, a child may focus more on the properties of the materials than on the ways in which they can be incorporated into fantasy. The child may spend more time wondering "What is it?" than "How can I play with it?"

On the other hand, the pattern of results for research on prop realism seems to depend on such variables as level of development and familiarity with dramatic play. Younger preschool children or those with little experience with make-believe may need a greater degree of realism in the props they are given. For example, Fields (1979) discovered that preschoolers played more imaginatively and in a more sustained manner with toys that seemed to have specific purposes (e.g., a cardboard box painted like a car or truck) than with those that were more abstract (e.g., a cardboard box painted in an abstract design). A similar finding was reported by Umek and Musek (2001), who observed that 4- and 5-year-olds showed more sophisticated dramatic play with realistic than with unrealistic props but that 6-year-olds played as easily with both types of materials.

The challenge to the preschool teacher is that children need to have some familiarity with play materials if they are to use them imaginatively, yet if the intended uses of toys are too obvious and too specific, the imaginations of the players might be constrained. Perhaps the dilemma can be best summed up by the results of a study by B. L. Mann (1984), who had 40 children ranging in age from 3.5 to 5.5 years listen to a story about the adventures of "Mole" and "Troll." They were then told to act out the story, and some were given realistic props that resembled the story's characters and events while others received unrealistic props. Finally, the children were asked questions about the story.

Children who had the realistic props acted out the story line in more realistic detail and had

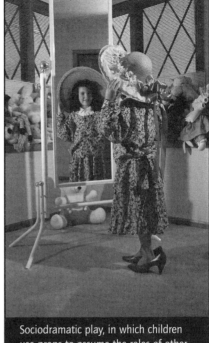

© Photodisc

Sociodramatic play, in which children use props to assume the roles of other people and then create scripts to describe the action, is the most popular form of pretend play in preschool children.

a better memory of the story when questioned about it. However, those with unrealistic props seemed to rely on cognitive activities requiring a greater degree of creative imagination; their renditions of the story were less technically accurate but more creative. Mann (1984) concluded that children may need realistic props to get them started and to sustain their play in the early stages but that as they become comfortable in the exercise of their powers of make-believe, unrealistic props suffice and serve to stimulate their creativity.

Functions of Dramatic Play

Psychologist Ruth E. Hartley (Hartley et al., 1952) described a number of important functions of dramatic play for preschool children. The first is *simple imitation of adults:* The child can play out scenes that he or she may have witnessed adults engaged in and, by doing so, may come to a better understanding of what the world of adulthood is all about. A second function is *intensification of a real-life role:* The child plays a role that he or she is accustomed to in everyday life and is familiar with, such as the role of the victim, the dependent role of a baby, or the role of a boss or leader of other children.

Dramatic play may serve the function of *reflecting home relationships and life experiences,* when simple imitation of what they have seen adults do is combined with intense emotion. Children in dramatic play may unwittingly reveal a good deal of information about their home lives and about the people who live with them. Hartley and colleagues (1952) described the case of 3-year-old Mary, the child of an anxious and controlling mother. Mary and her mother ordinarily related well, but the mother seemed overly concerned about neatness and often slapped Mary for touching things she wasn't supposed to or for getting her clothes dirty. In dramatic play, Mary became a gross exaggeration of her own mother: She slapped her "children" regularly, yelled at them, and complained about the messes they made.

Another function of dramatic play is to allow children to *express urgent needs.* As an example, consider the case of 3-year-old David, the youngest of four children and the baby of the family, who received much love from his parents and older siblings but who wanted to have someone he could nurture and protect. In dramatic play, David almost always assumed a parent role, holding, cuddling, calming, and reassuring a variety of dolls, stuffed animals, and even other children.

Dramatic play serves as an *outlet for forbidden impulses.* The child who fears the expression of aggressive impulses in real life might in play take the role of a highly aggressive character, or the child who is curious about the body's sexual parts and functions might express that curiosity by playing the role of doctor or nurse. The point is that in play the impulse is safe because it is acceptable, while in the child's everyday world it is not.

Finally, dramatic play also allows for the *reversal of roles:* A child who ordinarily feels helpless in the family situation may assume the role of parent and therefore become the source of power rather than the victim of it. By reversing roles, children can learn much about the points of view of other people and can thereby expand their own self-concepts. In the case of the parent-child role reversal, the child might also learn that parenting is more of a challenge than it ordinarily appears to be!

Benefits of Dramatic Play

The benefits of dramatic play are numerous and are found in three general areas of development: the affective, the intellectual, and the social (Mellou, 1994). The affective benefits include the development of self-awareness, self-confidence, and self-control (Singer, 1995). In pretend play, children have an opportunity to master an environment that is bound only by the limits of their fantasy. They can extend themselves beyond the real world in which they often feel powerless into a world in which they can experience the pleasure of exercising their powers of mastery. In doing so, they are often able to reduce conflicts in their lives—to compensate for unpleasant experiences by "undoing" them and playing them out with happier endings and by taking revenge on reality (Bretherton, 1986; Freud, 1974; Piaget & Inhelder, 1969).

The intellectual benefits of dramatic play are many. Such play, by allowing children to create alternative worlds, encourages them to engage in subjunctive representation of reality (Bretherton, 1986). That is, it stimulates the "what if" type of thinking that forms the basis for mature hypothetical reasoning and problem solving. Dramatic play stimulates children to think creatively and, in fact, is related to later creativity (Dansky, 1980). In addition, while the evidence is correlational, extensive involvement in dramatic play may improve children's memory, language development, reading ability, and cognitive perspective-taking skills (Burns & Brainerd, 1979; Dansky; Kavanaugh, 2006).

Finally, since dramatic play is usually highly social, it can have a significant impact on children's social development. Lev Vygotsky (1978), whose theory was discussed in Chapter 1, suggested that dramatic play has a critical role in self-regulation. Children seem to want to imitate adults, and when they do, they internalize adult norms and learn skills that are necessary to live up to those norms. The relationship between self-regulation and complex sociodramatic play was illustrated in a study by Elias and Berk (2002), who discovered that preschool children who engaged in the most episodes of group dramatic play were more likely to pick up their toys and clean up after themselves. However, the same tendency to self-regulate was not related to involvement in solitary dramatic play. Interesting too was the fact that the connection between complex sociodramatic play and self-regulation was most evident in children described by their teachers as impulsive.

Taking on imaginary roles forces children to control their own impulsive behavior in favor of the behavior that is consistent with those roles (Bodrova & Leong, 1996; Krafft & Berk, 1998). As a result, involvement in dramatic play seems to improve children's ability to cooperate when in group situations, to participate in social activities, and to understand human relationships (Lutz & Sternberg, 1999). When preschool children engage in social pretend play, they enter a delicate process of negotiation with other children as they assign and bargain about play roles (e.g., Todd: "I want to be the monster." Steve: "No! You were the monster the last time we played.") and themes (e.g., Jean: "We're a family going to the beach." Joan: "I don't want to go to the beach. That isn't any fun. I want to be a firefighter." Jean: "OK. You could put out a fire at the beach.") Such negotiations help children communicate with one another more effectively and resolve some of the inevitable conflicts that arise in the interaction of preschoolers (Howes, Unger, & Matheson, 1992; Singer & Lythcott, 2004).

FACTORS THAT INFLUENCE PRESCHOOL PLAY

Nutrition and Play

A point made often in this book is that the sophistication of children's play is related to the sophistication of their cognitive functioning, and it has long been recognized that a severely inadequate diet over a period of time can adversely affect a child's cognitive functioning. Malnutrition seems to result in a lowered level of activity in school, increased difficulty in staying on task, decreased social involvement, and poorer performance on standardized tests (McDonald, Sigman, Espinosa, & Neumann, 1994; Sigman, Neumann, Jansen, & Bwibo, 1989; Sigman et al., 2005). On a positive note, however, the effects of malnutrition are apparently reversible. Intellectual performance, as measured by tests of intelligence in an older child or of overall development in an infant or a toddler, can be enhanced in malnourished children by providing them with nutritional supplements (Pollitt, 1994; Pollitt, Gorman, Engle, Martorell, & Rivera, 1993), and there is evidence to suggest that intervention can have lasting positive effects (Grantham-McGregor, 2005; Grantham-McGregor, Powell, Walker, Chang, & Fletcher, 1994).

Since play and cognition are related, one might expect that the quality of a child's diet will influence the quality of his or her play. It might also be expected that the play of a malnourished child will be enriched by the availability of nutritional supplements. In fact, a number of studies indicate that play can be influenced by nutritional factors. In general, children who are malnourished tend to be less social, less active, less happy, and less playful (Espinosa, Sigman, Neumann, Bwibo, & McDonald, 1992; McDonald et al., 1994; Sigman & Sena, 1993). Malnutrition, particularly if it is moderate to severe, seems to be associated with (a) reduced amounts of overall play and (b) a lessening of the quality of play (Barrett & Radke-Yarrow, 1985; Chavez & Martinez, 1984; Sigman et al., 1988, 1989; Wachs, 1993; Walka, Pollitt, Triana, & Jahari, 1997). Specific types of dietary deficiencies have been found to affect play. For example, iron deficiency anemia in preschoolers has been associated with a delayed positive response to and a reluctance to approach novel toys (Jukes, 2005; Lozoff et al., 2007). It seems that play is most readily affected by the child's level of protein intake and that symbolic play, which has a strong cognitive component, is more likely to be affected by nutritional variables than are other play activities (Wachs; Wachs et al., 1993).

It is encouraging to realize, however, that, just as nutritional deficiencies can inhibit play, nutritional supplements can have the opposite effect. For example, in a study of 55 mildly to moderately malnourished children living in West Java, Indonesia, it was found that children given nutritional supplements played with more toys, had more interest in play, and displayed a longer span of attention when playing. These children were also less likely than those without a supplement to seek interaction with a caregiver, such as by breastfeeding, rather than playing when they had the opportunity to do so (Walka et al., 1997).

Parent Influences

Considering the importance of the roles they play in their children's lives, it should not be surprising that parents exert a major influence on their young children's play. Sometimes the influence is intentional and direct. For example, the amount of unrealistic fantasy play children engage in is related to their parents' appreciation for unrealistic fantasy (Boyatzis & Watson, 1993; Farver, 1999; Gleason, 2004; Haight, Parke, & Black, 1997). In addition, mothers often provide props for make-believe play, offer suggestions to get children started, and comment on the action once the play has begun (Farver; O'Connell & Bretherton, 1984). Sometimes it is indirect and unintentional, and while it isn't clear that maternal participation actually increases the sophistication of young children's make-believe play, it certainly increases the *amount* of fantasy that they engage in (Fein & Fryer, 1995).

Play and Attachment

It has long been recognized that there is considerable individual variation in the quality of parent-child attachment in our society (Ainsworth, 1979; Ainsworth, Blehar, Waters, & Wall, 1978; Bowlby, 1988; Creasey & Jarvis, 2007), and the quality of attachment is related to the quality of children's play. (In fact, play has been found to facilitate attachment between parent and child, a point that will receive further attention in Chapter 9.)

Children appear to be the most closely attached to parents who tend to be secure and who are confident in their parenting skills. Such parents make themselves readily available to their children from infancy onward and appear to be sensitive to their children's needs. They handle their children with affection, are interested in the various aspects of their lives, and truly enjoy spending time with them. On the other hand, the profile of the parent whose children are less closely attached is that of an anxious, irritable person who lacks sensitivity toward his or her child, has difficulty seeing the child's perspective, and projects a general sense of unavailability (Trapolini, Ungerer, & McMahon, 2008).

Attachment predicts the quality of play throughout the preschool years. Securely attached infants are more likely to explore the physical environment when in the presence of their mothers and are more likely to discover the appropriate uses of objects, as when they realize that a ball is to be rolled or a toy car is to be pushed across the floor (Bowlby, 1988; Rubin et al., 1999). Securely attached toddlers are more sociable, more likely to engage in rudimentary cooperative games with peers, and simply more enjoyable to be around (Creasey & Jarvis, 2007). Finally, preschoolers who are the most closely attached to their parents are the most likely to engage in fantasy play with objects, and their make-believe play is more sustained and more complex than that of insecure children (Creasey & Jarvis, 2003; Slade, 1987). They are more likely to function independently at the age of 2 years, and by the age of 5 years, they seem to have a greater amount of curiosity and behavioral flexibility and are more environmentally oriented in free play (Belsky, Garduque, & Hrncir, 1984; Joffe & Vaughn, 1982).

Closely attached preschoolers also appear to be more successful when engaging in social pretend play with peers. Howes and Rodning (1992) observed the social play of forty 3-year-olds, looking particularly at the number of dramatic play episodes they engaged in, the length of those episodes, and the amount of conflict they contained. Since all of these children had been participants since infancy in a research project, information was available about the closeness of their attachment to their parents during their first year of life. The researchers noticed that secure, closely attached children engaged in five times as many episodes of social pretend play and that these episodes lasted longer than those of insecure children. In addition, the secure children were only half as likely to experience conflict when they played. When conflict did occur, the secure children were likely to resolve the conflict and continue the game, while the insecure children responded by simply ending the play episode.

Play and Marital Disruption

In a classic study of the effects of divorce on preschool children's play, Hetherington and colleagues (1979) found that girls from disrupted families engaged in less dramatic play than did those from intact families both 2 months and 1 year after the divorce. When observed 2 years after the divorce, however, the differences between the two groups of girls had disappeared. Boys from disrupted families, on the other hand, engaged in fewer episodes of dramatic play at all three time periods studied, and when dramatic play did occur, these boys appeared to be more rigid and less imaginative in their roles than were their counterparts from intact families. Furthermore, sons of divorced parents engaged in more of the relatively immature solitary and parallel functional play, involving the simple repetition of motor behaviors, than did the boys from intact families.

Since much of a preschool child's play involves make-believe, it is not surprising that divorce has an impact on young children's fantasy. In a study by Page and Bretherton (2003), children of divorced parents were presented with the beginnings of stories dealing with aspects of family life and then asked to complete the story ("Show me and tell me what happens now"). One of the story themes that the authors examined was that of violence, and it was found that children whose stories contained high levels of violent activity between parents or of maternal violence toward children were also rated as less socially competent in the nursery school setting. This finding is not surprising since postdivorce conflict has been found to be a major predictor of young children's social and emotional adjustment to divorce (Emery, 1999; Hetherington, Bridges, & Insabella, 1998).

Peer Influences

Psychologists have long regarded the childhood peer relationship as the context in which a variety of important social skills emerge. Peer relationships are seen as playing a major role in a child's development of social competence and social adjustment (Ladd, Herald, & Andrews, 2006). In a relationship between a child and an adult, it is the adult who typically determines the rules for and provides the scaffolding for the interaction. The childhood peer relationship is a mutual one, in that the children themselves must establish the rules by which they will interact. As discussed in the previous chapter, this is a process that begins in the toddler years, and it promotes an understanding of cooperation and mutual respect, characteristics that are essential to the maintenance of successful social relationships of any kind (Brownell & Kopp, 2007).

Considering the overwhelming significance of peer interactions for children's social development, one would expect that peers, like adults, would have a substantial influence on children's play. In fact, they do, and the research indicates the presence of peer influence on play in three specific areas: peer familiarity, sex of playmates, and age of playmates.

Peer Familiarity

In general, the presence of stable, consistent peer relationships is related to a greater degree of overall social competence in preschool children, a greater likelihood of their being accepted by others, and a broader range of mature cooperative social play (Ladd, 2007). Children who have been in the same day care setting over a period of time, having a fairly stable group of peers to interact with, play in a more mature manner than do children of the same age who have not been exposed to a stable and consistent peer group (Howes, 1988). Perhaps it is not surprising, therefore, that children who enter kindergarten with a group of peers they knew in nursery school the year before seem to like school better and to display fewer symptoms of school-related anxiety (Ladd & Price, 1987).

Peer familiarity influences children's play in other, more specific ways. For example, children are more willing to engage in dramatic play when they are with familiar rather than unfamiliar peers. There is a greater amount of social organization and collaboration and a higher degree of enthusiasm and concentration when a peer is familiar (Tessier, de Lorimier, & Doyle, 1993). Finally, as children become more comfortable with a particular peer group, their fantasy play becomes more complex and reflects a higher level of cognitive functioning (Doyle, Connolly, & Rivest, 1980).

Sex of Playmates

The sex of a child's playmate also seems to influence the quality of social play. On the one hand, children are more likely to explore new objects and spend less time with familiar toys when playing with a same-sex playmate (Rabinowitz, Moely, Finkel, & McClinton, 1975). On the other hand, however, if boys play only with boys and girls play only with girls, they are more likely to engage in forms of play that are traditionally gender-typed (Serbin, Connor, Burchardt, & Citron, 1979). In other words, same-sex play seems to broaden a child's horizons in one sense but to limit them in another, indicating the value of both same- and mixed-sex play for young children.

Children tend to seek out same-sex playmates and have been found to do so even before the age of 2 years (Viernickel, 1997). Play with members of the opposite sex is rare in the preschool years, usually doesn't last very long, and is judged to be less sophisticated than same-sex play (Fabes, Martin, & Hanish, 2003). In addition, a preference for other-sex playmates is related to social adjustment difficulties. For example, for preschool boys at least, pretend play with girls is related to peer rejection and low teacher ratings of social competence (Colwell & Lindsey, 2005).

There is a difference, however, between a preference for other-sex playmates and a willingness to play with members of either sex, and there are approaches that facilitate mixed-sex play in the classroom. Mixed-sex play is more likely to occur if teachers comment approvingly on it (Serbin, Tonick, & Sternglanz, 1977), if the school curriculum emphasizes the teaching of nonstereotyped values regarding gender roles (Bianchi & Bakeman, 1978; Lockheed, 1986), and even if the room is designed so that boys and girls are more likely to interact (Kinsman & Berk, 1979). Illustrating this last point are the findings of Theokas, Ramsey, and Sweeney (1993), who first observed the typical behavior of 14 kindergartners and then modified their classroom by temporarily combining the housekeeping and block areas into an outer space environment. The teachers provided androgynous space clothing for the children, as well as space food, various foam and cardboard shapes, and even a space capsule constructed in the block area. The newly created area was designed to appeal equally to children of both sexes.

In the initial observation, boys spent 25% of their free-play time in the block area and only 2% in the housekeeping corner; girls were in the housekeeping area 10% of the time but spent only 2% of their playtime with the blocks. During the intervention, however, the pattern changed. Girls now spent 19% of their time in the block area, while the time boys spent in the housekeeping section increased from 2% to 10%! In addition, play with members of the opposite sex increased from its previous levels. Even a month after the block and housekeeping areas had been returned to their original states, the effects of their alterations could still be seen.

Age of Playmates

Young preschool children, aged 2 and 3 years, are likely to interact with playmates of almost any age, but as children develop, they are increasingly likely to select playmates of their own age. By the time they enter elementary school, children typically prefer same-age playmates to younger or older ones (Berk, 1989; Lederberg, Chapin, Rosenblatt, & Vandell, 1986; Roopnarine & Johnson, 1984).

Play with same-age peers differs from play in mixed-age groups in several ways. Same-age interaction tends to be more positive in general, there tends to be a greater incidence of verbal interaction, and cooperative dramatic play is more likely to occur in groups of same-age peers than in mixed-age groups (Lederberg et al., 1986; Roopnarine & Johnson, 1984). On the other hand, cooperative constructive play (e.g., building things together, working together on group projects) is found to occur more often in mixed-age groups than in same-age groups (Roopnarine et al., 1992). Thus it appears that both types of age grouping foster cooperation, albeit of different sorts. Not surprisingly, imitation of the behavior of peers is more likely to occur if peers are the same age or older, but it is unlikely if peers are younger (Berk, 1989; Brody & Stoneman, 1981). Finally, children are drawn more easily into social interaction by older playmates than by same-age or younger ones, perhaps because the older child tends to assume the role of social director, as it were, in structuring the play (Brody, Graziano, & Musser, 1983).

The benefits of structuring are especially obvious when a playmate is considerably older, as Feldman (1997a, 1997b) discovered when he observed naturally occurring episodes of play at a private school (age range: 4 to 19 years) that was organized as a "participatory democracy." In this setting, children of all ages played together spontaneously, without being required to, and the play interactions were very positive. Competitive play was rare because everyone realized that a young child cannot compete successfully against an older one. Cooperation was the rule; the older children instructed the younger ones and offered them help and advice. When a younger child asked for assistance, it was almost always given. The older children benefited from the mixed-age play as well. Since they had to structure the play activities to accommodate their younger playmates (e.g., by changing the rules of the game), the games were more challenging to them because of the adjustments needed. It seemed to be a win-win situation; everyone gained from the experience of playing in the mixed-age groups.

Group Child Care Experience

According to the most recent information provided by the U.S. Census Bureau, 63% of U.S. children under the age of 5 years (11.6 million of 18.5 million) were involved in some type of regular child care arrangement while their mothers worked (Johnson, 2005). As can be seen in Table 4.2, the arrangements for child care were varied. (In some cases, the numbers in the table exceed the numbers in the headings because many children were involved in multiple types of arrangements.) Four of 10 children were cared for by a relative, the child's father in 14% of the cases and a grandparent in 23%. One third were cared for by nonrelatives, and 23% of the total number were involved in regular group child care arrangements.

What are the effects of exposure to day care on children's development and, more specifically, on children's play? For the past 40 years, educators and psychologists have put considerable effort into seeking answers to these questions, but simple answers have yet to be discovered. In fact, there is little to report about the overall effects of home-based day care, since arrangements of this type are difficult to study. And even when researchers focus specifically on organized

Table 4.2   Child Care Arrangements for Preschoolers: Winter 2002

Arrangement Type	Number of Children (Thousands)	Percent in Arrangement
Total children under 5 years	18,454	100
Children in a regular arrangement	11,596	62.9
Relative care	7,411	40.2
Mother	654	3.5
Father	2,616	14.2
Sibling	462	2.5
Grandparent	4,180	22.7
Other relative	1,337	7.2
Nonrelative care	6,447	34.9
Organized day care facility	4,198	22.7
Day care center	2,335	12.7
Nursery or preschool	1,138	6.2
Head Start/kindergarten	981	5.3
Other nonrelative care	2,554	13.8
In child's home	690	3.7
In provider's home	1,890	10.2
Family day care	1,149	6.2
Other arrangement	769	4.2
Self-care	39	0.2

Note: From J. O. Johnson (2005).

day care centers, they often find themselves comparing apples and oranges because the qualifications of caregivers and their access to material resources are so varied (Belsky, 2001; Clarke-Stewart & Allhusen, 2002). Perhaps it should not be surprising that inconsistent and even contradictory findings have emerged from research conducted in child care centers: The general finding is that exposure to such environments may indeed influence the maturity of children's social interaction and social play, but the influence can be either negative or positive.

On the negative side, extensive group care involvement has been associated with negative affect, displays of aggression, and resistance to adult authority (Clarke-Stewart, 1984; Howes & Olenick, 1986; Phillips, McCartney, & Scarr, 1987). These findings are not consistent, however, and in one extensive Canadian study, higher levels of aggression were found in children cared for at home by their mothers than in children in group day care settings (Borge, Rutter, Côté, & Tremblay, 2004). The authors suggested as an explanation for this surprising finding that very high levels of aggression were found in children from high-risk homes, which are characterized by lack of communication and affection and by difficulties in solving problems and controlling unacceptable behavior. Children from such homes inflated the average of the aggression levels in the home care group. Any comparison of the relative effects of day care versus home care must take into account the characteristics of the homes and the group care settings.

On the positive side, experience in child care centers is related to advanced levels of social play, which are characterized by a greater degree of sophistication in children's social interactions (Belsky & Steinberg, 1978; Howes, 1988; Phillips et al., 1987). Illustrative of such positive findings were those of Schindler, Moely, and Frank (1987), who looked at the relationship between time spent in day care and social maturity of play in terms of Mildred Parten's (1932) classification system. Children ranging in age from 2 to 5 years were grouped according to (a) the number of months they had been in day care and (b) the number of hours they spent at a day care center each week. It was found that children who had spent and were spending the greatest amount of time in a day care setting were more likely to engage in socially mature associative play, as well as in constructive play, and were less likely to engage in solitary play, onlooker play, or what is termed unoccupied behavior.

Interestingly enough, time spent in day care was not related to the amount of cooperative play observed by these particular researchers, although other researchers (e.g., Howes, 1988) have reported that children who begin day care at an earlier rather than at a later age, such as 1 year as opposed to 3 years, engage in more cooperative social pretend play and have an easier time relating to their peers in general.

How can the apparent contradiction between the positive and negative social influences of group child care be explained? Much seems to depend on the quality of the centers themselves. For example, Phillips and colleagues (1987) found that positive social outcomes were most likely to occur when (a) the child care environment was verbally stimulating, in that adults and children regularly engaged in conversation; (b) the director of the center was relatively experienced in her or his role; and (c) the staff-to-child ratio in the center was high.

In summary, the group child care experience can enhance social maturity and lead to increasingly sophisticated levels of social interaction and social play. However, the effect depends on the characteristics of the setting in which children are placed, and unfortunately, considerable variation exists in the quality of child care in the United States today.

The Physical Environment

While children's social environments can certainly influence the quality of their play, the physical environment can easily do so as well. We shall now examine the influence of the physical environment on children's play by looking first at the characteristics of an area specifically designed (usually by adults) for children's play—the school or neighborhood playground—and then at the arrangement of play space in a nursery school classroom.

Playgrounds and Outdoor Spaces

When children play outdoors, compared with indoors, their play is noisier, messier, less likely to be under the control of adults, and supportive of a greater range of exploration and experimentation (Sutterby & Frost, 2006). Outdoor play often occurs in playgrounds, but it can occur anywhere.

Playgrounds were virtually nonexistent in the United States before 1900, but in the early years of this century the playground movement flourished, and by 1916 there were more than 3,000 playgrounds in nearly 500 American cities (Park, 1982). The earliest playgrounds were little more than paved areas enclosed by high fences, later followed by the addition of such stationary equipment as slides, swings, jungle gyms, and seesaws. These traditional playgrounds have remained virtually the same throughout the years, probably because they are easy to maintain and the metal equipment is nearly indestructible (Boyatzis, 1987).

How do young children play in these traditional playgrounds? Perhaps it should not be surprising that play is more restricted in such areas; social play and fantasy play occur rarely, and most of children's time is spent instead in physical play (Barbour, 1999; Boyatzis, 1987; Sutterby & Frost, 2006). In an analysis of preschoolers' play on specific types of equipment found in traditional playgrounds, Boyatzis discovered that while some equipment promotes social interaction and social fantasy, most does not. For example, less than 20% of the play episodes observed on the swings could be described as social, and sociodramatic play was *never* observed while children played on the swings. Social interaction occurred more often on the jungle gym and the slide, as well as in the sandbox, but even then it accounted for less than half of the play episodes: Children spent most of their time engaged in either solitary or parallel play. Some episodes of sociodramatic play were seen on the slides, jungle gym, and sandbox, but these were very rare, accounting for only about 5% of the total playtime.

Children's activities in newer, less traditional playgrounds, with colorful plastic or wooden "enclosures," such as tubes, tunnels, and structures resembling forts, as well as construction and dramatic play materials with loose and movable parts, provide an interesting contrast. The primary difference is that newer playgrounds encourage children to engage in a greater variety of activities (Barbour, 1999). As an example, in one study it was found that more than half of the play episodes that occurred in enclosures that a child could climb in and out of consisted of forms of social interaction, and 1 in 4 play episodes included social fantasy themes, such as house, jail, or spaceship games (Boyatzis, 1987). The author of that study concluded that enclosures actually brought children together and encouraged them to use their creative imaginations.

Newer, less traditional playgrounds also seem to be very effective in increasing children's activity levels, as measured by their heart rates when playing. Children in playgrounds with colorful enclosures and climbing structures seem to play more vigorously and more excitedly than do children in older, traditional playgrounds (Stratton, Marsh, & Moores, 2000; Sutterby & Frost, 2006). If society's goal is to encourage physical exercise, traditional playground equipment will be adequate. If, however, the goal is to stimulate social and imaginative play as well, nontraditional materials should be included—more complex materials that children can move, manipulate, explore, and incorporate into their play in a variety of different ways.

Playground equipment can range far beyond even the newer, colorful manufactured materials, of course. Much of the most interesting "equipment" is found in the natural environment, including gardens with flowers and plants, which children themselves can plant and tend, as well as sand, water, and animal habitats to explore. Such natural playgrounds were found in one study to decrease boredom and antisocial behavior in young children (Moore & Wong, 1997). Most important, children find areas with vegetation particularly appealing, and such green spaces are especially conducive to play (Freeman, 1995; Kirkby, 1989; Moore, 1989; Taylor, Wiley, Kuo, & Sullivan, 1997). In a study of the play patterns of children in inner-city Chicago, it was found that twice as many children played in an area with many trees as in an area with few trees (Taylor et al.). It was not simply that children prefer to be in green spaces but that they really prefer to play there because the frequency of nonplay activities was unrelated to the amount of vegetation. Furthermore, creative play (e.g., make-believe) was particularly likely to occur in green spaces. Finally, when children played in green spaces, they had greater access to adults and were more likely to interact with them. It seems that, for a variety of reasons, green is the most appropriate color for outdoor play.

In addition to environmental playgrounds, there are materials that children enjoy but adults do not associate with play, such as those found in so-called adventure playgrounds—lumber in various sizes and shapes, old tires, bricks, scrap metal, and—perhaps most important of all—adult supervisors to help children safely discover their creative potential (Boyatzis, 1987; Frost, Wortham & Reifel, 2005).

Children enjoy playgrounds, of course, but their outdoor play is hardly confined to specific areas. Play takes a child anywhere and everywhere (Parkinson, 1987). Sadly, however, the average urban neighborhood may be more dangerous and less hospitable a play environment than it was in the past (Frost & Jacobs, 1995), leading some child development experts to argue that society should set aside natural play areas—protected open spaces for informal play.

Classroom Arrangement of Space

Experienced caretakers of young children realize the wisdom of dividing overall play space into activity areas of different sizes. The major reason for the partition of play space is to maximize the flexibility and enhance the overall quality of play, since children have been found to play differently in different physical settings. For example, in smaller spaces there is less running around and less rough-and-tumble play, although there is more actual physical contact among the children. Furthermore, in smaller spaces the child's attention can be focused on the activity that the space was designed for, whether constructive play in the block area, dramatic play in the housekeeping corner, or creative play with paints or clay in the art area.

There is an important caution to be observed, however, in designing small play spaces: If the space becomes overly crowded, children's play can be interfered with rather than facilitated. In small crowded areas, some children feel a loss of the privacy that everyone needs on occasion, and some display increases in aggressive behavior, a natural consequence of overcrowding in human beings and lower animals alike (Bailey & Wolery, 1984). It is also important to remember that the sense of being crowded is a psychological experience, so it is difficult to define the ideal play space density. In other words, a child in one culture might feel crowded in a particular physical and social environment, while a child in another culture might not feel crowded in exactly the same environment (Driscoll & Carter, 2004).

Large open spaces, on the other hand, seem to suggest to children that large muscle activities (e.g., running, jumping, general roughhousing) are appropriate and may discourage quieter, more creative forms of play. Perhaps this is the reason that, as pointed out in the previous section of this chapter, outdoor play is messier and noisier than indoor play (Sutterby & Frost, 2006). A large undivided room might contain exactly the same play materials as a room divided into theme areas, but a child in the open room is more likely to be distracted from a particular activity by other children, other play materials, and other ongoing play activities. Perhaps it is not surprising that children are more likely to engage in imaginative play in smaller spaces with flexible boundaries than in larger ones (Peck & Goldman, 1978).

A final, more practical reason for the division of play space is to help the teacher maintain a degree of organization and structure over both materials and time. Materials are less likely to be misplaced or used inappropriately if their use is restricted to a theme area, and it is difficult to schedule activities for particular times of the day if the materials are scattered throughout the room rather than housed in specific places.

Summary

The years from 2 to 5 are characterized by a decrease in rigidity and stubbornness; by increasing degrees of stability, reliability, and predictability; and by a move from primarily large muscle play to that involving small muscle activities. Sensory exploration during play is on the decline, and increases occur in play that is social and reflects children's interest in and identification with adults.

Between the ages of 2 and 5 years, children move from solitary and onlooker play to parallel play and then to associative and cooperative forms of play, although all forms of play are found at all ages. The size of the play group increases with age, and the same play materials are used differently at different ages, with younger children typically playing with them in isolation and older ones integrating them into cooperative social activities.

Pretend play can be a solitary activity, it can occur in parallel, or it can involve extensive cooperation, as in the case of sociodramatic play. Solitary and parallel pretend play can be found among children of all ages, but a disproportionate amount of solitary—as opposed to cooperative—pretense is thought to be a sign of social immaturity.

The central roles in dramatic play are family roles, but children typically assume a variety of character and functional roles as well. The dramatic play props most likely to stimulate the processes of creative thinking are those that are the least structured. However, if props leave *too* much to the imagination, many children—particularly very young ones or older ones with little experience at dramatic play—may not know what to do with them. The functions of dramatic play are many and include simple imitation of adults, intensification of real-life roles, reflection of home relationships, expression of pressing needs and forbidden impulses, and the reversal of roles. Finally, dramatic play appears to have a number of affective, intellectual, and social benefits for the preschool child.

The play of preschoolers is influenced by family factors, such as the security of parent-child attachment and the stability of the marriage; by the familiarity of the child's peer group; and by the amount of experience the child has had in a group setting, such as a day care center. The quality of play is also affected by such elements in the physical environment as the size of the play space and the extent to which it is organized into definable activity areas.

Key Terms

Associative Play	p. 101	Onlooker Play	p. 100
Character Roles	p. 108	Parallel Play	p. 100
Cooperative Play	p. 101	Sociodramatic Play	p. 105
Family Roles	p. 108	Solitary Play	p. 100
Functional Roles	p. 108		

Issues for Class Discussion

1. Solitary play is seen as indicative of a low level of social maturity, and teachers may regard a 4- or 5-year-old child who prefers solitary over social play as a child in need of intervention. However, shouldn't there be an effort to recognize individual differences in the need for socialization? Aren't there some children—and some adults for that matter—who simply prefer to be alone, and shouldn't they be granted this privilege?

2. How can teachers balance a young child's need for realistic dramatic play props with the recognition that, when props are too realistic, play can lose a certain amount of creativity? What clues should indicate to teachers that props aren't realistic enough? When should they realize that props are too realistic?

3. The research on attachment indicates that children may need a secure home base in order to get the most out of their play opportunities. Is it possible that emotional security is a prerequisite for any form of spontaneous play to occur?

4. Realizing that children play differently in the presence of same-sex and opposite-sex playmates, should adults make a conscious effort to facilitate mixed-sex play among children? Should adults encourage children to select playmates of the opposite sex even if they prefer not to?

Chapter 5

Play in Later Childhood and Adolescence

Is there play after kindergarten? Judging from the relative number of studies of middle childhood and adolescent play compared with that of play during the preschool years, one might come to the conclusion that children stop playing after they enter the first grade. In fact, many psychologists suggest that the organized games of older children should not be thought of as play at all, a point with which we are only in partial agreement. As will be indicated throughout this chapter, play continues to be an important element in the lives of children beyond the preschool years, and it continues to mirror their overall pattern of intellectual, social, and personality development.

The first half of the chapter will be devoted to a discussion of some of the general intellectual, social, and personality characteristics of the school-age child and the adolescent. For obvious reasons, an exhaustive treatment of the principles of child and adolescent development will not be presented. Only the more general features of these phases of life will be examined, with particular emphasis on the relationship between development and trends in children's play.

In the remainder of the chapter, trends in play during later childhood and adolescence will be discussed, as will the ways in which play both reflects and enhances the internal processes of human development. For example, it will be seen that as children become more logical in their thinking, their play becomes more orderly and more rule dominated. As children socialize with one another in increasingly mature ways, their play becomes a vehicle by which they can better understand the perspectives of others and the hierarchical structures of their specific peer groups; such social awareness is often a prerequisite for entrance into the "culture of childhood."

Learning Objectives

After reading Chapter 5, a student should be able to:

✦ Understand the general characteristics of school-age children in terms of their developing need for order, belonging, and industry.

✦ Describe some general characteristics of concrete and of formal operational reasoning and explain the differences between operational and preoperational thinking.

✦ Describe a number of peer group functions and recognize the ways in which the peer group serves as a major socializing agent during middle childhood.

✦ Describe the differences between early childhood play and middle childhood play in terms of decreasing symbolic play and the emergence of organized rituals and games with rules.

✦ Understand the characteristics of games with rules and their implications for children's intellectual development as they enter the elementary school years.

✦ Understand the significance of organized sports for school-age children and realize that there are both advantages and disadvantages to sports participation.

✦ Explain the impact of organized sports participation on the child's (a) level of physical fitness, (b) self-concept, and (c) ability to relate to other children.

✦ Identify the most popular recreational activities of adolescents in our society and relate these to the adolescent's social, intellectual, and personality development.

GENERAL CHARACTERISTICS OF THE SCHOOL-AGE CHILD

Three general characteristics—corresponding to trends in the areas of intellectual, social, and personality development—capture the essence of the period of middle childhood (see Table 5.1).

From an intellectual standpoint, the major development is that the child's thinking is becoming more orderly, more structured, and more logical. Therefore, the school-age child at play is more realistic and more rule oriented than the preschooler. Play thus reflects a developing *need for order*.

The school-age child is more socially involved with age mates than ever before, and the peer group provides support that formerly was offered only within the family. Acceptance by one's peers is of great importance to children in this age group, and their play reflects an overwhelming *need to belong*.

Finally, in the realm of personality development, a major challenge to the emerging self-concepts of school-age children is to demonstrate to themselves and others that they are competent—that they have talents, skills, and abilities of which they can be proud. In their play, there is reflected this *need for industry*.

TABLE 5.1　Characteristics of the School-Age Child

A Need for Belonging	A Need for Industry	A Need for Order
A decreasing reliance on parents	Increasing self-assertion	Logical thinking
A power struggle with mother	Boasting ("That's easy." "I can do that!")	The appearance of games with rules 　Physical games, such as 　　organized sports 　Intellectual games, such 　　as video games or 　　board games
Rudeness, argumentativeness	Bossiness with siblings, beginning at age 6	
Refusal or slowness in following directions	A need to demonstrate physical skills	
A decreasing emphasis on life within the family 　Teasing, tattling on, pestering 　　siblings 　Quarreling (especially at 7, 8, and 9) 　Sibling rivalry	A need to take risks and chances	
An increasing reliance on the group as: 　A source of companionship 　A place to test oneself 　A context in which to discover one's 　　surroundings 　A place to solidify one's gender 　　identity		

The Emergence of
Logical Thinking: A Need for Order

Even as early as the beginning of their second year of life, children are able to represent the world mentally. They are starting to use symbols in that they can let objects represent one another and can let words stand for objects, people, or events. Therefore, as pointed out in Chapter 3, they can now begin to engage in make-believe play. In a sense, the preschooler's intelligence consists of mental activity, compared with the sensory and motor intelligence of the younger infant (Flavell, 1985; Piaget, 1970; Piaget & Inhelder, 1969).

Preschoolers are limited, however, in that their mental representations of reality are not regulated by a consistent system of thought. They are easily distracted. When solving problems, they often focus on irrelevant aspects of the materials they are working with while ignoring information that is highly relevant. They are influenced too easily by appearances and too often fail to attend to substance. A preschool child may conclude, for example, that a tall, thin glass of water contains more liquid than a wide bowl *even if* the child has watched beforehand the liquid being measured in exactly equal amounts into both containers. The tall glass looks bigger, so it must hold more liquid—never mind the fact that the taller glass is also wider. (See Chapter 8 for a discussion of the influence of play on the child's emerging awareness of the concept of quantity.)

Children of 5 or 6 years are entering a new stage in the development of thinking, what Piaget (1963, 1983) referred to as the stage of **concrete operations**. Now the child's mental representations of reality are organized into an overall system of related representations (Birney, Citron-Pousty, Lutz, & Sternberg, 2005). The result is that thinking takes on a more logical, more orderly appearance. When asked to sort objects into groups, for example, the child in concrete operations sorts with reference to the logically defining properties of the objects. Thus, a collection of geometric forms might be sorted according to size, color, shape, or the number of straight lines they contain. By contrast, the preschool child would have sorted the geometric shapes perceptually rather than logically and arranged them into what Piaget referred to as **graphic collections**, which are pleasing perceptual arrays: The preschooler may have arranged the shapes into a circle to make a necklace or into a straight line to make a train (Inhelder & Piaget, 1964).

The emergence of a logical system to govern one's thinking allows children to perceive the universe as an orderly place. In addition to acquiring the ability to classify materials logically, the child develops an understanding of cause-and-effect relationships, a mature understanding of the concepts of time and space, and an ability to reason by induction, which involves the postulation of general principles on the basis of particular observed instances.

Now, because the child's thinking is patterned and orderly, the universe assumes the patterns of the child's mind. As will be seen, children's play during the years of middle and later childhood reflects the transition from the stage of prelogical thinking to that of concrete operations, in the sense that play becomes increasingly realistic and increasingly characterized by a need for order.

The Childhood Peer Group: A Need to Belong

Preschool children, even if they spend considerable amounts of time in nursery school or day care settings, are primarily home centered in orientation. That is, the family is the social unit around which most of their social activities are focused. By the age of 5 or 6 years, however close, children in most cultures engage in a major social transition. In modern industrialized societies, the transition involves the beginning of formal schooling, while in societies with no formal schooling, children may have to leave the protection of the family, stop playing childhood games, and become more productive members of the community (Cole, 2005). In other words, children become increasingly peer oriented and decreasingly family oriented, and they spend a greater and greater proportion of their waking hours in the company of peers.

Developmental psychologists suggest that the transition from the world of the family to the world of peers represents a major challenge for school-age children (Rubin, Bukowski, & Parker, 2006). Having recently mastered the ability to play with other preschool children in one-on-one or small-group settings, now they must negotiate their way through a peer group system, which is a close-knit society with definite, if unwritten, rules for membership. The characteristics of the peer group may differ from neighborhood to neighborhood and from school to school and may also differ over time because children's peer relationships are relatively unstable compared with those of adults. Even by early adolescence, only about half of children's close friendships extend beyond 1 year (Bowker, 2004), so it is not surprising that the composition of the larger peer group is variable as well. Nevertheless, in his or her particular peer group, the child who is different in any way—whether because of physical characteristics, personality traits, style of dress, access to material possessions, or socioeconomic status—may be quickly excluded (Lease, Musgrove, & Axelrod, 2000; Parker & Gottman, 1989).

The importance of acceptance by other children cannot be overestimated. In fact, successful interaction with peers seems to facilitate adjustment to school. Kindergarten children have a more positive attitude toward school and adjust to it more successfully if they form a close friendship in kindergarten or bring a friend with them from nursery school (Dunn, Cutting, & Fisher, 2002; Ladd &

Kochenderfer, 1996). In addition, the peer group is a major socializing agent in middle childhood. It is from their peers, rather than from their parents or teachers, that children learn about the culture of childhood. Peers teach a child effectively—and sometimes harshly—about social rules and the importance of obeying them. Peers establish a certain moral order that may differ somewhat from that established by adults. For example, parents may teach their children to inform on a child who is misbehaving, but in the peer culture tattling may be a major crime that qualifies the child for exclusion from the group.

Peers teach a variety of physical and intellectual skills that are necessary for group acceptance. Parents may provide instruction in riding a bicycle, but rarely do they teach their children how to ride on only the back wheel or how to jump their bicycle across ditches! Such education is usually provided by more experienced children in the peer group. Similarly, many of the jokes, stories, riddles, and slang expressions heard among the "coolest" of grade-school children were never taught to them by adults but were transmitted by the peer group.

The significance of the childhood peer group as a socializing agent cannot be overestimated; nor can the importance to grade-school children of being accepted by their age mates. What is the context in which the transmission of peer culture takes place? What is the battleground on which children fight to gain acceptance and to avoid rejection by the group? It should not be surprising, considering the amount of free time children spend on play, that the battleground is often the playground—both figuratively and literally. Indeed, it would be surprising if the play of school-age children did not comprise a large portion of their socialization experience and enhance the socialization process. In fact, play serves that very function and is often used to satisfy the school-age child's preeminent need to belong.

The Developing Self-Concept: A Need for Industry

One of the most pressing needs of elementary school children is the need for what psychoanalytic theorist Erik Erikson (1963) called a sense of **industry**. As children develop, Erikson wrote, they come to realize that there is no future for them "within the womb of the family" (p. 259), so they begin to apply themselves to a variety of skills and tasks that are necessary for success in the larger world of adults. They become eager to be productive, to achieve a sense of mastery and a feeling of accomplishment. In more traditional cultures, children's feelings of accomplishment are acquired by their learning to use the tools, utensils, and weapons that adults in their culture need for survival; in the United States, the "tools" are often acquired in the classroom.

PUTTING THEORY INTO PRACTICE 5.1

Encouraging a Sense of Industry

Children in the elementary school years have a particularly strong need to develop a sense of industry. They need to feel productive and to achieve a sense of mastery. Sensitive and caring adults can be particularly helpful in encouraging a sense of industry.

A sense of industry can be nurtured in children if parents and teachers keep in mind the following suggestions:

- Provide a broad range of opportunities for success. The greater the range of areas in which a child can succeed, the more likely the chance of success. If the only type of success that adults value is academic success or success in sports, children will have fewer opportunities to succeed and fewer opportunities to develop a sense of industry.

- For every child in a classroom, identify at least one activity that he or she is particularly good at. Not all children are great students or great athletes, but everyone is good at something. Some are great storytellers, some have a great sense of humor, some are loyal friends, and some are great at erasing the blackboard.

- Be constructive in statements critical of children. Every time an unacceptable behavior is identified, an acceptable alternative should be specified.

- Do not use excessive means to prevent children from failure. Occasional failure is realistic and will not seriously damage a child's developing self-concept. In fact, failing will help children cope with the experience of failure. However, some children experience repeated failure in all areas of their lives, and these are the ones for whom special efforts need to be made to provide success experiences.

- Do not be afraid to make negative comments about children's behavior. Adults will sometimes remark that they feel they are saying no all the time. Try to say yes more often to positive behaviors. It is a mistake to fall into the trap of criticizing negative behaviors while ignoring positive ones.

When Erikson (1963) spoke of the need for industry, he was referring to accomplishment in the world of work, however that may be defined. He was not speaking specifically of play, and in fact, he even suggested that as children strive for industry, they leave behind the "whims of play" (p. 259). It seems, however, that an ego-building sense of mastery can be acquired in the performance of activities other than those that have as their specific purpose the acquisition of skills. Indeed, why could a sense of mastery not be acquired from the performance of activities that have no external purpose at all, such as activities that fall under the definition of play? As will later be indicated, the need for industry is often reflected not only in the classroom activities of grade-school children but also in their play.

GENERAL CHARACTERISTICS OF THE ADOLESCENT

We now turn to an examination of some general characteristics of the period of adolescence, again referring to needs in the areas of social, intellectual, and personality development. We shall later attempt to relate these three types of needs to the forms of play that are often observed during the adolescent years.

In terms of intellectual development, the adolescent is experiencing a transition from the concrete form of reasoning that typifies the middle childhood years to a reasoning that is abstract and hypothetical. The intellectual need of the adolescent is a *need for abstract conceptualization.* In social terms, the adolescent needs more than simply to belong within the peer group; now there is a need to single out particular individuals with whom one can have an intimate relationship. In their social interactions and in their play, adolescents express a compelling *need for communication.* Finally, the adolescent is engaged in a struggle to create a stable and permanent sense of self—to achieve a degree of self-awareness and self-acceptance. Again, play will be the context within which this *need for identity* can often be met.

Formal Operations: A Need for Abstract Conceptualization

The use of a logical system of thinking appears, as we have pointed out, at the beginning of the elementary school years and brings with it a passion for order that is seen in children's **games with rules.** As adolescence approaches, however, there is again a qualitative change in the processes of thought. The adolescent, according to Piaget (1983), is ready for a transition from thinking in concrete to thinking in **formal operations.**

The child who is using logic is still limited in terms of the types of issues and problems that can be reasoned about. Children can reason about the concrete, but they are not yet able to reason about abstractions. They can apply their logic to questions involving objects, people, places, and events but cannot reason about ideas, theories, and concepts. It is during adolescence that people are first able to scrutinize their own thought processes and personality characteristics; to question the meaning of political structures and religious ideologies; to analyze the nature of feelings, such as love and hate; and to attempt an understanding of the significance of life itself.

Formal operations allow the user to be more planful in problem solving. Instead of relying on trial-and-error approaches to problems, the formal thinker sets up a variety of hypotheses, or "if-then" statements; ranks them in order of probability; and then tests them out systematically in sequence. This is known as **hypothetico-deductive reasoning**, and it allows the formal thinker, in contrast with the child who is using concrete operations, to generate a universe of alternatives when dealing with a problem. Thus, formal thought is possibility oriented, while concrete reasoning is focused on the real rather than the possible.

The possibility orientation of formal reasoning also allows the adolescent to go beyond the world as it exists and to speculate about a world that might be or that might have been but never was. Indeed, young adolescents often become so absorbed in the realm of possibility that they forget the realistic limitations on their dreams. The ability to consider numerous life possibilities other than those that actually exist often leads the adolescent to become overly idealistic. "Why can't the world be different?" adolescents ask; adults reply that someday they will realize that an outcome's being theoretically possible does not mean that it is likely to occur.

We shall see later that the types of play engaged in by adolescents in our society reflect the transition to formal operational thinking, with its emphasis on abstraction, explorations of the realm of possibility, and the early confusion in reconciling one's own thoughts and those of other people. Play also enhances adolescents' thinking processes by offering them an opportunity to indulge their need for abstract conceptualization.

The Redefinition of Friendship: A Need for Communication

As children move into the teen years, there are changes in the types of knowledge they have about their friends, in basic definitions of friendship, in expectations of friends, and in the perceived obligations of friendship. The general trend is a shift from external, action-oriented conceptions to those that are internal and communication oriented. Compared with elementary school children, adolescents expect a greater degree of intimacy and stability in their friendships and a greater possibility of self-disclosure (Hartup & Stevens, 1997; Phillipsen, 1999; Richard & Schneider, 2005). In other words, they see a relationship as an opportunity to satisfy their need to communicate. Mere playmates—people whose preferred recreational activities are the same as one's

Much of the play of adolescents is unstructured and involves simply hanging around with friends.

© Digital Vision

own—are no longer sufficient, and shared personality characteristics replace shared activities as the basis for friendship. It should not be surprising, therefore, that a major function of play during adolescence is to satisfy this need for intimacy. We shall see that although much of adolescent play is less structured than that of children and often consists of simply "hanging out," such play is no less important developmentally than the games of childhood.

The Growth of Self-Awareness: A Need for Identity

As children enter their teenage years, a number of circumstances occur that cause them to reevaluate their definitions of self. The first is a series of major physical changes attributable to the onset of puberty. Erikson (1963) maintained that as a result of pubertal changes "all samenesses and continuities relied on earlier are more or less questioned again" (p. 261). In other words, because the transitions of early adolescence are so rapid and so dramatic, children must, in a sense, reacquaint themselves with their own bodies.

A second major change at adolescence is the change in social roles and expectations; the adolescent is no longer expected or allowed to behave like a child and now must make serious plans for his or her future as an adult. For example, frivolous or unrealistic career goals are no longer seen as appropriate by adults, and the adolescent is encouraged to think seriously about future work roles.

Finally, as mentioned earlier, adolescents can reason in abstract terms and are now able to analyze themselves, to stand back and assess themselves as others see them. In fact, Erikson (1963) believed that although the major concern of children is with what *they* feel they are, the concern shifts during adolescence; teenagers become concerned with what they appear to be in the eyes of other people.

Physical changes, changed social roles and expectations, and the intellectual changes related to formal reasoning all combine to challenge the adolescent to integrate past, present, and future in such a way as to establish a stable and consistent sense of self. This is the crisis of **identity**. A stable identity will not be established quickly, however, and it is during the period of adolescence that there is a slow trial-and-error process of identity resolution. Teenagers test themselves in a variety of ways as they seek deeper levels of self-awareness, and it is often through relationships that adolescents come to understand themselves. Self-awareness often comes about through play, so when we speak of adolescent play, we should try to think of it in the context of the adolescent's attempts at identity resolution. While Erikson did not directly address the issue of play during the teenage years, his conceptualization of ego development explains much about the play of adolescence. Adolescent play, as we shall see, is both a reflection of and an effort to satisfy the adolescent's *need for identity*.

PLAY IN MIDDLE CHILDHOOD

If we combine the trends we have described as characteristic of the elementary school child (the development of an orderly and logical system of thought, the increasing peer orientation and the effort to gain acceptance into the "culture of childhood," and the need to demonstrate one's skills, talents, and abilities), we might expect the play of grade school children to be more patterned, logical, and orderly than that of the preschooler. It would be more realistic, less dominated by the world of fantasy, and more adult-like. It would also be more intensely social and often group focused in its orientation. Finally, it would be designed to allow children to demonstrate their newly emerging intellectual, physical, and social skills and to receive the approval of their peers for doing so.

As we now examine some of the characteristics of the play of school-age children, it will become obvious that their play does, in fact, reflect the general trends in social, intellectual, and personality development.

A Decline in Symbolic Play

Make-believe play occurs in children of all ages. However, beginning at about the age of 5 years, there is a significant decline in the prevalence of such play. Piaget (1962) suggested three reasons for the decline. The first is that children no longer need make-believe to serve their ego needs; as they come to feel more powerful and less helpless in the real world, they are less likely to use play to compensate for perceived inadequacies. Second, symbolic play naturally evolves into games that have rules whenever more than one player is involved. And finally, as children develop, they make greater and greater efforts to adapt to reality, rather than distorting reality as in make-believe play.

Play and the Acquisition of Skills

The young elementary school child takes pride in developing and refining a variety of motor and intellectual skills that, on the one hand, enhance the child's sense of industry and, on the other, are likely to promote acceptance by the peer group. Whether by skateboarding, shooting baskets, roller-skating, wrestling, jumping rope, performing stunts on a bicycle, throwing a Frisbee, or climbing a tree, each generation of children inherits or invents a wide assortment of motor activities that allow them to show off in front of peers and adults and to establish their positions within the peer group.

Skills can be demonstrated intellectually as well, and elementary school children will take great satisfaction in demonstrating how well they can play a game of cards, read a book all by themselves, tell a joke, guess the answer to a riddle or ask one that no one else is able to guess, or negotiate their way through a tongue twister.

The Child as Collector

Maybe it is because grade-school children think in a more logical, orderly manner than they did at a younger age. Maybe it is because they are able to see the world in terms of logical classes and categories. Whatever the reason, children in elementary school often acquire a genuine passion for collecting. They collect almost anything that interests them: bubble gum cards, bottle tops, comic books, stickers, coins, Barbie dolls, or any of the assorted trinkets found in Happy Meal boxes at fast-food restaurants. Collected materials may be used in play, as when collectors read their comic books or play with their dolls. Often, however, the play is the collecting itself, and the objects are not used at all but are only taken out occasionally to be looked at.

Collections of any sort can be of great significance to the child's social, intellectual, and personality development. One social value is that a collection may enhance the child's popularity within the peer group if it is seen by peers as interesting. Another social value of collecting is that collectors often share or trade their possessions. Lending and borrowing can teach a child to be responsible and to respect the property of other people. Trading can teach negotiation skills as well as concepts of equivalence and fairness.

The intellectual value of collecting is that children can learn a good deal about the materials in their collections and may even need a certain amount of knowledge to begin their collections. Through the experience of collecting, one child can gain a wealth of information about the players in the National Football League, another can become the family expert on rock formations, and a third can learn about world geography by assembling a collection of stamps from various countries.

Children who collect may also refine their counting skills. They may acquire more mature concepts of logical classification, as when they realize that their collectibles can be sorted into groups and subgroups in a variety of different dimensions. Finally, the experience of collecting often requires the collector to attend to the sometimes very minor distinguishing features of the objects within the collection; there is often little point in having two identical items in the collection, so collectors must attend closely to notice exactly how a new rock, stamp, or coin differs from the ones they already have.

Finally, a collection is an accomplishment, and as the collection enlarges, so does the magnitude of the accomplishment. The experience of collecting can, therefore, boost children's self-esteem by providing them with the sense of industry that is so important during the elementary school years.

Play Rituals

"If you step on a crack, you'll break your mother's back." "One potato, two potato, three potato, four . . ." "You can't hit a kid with glasses on." Such rhymes, counting rituals, and superstitions are familiar to everyone, regardless of where in the United States or even what part of the world one is from. They are an integral part of what is often regarded as the culture of childhood.

Children's play during the elementary school years is replete with such chants and rituals, and they reflect both the orderliness of children's thinking and the extent to which ritual is involved in the socialization process. The point is that the children usually take these rituals very seriously, as they do counting rules like "One potato, two potato" or "Eeny meeny miny mo"; if a child attempts to cheat or refuses to accept the role determined by the count, that child will be harshly criticized by peers. Learning the rituals puts a child "in the know"; learning to abide by them teaches a child how to obey rules and follow a moral order.

Games With Rules

We noted earlier that as children become increasingly logical, they become increasingly likely to see the world as a logical and orderly place that is governed by a system of rules. This orderliness of thought finds its way into children's play in the form of what Piaget (1962) described as the major play activity of the civilized being, the game with rules.

Games with rules may be sensorimotor in nature, as in the case of marble or ball games, tag, hide-and-seek, hopscotch, blind man's buff, or jacks. They may also be of an intellectual variety, such as checkers, cards, or Monopoly and other board games. Whether they are sensorimotor or intellectual, however, they contain two essential characteristics. First, they involve competition between two or more players. Second, they are governed by a set of regulations that are agreed to *in advance* by all the players and that may not be changed midgame unless the players have previously determined that modifications will be acceptable. The rules themselves may be handed down by code, as in a game of chess, or may exist in the form of a temporary agreement between players. In other words, children may either learn the rules from their older peers or establish their own rules at the outset of a particular game.

Piaget (1962) maintained that games with rules require (a) the ability to engage in rule-dominated forms of thinking and (b) the presence of two or more potential players. A prelogical child will not engage in such games, nor will an older child who is playing alone, for that matter. Consider the example of the play activities of a 3-year-old girl observed by Piaget when she was offered some marbles. She did not engage in a rule game but instead either initiated sensorimotor play with the marbles (e.g., by throwing them) or incorporated them into symbolic play: She pretended they were eggs in a bird's nest!

Preschool children use rules in their play to assign roles and sustain the make-believe plan of action. For example, children will often engage in complex negotiations about designated roles (e.g., "You can be the bus driver next time if you will be a passenger this time"), and such negotiations naturally involve a measure of give-and-take. However, the roles and themes of make-believe play may change continually, and thus the rules in symbolic play have none of the rigidity of the more mature games with rules. As we have already indicated, in genuine games with rules the rules are decided upon in advance, and changes may not be made during the course of the action unless all the players decide at the outset that such changes are allowable (Rubin, Fein, & Vandenberg, 1983).

Finally, we should point out that games with rules are seen by many psychologists as falling outside of the definition of play. Play is an activity engaged in for its own sake; it contains no external goals. Games with rules, however, involve competition and thus have an external goal: the goal of winning. Why, then, should we consider games with rules as a topic in a book about children's play? It is because, the competitive element notwithstanding, much of the activity that occurs during a game with rules really is play, particularly for the young grade-school child. A group of first and second graders playing soccer certainly realize that their purpose on the field is to win and not to lose, but they are also able to enjoy the activity simply as an end in itself; the game offers them a chance to run around and interact with friends, and in doing so they may even lose sight of their intended purpose.

Organized Sports

While games with rules can take many forms, a form that is increasingly in evidence throughout the childhood years is the organized sports activity. More than 41 million children participate in youth sports every year in the United States, and this number has been increasing dramatically. While involvement in Little League baseball has decreased slightly, there are still more than 2 million children who play in Little League every year. Children are playing soccer and Pop Warner football at significantly higher rates. Approximately 17.5 million children play soccer today, up from 15 million in 1987, and involvement in Pop Warner football has doubled in the last 15 years (Hilgers, 2006).

With so many children involved in youth sports, it is reasonable to ask about the benefits of sports participation during childhood. Presumably one would expect to discover benefits in three areas: in overall physical fitness, in self-esteem, and in the ability to get along with others and work cooperatively within a group.

PUTTING THEORY INTO PRACTICE 5.2

Helping Children Develop a Task Orientation in Sports

Encourage children to develop a task orientation rather than an ego orientation toward their involvement in sports. In this way, they will enjoy the sport more and will develop better habits of sportsmanship.

A child's attitude toward sports is easily influenced by the attitudes of adults. Make an effort to direct statements to children that encourage a task orientation.

Develop the habit of examining the remarks made by adults to see if they encourage a task or an ego orientation. For example, try to determine which of the following remarks encourage children to be task oriented and which encourage an ego orientation. More important, explain why the statements fit into each category:

1. You can be very proud of the way you played today.
2. That referee stole the game from you.
3. You didn't play a great game, but at least you played better than most of the other kids on the team.
4. I'm very proud of the way you played today.
5. Don't be so hard on yourself. Let's face it. You're just not as fast as that kid who scored a goal on you.
6. Your game would improve if you passed off a little sooner.
7. Are you satisfied that you gave the game your best effort?
8. I was watching the coach, and he seemed to be pretty happy with the way you played tonight.
9. Maybe you can spend some time working on your free throws to increase your percentage.
10. I thought you played well today, but what really matters is what you think.

Answers:
Task (1, 6, 7, 9, 10)
Ego (2, 3, 4, 5, 8)

Sports and Physical Fitness

Adults in the United States today are urged continually to incorporate exercise into their daily lives in order to reduce the likelihood of cardiovascular disease; in fact, the cardiovascular benefits of regular exercise have been repeatedly demonstrated

Children in elementary school can play rules games, many of which involve organized sports. They should be taught the skills necessary to play the game, since perceived ability level is the best predictor of sports enjoyment.

© Comstock

in the adult population (Perkins, Jacobs, Barber, & Eccles, 2004). Are there short-range and long-range physical benefits for children that result from their participation in sports programs? It may be surprising to discover that this is a difficult question to answer. There is certainly a relationship between involvement in sports and cardiovascular health, muscle strength and endurance, flexibility, and weight control (Hoffman, Kang, Faigenbaum, & Ratamess, 2005), but the difficulty is that the existence of a relationship tells us little about specific causal factors. It may be that intensive sports involvement causes children to be more physically fit than their peers, but it may also be the case that children who are initially more physically fit are the ones who seek out competitive sports activities.

Another issue to be considered is that the fitness benefits of sports vary considerably depending on the sport in question. In other words, specific sports promote specific types of fitness, but it is difficult to find one that promotes all aspects of fitness. Some sports focus on muscle strength, some on muscle coordination, some on aerobic development, some on total body coordination, and some on flexibility (Ewing, Gano-Overway, Branta, & Seefeldt, 2002). It seems that the greatest fitness benefits would be achieved if children were exposed to a variety of sports, but in reality specialization in one sport is often encouraged at an early age in hopes of producing elite athletes (Fraser-Thomas & Côté, 2006).

Turning to the question of long-range physical benefits, it would be difficult to demonstrate that sports involvement during childhood has an impact on the likelihood of cardiovascular disease in middle and later adulthood. Nevertheless, the general consensus among researchers is that there is indeed a significant long-range physical benefit to athletic participation during childhood: Children and adolescents who are active in sports seem to maintain their activity level into young adulthood and are likely to carry with them into adult life a positive attitude toward physical exercise (Perkins et al., 2004).

Sports and Self-Esteem

Does participation in sports help children feel better about themselves? To answer that question, we must first refer to a growing body of opinion among psychologists that "self" is not a global concept but that children acquire images of themselves in a variety of different capacities. That is, they may develop a *self-schema* for their physical selves, their social selves, their intellectual selves, and so forth. These self-schemas, which typically begin to differentiate during the elementary school years, focus on the domains that are of lasting relevance, investment, and concern (Markus & Nurius, 1984). To discuss the effects of sports participation on the self, therefore, we need to specify which aspect of the self we are referring to.

A number of researchers in the past 20 years have discovered in children a relationship between successful athletic participation and a positive image of the self-as-athlete (Anshel, Muller, & Owens, 1986; Smith, 1986), but, as is true of all correlational studies, the existence of a relationship says little about the direction of cause and effect: Does participation in sports cause children to feel better about their physical selves, or are the children who already have a positive physical self-image the most likely to go out for sports? It has been found, in fact, that children who believe they are athletically skilled and expect to do well in sports are more likely to choose sports as a preferred activity, while those who feel they lack physical ability may avoid sports involvement (Fredricks, Simpkins, & Eccles, 2005). Furthermore, there are no consistent indications that being a successful athlete improves a child's overall self-concept or that athletic success improves children's opinions of themselves from an intellectual or a social standpoint.

Athletic success will be of little consequence to a child who lacks a self-schema that pertains to athletics. In other words, if there is no investment in the athletic component of the self, success or failure on the playing fields will have no effect on a person's self-image. Perhaps this explains why successful sports experience is related more clearly to the self-concept of a boy than to that of the average girl: Girls, traditionally, are less likely than boys to define themselves in terms of athletic prowess.

The degree to which children actually enjoy sports participation depends on the type of achievement orientation they bring to it. A *task orientation* emphasizes internal standards of mastery and self-improvement. Task-oriented players focus on living up to their own personal standards and are satisfied if they feel that they played well. They believe that success in sports is defined by the effort they put into it. On the other hand, an *ego orientation* emphasizes external standards of performing well compared with others, and a child with this orientation might be excessively concerned about winning—or at least about performing better than other players. Children with this orientation believe that success is defined by ability rather than by effort (Duda & Nicholls, 1992; Duda & Ntoumanis, 2005; Duda & White, 1992). Of the two types, task-oriented players are more cooperative, better sports, and more intrinsically motivated. They are more likely to enjoy their sport. Ego-oriented players are less sportsmanlike and more likely to view highly aggressive play as acceptable. They tend to see sports involvement as a way of enhancing their social status, and they are more likely to miss practices, indicating an unwillingness to work hard to improve (Ommundsen, Roberts, & Kavussanu, 1998). Most important, they don't appear to enjoy their sport as much as task-oriented players do (Boyd & Yin, 1996), and if an activity is not enjoyable, it is inappropriate to call it play.

Adults who want children to gain the most benefit from sports participation might consider a number of steps. First, children should be taught the skills necessary to play the game, since perceived ability level is the best predictor of sports enjoyment (Boyd & Yin, 1996). The ideal situation for the enhancement of physical self-esteem is to teach skills, help the players develop a feeling of competence, and provide them with a setting in which their competence can be displayed (Coakley, 2002). Second, children should learn that winning is not all-important and that the goal of athletic participation is to play as well as one can regardless of the outcome. This attitude in parents and coaches has been found to be important in helping children develop a task orientation (Boyd & Yin; Waldron & Krane, 2005; White, 1998). Third, children should be exposed to a variety of sports, both of an individual and a team variety, so that if one sport is unappealing, others are available. Fourth, children should not be forced to play if they choose not to. Finally, adults must remember that the game belongs to the children and that it should not be contaminated by any hidden agenda the adults may have. Children should not have to prove their worth to parents or coaches, either in the sports arena or anywhere else!

Do Sports Build Character?

It is often said that involvement in sports builds character, in that children learn how to play fair, act responsibly, follow rules, and function as team players—all characteristics that might serve a child well in many other areas of life. Is it true that a child's moral fiber is built up by his or her sports participation? The answer depends on (a) the attitudes of the players, coaches, and parents; (b) the extent to which the goals of the sports program are consistent with the moral values of the larger society; and (c) the willingness of adults to use the sport to teach children about morality, cooperation, tolerance, and fairness. If a child is involved in a sport and is taught to win at any cost, he or she will learn little about the sportsmanship that is presumed to build character (Duda, 2007; Ewing et al., 2002; Shields & Bredemeier, 2007).

Psychologists Brenda Bredemeier and David Shields (1985, 1986; Shields & Bredemeier, 1995, 2007) have done extensive research on the relationship between sports participation and moral development, and their findings would probably disappoint those who argue that sports build character. They proposed the concept of "game reasoning" in sports, meaning that decisions made in sports are different from the decisions of everyday life, which is not surprising since the world of sports is in many ways set aside from the everyday world, in terms of the times and places, artificial roles and roles, and goals that have no intrinsic meaning or value. In one of their earliest studies, Bredemeier and Shields (1985) examined the moral reasoning skills of 120 high school and college students, some athletes and some nonathletes, asking them questions about moral situations related to and unrelated to the world of sports. As an example of a sports-related dilemma, students were told about Tom, a football player whose coach tells him to injure an opposing player deliberately in order to win the game. What should Tom do? A moral dilemma unrelated to sports included a question about whether a person should keep a promise to deliver a sum of money to a rich man or spend the money instead to help feed his or her own hungry relatives.

The researchers discovered that adolescent and young adult athletes and nonathletes alike believed that a different set of moral principles applied to sports than applied to everyday life situations. Specifically they expressed the view that a lower moral code may be followed in a sporting event. One high school girl commented that in sports it is often difficult to tell right from wrong, so it is necessary to use "game sense." A male college basketball player noted that you may do what you want in sports because you are free to think only of yourself, while in everyday life you must be attentive to the feelings of other people. The general consensus seemed to be that in real life one should try to be considerate, while in sports, because of the emphasis on winning, one need not treat opposing players as one would like to be treated.

Bredemeier and Shields (1985) did not suggest that playing in organized sports actually *causes* a player to function at a lower moral level; perhaps it is the case that people with a less well-developed moral sense are more easily attracted to highly aggressive sports. Many successful athletes, however, are morally mature people who apparently try to coordinate their everyday moral principles with their sports behaviors (Bredemeier & Shields, 1985). Nevertheless, this study and a number of others (Bredemeier & Shields, 1986; Bredemeier, Shields, Weiss, & Cooper, 1986; Romance, 1984; Shields & Bredemeier, 1995) clearly indicate a relationship between interest in or participation in aggressive sports and level of moral reasoning—in children, adolescents, and adults. People who have the greatest interest in highly aggressive contact sports or have participated in them for the longest amounts of time tend to score lower on tests of moral reasoning; interestingly enough, athletes who do earn high moral reasoning scores are the least willing to display hostile aggression during a game.

In summary, it would be difficult to make the case that participation in sports, at least in those that involve high levels of aggression and physical contact, improves the moral character of a child. As long as anyone sees deliberate injury to another person as conceivable under *any* circumstances, involvement in high-contact sports may be counterproductive to the moral development of the grade-school child (Bredemeier et al., 1986).

Parents, teachers, and coaches may encourage children to participate in sports for many reasons (for the health benefits, for the opportunity to socialize, for the sheer pleasure that is found in the activity), but if the reason for involvement is to build the child's character, adults may want to rethink their motives.

ADOLESCENT PLAY

By the age of 12 and into the adolescent years, the most popular recreational activities include many that reflect a need for self-awareness, heterosexual socialization, and intimate communication. Most of their unstructured time has been described as falling into one of two categories: (a) media use, including watching television, watching movies, reading, listening to music, and playing computer games, and (b) active leisure, including participation in sports, talking, or simply hanging out with friends (Larson & Verma, 1999). Adolescents like to attend movies, watch television, read, go to dances and parties, and listen to music (or watch music videos). They also like just hanging around with friends, and much adolescent play is of this unstructured variety. While play as a category of activity all but disappears during adolescence in most non-Western cultures, it is replaced in the United States and European countries by talking, primarily with peers. American high school students simply talk to one another for approximately 2.5 hours a day (Larson & Verma). Consistent with the transition from a concrete and action-oriented view of friendship to one that involves a greater degree of abstract conceptualization, socialization is defined less as *doing* something with friends and more as simply being together.

There is a decline overall in the frequency of the rule games that adolescents play, as well as a greater selectivity (Damon, 1983). Recognizing their particular strengths and weaknesses, most teenagers choose to specialize in one or two sports rather than trying to play all of them. Sports continue to play an important role in their lives, however, providing enjoyment, exercise, an opportunity for socialization, and—particularly for males—a means of coping with life stress. Adolescent boys in the United States devote an average of an hour per day to sports participation, and girls devote approximately half that time (Larson & Verma, 1999).

Adolescent play serves a wide variety of functions. When peers are involved, as they frequently are, leisure offers teenagers a chance to develop social skills, to develop their interests by interacting with peers who have similar interests, to achieve a sense of belonging, and to understand themselves better by seeing how their peers react to them, thus enhancing their sense of personal identity (Csikzentmihalyi & Larson, 1984; Gottman & Mettetal, 1986; Hultsman, 1992; Zarabatny, Hartmann, & Rankin, 1990). When adolescents engage in solitary leisure—when they read, watch television, or listen to music, for example—they have a chance to understand themselves better, to analyze their interests and abilities, and to develop their talents.

Watching television is by far the most popular form of media use among adolescents. Adolescents in the United States watch approximately 2 hours of television a day, with boys watching more than girls do. By contrast, reading as a leisure activity (not required for school) consumes an average of 15 to 30 min per day of a teenager's time, and in most countries studied, girls have been found to engage in more leisure reading than boys do. Adolescents in the United States spend an average of 13 to 15 min a day listening to music (Larson, Kubey, & Colletti, 1989; Larson & Verma, 1999).

Movies and television serve a number of functions for teenagers. For example, both provide an opportunity for interaction with peers of both sexes. A film may also allow adolescents to understand themselves better by testing out their own emotions—discovering what makes them laugh, what saddens them, what fills them with terror. Perhaps the popularity of the "slasher" genre of films is not an indication of adolescent indifference to human suffering, as adults fear, but is an indication of adolescents' need to test their limits. Sitting through a frightening film is admittedly a safe risk, but it may be for many U.S. adolescents a rare opportunity to test themselves in a world that is ordinarily risk free.

Adolescents also come to a greater understanding of themselves by identifying with the characters whose lives they are observing in television and movies. They often find themselves wondering, "What would I do in that situation? What would I have said? How would I react?" And, of course, an adolescent may be inspired by the life of a film character or by that of the actor who plays the role. Many adults report that they made important decisions about establishing their life direction after seeing an inspiring film or play or reading a book that captured their imagination.

Finally, the intellectual appeal of the media is that the viewer or reader has the opportunity to see the world not as it is but as it might be or as it might have been. As mentioned earlier in the chapter, adolescents are likely to engage in a considerable amount of speculation about a hypothetical world. In everyday life, it is often difficult to do this because one must live in the real world even as one fantasizes about the imaginary one, and adolescents are often accused of being dreamers whose feet are 10 ft off the ground. Through the use of the media, however, a teenager may give free rein to his or her idealistic imagination and is allowed—and even encouraged—to engage in the type of hypothetical, contrary-to-fact reasoning that is so typical of the adolescent. One of the more popular forms of adolescent play is the computer game, including video arcade games, console boxes attached to a television set, and multiplayer Internet role-playing games. However, computer play can hardly be described as an adolescent form of activity. Even though most of the research on computer games has focused on the play of adolescents, games of this type are even more popular with adults. This is illustrated by the fact that in a recent online survey of computer game playing, only 1 in 10 respondents was between the ages of 12 and 17. Nearly 60% were between the ages of 18 and 30, and the average age of the group was 28 (Griffiths, Davies, & Chappell, 2004a).

Three fourths of teenagers play computer games, once a day on average, with boys playing more often than girls and for longer periods of time. Approximately 85% of computer game players are males. Boys, incidentally, are more likely than girls to neglect their responsibilities, such as homework, in order to play these games (Phillips, Rolls, Rouse, & Griffiths, 1995).

As computer games become increasingly popular, concerns have been raised that players may become "addicted" to them, spending excessively long hours at play to the neglect of work, family, and even sleep. Addiction is difficult to define. A teenager may spend excessive amounts of time with a new game but then may spend less and less time as the novelty wears off. A teenager may use a game as a way of avoiding life's problems one week but may not do so the following week. Estimates of genuine addiction range from 6% to 20% of players (Meenan, 2007; Salguero, Moran, and Bersabe, 2002). The encouraging news is that only a small minority (7.5%) of teenagers can be described as truly addicted to computer games. Despite the fears of many parents that their children will become socially isolated if they engage too often in computer play, most adolescents who frequent the video arcade are casual visitors who go there simply to hang out and to meet friends (Fisher, 1995). What's more, multiplayer online role-playing games, such as EverQuest, allow for a good deal of social interaction. Most teenagers play these Internet games with friends, and most report that their favorite characteristic of the game is the opportunity to social-ize (Griffiths, Davies, & Chappell, 2004b). In fact, it was found in one study that 3 of every 4 players developed one or more close friends while involved in an Internet role-playing game (Cole & Griffiths, 2007).

Teenagers are likely to play computer games more often than adults, perhaps reflecting the fact that teenagers have more disposable free time. Teenagers are also more likely than adults to report that the violence is their favorite aspect of the game (Griffiths et al., 2004b). Indeed, violence is characteristic of the most popular video games; an analysis of 55 games designated as appropriate for players of all ages indicated that 64% of them contained violence resulting in injury or death (Thompson & Haninger, 2001). When a player assumes the role of a violent character, he or she is given permission to act in a violent way, and this may explain why violent computer game play is associated with increased

© Photodisc

As computer games become increasingly popular, concerns have been raised that players may become "addicted" to them, spending excessively long hours at play.

levels of aggressive behavior, a decline in empathy for other people, and increased tolerance for violent behavior (Anderson, 2004; Anderson & Bushman, 2001; Konijn, Bijvank, & Bushman, 2007; Wei, 2007). Adults may not see a computer station, a video arcade, or a street corner for that matter as a wholesome place to engage in leisure activities. Teenagers respond to this criticism by arguing that often there are no suitable places for unstructured activities. There are theaters for movie-going, gymnasiums and playing fields for sports, and recreation halls for dancing, but, whether they live in cities, suburbs, or rural areas, teenagers consistently complain about a lack of places to go when they just want to "hang out" (McMeeking & Purkayastha, 1995).

Summary

There are three general characteristics that capture the essence of the period of middle childhood, corresponding to trends in the areas of intellectual, social, and personality development. From an intellectual standpoint, the major development is that children's thinking becomes more orderly, structured, and logical. As a result, their play will reflect a developing need for order. The major social change in middle childhood is that the peer group provides support that formerly was offered only within the family. Acceptance by peers is of great importance to children in this age group, and their play reflects an overwhelming need to belong. Finally, in the realm of personality development, a major challenge to the emerging self-concepts of school-age children is to demonstrate to themselves and others that they have talents, skills, and abilities that they can be proud of. This need for industry is reflected in their play.

Adolescence is characterized by major transitions in the areas of intellectual, social, and personality development. In terms of intellectual development, the adolescent is experiencing a transition from the concrete form of reasoning that typifies the middle childhood years to a reasoning that is abstract and hypothetical. The intellectual need of the adolescent is a need for abstract conceptualization. In social terms, the adolescent needs more than simply to belong within the peer group: Now there is a need to single out particular individuals with whom one can have an intimate relationship; the overwhelming need is for communication. Finally, the adolescent is engaged in a struggle to create a stable and permanent sense of self, and play often forms the context within which this need for identity can be met.

Middle childhood brings with it a decline in make-believe play, perhaps because (a) children no longer need make-believe to serve their ego needs, (b) symbolic play naturally evolves into games that have rules, and (c) as children develop, they make greater efforts to adapt to reality, rather than distorting reality as in make-believe play.

Young elementary school children take pride in a variety of motor and intellectual skills, which both enhance their sense of industry and are likely to promote acceptance by the peer group. Collecting becomes a passion for many children of this age and allows them to gain a sense of accomplishment, as well as being an educational pastime. The organization of thought at this age leads to rule-oriented play, such as solitary rituals and games with rules, including organized sports.

Organized sports for children can be highly enjoyable, promote a sense of accomplishment, and provide an opportunity for social acceptance. Nevertheless, there is little evidence in support of the beliefs that sports are necessary for physical fitness, that participation in sports will automatically enhance a child's self-esteem, and that sports build moral character in any meaningful sense.

By the age of 12—and into the adolescent years—the most popular recreational activities include many that reflect a need for self-awareness, heterosexual socialization, and intimate communication. For example, adolescents like to attend movies, watch television, read, go to dances and parties, and listen to music or watch music videos. They also like simply to hang around with friends, and much adolescent play is of this unstructured variety.

Key Terms

Concrete Operations	p. 132	Hypothetico-Deductive Reasoning	p. 136
Formal Operations	p. 136		
Games With Rules	p. 136	Identity	p. 139
Graphic Collections	p. 132	Industry	p. 135

Issues for Class Discussion

1. Why does the peer group take on such importance during the elementary school years? Do parents and other adults lose some of their importance in the process of socialization? What specific behaviors do children exhibit that illustrate the growing importance of peers?

2. Some psychologists argue that the competitive rule-dominated games of school-age children are not play at all because the goal of winning becomes more important than the sheer enjoyment of engaging in the activity. Can an activity still be playful if there is an external goal of winning?

3. Knowing what we do about the advantages and disadvantages of sports involvement, should we allow our children to participate in such activities at all? If the answer is yes, are there conditions that adults might want to set in order to help the child get the most out of such activities?

4. Is it fair to speak of the morality of sports as being different from the morality of everyday life? Do we allow behavior to occur in sports activities that we would not tolerate in children under other circumstances? If so, what do we allow?

PART III

Individual Differences in Play

In this section, we highlight some of the major factors related to variations in play within our own culture. Among the most heavily researched areas related to variations in play are gender, physical impairment, intellectual differences, and emotional problems that range from chronic conditions, such as autism, to temporary life stresses. We address the question of why these variations exist and how an adult who works with children can effectively respond to them. A review of the current literature on play reveals that a large percentage of studies deal with the play of children who differ from the typically developing child. It is rewarding to realize that regardless of their life circumstances, all children want and need to play.

Chapter 6

GENDER DIFFERENCES IN PLAY

When he was 3 years old, Jonathan found in the attic a doll that his mother had kept since her own early childhood. Jonathan enjoyed playing with the doll but was confused by its appearance. He claimed it was a "boy" doll and therefore should not be clad in a dress. No, he was told; the doll is a little girl. He insisted, however, that it was a boy and, when asked why he was so certain, remarked that it had "boy hair." What did that mean? "Boy hair goes this way," he said, waving his hand back and forth in the air, "and girl hair goes this way," turning his hand in circles. When his mother finally succeeded in convincing him that the doll was intended to be a baby girl and that it was the dress and not the hair that indicated its gender, Jonathan reacted by saying that he didn't want to play with it anymore!

Where did Jonathan get his ideas about the physical characteristics of gender? Did he learn it from his parents? His peers? Television? We begin this chapter with a discussion of the two major theoretical views on how the concept of gender is acquired. Then the research on gender differences in children's play will be discussed, and this has been concentrated in four areas: (a) toy selection, (b) fantasy play, (c) rough-and-tumble play, and (d) games with rules.

THE CONCEPT OF GENDER

No one knows for certain why very young children make clear distinctions among play materials and activities suitable for girls and those appropriate for boys. However, there are several theoretical interpretations of gender typing, and these are (a) learning theory, (b) cognitive-developmental theory, and

Learning Objectives

After reading Chapter 6, a student should be able to:

✦ Understand the mechanisms of gender typing as outlined by learning theory and cognitive-developmental theory and recognize the differences between the two theoretical approaches.

✦ Realize how the "gender appropriateness" of toys is determined and identify the toys most often described as gender appropriate for each sex.

✦ Understand the influence of cultural factors on the selection of gender-appropriate toys by young children.

✦ Be aware of the well-established gender differences in the fantasy play of young children in terms of the props that are used, the roles that are assumed, and the themes that are frequently expressed.

✦ Define rough-and-tumble play, identify its various functions, and differentiate it from other forms of vigorous activity play that occur in childhood.

✦ Identify gender differences in rough-and-tumble play that have been found in both human beings and in lower animals and understand the possible explanations for such differences.

✦ Discuss the evidence to suggest gender differences in children's games with rules.

✦ Identify and contrast the cultural and biological interpretations of gender differences in games with rules.

(c) biological, or hormonal, theory (Miller, Trautner, & Ruble, 2006). The viewpoint of *learning theory* is that children learn by the mechanisms of imitation and reinforcement to behave in gender-appropriate ways, such as by playing with certain toys and not with others (Bandura, 1977; Bussey & Bandura, 1999). The process of imitation is illustrated by a 2-year-old who acquires his preference for rough-and-tumble play simply by watching the activities of older boys and using them as models. Direct reinforcement occurs when a boy is praised for showing interest in owning a football, when a girl is praised for wanting a baby doll, or when either a girl or a boy is criticized for playing with toys seen as more appropriate for the other sex.

The basic premise of *cognitive-developmental theory* is that children gradually develop an awareness of the concept of gender and then engage in gender-appropriate activities because such activities are consistent with their emerging gender concept. According to this theory, children gradually acquire a sense of gender constancy, and this includes (a) **gender identity**, the recognition that males and females are different on the basis of their physical characteristics; (b) **gender stability,** the realization that gender will always remain the same and that boys and girls will grow up to become either men or women; and (c) **gender consistency**, the realization that gender always remains the same regardless of surface physical changes in appearance (Kohlberg, 1966; Martin, Ruble, & Szkrybalo, 2002; Ruble & Martin, 1998; Ruble et al., 2007).

Once they have begun to understand the concept of gender, engaging in gender-appropriate behaviors, such as playing with supposedly appropriate toys, becomes satisfying and rewarding because it affirms the correctness of the child's schema of categorization. As Kohlberg (1966) noted, the child concludes: "I am a boy (or girl), and therefore I want to do boy (or girl) things; therefore, the opportunity to do boy (or girl) things is rewarding" (p. 89).

Finally, there is a *hormonal theory* of gender development, which states that sex hormones affect the sexual differentiation of the brain during critical periods of development and, as a result, gender-linked behaviors are permanently altered (Goy & McEwen, 1980; Hines, 2004).

TOY SELECTION

One of the most intriguing aspects of young children's play is their preference for gender-typed toys well before they could have developed a concept of gender. In one study it was found that boys at 9 months of age spend more time looking at traditional boys' toys than at those judged appropriate for girls, and children of both sexes show such looking preferences at 18 months (Campbell, Shirley, Heywood, & Crook, 2000). Another researcher found that girls preferred dolls to other playthings at 10 months of age, although boys of the same age showed no such preference (Roopnarine, 1986). A number of studies have demonstrated that some children show preferences for gender-appropriate toys as early as 18–24 months of age (Caldera, Huston, & O'Brien, 1989; Campbell, Shirley, & Caygill, 2002; Fagot, 1978; Huston, 1983; O'Brien & Huston, 1985; Perry, White, & Perry, 1984).

It is widely accepted today that the majority of children acquire a preference for gender-typed toys at some time between the ages of 2 and 3 years, and most 3-year-olds easily separate stereotypical female toys from stereotypical male toys and know which toys their parents would and wouldn't approve of their playing with (Freeman, 2007). If children show a preference for gender-typed toys even before they have acquired a concept of gender, where does this toy preference come from? It has been suggested that there must be some characteristics of the toys that either boys or girls find especially appealing—their

When girls play with dolls, they often select mother and baby figures. In contrast, boy dolls tend to be action figures, which often have aggressive roles in play.

appearance or their potential to be manipulated in certain ways—but psychologists have yet to determine these characteristics (Campbell et al., 2002).

The assignment of toys to a gender category is usually done in response to actual play preferences of children, ratings of gender appropriateness made by adults, or both. In other words, there is nothing inherently masculine or feminine about any particular plaything. A toy is seen as gender appropriate if children of one sex typically choose to play with it while children of the other sex do not or if adults are in general agreement that it is more suitable for children of one sex than for those of the other. The application of these criteria results in a classification of toys according to gender, as illustrated in Table 6.1.

Adult Interaction With Gender-Labeled Infants

To what extent are adult interactions with an infant determined by the child's gender? Ordinarily it would be extremely difficult to answer this question because gender is an inseparable component of the self, and adults typically know whether the child they are cuddling or bouncing on their knee is a boy or a girl. What might happen, however, if the adults' knowledge about the child's gender was based solely on a designated label and if the same baby were identified as a boy to some adults and as a girl to others? Would adults respond differently to the same child based on their *perceptions* of its maleness or femaleness? Would they handle the baby differently? Would they use different words to describe its behaviors? Would they offer it different types of toys? Apparently the answer to all three questions is yes.

In a variety of different studies, adult strangers have been introduced to the identical baby labeled either as a boy or as a girl, depending on the experimental condition. Both gender-typed and neutral toys were made available, but the adults were not told how they should be used. The typical finding was that adults of both sexes more often offered supposedly female toys, such as dolls, to what they

TABLE 6.1 Toys Designated as Gender Appropriate Based on Actual Play Preferences of Children or on Independent Ratings by Adults

Boy Toys	Girl Toys
Road racing sets	Fashion dolls
Trains	Fashion doll accessories
Toy guns and gun sets	Mother and baby dolls
Sports-oriented games	Doll carriages and strollers
Blocks	Dollhouses
Cars and trucks	Housekeeping/cooking toys
Electronic toys	Beauty kits
Construction toys	Doll furniture
Model kits	Stuffed dolls
Sports equipment	Feminine clothing
Workbenches and tools	Beads
Walkie-talkies	Crayons, art materials

Note: Adapted from C. P. Benbow (1986), J. M. Connor and L. A. Serbin (1977), N. Eisenberg (1983), M. Giddings and C. F. Halverson (1981), L. A. Schwartz and W. T. Markham (1985), D. M. Tracy (1987).

believed were baby girls; when the same baby was believed to be a boy, conventionally male toys, such as footballs and hammers, were more likely to be offered, although the effect with the presumed male babies was less consistently observed (Beal, 1994; Etaugh, 1983; Huston, 1983; Sidorowicz & Lunney, 1980; Smith & Lloyd, 1978; Stern & Karraker, 1989; Will, Self, & Datan, 1976).

Implications of the findings from research on adult interaction with infants presumed to be male or female are far-reaching. It is obvious that the children were not providing specific behavioral cues about toy preferences, since the identical baby was thought of as either male or female depending on the introduction provided by the experimenter. Gender-related behavior, like beauty, seems to be in the eye of the beholder. If told that a baby is a boy, adults are likely to see "him" as strong, active, and muscular, but if told the same baby is a girl, they describe "her" as having soft and sweet features (Burnham & Harris, 1992; Will et al., 1976).

The Parent's Role in Gender Typing

Do parents, like the adult strangers in the studies mentioned above, choose gender-typed toys for their very young children? Most researchers find that they do. Eisenberg, Wolchik, Hernandez, and Pasternack (1985) asked parents to let them observe their normal patterns of interactions in the home with their 1- and 2-year-old children. Two 20- to 25-min interaction sessions were videotaped, with the parent and child in a room with some of the child's own toys that the parent had selected for use in the observations. It was found that parents picked gender-typed toys for their children, particularly when the children were male.

Differences were not observed by Eisenberg and associates (1985) in parents' reactions to their children's play with gender-appropriate and gender-inappropriate toys. That is, the parents did not seem to actively reinforce their children for playing with gender-appropriate toys or discourage them from playing with those that were inappropriate. It should be pointed out, however, that differential reactions by parents to young children's toy selections have been observed in other studies (Caldera, Huston, & O'Brien, 1989; Langlois & Downs, 1980; Snow, Jacklin, & Maccoby, 1983). For example, Caldera and colleagues noticed subtle parental reactions to the gender appropriateness of toys. While they didn't openly encourage the use of one type of toy or another, parents appeared to be more excited when they discovered that gender-appropriate toys were available, and they were more likely to become involved in their children's play.

In the Langlois and Downs (1980) study, parental influences on their children's play with gender-appropriate and gender-inappropriate toys were not quite so subtle. Children aged 3 to 5 years were brought into a room and given either "girl" toys (a dollhouse with furniture, pots and pans, female clothing) or "boy" toys (toy soldiers, a gas station with cars, cowboy gear). Some were given gender-appropriate toys while others were not, and as the children played, their mother, their father, or a same-sex friend entered the room. The researchers found that when boys were playing with conventionally masculine toys, they were ignored by their peers, received mild approval from their mothers, and were strongly encouraged and rewarded by their fathers. When boys played with conventionally feminine toys, however, they were encouraged by their mothers but strongly discouraged both by fathers and by peers, who openly made fun of them, interfered with their play, or encouraged them to find other toys to play with.

By way of contrast, mothers, fathers, and same-sex peers all expressed their approval of girls' play with gender-appropriate toys, and all expressed their disapproval of girls' play with "boy" toys. Thus it appeared that girls were treated more consistently than boys; that, in general, fathers and peers responded more strongly than mothers; and that, of all the visitors to the playroom, fathers seemed to exert the greatest amount of influence on the preschoolers (Langlois & Downs, 1980).

The Contents of Children's Rooms

One of the most frequently cited studies of the toys made available to young children is an analysis by psychologists Harriet Rheingold and Kaye Cook (1975) of the contents of children's bedrooms. The researchers obtained permission to enter the homes of 96 children ranging in age from 12 to 72 months, all of whom slept in their own rooms, and to take inventory of the toys and furnishings that the rooms contained. The 13 classes of categories they identified are listed alphabetically in Table 6.2.

The researchers discovered that the average 1-year-old had 28 different toys; this number increased to 96 by the time the child approached the age of 6. The number of animal furnishings decreased with age, as did the number of floral furnishings. Increasing age brought increases in the number of books and dolls and in the size of the child's supply of educational and art materials.

TABLE 6.2   Contents of the Bedrooms of 96 Children Ranging in Age from 12 to 72 Months

1. *Animal furnishings* (furniture, bedspreads, pictures, posters, mobiles, rugs and pillows that contained animal characters)
2. *Books*
3. *Dolls* (baby and figures, toy soldiers, cowboys and Indians, and so forth)
4. *Educational/art materials* (charts with letters or numbers, materials for drawing, painting, coloring, or sculpting)
5. *Floral furnishings* (bedspreads, pictures, wallpaper, sheets, pillows, and rugs that depicted plants and/or flowers)
6. *Furniture*
7. *Musical items* (toy or real musical instruments, radios and radio players)
8. *Ruffles* (bedspreads and curtains decorated with fringes or lace)
9. *Spatiotemporal objects* (materials, such as magnets, clocks, maps and outer-space toys, designed to teach children about space, time, energy, and other aspects of the physical world)
10. *Sports equipment*
11. *Stuffed animals*
12. *Toy animals* (including housing, such as barns or zoos)
13. *Vehicles*

Source: From H. L. Rheingold and K. V. Cook (1975).

Perhaps the most striking results of the Rheingold and Cook (1975) study, however, were those pertaining to gender differences in bedroom contents. Boys' rooms contained more animal furnishings, more educational and art materials, more spatiotemporal toys, more sports equipment, more toy animals, and more vehicles. The only content categories in girls' rooms that surpassed those found in boys' were dolls, floral furnishings, and ruffles. Finally, no gender differences were found in the number of books, musical objects, and stuffed animals or in the amount of furniture.

Looking not at the specific toys themselves but at general patterns of gender differences, we see a most revealing contrast. First, although neither sex had more actual toys than the other, boys had a larger *variety* of toys; the range of toys for girls was considerably more restricted. Second, boys had more toys that were *educationally oriented*. Third, boys' toys seemed to have an "away from the home" emphasis, as in the case of vehicles, military toys, machinery, and sports equipment, while girls' toys, such as baby and mother dolls and miniature household equipment, were more domestic.

Have there been changes in gender-typed toy play in the years since the Rheingold and Cook (1975) study was done? If so, this was not reflected in the findings of Nash and Fraleigh (1993). Their examination of the bedrooms of 60 preschool children revealed that boys' rooms still contained a larger number of what they termed "toys of the world" (p. 5) (vehicles, military toys, action figures, tools, and sports equipment) while girls' rooms contained more "toys of the home" (p. 5) (dolls, doll paraphernalia, and housekeeping toys).

One might wonder if the same pattern of gender differences in children's toy collections would be found in a country with a stronger tradition of gender equality. Sweden has been described as such a country and in one study was described as the most egalitarian of the 63 countries studied (Inglehart & Norris, 2003). Nevertheless, the same pattern described in American studies can be seen in Sweden as well (Nelson, 2005). For example, Swedish boys had more sports equipment and adult male action figures, while girls had more female dolls and baby dolls.

Toy Preference as a Two-Directional Process

In discussing the gender-typed toys provided by parents to their children, we must remember that toy purchases usually reflect more than just the parent's preferences and values. Parents are not likely to force unwanted toys on their children, and a child will begin to make requests for specific toys as early as the age of 2 years and possibly even before. After that point, it becomes extremely difficult to know how active parents are in promoting the use of gender-appropriate as opposed to gender-inappropriate toys by their preschoolers. If accused of perpetuating gender stereotypes by providing their 5-year-old daughter with a junior makeup kit instead of a dump truck, parents might justifiably respond that she *wanted* a makeup kit and wouldn't even consider a dump truck as a birthday gift.

There is evidence, in fact, to suggest that children themselves are *more* gender typed than their parents in their toy preferences. Robinson and Morris (1986) examined the Christmas toy requests of 86 children aged 2.5 to 5.5 and then looked at the characteristics of the nonrequested toys that their parents also bought for them. A panel of six child development professionals estimated the gender appropriateness of the various toys as "toys for boys," "toys for girls," and "toys for both."

The researchers found that most (63%) of the toys actually requested by children of all ages combined were gender typed; approximately 75% of toys requested by boys aged 3, 4, and 5 were "toys for boys." The remainder of the boys' requests were gender neutral, and only one boy in the entire sample asked for a cross-sex toy. The pattern of girls' toy requests was somewhat different, however. In the first place, it seemed that boys developed gender-typed toy interests at a younger age than girls did. Only one third of the toys requested by 3-year-old girls were designated "toys for girls," although this percentage rose to 51% at age 4 and to 73% at age 5. In addition, girls differed from boys in that several of them asked for such "toys for boys" as vehicles or weapons, a finding consistent with other research indicating that boys tend actively to dislike "girl" toys more than girls do "boy" toys (Eisenberg, Murray, & Hite, 1982; Hanna, 1993).

Boys of all ages showed a strong preference for conventionally masculine toys like cars, trucks, weapons, and action figures and were, in fact, more likely to receive these than were girls. By the time they were 5, girls typically requested conventionally feminine toys like baby dolls, cradles, and tea sets and were more likely than boys to receive dolls, doll accessories, and domestic toys (e.g., play food, toy ovens, pots and pans). In fact, boys never asked for and never received such items.

Approximately 60% of the nonrequested toys, on the other hand, were categorized as gender neutral. These included art supplies (paints, felt-tip pens, crayons), musical toys (radios, musical instruments), and educational toys (books, puzzles, microscopes, magnetic letters and numbers, computers). It would seem, therefore, that children themselves are more attentive than their parents to gender appropriateness in toys. At least parents appear to make efforts to balance out their children's toy collections by providing gender-neutral play materials.

Are parents likely to go even further by offering cross-sex toys to their children? To some extent they are but only to their daughters. One third of girls in the Robinson and Morris (1986) study received a nonrequested toy in the category of "toys for boys"; not a single boy received a nonrequested toy from the "toys for girls" category. This finding is consistent with a pattern typically observed in research on gender roles in the United States: Males feel a greater pressure than females to behave in gender-appropriate ways (Maccoby, 1998).

Messages From Toy Advertising

Ever since the advent of the television era in the 1950s, toy makers have recognized the power of this medium to reach a vast audience of children. It would not surprise any parent to hear that two of the five major advertisers on children's television are toy manufacturers (the other three market food products) (Strassburger & Wilson, 2002). Toy advertising seems to be effective because children who watch the most television seem to send the longest Christmas lists to Santa Claus (Pine & Nash, 2002). Although advertisers in the United States are limited to 10.5 min per hour on children's television on weekends and 12 min per hour on weekdays, this is a less restrictive standard than is found in all European countries (Strassburger & Wilson; Valkenburg, 2000). In addition, the restriction doesn't apply to those television programs that dominate the children's market in which the characters themselves market products to viewers; dolls and other materials seen in the programs are available for purchase (Kline, 1995; Pecora, 2007). One study found that approximately 1 in every 4 young children was unable to tell the difference between the cartoons and the commercials (Wilson & Weiss, 1992).

Television advertising is found to contain powerful messages about the gender appropriateness of toys. The gender appropriateness of a toy is rarely directly stated, of course, but it seems obvious that if members of one sex exclusively are shown playing with a toy in a commercial, the toy is being suggested specifically for children of that sex. Indeed, it is typical for commercials to include children of only one sex. Boys do not appear in commercials for female dolls, doll accessories, or household items (e.g., stoves, pots and pans), while girls are not seen in commercials for male dolls, weapons, construction toys, or sports equipment (Feldstein & Feldstein, 1986). In fact, there is research to support the obvious. When children are exposed to commercials with only boys or only girls playing with a toy, they are indeed more likely to define that toy as for girls or for boys but not for both (Pike & Jennings, 2005).

The voice-overs in toy commercials clearly suggest gender appropriateness. Male voices are used in commercials targeted at boys, female voices are used in those targeted at girls, and both types of voices tend to have exaggerated gender characteristics. The female voices tend to be particularly high-pitched and singsong, and the male voices are overly gruff and aggressive (Johnson & Young, 2002). Feelings and nurturing verbs (*love, care, cuddle*) are used in "girl toy" commercials, while "boy toy" commercials emphasize aggression, violence, and competition and use such aggressive verbs as *bash, wreck,* and *battle* and such control verbs as *rule* and *drive* (Jennings & Wartella, 2007; Johnson & Young). Commercials aimed at boys are louder, more likely to depict scenes of violence, and more likely to include quick cuts instead of soft dissolves (Chandler & Griffiths, 2000). In addition, commercials intended for girls are more likely to take place in home settings (Jennings & Wartella; Larson, 2001).

Television is not the only source of information about children's toys, of course. Catalog and package advertising often depicts children of only one sex playing with a toy and almost always does so when the toy in question is even moderately gender typed (Schwartz & Markham, 1985). In addition, girls' and boys' toys are often shown separately in different sections of catalogs, and even toys intended for use by both sexes contain references to gender appropriateness. Plastic tricycles for girls come in pastel colors and contain floral designs, while the same toys for boys come in dark colors and have seemingly heavy-duty tires and a rugged-sounding name. Costumes for girls are typically those of brides, ballerinas, nurses, or cheerleaders, while boys' costumes are those of traditionally masculine roles, such as soldier, astronaut, or police officer.

Not known, of course, is whether toy manufacturers actually shape children's interests or merely respond to them. Is the message of the advertiser that children *should* play with supposedly gender-appropriate toys, or is it simply that they do? If advertisers are shaping children's opinions about the gender appropriateness of their toys, we might expect that children exposed to the greatest amount of advertising would hold the most rigid gender stereotypes. However, a connection between the amount of television (and presumably television advertising) that is watched and the tendency to engage in gender typing of toys has been observed in some studies but not in others (Repetti, 1984; Tracy, 1987). Thus it seems that, again, as in the question of the influence of parents on children's toy preferences, we are faced with a complex interaction in which it is difficult to separate causes from effects.

Can any definite conclusions be drawn about gender differences in the toy preferences of U.S. preschool children? Perhaps there are a few. It seems clear, first of all, that parental attitudes play at least some role in toy selection, since adults are likely to offer gender-typed toys even to infants too young to express a preference. It is clear also that by the age of 3 years and probably earlier, children express definite preferences for gender-typed toys; these preferences appear sooner and are considerably more emphatic in boys than in girls. What is not clear is the extent to which cultural conditioning accounts for the toy preferences of older children;

it becomes increasingly difficult as children develop to separate out the specific factors that influence their choice of play materials. Unfortunately, the children themselves are usually unable to give reasons for their preferences.

As a final comment on gender differences in toy preference, let us look at the ways in which boys and girls play with *identical* toys. Grinder and Liben (1989) observed 40 preschool children at play with toys that were stereotypically masculine (e.g., a workbench and tools) and stereotypically feminine (e.g., a tea set). They found that when children played with gender-appropriate toys, they were likely to engage in typical toy play, meaning that they played with the toy according to its intended use, such as hammering nails at a workbench or pouring tea with a tea set. When they initially played with cross-sex toys, however, children were not as likely to use them as intended. The authors concluded that simply providing boys and girls with the same play materials will not guarantee that they will play with them in identical ways.

Correlates of Gender-Typed Toy Preference

Although the actual reasons for gender-typed toy preferences are not fully known, a growing body of research examines the correlates of such preferences. It has typically been found, for example, that a preference for masculine, feminine, or neutral toys among preschoolers is related to the extent to which children assume traditionally masculine or feminine gender roles; toy choice is therefore thought to indicate the degree of a child's traditional gender role adoption (Cameron, Eisenberg, & Tryon, 1985; Eisenberg, 1983; Eisenberg, Tryon, & Cameron, 1984). Perhaps it is not surprising that gender-typed toy choice among children is related also to the extent to which the child's parents assume traditional or nontraditional gender roles (Repetti, 1984).

The sex of one's playmate is also related to the tendency to select gender-appropriate or -inappropriate toys. When children play with same-sex peers, they are more likely to make use of gender-appropriate toys (Connor & Serbin, 1977; Eisenberg et al., 1984; Lloyd & Smith, 1985); in fact, a tendency to choose same-sex rather than opposite-sex playmates is correlated with a tendency to prefer gender-appropriate toys (Eisenberg, Boothby, & Matson, 1979).

There is a relationship between the tendency to play with gender-stereotyped toys and certain aspects of children's intellectual functioning. Specifically, it has been shown that school-age boys who indicate the strongest preference for masculine-stereotyped toys demonstrate superior performance on tasks requiring spatial skills and score higher on mathematics and science achievement tests; girls who are the most likely to play with feminine-stereotyped toys are the most likely to give evidence of superior verbal skills. In other words, highly gender-stereotyped toy play is related to traditional patterns of male spatial

> **PUTTING THEORY INTO PRACTICE 6.1**
>
> ## Selecting Toys for Gender Equality
>
> For children of both sexes, select toys that are equally educational and science oriented. Carefully examine the messages about future expectations of the toys that are available for young children.
>
> This is not to suggest that all toys should be designed to teach educational concepts but only that we should be equally sensitive to the educational potential of toys for our daughters as we are to that of toys for our sons. Key questions to keep in mind when attending to the gender implications of toys are:
>
> - When children are playing with this toy or game, what can they learn about the natural world that they didn't know before? What can they learn about space, time, energy, letters, or numbers? Make a list of your answers. This may seem to be excessive attention to detail, but it's much more informative than just thinking about answers to the questions.
>
> - Does this toy teach children about "the way things work"? To what extent does the toy incorporate the concept of putting things together and taking them apart?
>
> - Is this a toy or game that boys and girls can share and use at the same time?
>
> - Does this toy or game suggest that the roles of adult women and men in our society are or should be different from one another?
>
> - Is there anything about the way the toy is packaged, in terms of colors or children pictured on the box, that suggests it is a toy only for boys or only for girls?

superiority and female verbal superiority (Ruble & Martin, 1998; Tracy, 1987; Wolfgang, Stannard, & Jones, 2003).

It has been suggested that "boy" toys (e.g., Legos, Lincoln Logs, vehicles, Erector sets) are more likely than "girl" toys to require construction, the manipulation of objects and patterns, and movement through space; "girl" toys (e.g., dolls and doll equipment, board games, art supplies) facilitate verbal interaction (Cherney & London, 2006; Robert & Héroux, 2004; Ruble & Martin, 1998; Tracy, 1987). Nevertheless, it has yet to be demonstrated that the use of certain play materials actually *causes* gender differences in verbal and spatial skills. Perhaps it is boys' superiority in spatial skills and girls' superiority in verbal skills that leads them to seek out gender-appropriate toys.

Finally, although most research on toy preferences has examined cultural variables, an interesting line of inquiry in the past 20 years has explored the possible influence of biological factors on toy selection. For example, there have been a number of studies of the toy preferences of girls who have a condition known as **congenital adrenal hyperplasia (CAH)**, which causes the adrenal glands to secrete excessive amounts of male sex hormones during prenatal development. These hormones are believed to masculinize the developing brain, and in lower animals excessive androgen secretion in the womb results in masculine behavioral characteristics in the female (White, New, & Dupont, 1987).

Several of the studies found that the girls with congenital adrenal hyperplasia, compared with control groups made up of their sisters and female cousins, were significantly more likely to play with such traditionally male toys as a helicopter, cars, a fire engine, blocks, and Lincoln Logs than with such traditional female toys as dolls, kitchen supplies, crayons, and paper (Berenbaum & Hines, 1992; Nordenstrom, Servin, Bohlin, Larsson, & Wedell, 2002; Pasterski et al., 2005; Servin, Nordenstrom, Larsson, & Bohlin, 2003).

What are we to make of these results? They are certainly intriguing, although we should point out that CAH is a rare condition in human beings, affecting from 1 in 5,000 to 1 in 15,000 children in the United States and Europe (New, 1998). Therefore, the sample sizes in the studies mentioned above were small, so our knowledge of the behavioral consequences of excessive masculinization of the female fetus is still extremely limited. We must be very cautious in interpreting results of studies of such small and atypical populations.

FANTASY PLAY

Before discussing gender differences in fantasy play, we should point out that make-believe is influenced by a variety of factors in addition to the sex of the player. As indicated in Chapter 4, the child's developmental level is an important predictor of the amount and the quality of fantasy play, with older preschoolers engaging in this activity to a considerably greater extent and more imaginatively than younger ones. Factors of physical location, spatial density, and toy availability must be considered. Fantasy play is more likely to occur indoors than outdoors; in smaller, enclosed spaces than in wide-open areas; and when suggestive props are available to stimulate the imagination (Connolly, Doyle, & Ceschin, 1983; Mann, 1984; Peck & Goldman, 1978).

A number of fairly well-established differences in fantasy play, however, are related to the sex of the player. Girls seem to engage in fantasy play more often than boys, their episodes of fantasy play last longer than those of boys, and the themes of their fantasy play compared with those of boys' are more complex and better developed (Pellegrini & Bjorklund, 2004). In addition, gender differences can be found in (a) the props used, (b) the roles assumed, and (c) the themes enacted.

PUTTING THEORY INTO PRACTICE 6.2

Examining Gender and Dramatic Play

Offer the same or similar dramatic play props to children of both sexes. Give children of both sexes the opportunity and the encouragement to play domestic roles as well as exotic fantasy roles.

The first thing a teacher should do is examine the placement of materials in the room to determine whether the sections that typically are more attractive to members of one sex or the other (e.g., the block corner, the housekeeping area) have permeable boundaries. For example, must boys make an effort to come over to the housekeeping area? Would it be unusual for a girl to enter the block area? If the areas were combined, children of both sexes might be more likely to enter them and play together.

Second, a teacher should attend to the availability of props and the gender implications of the materials provided for children to play with. Are there more female or male props in the areas that boys or girls will typically gravitate to? For example, are there as many traditionally male props and articles of clothing for dressing up in the housekeeping corner as there are traditionally female props and clothing? If the housekeeping area included tools, lawn mowers, and snow shovels as well as pots and pans, would children of both sexes be equally comfortable there?

Third, a teacher should be supportive of activities that defy gender stereotypes and should be willing to address the issue directly if children are subject to ridicule from their peers. If Jon wants to bake a cake and the other boys laugh at him, the time would be right for a discussion of why we think only women can bake cakes.

Finally, a teacher should be a model of familiarity and comfort in the use of materials thought of as appropriate for children of both sexes. The author was conducting research in a preschool classroom in which the teacher was eager to project an attitude of flexibility toward gender roles. However, she commented one day that it was nice to have a man in the room so that the children could play with the workbench and tools. She was completely unaware of the gender stereotype she was modeling.

Props for Fantasy Play

The props for fantasy play are the materials that stimulate a child's imagination. As indicated in Chapter 4, such materials vary considerably in their degrees of realism; for example, a child playing out a kitchen scene may be equipped with a toy stove or only with a stack of blocks on top of which eggs are fried and water is boiled. We pointed out in Chapter 4 that children differ in their need for realistic props to stimulate their creative play and that these differences

© Photodisc

Drama, danger, adventure, and the use of weapons are more typical of boys' fantasy play than they are of girls'.

depend primarily on the familiarity of the play materials. However, there is some evidence that boys and girls differ in their need for realistic props; during the preschool years, when most fantasy play occurs, girls seem to be slightly ahead of boys in their ability to initiate fantasy play without the benefit of realistic props, although this difference has been found only in play settings that have been somewhat structured by adults; in free-play situations, gender differences have rarely been observed (Fein, Johnson, Kosson, Stork, & Wasserman, 1975; Johnson & Roopnarine, 1983; Matthews, 1977; McLoyd, 1980). Boys prefer masculine and neutral props and tend to avoid feminine props to a greater extent than girls avoid masculine props. When boys do play with feminine props, their play is less sophisticated than it is when they play with masculine or neutral props (Pellegrini & Bjorklund, 2004).

Fantasy Play Roles

Gender differences in fantasy play roles have been clearly established in the literature on children's play. Girls are much more likely than boys to choose domestic and family roles, such as mother and baby, while boys prefer roles that are more adventurous, more action oriented, more fictitious than real, and further removed from the domestic environment. Boys often choose superhero and supervillain roles, for example, while girls are not likely to do so (Boyatzis & Watson, 1993; Johnson & Roopnarine, 1983; Maccoby, 1998; Sutton-Smith, 1979).

Children of both sexes typically assume roles of same-sex characters, although girls are more willing than boys to play opposite-sex roles. Boys are reluctant to assume the role of a female character (e.g., mother in a game of house) or even to assume a functional role that is typically regarded as female (e.g., the person who makes and serves the food) (Garvey & Berndt, 1977).

Themes of Fantasy Play

Finally, gender differences have been observed in the themes of preschoolers' fantasy play. High drama, adventure, and danger characterize the make-believe play themes of boys, and vehicles and weapons of various sorts are likely to be incorporated into the action. Girls more often play out scenes pertaining to family relationships, use dolls as characters in their play, and rely more on verbal interaction and less on physical activity than do boys (Maccoby, 1998). A typical girls' theme might involve a family interaction, for example, in which there is extensive conversation among the characters, while a group of boys might pretend to be pilots, astronauts, or the crew of a submarine dealing with the many adventures and dangers such roles entail.

ROUGH-AND-TUMBLE PLAY

Rough-and-tumble play is characterized by play fighting, including hitting and wrestling, and chasing with the intent of fighting. However, there are many differences between such play and genuine acts of aggression (Smith, 1989). First, aggression is often triggered by children's competition for resources, such as space or equipment; rough-and-tumble play involves no such competition. Second, during acts of aggression, the participants behave seriously (staring at each other, frowning, crying), while in rough-and-tumble play there is much smiling and laughter. Third, in cases of real fighting, rarely are more than two children involved, while many children at a time may engage in play fighting. Fourth, play fighting draws and keeps the players together rather than driving them apart, as would be the outcome of genuine aggression. Finally, children engaging in rough-and-tumble play usually do not use their strength to the maximum; they restrain themselves lest another child be injured. In a sense, then, rough-and-tumble play is *mock* aggression (DePietro, 1981; Humphreys & Smith, 1984; Pellegrini & Archer, 2004; Power, 2000).

Rough-and-tumble play must also be distinguished from what has been referred to as **vigorous activity play** (Humphreys & Smith, 1984). Running, swinging, climbing, jumping, and pushing and pulling large objects are certainly vigorous physical activities, yet they differ from rough-and-tumble play in two important ways. First, such energetic motor play can be either a solitary or a social activity, while rough-and-tumble play is *always* of a social nature. Second, as noted, rough-and-tumble play always contains components of mock aggression, but vigorous activity play does not.

Functions of Rough-and-Tumble Play

Reasons for the occurrence of rough-and-tumble play in human beings are difficult to establish. For example, it seems clear that such play provides children with an opportunity for physical exercise. However, since it constitutes only about 15% of all of their vigorous physical play, it is unlikely that play fighting is engaged in primarily for exercise. Vigorous physical play seems more likely to serve that exercise function (Fagen & George, 1977; Humphreys & Smith, 1984).

Rough-and-tumble play is explained by some theorists as practice for hunting and fighting, and these skills would have been adaptive in earlier times (Bjorklund & Ellis, 2004). Perhaps the practice explanation makes sense, however, if viewed in evolutionary terms. Children do engage in rough-and-tumble play more often with peers who are close to them in strength than with considerably stronger or weaker peers (Humphreys, 1983), lending some support to the notion that an element of practice is involved. After all, people are considerably more likely to improve their motor skills when they test them against opponents who are closely matched in ability.

Rough-and-tumble play has also been described as a means of achieving status in one's peer group. When a peer group is forming, children attempt to sort themselves into hierarchies and to achieve dominance by aggression and competition. Once the hierarchies have been established, aggressive behavior declines (Pellegrini, 2003; Pellegrini & Archer, 2004). As shown in Chapter 2, other primates often use play to establish their social rankings, and there is little doubt that children's peer groups are hierarchically divided in terms of popularity and social desirability. On the other hand, in our modern world children's social hierarchies are based on criteria other than proficiency at rough-and-tumble play. Quite often, the most popular and admired children, the natural group leaders, never engage in play fighting of any sort (Humphreys & Smith, 1984). Children are not expected to fight their way, in a literal sense, to the top.

While the specific reasons for its occurrence and the benefits that it offers are not always clear, adults might be comforted to know that rough-and-tumble play does not apparently cause greater aggression at later points in life (Humphreys & Smith, 1984). Perhaps the wisest course of action for harried parents and teachers is to accept such play as normal and to try to prevent it from turning into real aggression, as it often does.

Gender Differences in Rough-and-Tumble Play

One of the most consistently observed gender differences in children's play is that males engage in considerably more play fighting than do females (Pellegrini & Archer, 2004; Rubin, Fein, & Vandenberg, 1983); the gender difference is particularly clear in the area of wrestling for superiority, although it is less so in the area of chasing. This male-female difference is found among children of all ages but is especially noticeable among elementary school-age children (Blatchford, Baines, & Pellegrini, 2003; Humphreys & Smith, 1984; Pellegrini & Archer). Furthermore, the difference has been observed in a variety of cultures throughout the world, including that of the United States (DePietro, 1981; Whiting & Edwards, 1973), England (Blurton-Jones, 1967; Blurton-Jones and

Rough-and-tumble physical play is more typical of males than of females in all human cultures and in many lower animal species as well.

© Photodisc

Konner, 1973; Brindley, Clarke, Hutt, Robinson, & Wehtli, 1973; Heaton, 1983; Smith & Connolly, 1980), Mexico, the Philippines, Okinawa, and India (Whiting & Edwards). And finally, gender differences in rough-and-tumble play have been observed consistently in animal research: Among every species of ape and monkey that has been studied to date, as well as in such other animals as rats, play fighting is significantly more likely to occur among males than among females (Gandelman, 1992; Humphreys & Smith; Meaney, 1988).

Explanations for Gender Differences

As might be expected, two lines of argument have been set forth in attempting to explain gender differences in rough-and-tumble play. The first stresses the influence of culture, and attributes the observed gender differences to differential reinforcement by parents—and others—of play fighting in young children. The second argument is based not on environmental factors but on internal biological mechanisms—and specifically on the influence of sex hormones—in predisposing young males to take pleasure in rough-and-tumble play.

Differential Reinforcement?

Infants do not initiate rough-and-tumble play activities as we have defined them; they are not socially mature enough to do so. However, it is possible that children in their first year of life may already be learning that play fighting is intended as a male activity. In ways they do not realize, adults may be communicating subtle messages about the gender appropriateness of certain behaviors.

In order to examine the subtle messages that infants often receive, Fagot, Hagan, Leinsbach, and Kronsberg (1985) observed 34 babies, aged 13 to 14 months, at play in a child research laboratory. Among the types of infant and toddler activity the researchers were interested in documenting was physically assertive or aggressive behavior—for example, grabbing for an object or hitting, pushing, or kicking another child. Interestingly enough, boy and girl babies engaged in roughly the same amounts of aggressive behavior. However, adult reaction to aggressive behavior appeared to depend on the sex of the baby. Aggression in 13-month-old boys was likely to draw a reaction from an adult; teachers would respond by picking the child up, offering him a new toy, or physically removing him from the situation. Aggression in female babies was typically ignored.

The researchers suggested that adults may expect boys to be more aggressive than girls and so may monitor aggressive behaviors more closely when a boy displays them. The net result is that male babies learn that behaving aggressively pays off. It earns attention from adults, and it brings about a change of one sort or another in the play situation. For female babies, on the other hand, assertive or aggressive acts, being followed by no consequences of any sort, are less likely to be continued.

There are other lines of research that support a differential reinforcement explanation of gender differences in rough-and-tumble play. As discussed in Chapter 3, fathers are more likely than mothers to engage in rough-and-tumble play with children, both during infancy and during the toddler years (Hewlett, 2003; Lamb, 2004; MacDonald & Parke, 1986; Parke & Tinsley, 1987; Stevenson, Leavitt, Thompson, & Roach, 1988; Tamis-LeMonda, 2004). Fathers are also more likely to initiate such play with their sons than with their daughters (Lamb, 2004) and so may be teaching their children, both by direct reinforcement and by serving as models, that such play is masculine behavior.

By the time their children are 2 years of age, most parents in the United States already hold stereotypes of rough-and-tumble play as an appropriate activity for boys but not for girls, and children realize, even before they are 3 years old, that certain forms of play are more appropriate for and with males than for and with females. Fagot (1984) found, for example, that a toddler is more likely to engage a male adult than a female adult in a game of throwing a ball back and forth but is more likely to seek various forms of help from a woman than from a man. Those who support a differential reinforcement position maintain that such stereotypes result from a cultural conditioning that is subtle but pervasive and begins in the early weeks of an infant's life, if not before.

A Biological Predisposition?

Earlier in this chapter we discussed the condition known as congenital adrenal hyperplasia, which results when the adrenal glands produce excessively high levels of androgens in a female fetus. We pointed out that CAH patients in one study were more likely than other girls to prefer traditionally masculine toys, such as cars and blocks. There is research to suggest that CAH may be related to differences in rough-and-tumble play as well. It has been found that girls with CAH are more active and more aggressive, more likely to be described as tomboys, and more interested in rough-and-tumble play than their sisters and cousins who do not have CAH (Ehrhardt & Meyer-Bahlburg, 1981; Hines & Green, 1991; Money & Ehrhardt, 1972; Pasterski et al., 2007).

It would be difficult to argue that research on CAH offers conclusive proof that biological predispositions account for gender differences in rough-and-tumble play, however. In the first place, there is no way to ascertain that cultural as well as hormonal factors are not involved. Those who reject biological explanations argue that childrearing practices must also be considered as influences on the supposedly masculine play patterns of girls experiencing the adrenogenital syndrome. They suggest that, since girls with CAH begin life with rudimentary male genitalia, the parents may unconsciously encourage more masculine play in their initially masculine-appearing daughters. Ehrhardt and Meyer-Bahlburg (1981) replied that the opposite parental reaction is actually more likely: Parents would try harder to feminize daughters who displayed physical signs of masculinization at birth.

A more compelling reason for caution in interpreting the evidence for biological predispositions in rough-and-tumble play centers on the research design itself. As mentioned above, genuine experimental research on the effects of sex hormones on human brain tissue is not possible; that is, ethical constraints prevent researchers from experimentally manipulating the amount of sex hormone that is secreted in the womb in order to observe the results on later childhood play. Therefore, research on the effects of hormonal abnormalities in humans is correlational by nature; it is limited to examining relationships among variables. A relationship between hormone secretion during pregnancy and characteristics of later childhood play does not prove that the influence of hormone levels on the fetal brain actually caused certain forms of play to occur later on. And since conditions such as CAH in females and androgen insensitivity in males are quite rare, there are very few cases on which to base conclusions.

GAMES WITH RULES

In Chapter 5, games with rules were described as forms of play that emerge when children begin to apply the structure of logic to their thinking; this happens when the child reaches the age of 5 or 6 years and begins to use what Piaget (1962) referred to as concrete operations. Remember that games with rules require the involvement of two or more children in a competitive activity, the rules of which are agreed upon in advance.

Evidence of Gender Differences

In describing the games with rules that he observed in children, Piaget (1962) pointed out that such activities were engaged in primarily by boys.

After extensive analysis of the marble games of elementary school children, Piaget (1965) remarked, "We did not succeed in finding a single collective game played by girls in which there were as many rules and, above all, as fine and consistent organization and codification of these rules as in the games of marbles [played by boys]" (p. 77).

Consistent with Piaget's (1965) analysis, it has often been observed that traditional girls' games (e.g., hopscotch, skipping rope) are simpler in their rule structure than the games of boys (Parker, 1984). Usually there are no teams with specialized roles, no umpires, and no referees. Boys are more likely to become involved in sports, and their games are played in larger groups, are more competitive, last longer, and seem to require a greater amount of skill than do the games of girls (Bradley, McMurray, Harrill, & Deng, 2000; Cherney & London, 2006; Crombie & Desjardins, 1993; Lever, 1976). We should remember, however, that this gender difference is a matter of degree. Traditional girls' games definitely require skill, have rules that are often very complex, and can be highly competitive, as an analysis of playground games of skipping rope makes very clear (Goodwin, 2006).

Cultural Explanations for Gender Differences

Cultural explanations typically focus on the significance of play and the role of games in preparing children for their positions and functions in adult life. An emphasis on rules, in play as well as in other areas of life, is thought to provide a basis for the ranking of male dominance hierarchies in a safe, nonthreatening way. In organized games, children are grouped according to ability; they quickly learn their positions within the hierarchy from observing the significance of their positions on the team or from their assignments as first-stringers, second-stringers, or benchwarmers (Cherney & London, 2006).

Not only do children learn their status rankings from their games, but as a result of the grouping process, they also have opportunities to develop their skills to the fullest by competing with peers who are similar to them in ability. This early status ranking and opportunity to refine competitive skills may prepare children to assume the status roles in which they can compete most effectively as adults for scarce resources; such preparation may have been, at some point in the process of human evolution, a reason for the emergence of games with rules.

Anthropologists point out that many of the children's games with rules that are commonly seen in our society bear a resemblance to certain forms of adult competition for scarce resources (Parker, 1984): Soccer, basketball, and football offer practice in territorial invasion; baseball prepares one for territorial raiding;

checkers and chess allow for practice invasion and the capture of one's enemies; "snakes and ladders" gives practice in overcoming a series of obstacles in order to achieve one's goals; and card games like Old Maid offer practice in bluffing and in calculating the odds. All games offer practice in rule manipulation, memory, quantification, and strategic coalition.

The Possible Role of Biology

Biological explanations for gender differences in games with rules typically emphasize the effects of male sex hormones on the fetal brain, which, as in the case of rough-and-tumble play, are thought to predispose males to engage in competition via games with rules. As a matter of fact, girls with CAH have been found to be more active and to show a greater preference for playing outdoor sports and games (as well as for playing with cars, trucks, and blocks) than do other girls (Ehrhardt & Baker, 1974; Hines & Green, 1991; Pasterski et al., 2007). Again it should be pointed out, however, that research of this type is correlational and is based on a very small number of cases.

It seems fair, at least at this point, to conclude that cultural explanations of gender differences in games with rules are more compelling than biological ones, particularly in light of the ethical constraints on biological research with human beings. Whether or not biological predispositions exist, cultural influences cannot be ignored. The impact of culture on children's games in general has certainly long been recognized (see Chapter 2). What is more, the cultural argument is supported by an examination of recent trends, both in the play of U.S. children and in their roles as adults. Perhaps it is not surprising that as women are increasingly likely to find themselves competing with men in the work world, girls are increasingly likely to engage in traditional male activities such as sports, while traditional female games (e.g., jumping rope, playing jacks, playing board games) have declined in popularity (Beal, 1994; Bensoussan et al., 1992; Parker, 1984). Finally, it's interesting to note that women in nontraditional professions (e.g., business) are more likely than those in traditional female professions (e.g., teaching) to have played competitive sports as children (Coats & Overman, 1992).

Summary

The vast majority of the research on gender differences in children's play has been concentrated in four areas: (a) toy selection, (b) fantasy play, (c) rough-and-tumble play, and (d) games with rules. No one is certain why differences are found in any of the four areas, but there are two major theoretical viewpoints on the origins of gender stereotyping.

According to *learning theory*, children learn by imitation and reinforcement to behave in gender-appropriate ways, even before they understand the concept of gender. The basic premise of *cognitive-developmental theory* is that children engage in gender-appropriate activities because such activities are consistent with their gradually emerging gender concept.

Gender differences in toy selection are usually attributed to cultural factors, in particular to the socializing influences of adults, peers, and the mass media. Adults are likely, for example, to offer gender-appropriate toys to very young children and to reinforce children, in often very subtle ways, for playing with gender-appropriate toys. Research on the contents of preschool children's bedrooms indicates that boys and girls have decidedly different play materials and that boys' toys are characterized by greater variety, a greater educational focus, and an "away from the home" rather than a domestic emphasis.

Gender differences in fantasy play appear in (a) the props that are used, (b) the roles that are assumed, and (c) the themes that are played out. During the preschool years, when most fantasy play occurs, girls may be slightly ahead of boys in their ability to initiate fantasy play without realistic props. Girls are much more likely than boys to choose domestic and family roles, while boys prefer roles that are more adventurous, more action oriented, more fictitious than real, and further removed from the domestic environment. Finally, high drama, adventure, and danger characterize the make-believe play themes of boys, while girls more often play out scenes pertaining to family relationships.

Gender differences in rough-and-tumble play have been observed consistently in human and animal research, with males engaging in this activity much more frequently than females. Explanations for the gender difference focus either on differential patterns of reinforcement or on biological predispositions related to the effects of male sex hormones on the developing fetal brain.

Finally, games with rules are characterized by gender differences, with boys' games occurring more frequently than girls' and being more complex, more competitive, and longer lasting. Cultural explanations of such gender differences emphasize the role of games in preparing children for competition in adult life and the greater need for the male to compete, at least in traditional societies. Biological explanations again focus on the influence on hormones on the fetal brain, but research on gender differences in fetal hormone production is by nature correlational and is based on a very small number of cases.

Key Terms

Congenital Adrenal Hyperplasia (CAH)	p. 169	Gender Stability	p. 159
Gender Consistency	p. 159	Rough-and-Tumble Play	p. 173
Gender Identity	p. 159	Vigorous Activity Play	p. 174

Issues for Class Discussion

1. Should parents make a conscious effort to buy gender-neutral toys for their children, even if the children ask for gender-stereotyped toys? Should parents encourage children to play with toys designed for the opposite sex?

2. What do the contents of young children's bedrooms tell us about existing gender differences and about long-range parental expectations for their children?

3. If a person had never seen a particular gender-stereotyped toy and came across it accidentally on a department store shelf, how could he or she tell that it was intended for a child of one sex rather than the other?

4. How do you feel about the marketing of promotional toys, which are based on characters in television programs? Since 1 in 4 preschool children can't tell the difference between a television program and a commercial, is it ethical to market toys of this type?

Chapter 7

PLAY IN SPECIAL POPULATIONS

The Sandersons were pleased when their 7-year-old son Todd announced that he had been invited to a classmate's birthday party. Their pleasure changed to apprehension, however, when they discovered that the party was in honor of a child who was both mentally and physically impaired. Roger, who had been admitted to Todd's class as a result of the school's new mainstreaming policy, was judged to be moderately mentally retarded and was confined to a wheelchair as well.

Mr. and Mrs. Sanderson had no negative feelings about impaired children. In fact, they were strong advocates of the mainstreaming concept. Nevertheless, they now found themselves wondering whether they should prepare Todd in some way for the experience of attending Roger's party. What would the party be like? Would the children play games? Would Roger be able to participate in games? What kind of gift should Todd bring? What kind of toy would a child like Roger play with? Do children like Roger play at all?

The Sandersons's confusion about an appropriate birthday gift for Roger should not be surprising. Little is known, even by child development professionals, about the play of children with disabilities, and the scarcity of information is attributable to the shortage of carefully designed studies of the subject (Rubin, Fein, & Vandenberg, 1983). Furthermore, even the findings from well-constructed studies tell us little about the reasons for observed play differences. Too often it has been assumed that disabled children have inherent play deficits when, in fact, differences in play might be explained more easily by environmental variables. Children like Roger differ from the norm by virtue of their disabilities, but they also grow up in a different sociocultural environment from that of the average child.

Learning Objectives

After reading Chapter 7, a student should be able to:

✦ Describe the observed differences in play between children with and without visual impairments, explain these differences in terms of adult expectations, and identify suggestions offered by psychologists and educators that might help all children play to their fullest potential.

✦ Identify the differences in symbolic play between typically developing children and those with language impairment.

✦ Describe the differences between the object and symbolic play of typical children and that of children with intellectual and emotional disabilities and understand the frequently cited explanations for these differences.

✦ Understand the basic characteristics of childhood autism and the relationship between autism and play. Describe the intervention approaches used to enhance the play of children with autism.

✦ Explain the concept of a theory of mind and why it is central to successful social development.

✦ Identify and describe the various forms of hospital play programs that have appeared in the United States in the past 50 years.

✦ List and describe what have been called the necessary conditions for play in the hospitalized child.

✦ Describe the characteristics of the play of children who are victims of physical and/or sexual abuse.

In this chapter, we shall deal with the play of children whose development is atypical for a variety of reasons. Included will be a discussion of children with impaired vision or hearing, cognitive delays, chronic emotional problems, and temporary life stresses (see Table 7.1). The drive to play is fundamental in all children, and it will be shown that not only do all children play, whether they are typically developing or not, but play can be particularly beneficial to children dealing with particular life difficulties.

CHILDREN WITH PHYSICAL DISABILITIES

Studies of play among children with physical disabilities have been concentrated in the three areas of visual impairment, hearing impairment, and language disorder. It should be remembered, however, that these areas are not completely independent. For example, children with visual impairments often experience delays in language and motor skills as well (Warren, 1984), and impairments in hearing are correlated with impairments in speech.

TABLE 7.1   Characteristics of the Play of Children Whose Development Is Atypical Compared With That of Typically Developing Children

Condition	Characteristics of Play
Visual Impairment	Greater amount of solitary play Less imaginative in fantasy play Less likely to explore the physical environment in play Less varied and less flexible in play
Hearing Impairment	Less likely to engage in cooperative make-believe play Less likely to use objects symbolically
Intellectual Deficit	More interested in the physical characteristics of play materials than in their representational possibilities More likely to simply manipulate and handle play materials More repetitive and less varied in toy play Later appearance of symbolic play and lower likelihood of reaching higher levels of sophistication
Language Impairment	Less make-believe play More likely to receive a negative reaction from peers when making efforts to join them in play
Autism	More likely to engage in repetitive, stereotyped manipulation of play materials Less likely to use objects symbolically in make-believe

Children With Visual Impairments

Research on the play of children with visual impairments (e.g., Parsons, 1986a; Recchia, 1997; Rettig, 1994; Troster & Brambring, 1994) leads to two general conclusions. First—and perhaps most important—visual impairments do not result in a basic inability to play. Like all children, blind children *do* play. Second, despite the universal similarities in play, some play differences related to visual impairments have been observed.

One of the most striking differences between the play of blind children and that of the sighted is that children with limited vision engage in greater amounts of solitary play (Celeste, 2006, 2007; Erwin, 1993; Rettig, 1994; Schneekloth, 1989). For example, Schneekloth found that the amount of solitary play was related to the severity of the visual impairment: Children with the

PUTTING THEORY INTO PRACTICE 7.1

Enhancing the Feel of the Environment

Recognize that all children have a natural tendency to play, even though some are limited in their opportunities to do so.

Make certain that the physical environment of children with visual impairments is an inviting play atmosphere:

- Explain to the children what can be found in the physical environment. Identify and describe the play materials and the play equipment. Tell them where in the room these are located. Tell them about the other children in the room. How many are there? How many are boys, and how many are girls? What are their names?

- Make clear to them that it is fully expected that they will take full advantage of the play environment by asking them what activities they like and how they plan to play with the available materials.

- Encourage and provide adequate time for children with visual impairments to freely explore the physical environment.

- Make the environment as "colorful" for a child with a visual impairment as it is for a sighted child by providing as much variety as possible in the feel of the materials in the classroom. Talk about the way things feel, as well as about the way they look. Have the sighted children engage in tactile exploration by asking them to close their eyes and explore materials just by feeling.

- If possible, use distinctive texturing on the floors, walls, or ground in different areas of the room or playground. This will help children with visual impairments recognize different areas by their feel.

most severe visual limitations spent 56% of their time playing alone, those with partial limits on their vision were alone at play 33% of the time, and sighted children played alone only 14% of the time. A possible reason for the greater tendency of children with visual limitations to play alone is that the play of young children is often sporadic, with rapid movement from one activity to another, and children with low vision may be disoriented by the unpredictable transitions (Recchia, 1997).

A second distinction between the play of blind children and that of the sighted is that those with visual limitations are less imaginative in their fantasy play and less likely to manipulate and explore the physical environment (Parsons, 1986b; Recchia, 1997; Rettig, 1994; Warren, 1984). For example, Singer and Streiner (1966) found that blind elementary school children played in a manner that was more concrete, less varied, and less flexible than what ordinarily occurs among sighted children.

How can parents and teachers guarantee that children with visual impairments will be able to play to their full potential? Child development professionals (e.g., Cutter, 2007; Fazzi & Klein, 2002; Recchia, 1997; Rettig, 1994) have offered a number of suggestions. First, it is important for the teacher to plan for free play. The teacher should discuss with the children in advance all the options available in terms of play materials, equipment, activities, and playmates. The children should be encouraged to identify their favorite activities and to tell how they plan to use the upcoming playtime. Second, adults should resist the tendency to discourage blind children from exploring their environments since it is through such exploration that concepts are formed; even in a safe environment, a blind child may acquire a few bumps and bruises from exploration, but the same is true of sighted children. Third, adults should suggest

© Eyewire

One of the most meaningful findings from research on play in special populations of children is that all children want and need to play.

make-believe activities to blind children, beginning with simple objects or routines that the children are already familiar with (e.g., "Let's pretend to be a cat"), graduating to make-believe activities that involve more than one player, and eventually increasing the level of abstraction, such as by using the same object to represent different things at different times (Fazzi & Klein, 2002). Adults might need to offer blind children specific instruction in symbolic play. They might demonstrate pretend activities, encourage the children to try them for themselves, and reinforce the children for doing so.

Fourth, adults should provide real-world playthings (e.g., keys, sponges, pots and pans, doorknobs) for the child to manipulate since hands-on experience is necessary for children with visual limitations to gain information about the world. Fifth, adults should remember to choose play materials for their tactile qualities as well as for their appearance. In fact, they should attempt to create a sensory-rich play environment—a setting with sensory cues to guide the child with a visual impairment. Materials that vary in texture might be used; tactile maps might be placed in strategic locations throughout the environment, as might audiocassette recorders with taped directions. Areas of the room or outdoor playground might be made distinctive through the use of texturing, such as by placing sand or wood chips on the ground or different styles of carpeting or linoleum on the floor. Such an environment will provide tactile stimulation and help a child with low vision feel comfortable and secure enough to explore. As Rettig (1994) concluded, the ideal play environment for children with visual limits is a place where they feel free to throw their bodies around.

Finally, to prevent a blind child from feeling overwhelmed in a large group setting, a teacher might select just one sighted peer as a playmate at first and then gradually increase the number of sighted children in the play group. As preparation for this experience, the teacher might discuss with the sighted playmate(s) the practical implications of visual limitations.

Children With Language Impairment

Human language and symbolic, or make-believe, play both require the ability to use symbols: to let one thing stand for, or represent, something else (McCune, 1995). Because of the relationship between the two, it should not be surprising that language and symbolic play assume parallel courses of development. As pointed out in Chapter 3, both initially appear at the same time, early in the child's second year, and the shift in symbolic play from an uncoordinated collection of activities to one that is coordinated and schematic parallels the transition at the end of the second year from one-word utterances to original two-word combinations in speech. What is more, individual differences among children in their rates of language development seem to mirror individual differences in the development of symbolic play (Gould, 1986).

The language–symbolic play relationship raises interesting questions about the make-believe play of children who have specific language impairment, which is the atypical development of language in the absence of neurological, emotional, or intellectual deficits or hearing difficulties. Would children delayed in language but free of specific intellectual impairments show symbolic play deficits as well? In fact, a number of researchers have discovered a relationship between language deficits and deficits in symbolic play (Lewis, Boucher, Lupton, & Watson, 2000; Lyytinen, Poikkeus, Laakso, Eklund, & Lyytinen, 2001; McCune, 1995; Watt, Wetherby, & Shumway, 2006). But what do these findings mean? Do children with delayed speech exhibit basic deficits in overall symbolic functioning?

Some psychologists argue that the research fails to demonstrate the existence of a broad symbolic deficit among speech-delayed children because in many of these studies the children actually do engage in make-believe play, although less often than typically developing children. In addition, preschool children who have difficulty understanding the language of other children or expressing themselves in words tend to receive a negative reaction from peers and in turn may behave aggressively or simply withdraw. They tend to be less capable of handling peer conflict (Brinton & Fujiki, 2004; Horowitz, Westlund, & Ljungberg, 2007). They are not adequately assertive, get frustrated easily, and are more dependent on adults for assistance than are other children (McCabe & Marshall, 2006; Picone & McCabe, 2005). It is not surprising, therefore, that they are less likely than the typically developing child to engage in cooperative make-believe play. In other words, the explanation may be environmental in nature rather than the result of a representational deficit. Language can make it easier for children to engage in social varieties of make-believe, as in the case of complex forms of sociodramatic play (McCune, 1995).

Children With Hearing Difficulties

As noted in the previous section, children whose speech is delayed often exhibit less mature forms of play during the early childhood years, particularly with regard to their interest in social forms of make-believe. A similar—and related— finding is that young children with hearing difficulties engage in lesser amounts of cooperative make-believe play and are less likely to make symbolic use of objects than are children of normal hearing ability (Esposito & Koorland, 1989; Hughes, 1998; Mann, 1984; Morelock, Brown, & Morrissey, 2003). Again, however, it has not been demonstrated that such children have specific play deficits. It seems more likely that the play differences observed in comparisons of children with and without hearing impairments are differences in performance rather than potential. Depending on their surroundings and on cultural expectations, children do not always display the behaviors of which they are truly capable.

Esposito and Koorland (1989) discovered, for example, that the play of the same children in settings that were integrated (i.e., with non-hearing-impaired children) or segregated (i.e., with other hearing-impaired children) was substantially different. Three-year-old Michael and 5-year-old Vicki, both diagnosed as having severe hearing loss, were observed at play in their self-contained class for hearing-impaired children and in the regular day care centers they also attended. The number of children in the play groups and the specific roles of the adults were the same in both environments.

The play of children in the integrated settings was judged by observers to be more socially sophisticated. Parallel play was more often seen in the class for hearing-impaired children, while associative play was more typical in the day care centers. Remember from Chapter 4 that parallel play is thought to be less socially mature than associative play and more typical of the very young preschooler.

CHILDREN WITH INTELLECTUAL IMPAIRMENTS

As is the case for all children whose development is atypical, it is difficult to separate how children with intellectual deficits actually play from how they are able to play in ideal circumstances. This is because so much of the typically developing young child's play is social, and if a child has difficulty initiating and maintaining social interaction, his or her play will be restricted as well. Children with even minor intellectual deficits seem to be at risk for social isolation, are less likely to be accepted by peers, and have fewer friendships that are reciprocated. Those with more significant impairments such as Down syndrome have a good deal of difficulty interacting with peers and few peer contacts other than siblings, and 1 in 3 has no play contacts at all (Guralnick, 2002). Nevertheless, children with a range of intellectual deficits will play if given the opportunity. Opportunity is critical because these children benefit greatly from having adults arrange play experiences for them. Arranging could include inviting a playmate to one's house, suggesting play activities, and checking on the children when they are playing.

Object Play

Throughout the years there have been many studies of the uses of toys in free play by children with cognitive deficits, and the group most often studied is children with Down syndrome. The findings from these studies are that, compared with typically developing children, children with cognitive deficits display a variety of characteristics. They are interested in the physical rather than the representational characteristics of objects. They spend more time than the typical young child in nonspecific manipulation of objects, such as simply touching or holding them, dropping them, throwing them, or mouthing them. They have more difficulty sustaining an interest in the toys. Their toy play is repetitive and lacks variety. They are less likely to combine toys in play, less goal oriented, and more passive. In general, they seem to derive less pleasure from the toys than do typically developing children (Vig, 2007).

When comparing children who vary in intellectual ability, the quality of toy play seems to relate more to mental age than to chronological age (Malone, 2006), and this suggests that cognitive impairment is more of a developmental delay than a qualitatively different developmental path. In addition, it is important to remember when examining the toy play of children with Down syndrome that the complexity of object play depends on the social context. For example, play at home seems to be a better predictor of mental age than play in a school setting, and independent play looks to be more sophisticated than play in groups (Malone). Finally, children play with what is made available to them, and adults often provide children with Down syndrome with toys that have less creative potential. In fact, even in supposedly free-play situations, mothers of Down syndrome children tend to be very controlling and very directive, choosing the toys for their children and showing them exactly how the toys should be used (Hauser-Cram & Howell, 2003).

Symbolic Play

Symbolic, or make-believe, play emerges during the second year of life as children acquire the ability to mentally represent the world. As discussed in Chapter 3, the normal pattern is a gradual developmental progression into the world of make-believe. But what can be said about the make-believe play of children with cognitive delays? Three main conclusions can be drawn.

First, symbolic play has been observed consistently in such children; there is no evidence that intellectual impairment prevents children from engaging in imaginative acts of make-believe (McCune, 1995; O'Toole & Chiat, 2006; Venuti, deFalco, Giusti, & Bornstein, 2008). Second, mental age is a better predictor of the onset of symbolic play than is chronological age; thus, symbolic play typically appears later in children with intellectual deficits than in those whose intellectual development is typical. For example, Wing, Gould, Yeates, and Brierly (1977) examined the symbolic play of 108 children with severe intellectual deficits who ranged in age from 5 to 14 years. Symbolic play was found, but it did not occur before the children had attained a mental age of 20 months. As indicated in Chapter 3, this mental age is approximately the same as the age at which typical children begin to become involved in make-believe.

The third conclusion is that play is related to language skills in children with Down syndrome. In one study, children with Down syndrome were observed in three play sessions with their mothers (Fewell & Ogura, 1997). The mothers and children were supplied with a variety of play materials (e.g., dolls, toy eating and cooking utensils, blocks). It was found that the children who demonstrated the most sophisticated ability to play were also the most likely to make spontaneous utterances during the sessions. They spoke more, they used a greater variety of words, and their utterances were longer.

A final conclusion pertains to the fact that symbolic play does not appear suddenly; its onset is gradual, and there seems to be a series of stages through which children progress, as discussed in Chapter 3. While the stage progression seems to be identical in children at all levels of intellectual ability, children with impairments lag behind able children and are less likely to reach the most sophisticated levels (McCune, 1995; O'Toole & Chiat, 2006).

In conclusion, it seems that children of all intellectual levels involve themselves in functional play with objects, and children at all levels engage in make-believe play. While the research tends to emphasize group differences, the overwhelming impression is one of similarity. That is, it appears that children of different intellectual levels are not qualitatively different in their attitudes toward and their approaches to play. Those with impairments are simply delayed but can play as other children do if groups are equated in terms of mental rather than chronological age.

CHILDREN WITH AUTISM

Play in the preschool years is intimately connected with a child's ability to communicate with others and to engage in successful social interactions. There are a number of conditions (e.g., childhood autism, Asperger's syndrome, pervasive developmental disorder) that are characterized by social interaction difficulties, and these conditions typically have some but not all of their symptoms in common. For example, Asperger's syndrome is characterized by the social difficulties and repetitive behaviors found in autism, but autism is also characterized by significant communication problems. As a group, these conditions are referred to as autism spectrum disorders (Bishop & Lord, 2006; Risi et al., 2006). The specific disorder that has received the most attention from researchers in terms of its impact on play is childhood autism.

Childhood autism, a neurologically based emotional disorder that affects 34 in every 10,000 children, is characterized by significant impairments in social interaction and communication skills, as well as restrictive, repetitive, stereotyped patterns of behaviors, activities, and interests (American Psychiatric Association, *Diagnostic and Statistical Manual of Mental Disorders*, 2000). Children with autism may also be diagnosed as having cognitive deficits, although many are of average or above-average intelligence. The common characteristic shared by all of them, however, is a basic communication difficulty, a profound inability to understand and function within the normal social environment; the child with autism apparently fails to differentiate between the self and the external world (Baron-Cohen & Swettenham, 1997; Kanner, 1971; Rutter, 1983).

The Lack of a Theory of Mind

Children with autism have been found to lack representational skills. They seem to lack the ability to impute mental states to themselves and other people, an ability described as a **theory of mind** (Baron-Cohen, 1987; Baron-Cohen, Leslie, & Frith, 1985; Baron-Cohen & Swettenham, 1997). A theory of mind allows a person to understand that there is sometimes a difference between one's feelings, thoughts, and beliefs about reality and actual reality itself. It is acquired in the typically developing child between 3 and 5 years of age, and it allows the toddler to go from literally observing human behavior to understanding that there is motivation behind it (Slaughter & Repacholi, 2003). This is an important component of overall social understanding that is essential for making sense of and predicting other people's behavior (Colle, Baron-Cohen, & Hill, 2007).

The lack of a theory of mind becomes evident in situations when belief contradicts reality, as illustrated in the false-belief experiment, which is the most widely used task to indicate the presence of a theory of mind (Slaughter & Repacholi, 2003). An interesting example is the classic "Sally and Anne" study conducted by Baron-Cohen and colleagues (1985). The researchers included three groups of preschoolers, one including children whose development was typical, one including children diagnosed with autism, and one including children diagnosed as having Down syndrome. The children were seated at a table and shown two dolls, Sally and Anne, as well as a basket for Sally and a box for Anne. Sally placed a marble in her basket and then departed. Anne removed the marble from Sally's basket and placed it in her box. Then the children were asked three questions. First, "Where is the marble really?" The answer to this would indicate the child's understanding of reality. Second, "Where was the marble at the beginning?" This was designed to test their memory. Finally, "Where will Sally look for her marble?" was a question designed to determine if the children realized that Sally had a belief system independent of their own. In other words, the children knew that the marble was in Anne's box, but one might expect that Sally would hold the false belief that it was in her own basket, since she put it there before she went away.

All three groups of children answered the first two questions correctly. All apparently had the same sense of reality and the same ability to remember the placement of the marble. However, the responses to the third question were quite revealing. Neither the typically developing children nor the children with Down syndrome had difficulty realizing that Sally would *think* the marble was still in her basket, even though they knew that it was not. Of the children with autism, however, 4 out of 5 failed the belief question; they indicated that Sally would look for the marble in the box, apparently failing to differentiate between their knowledge of the situation and that of the doll.

The Sally and Anne study obviously required the use of language, leading to speculation that the difficulties faced by children with autism may really be linguistic deficits. Is it possible that children with autism may simply not understand what is being asked of them on false-belief tests? Language requires representational ability, and autism is characterized by language deficits. Early estimates were that as many as one third of children with autism show no signs of language at all, although these estimates have been revised downward as autism has become better understood (Baird et al., 2001; Rutter, 1978). In fact, like those with autism, children who do not have autism but have specific language deficits do not perform well on verbal false-belief tests. However, in false-belief experiments that are presented nonverbally, children with specific language deficits perform as well as typically developing children, while children with autism still cannot impute a theory of mind to other people. In other words, the lack of a theory of mind cannot be explained simply as a result of a language deficit (Colle et al., 2007).

Autism and Play

In terms of their toy and object play, children with autism are more likely than typical children to engage in repetitive, stereotyped manipulation and less likely to use objects symbolically in make-believe (Thomas & Smith, 2004; Vig, 2007; Wing et al., 1977). Compared with typical children, children with autism are less likely to engage in complex toy play and less likely to use toys appropriately. This is because they apparently do not see the toys as representative of other objects. Instead of playing with toys, a child with autism might simply line them up in a very specific way and then become upset if anyone arranges them differently (Nebel-Schwalm & Matson, 2008). Or instead of seeing a toy car as representing a real car and "driving" it by pushing it around the floor, a child with autism might simply spin the wheels repeatedly (Bishop & Lord, 2006).

The most extensive area of research on the play of children with autism concerns the use of symbolic play. When children pretend, they are by definition holding a view of the world that differs from reality, a theory of mind. Children who are autistic, however, have difficulty understanding pretense and are unable to generate ideas for pretend play (Bigham, 2008). It is not surprising, therefore, that children with autism rarely engage in symbolic play, and when they attempt to do so, they are less successful than the typically developing child (Baron-Cohen & Swettenham, 1997; Bishop & Lord, 2006; Keenan, 2003; Schwebel, Rosen, & Singer, 1999). The extent of the deficit in symbolic play is related to the extent of the child's cognitive impairment, as well as the extent of the impairment in the child's expressive language (Stanley & Konstantareas, 2007).

Intervention Approaches With Autism

Difficulties with representational ability certainly make social interaction, including social play, particularly challenging for a child with autism. Nevertheless, children with autism can experience dramatic improvements in the quality of their play if provided with instruction and a supportive social environment. Specific play training has resulted in significant improvement in symbolic play skills, appropriate language use, and what is known as joint attention (coordinated looking at toys and people, showing toys to others, or pointing to events and objects) in children with autism (Herrera et al., 2008; Kasari, Freeman, & Paparella, 2006; Kasari, Paparella, Freeman, & Jahromi, 2008; Liber, Frea, & Symon, 2008). Consider as an illustration the research of psychologist Connie Kasari and her associates (2006), who worked with 58 children aged 3 and 4 years for a half-hour a day for 5 or 6 weeks. The specific skills that were taught depended on the child's individual profile of developmentally appropriate skills that had not yet been mastered. For example, the skill in question might be showing an object to another person. The interventionist would sit on the floor with one child and use a teaching approach that included following the child's interest in activities, talking about and elaborating on what the child was doing, repeating what the child had just said, giving corrective feedback, making eye contact, and making environmental adjustments to maintain the child's attention. The results were very encouraging. There were improvements not only in joint attention and symbolic play but also in communication skills, and these changes seemed to last until at least a year after the training sessions.

The characteristics of the social environment, even in the absence of specific skill training, can influence the play of children with autism. For example, when preschool children with autism are closely attached to the caregiver in a play environment, their play is more sophisticated than when they are not closely attached. In fact, when developmental age is taken into account, closeness of attachment to a caregiver is a better predictor of the quality of play than is the presence or absence of autism itself (Naber et al., 2008). Improvements in the symbolic play of a child with autism have also resulted from one's involvement in an integrated play group (Wolfberg & Schuler, 1993): The child is encouraged by an adult to join a small group of peers, individually selected on the basis of their familiarity and the degree to which their interests, interaction styles, social skills, and personality characteristics complement those of the child with autism. The child entering the group is taught to negotiate play routines, to respond to the social cues of peers, and to initiate social activities. The adult takes an active role at first but gradually withdraws as the child's social skills improve. In other words, this is not a spontaneous coming together of children but the intentional creation of a supportive environment for socialization and play with peers. In such a setting, dramatic improvements have been seen in the make-believe play of children with autism, reinforcing the view that autism is not necessarily characterized by a deficit in representational skills.

The Special Child in the Classroom

While we cannot draw sweeping conclusions about the play of children with special needs, it seems clear that (a) all children play, regardless of their physical condition, level of intellectual functioning, emotional state, or environmental circumstance, and (b) children with disabilities play less effectively than those without them since they are less likely to explore the physical environment, to form mental representations of reality, or to initiate and sustain social play.

For some groups, such as children with intellectual impairments, the issue is primarily one of delay, and compared with groups of normal children of the same mental age instead of the same chronological age, the play differences disappear. For others, including children with physical disabilities and children who have been abused, the issue may be one of opportunity. The observed play differences are most easily explained by circumstances in the social environment that are not conducive to play but might be made so with appropriate intervention. In fact, the social environment can have a major influence on children's play. Consider the findings of Skellenger and Hill (1994), who demonstrated the value of teacher-child play experiences. Working with three children aged 5 to 7 years, a teacher modeled appropriate play activities, served as a play partner, and followed the children's lead in play. Over a period of 4 months, the sophistication of the children's play improved markedly.

Unfortunately, the social environment of children with disabilities may not be at all supportive of play. Some adults may believe that children with disabilities are unable to play and may therefore neglect to plan for and encourage their play. Adults may also allow children with disabilities to associate only with similar children in early childhood special education programs that put greater emphasis on academic skills and less on free play than is found in typical early childhood programs. Since social interaction occurs more often during play than during preschool academic activities (Odom, Peterson, McConnell, & Ostrosky, 1990), children with disabilities may simply have fewer opportunities to socialize with peers. This is despite the fact that numerous studies have found that when they are included in groups with typically developing children, the play of special children is richer, more varied, and more sophisticated than when they are placed in separate settings (Buysse, Goldman, & Skinner, 2002; Guralnick, 1999).

An obvious approach to increasing their opportunities for social play is to include children with special needs in programs that also contain children whose development is typical. The inclusion approach is increasingly common today, and even 20 years ago 3 out of every 4 preschool classrooms included at least one child with a disability (Diamond & Hestenes, 1994; Wolery et al., 1993). Physical integration does not guarantee social integration, however, as evidenced by what actually happens in mainstream preschool settings. Children with disabilities are not totally isolated, but neither are they completely accepted. Young children usually prefer a playmate whose development is normal to a playmate with a disability (Guralnick, Connor, Hammond, Gottman, & Kinnish, 1996). Positive social interaction is considerably more likely among children without disabilities than among children who have them (Roberts, Pratt, & Leach, 1991), and there may be very little spontaneous interaction between the two groups (Beh-Pajooh, 1991). On the whole, children with special needs develop fewer friendships and are rated lower in terms of popularity (File, 1994). In summary, inclusion doesn't guarantee that typical children will play with—or even interact with—children with disabilities (Odom et al., 2005), and this is probably a major reason why the evidence for the success of inclusion is somewhat inconsistent (Lindsay, 2007; Odom et al., 2004; Webster & Carter, 2007).

It seems likely that the lack of complete acceptance by peers is related to a lack of social skills rather than to a specific disability. What looks like inability to play is often an aspect of a larger communication difficulty. For example, young children with cognitive delays typically lack the social skills needed to gain entry into the peer group and have trouble sustaining social activities and resolving the inevitable conflicts that arise in social relationships (Guralnick, 1999; Guralnick, Hammond, Connor, & Neville, 2006; Guralnick, Neville, Hammond, & Connor, 2007). Children with disabilities have a tendency to be overly direct and even disruptive when making an effort to enter a play group (Lieber, 1993), and even among children with no disabilities such a pushy approach tends to lead to peer rejection. Finally, children with disabilities engage in a greater amount of solitary play and a lesser amount of cooperative play than expected (Beh-Pajooh, 1991; Hestenes, Carroll, Whitley, & Stephenson, 1997).

Despite the fact that physical integration does not guarantee total social integration, mainstreaming can have a strongly positive effect on the play of young children with disabilities and on their social competence (Esposito & Koorland, 1989; Pickett, Griffith, & Rogers-Adkinson, 1993). An essential component of the mainstreaming experience, however, is some degree of adult intervention. What type of intervention should it be? First of all, it should not be overly directive. Adults may assume that children with certain disabling conditions, particularly those that are intellectual in origin, need a greater amount of direction in order to play. This direction, however well intentioned, may become intrusive and may reduce the spontaneity of play and diminish its quality. Odom, Skellenger, and Ostrosky (1993) found, for example, that teacher-initiated activity occurs more often in special education classes than in early childhood education classes for able children, and play was three times as likely to be seen in the classes of typically developing children.

Children with disabilities need direction, but it should be of a different type. For example, if teachers engage in direct social skills training with these children, emphasizing such skills as sharing, asking to share, asking for help, and persisting with an activity, social interaction ability improves significantly (Odom et al., 1999). In one successful program the staff used peer modeling, puppets, role-playing, and generous amounts of reinforcement to teach children how to greet one another, ask for things appropriately, share, and initiate play. They also taught children that it is socially inappropriate to behave too aggressively, such as by grabbing toys away from other children who are playing with them (Matson, Fee, Coe, & Smith, 1991).

When children with disabilities are given specific training in the social skills necessary to initiate and sustain social play, there seems to be an increase in positive peer responsiveness to them, in the amount and sophistication of the peer interactions they engage in, and in the amount of social play that is observed (Hundert & Houghton, 1992). As a matter of fact, when teachers are trained to encourage peer interaction in preschool children, there is an increase in peer interaction among *all* children, whether they have a disability or not, although it isn't clear from the research that such educational experiences generalize from one social situation to another (Hundert & Houghton; Lifter, Sulzer-Azaroff, Anderson, & Cowdery, 1993).

Finally, it should be mentioned that structured approaches can do more than facilitate social play. The use of modeling and reinforcement by teachers can also encourage imaginative play, even in the case of children who are least likely to engage in acts of make-believe. In one study, children with autism who were taught to engage in dramatic play by the use of scripts and teacher prompts did, in fact, display more spontaneous theme-related social behavior (Goldstein & Cisar, 1992). In a variety of other successful approaches, teachers would select a typically developing classmate to work with a child with autism, and this classmate would ask the child to play, would suggest play activities, would offer to share toys, and would prompt, model, and verbally reinforce appropriate behaviors in the child with autism (Harrower & Dunlap, 2001; McConnell, 2002; Odom et al., 2003).

The necessity of staff intervention to facilitate the play of children with disabilities suggests that it is not enough to remove the physical or social barriers to play. Affirmative action is also needed. The special child may need special support and encouragement from adults in order to play to his or her maximum potential—similar, perhaps, to the support that all children need to play when they are very young.

CHILDREN UNDER STRESS

As pointed out many times in this book, children's play is most likely to occur in the absence of stress. In fact, the quality of play might be seen as an indicator of the degree of stress a child is experiencing. Securely attached children, for example, are more likely to engage in free play, and children play more freely when their surroundings are safe and familiar, as when they are with playmates they are acquainted with. Furthermore, it was pointed out in Chapter 4 that the stress of marital disruption appears to have a negative effect on the play of preschoolers.

Let us turn now to examination of play in two populations of children who differ from the norm in the amount of stress that is occurring in their lives. First, we shall look at the play of children who are victims of abuse—emotional, physical, sexual, or multiple abuse—at the hands of their caretakers. Second, we shall discuss the play of children who are ill and facing the stress of hospitalization and look at the ways in which play can make the hospital experience a more positive one for the child, the parents, and the hospital staff.

Victims of Child Abuse

The maltreatment of children, whether physical, sexual, emotional, or a combination of these, seems to have an impact on their play, although the impact differs depending on the age of the child. In a study of 1-year-old infants, the researchers found that those identified as maltreated displayed more imitation and less independent behavior in a free-play session with their mothers than did children who had not been maltreated. However, the overall intellectual maturity of the play did not differ between the two groups (Valentino, Cicchetti, Toth, & Rogosch, 2006). The researchers suggested that the lack of an impact on the cognitive sophistication reflects the fact that infant play is primarily biologically determined. It is primarily sensory and motor in nature, as discussed in Chapter 3. However, the excessive imitation and lack of independence could reveal another type of developmental delay—a delay in the normal process of differentiation between oneself and other people. This in turn could be a predictor of later difficulties in relating to peers.

In an older preschool child, play relies more heavily on cognitive factors and social skills, and one might expect the effects of maltreatment to be more pronounced. In fact, this is the case. For example, Allesandri (1991) compared the play of 15 children in a preschool program, aged 4 to 5 years, who had a history of being abused with that of 15 matched (on gender, socioeconomic status, parents' age, ethnic background, parents' education, number of siblings, etc.) controls. The maltreated children played in less mature ways, both socially and cognitively, than did the children who had not been maltreated. The maltreated children engaged in less play overall, involved themselves less often in group and parallel play, and used the play materials in less imaginative and more stereotyped ways. In addition, their fantasy themes were more imitative and less creative. They repeatedly played out domestic scenes, for example, whereas the control group also played the roles of fantasy characters, such as monsters or superheroes.

The relationship between maltreatment and a lack of social skills in preschool children has been found in other studies as well. For example, Darwish, Esquivel, Houtz, and Alfonso (2001) found maltreated children to have significantly poorer skills in initiating interactions with peers and maintaining self-control, although, in contrast with Allesandri's (1991) results, there were no differences in the cognitive aspects of play.

Even though young victims of various forms of maltreatment are often grouped together for research purposes, some researchers have attempted to compare the play of the different abused groups. For example, Fagot, Hagan, Youngblade, and Potter (1989) observed the free-play behavior of three groups of preschool children: sexually abused, physically abused, and not abused. Consistent with other studies was the finding that the nonabused children played more than the children in the other two groups and spent less time doing nothing. They also reacted more positively to other children, spoke more to them, and engaged in a greater amount of associative play.

The differences between the victims of sexual abuse (SA) and the victims of physical abuse (PA) were quite interesting. The SA children were more passive than the children in the control group, but they were not antisocial or negative. They didn't make trouble and usually played quietly by themselves. By contrast, the PA children, although generally passive, engaged in quite a bit more aggression than the norm. They were disruptive, uncommunicative, and antisocial, offering clues that might lead a teacher to suspect there were problems in their lives that needed closer examination. The SA children, however, did not call attention to themselves. Their play was certainly different from the norm, but this difference might not have been noticed by someone who knew little about normal play and failed to realize that play can offer fascinating glimpses into a child's psychological world (Fagot et al., 1989).

An interesting line of research involving child victims of sexual abuse has been to observe their play with anatomically correct dolls. Since 1977, dolls with realistic-looking genitals have been used in interviews with children suspected of being abused, under the assumption that a child in play will reveal what he or she cannot reveal in words (August & Forman, 1989; Cohn, 1991; Everson & Boat, 2002; Freidemann & Morgan, 1985; Leventhal, Hamilton, Rekedal, Tebano-Micci, & Eyster, 1989). It is important to note, however, that the research findings on the effectiveness of anatomically correct dolls in eliciting information from children are definitely mixed. In the first place, few studies have compared allegedly abused children to those who have not been abused. Most studies include only those children who have allegedly been abused, so there is little opportunity for comparison with the "norm." We should point out, however, that in those studies where comparisons have been made, it has been found that sexually abused children play in more sexualized ways with anatomically correct dolls (August & Forman; Faller, 2007; Jampole & Webber, 1987; White, Strom, Santilli, & Halpin, 1986). For example, August and Forman compared the play of 16 sexually abused girls, aged 5 to 8 years, with that of 16 nonabused girls, offering them anatomically correct dolls to play with while an adult interviewer left the room for 5 minutes. The girls who had been abused engaged in less overall free play, a finding consistent with the results of other studies of maltreated children, and were more likely to attend to the sexual features of the dolls. They would touch the dolls' breasts or genitals, for example, and giggle when they did so, and they would remove and examine the undergarments.

When preschool children are involved, the use of anatomically correct dolls seems to be particularly questionable. The use of dolls seems to be a less effective technique than simply asking young children to point to areas on their bodies that a suspected abuser may have touched. This is because children aged 4 years and younger often fail to understand that in an abuse interview the doll is intended to represent them (DeLoache, 1995; Hungerford, 2005) and because they provide a greater amount of inconsistent information with the dolls than without them (Bruck, Ceci, & Francoeur, 2000; Goodman, Quas, Batterman-Faunce, Riddlesberger, & Kuhn, 1997; Thierry, Lamb, Orbach, & Pipe, 2005). It is particularly troubling that when interviewers use suggestive questions pertaining to dolls (e.g., "Show me on the doll how he touched your butt," when touching did not occur) the responses from 3- and 4-year-olds are less accurate than the responses they give when asked suggestive questions not pertaining to dolls (Bruck et al.).

It is critical to point out that sexual play with dolls does not in itself constitute proof of sexual abuse. In fact, evidence of this type has frequently been challenged in courts of law. This is because, as already mentioned, few studies have been done on this subject. To complicate the matter, most sexually abused children never play in sexual ways with the dolls (Friedrich et al., 2001; Friedrich &

Trane, 2002: In one study abused and nonabused children were equally likely to play in sexual ways with dolls (Cohn, 1991), and sexual play with dolls is more likely to indicate a child's knowledge about sex, however it was obtained, rather than to constitute proof of sexual abuse (Faller, 2007).

There is an important lesson here about the need for caution in interpreting the play of children. Children's play reflects their psychological world and allows them to express themselves more freely than they do in words. Nevertheless, while an episode of play can offer clues to a child's emotional state and may lead trained professionals to ask further questions, play alone cannot provide the final answers, especially when the subject is as serious as child abuse.

The Stress of Hospitalization

The experience of hospitalization contains a number of specific stressors for a child, as well as many stressors for adults. Children are stressed by doctors' examinations and tests, limits placed on their physical activity, separation from their families, a general sense of loss of control, and, of course, physical pain (Bowden & Greenberg, 2008; Hendon & Bohon, 2008). Hospitalization is often so stressful an experience for young children that it can actually delay recovery since negative emotions increase stimulation of the sympathetic nervous system, increasing heart rate and blood pressure (Rozanski & Kubzansky, 2005). Hospitalization can result in emotional withdrawal, various regressive behaviors, prolonged crying, disrupted sleep patterns, and forms of destructiveness as children lash out in anger at the indignities being forced upon them (Bolig, 1984; Wilson, 1986).

The stress of hospitalization results from the fact that a stay in a hospital represents a radical departure from everything that is comfortable, safe, and familiar in a child's world. There is a temporary loss not only of family and friends but also of the many rituals that structure a child's life, ranging from eating and sleeping patterns to favorite television programs. And what is more normal in the everyday life of a child—and more alien to the routine of the hospital environment—than play? It is interesting that the feeling of being happy and the experience of laughing can actually promote physical recovery, and laughter and happiness are intimately connected to the experience of play (Gariepy & Howe, 2003).

To reduce the stresses of hospitalization for children, it is important to bring to the hospital ward as many as possible of the elements that are familiar in the child's outside world. These elements include familiar people, articles of clothing, stuffed animals, favorite toys (if it seems reasonable to do so), and opportunities for play with other children. Let us look now at some of the research on the ways in which play has been incorporated into the hospital routine and the subsequent benefits for the hospitalized child.

PUTTING THEORY INTO PRACTICE 7.2

Playing With a Medical Theme

Since no one can predict when hospitalization will be necessary, all young children should have the opportunity to play with miniature life toys or dramatic play props that pertain to medical treatment.

Medical experiences are often frightening to young children as well as to many adults. Fears about illness, pain, and separation can be lessened if a child has an opportunity to deal with these fears in play, and play in hospital settings is widely recognized as a right of children and their families. Medical play, however, should be encouraged before children undergo medical procedures, and such play is beneficial for all children, whether or not they have been hospitalized or expect to be in the near future. Medical play belongs in a preschool classroom.

When providing props for sociodramatic play, teachers should include materials that pertain to medical or hospitalization experiences. Included should be toy syringes, toy stethoscopes, hospital gowns, surgical masks and hats, bandages, and tongue depressors. Hand puppets are especially useful in helping children deal with anxieties about medical procedures, and doctor and nurse puppets make it easy for children to express their feelings about illness. In addition, there are many excellent books for children that deal with hospitalization, including the perennial favorite *Curious George Goes to the Hospital* by H. A. and Margret Rey.

Finally, the fear of medical procedures will be lessened if children are familiar with the setting in which these procedures are carried out. It is unfortunate that the first visit to a hospital or clinic is often the time at which a medical procedure occurs. An advance visit, during which no procedure is done, will relieve some of a child's anxiety. Many hospitals allow children to tour their pediatric facilities, and even if group visits cannot be arranged, parents should be encouraged to consider a hospital field trip for their own children.

Hospital Play Programs

Because play is a natural component of every child's life and because adults usually recognize this fact, play seems to occur wherever children are found. When children are hospitalized, there is play in the hospital. It was not until the 20th century, however, that formally organized programs of play were seen in U.S. hospitals. Some of the earliest programs were developed during the 1920s and 1930s, but the greatest period of expansion occurred during the 1960s and 1970s (Wilson, 1986).

Hospital play programs vary considerably in their emphases, methods, and particular goals (Bolig, 1984). The type of program that exists depends on many factors, the first of which is the *degree of institutional support* that the program receives. Do the hospital administrators view play as a necessary component of a child's life? Are they willing to staff a play program with regular employees, provide adequate space, and purchase the necessary play materials?

A second influence on the hospital play program is the *educational background of the staff*. Are the staff members familiar with basic principles of child development? More specifically, are they knowledgeable about the physical, intellectual, social, and emotional benefits of play? Do they know how to foster and support play, or is their training almost completely in the area of medical procedure?

Third, programs vary in emphasis depending on who is seen as the *primary intended beneficiary*. It may appear obvious that play programs are designed to benefit hospitalized children. However, an inquisitive parent might discover that play is often used less to promote the optimal development of the child than it is to make life easier for the staff. There is no reason, of course, why *both* patient and staff should not benefit from a play program, but programs that exist primarily for the convenience of staff are often based on a limited understanding of the needs of children and often treat play merely as a convenient way to distract a young patient while necessary hospital procedures are carried out.

The broad spectrum of play programs in U.S. hospitals has been conceptualized in terms of a continuum, with simple diversionary programs on one end and comprehensive "child life" programs on the other (Bolig, 1984). The basis of assignment to position within the range is the degree to which a program (a) recognizes the particular developmental needs of children and (b) strives to promote children's optimal psychological development through the use of play. We turn now to an examination of the types of programs that fit into the various categories.

Diversionary Programs

On one end of the continuum of hospital play programs are those that use play as a diversion, an activity that will keep children occupied, entertained, and relaxed during a hospital stay. Children are typically given toys or encouraged into product-oriented activities, such as drawing pictures, that are in no way related to the experience of hospitalization. In addition, children are often put into passive roles as they are entertained by music, films, clowns, or puppet shows that have distraction as their primary goal.

In **diversionary play programs**, there is rarely any recognition of developmental differences among children; all receive the same types of toys or attend the same types of performances. Furthermore, there is an implicit assumption that children are better off if they do not directly confront the stressful experience of hospitalization. The goal of the play program is to encourage them not to think about being in a hospital.

Diversionary programs can certainly distract children, make them laugh, and make them happy. Listening to music, for example, has been found to make children smile more often and even to recover from their illnesses more quickly (Hendon & Bohon, 2008). Nevertheless, as more is known about the benefits of therapeutic play, the diversionary hospital play program is becoming the rare exception. Such programs tend to be found in hospitals having no professionals trained to meet children's psychological needs, no consistent adult supervision of the play space, and limited access to a special area in which to play (Bolig, 1984).

Activity/Recreation Programs

A second type of program is based on the belief that active children are happy children. The emphasis of such **activity/recreation play programs** is on *doing* things, on work with arts-and-crafts projects so that the child can gain the sense of accomplishment that comes from being busy and productive. The purpose of the activity is not simply to distract the child but to enhance his or her sense of well-being.

Activities in such programs might include drawing, painting, woodworking, stringing beads, reading, playing cards, playing a musical instrument, or making paper sculptures. Often the activities that are planned are intended for adult patients as well as for children, and adults and children may even engage in them together (Bolig, 1984).

Play Therapy Programs

Some hospital play programs use play as a form of therapy for their young patients. The underlying assumption is that children are better adjusted if they can release their feelings freely. Only by confronting those feelings can children overcome the anxieties triggered by the various elements of a hospital stay. Since play therapy is a form of psychotherapy, it is conducted by a trained psychotherapist rather than by a member of the hospital staff (Bowden & Greenberg, 2008).

Children in **therapeutic play programs** are given materials designed to encourage the expression of feelings—for example, dolls, puppets, miniature hospital equipment, and creative art supplies. With these materials, children can confront and "work through" their fears and hostilities.

Consider as an example of this approach the case of 8-year-old Brian, who was confined to his bed for a lengthy hospital stay. Brian was grieving for his normal life. As one component of that grief, he was furious at his parents for putting him in the hospital and at the doctors and nurses for keeping him there.

He became rude and sarcastic each time his parents came to see him, and his father reacted by saying, "You have no reason to be mad at us. We couldn't help it." Brian's mother remarked that if her son was going to be unpleasant when she came to visit, perhaps she should visit less often!

The hospital play therapist realized that Brian's angry response to hospitalization was normal but felt that the boy would do better to release his anger in more constructive ways. She told Brian that exercise was an important element in his recovery and had a punching bag suspended from a wire above his bed. Brian was free to use it whenever he wanted to, and he did so with great enthusiasm—channeling his angry feelings into a form of expression that was safe and, in doing so, perhaps coming to understand the feelings a little better.

Child Development Programs

A number of hospital play programs in recent years have based their philosophical orientation on general principles and theories of child development. They tend to focus on the whole child—on his or her intellectual, social, physical, and emotional development—and they see the role of the adult supervisor of hospital play as both counselor and nondirective educator.

Typical **child development play programs** include curricula that are found in preschool or elementary school classrooms. Children may listen to stories, draw, paint, sculpture, assemble puzzles, build with blocks, and learn a variety of quantitative, scientific, and verbal skills. In that sense, life in the hospital comes to resemble life in the outside world, and because it appears relatively normal to the child, the hospitalization experience seems to be less threatening.

Child Life Programs

During the 1960s, there emerged a type of hospital play program that was referred to as child life (Bowden & Greenberg, 2008). Stimulated by the work of the Association for the Care of Children's Health, the focus of **child life play programs** is on *all* aspects of the hospitalized child's development, seen in both an individual and a social context. Most pediatric hospitals today have child life programs, and it is estimated that there are approximately 400 such programs throughout the United States, which is twice as many as there were in 1965 (American Academy of Pediatrics, 2006). The objective of such programs is to reduce children's anxiety, as well as that of their families, and help them maintain their self-esteem throughout the hospital experience. Working toward that goal is a health care team that includes a child life specialist, an experienced counselor who is trained in such a field as education, psychology, or child development.

The child life specialist helps prepare the child and the family for the hospital experience. He or she works with entire families rather than only with children. Siblings are often confused or frightened by the illness of a hospitalized child, and parents may feel stressed and helpless because they are removed from their typical roles (Bowden & Greenberg, 2008; Dudley & Carr, 2004). The child life specialist educates the family about the child's illness and about hospital procedures, helps family members communicate with one another during their stressful ordeal, and encourages parents to maintain their positions of influence over their children's lives. In a sense, the child life specialist is an advocate for the family with the hospital staff.

Play is not the only emphasis of a child life program. Nevertheless, play retains a central position within the child life model. Children—and their parents—are encouraged to play in order that they can continue to grow intellectually, socially, and emotionally while in the hospital and in order that they can communicate their feelings and, in doing so, come to understand them better. In that sense, the comprehensive child life program represents a blend of both the child development and the release-oriented models (Bolig, 1984).

Providing the Conditions Necessary for Play

The most effective hospital programs, by whatever names they are called, are those that most adequately provide the conditions necessary for play to occur. In order for play to occur in a hospital setting, the following three conditions must be present (Chance, 1979). First, there must be a *child-oriented atmosphere*. Second, there must be available a supply of *appropriate play materials*. Finally, an essential component is the guidance of a *supportive adult supervisor*.

A Child-Oriented Atmosphere

Unlike most other areas of the hospital, the children's ward should be a warm and inviting place, decorated with colorful mobiles, pictures, and wall paintings and containing a variety of toys and play materials. If possible, a separate playroom—a place to which children will want to come, one that they will see as a point halfway between the hospital and the home—should be made available. The playroom should be a sanctuary for children in that no medical procedures can be performed there, and it should be accessible to *all* children, even those who are not ambulatory. In the playroom, children should have the opportunity to demonstrate the kind of independent behaviors that may not be tolerated elsewhere in the hospital, to express all their feelings freely and openly, and to engage in social play with other young patients (Bolig, 1984).

Appropriate Play Materials

Play materials in the hospital should be familiar to the child so that the psychological distance between home and hospital is minimized. In addition, they should be characterized by a high degree of diversity in order to be suitable for children who vary in their developmental levels and their interests. Included might be art supplies, crafts, books, games, musical instruments, and electronic equipment, such as films, tape recorders, radios, record players, television sets, and video games. If such activities are possible, the hospitalized child might also benefit from the use of outdoor play equipment.

Hospital play materials should certainly include toys that are medically oriented: stethoscopes, syringes, bandages, blood pressure kits, nurse and doctor costumes, toy ambulances, and an assortment of dolls and puppets that can be assigned the various roles in a hospital drama. By rehearsing the medical procedures they expect to go through, children can come to understand them better and fear them less. In these rehearsals, children often reveal to adult observers some frightening misconceptions about hospital care.

In addition to educating children and helping them cope with their fears, dramatic play with a medical theme can give them a sense of control that is usually lacking during their hospital stay. The child can reverse roles in playing with dolls and become the powerful doctor instead of the helpless patient. This temporary illusion of power can help build self-confidence and make the hospital experience a less threatening one.

Finally, when children, medical staff, and parents are involved together in a dramatic play experience, a sense of community is formed—a sense that the child is not undergoing treatment alone. In fact, parents who participate in such play, as is desirable in the case of a preschool child, become more comfortable in the hospital setting and transmit to their children an increased sense of well-being about the hospital experience. The children tend to recover faster, as indicated by physiological measures like heart rate, temperature, and blood pressure, and the parents are enlisted as partners in the healing process rather than simply as supportive bystanders (Wilson, 1986).

A Warm, Accepting Supervisor

The hospital playroom should be directed by an adult who is warm, accepting, permissive, and consistent. In the absence of an adult supervisor, young children may simply not be able to play; even older children usually need caring adult support until they are ready to develop relationships with their hospitalized peers (Bolig, 1984).

Because separation from the family is largely responsible for a child's negative reaction to a hospital stay, it is important that the play supervisor be a consistent figure, not just one of many. Such consistency promotes the development of attachment between caretaker and child and thereby reduces the child's sense of separation from his or her parents. In fact, for this very reason, it is increasingly common to have young patients cared for by fewer nurses assigned to them on a case basis rather than by many nurses assigned on the basis of task (Bolig, 1984).

Summary

Relatively little is known about the play of children with impairments, primarily because of numerous methodological problems that characterize much of the research on the topic. In addition, it has not been easy to determine the origins of differences that have been observed between typical children and those with disabilities. Children with disabilities experience physical, mental, emotional, or a combination of difficulties, but they also grow up in environments that are different from those of typical children. For example, they may lack appropriate physical surroundings to play in, adult supervisors to help them plan and carry out their play routines, and suitable playmates. These elements may conspire to foster an impression that children with disabilities experience basic play deficits. In fact, this impression may be completely false since the observed play differences could be environmental in origin.

Children with visual impairments play less imaginatively than sighted children and engage less often in games of make-believe. Nevertheless, they do enjoy play, and their play can be enhanced if adults encourage them by helping them plan for play and providing them with sensory-rich play environments. Children with language and hearing impairments engage less often than typical children in symbolic play, but the differences are quantitative rather than qualitative; there is no evidence of a far-reaching symbolic deficit in those with hearing difficulties or whose language is delayed.

In terms of their play with objects, children with intellectual deficits seem to prefer structured materials, such as puzzles and jacks, while typical children of the same mental age prefer open-ended materials (e.g., art supplies) that allow them to be creative and imaginative. In addition, children with intellectual deficits are less likely than other children to combine objects appropriately in play. Symbolic, or make-believe, play has been observed consistently in all children; there is no evidence that intellectual impairment prevents children from engaging in imaginative acts of make-believe. It should be noted, however, that mental age is better than chronological age as a predictor of the onset of symbolic play; thus, symbolic play typically appears later in children who are intellectually impaired than in those whose intellectual development is not impaired.

Children with autism show evidence of a basic communication difficulty, a profound inability to understand and function within the normal social environment; the child with autism apparently fails to differentiate between the self and the external world. In toy and object play, children with autism are likely to engage in repetitive, stereotyped manipulation and less likely than typically developing children to use objects symbolically in make-believe. They are also less likely to engage in complex toy play or to use toys appropriately. Children with autism rarely engage in symbolic play, and the reasons for this pattern are not fully understood. Children who are undergoing severe stress in their lives, such as that caused by physical, emotional, or sexual abuse, or the temporary stress of hospitalization do not play as freely as they otherwise would. Children who have been abused play in less mature ways than do those who have not been abused. They play less often and with a more limited range to their imagination.

Play can be very beneficial for children undergoing temporary stress, such as that involved in the experience of hospitalization. In recognition of this fact, a broad range of hospital play programs has emerged, particularly within the past 40 years. Some merely attempt to distract the child so that hospital routines can be more efficiently carried out. Others are firmly rooted in child development principles and work to maintain the emotional, social, and intellectual well-being of hospitalized children and their families.

It seems clear that play is unlikely to occur in a hospital setting, however, unless certain conditions are present. There must be a child-oriented atmosphere, a supply of appropriate play materials, and the guidance of a supportive and continuing adult supervisor.

Key Terms

Activity/Recreation Play Programs	p. 204	Diversionary Play Programs	p. 204
		Theory of Mind	p. 193
Child Development Play Programs	p. 206	Therapeutic Play Programs	p. 205
Child Life Play Programs	p. 206		

Issues for Class Discussion

1. Choose a typical preschool play activity, such as building blocks, playing house, or singing "Farmer in the Dell," and try to envision the experience from the perspective of a child with a sensory impairment, an intellectual deficit, or an emotional problem.

2. If a person didn't have a theory of mind, how would he or she interpret the behaviors of other people in the social environment? Why is a theory of mind necessary for successful social interaction?

3. Why would anyone assume that a child with an intellectual impairment does not want or need to play? Is there anything in the behavior of such a child that might lead an adult to draw this conclusion?

4. If a person wanted to implement a play program in a hospital that never had one before, what kinds of resistance might he or she expect to face from the staff?

PART IV

The Benefits of Play

This section specifically addresses the benefits of play for all aspects of children's development. The chapter on intellectual development describes the ways in which some of the most commonly found play materials and activities can enhance children's intellectual functioning and the ways in which play is related to emergent literacy and problem solving. In the following chapter, we deal with the benefits of play for parent-child attachment and social integration with peers. Finally, we address the emotional benefits of play by discussing the uses of play in therapy. It is not anticipated that users of this book will seek careers as therapists, although some may. However, anyone who works with children is a therapist in the sense that he or she provides a climate that fosters emotional well-being.

Chapter 8

PLAY AND INTELLECTUAL DEVELOPMENT

In large red letters, the magazine advertisement described the computer game as not only fun for children but also helpful in teaching them the basic mathematical concepts most necessary for success in life. On another page of the same magazine was an ad boasting that infants who played with the manufacturer's brand of toys would develop "handling skills" and "tracking abilities" and would also come to master "eye focusing." The advertisement went on to say that "even though these are playthings for your baby, they're also the most advanced learning instruments to be called toys." A third advertisement suggested that children should be enrolled in a read-aloud book club because child development experts agree that an early love of reading builds a love of learning, which leads to "future success." Indeed, it is striking how often the word *success* appears in advertisements for children's toys. Is the reader to assume that children deprived of these particular toys will grow up deficient in quantitative skills, never develop proper eye-focusing or handling skills, or—even worse— be generally unsuccessful in life?

What exactly is known about the influence of play on children's intellectual development? There has been very little experimental research on the effects of specific types of play on later cognitive development. Most of the research is correlational, with the result that the direction of cause and effect is unclear. For example, it is known that infants who have a wide variety of play materials available score higher on some intellectual measures, but it has not been proven that the play materials actually caused any intellectual advancement. It may be the case that children who are brighter initially may seek out and receive from their parents a wider variety of toys.

Learning Objectives

After reading Chapter 8, a student should be able to:

✦ Identify the types of play materials that are most likely to facilitate the intellectual development of children throughout the preschool years.

✦ Recognize the advantages of block play in helping children understand the concepts of measurement, logical classification, equivalency, and balance and improve their spatial awareness.

✦ Understand the concept of conservation and its significance in children's intellectual development and explain how an understanding of conservation can be facilitated by play with materials such as clay and water.

✦ Recognize the intellectual benefits of creative movement activities.

✦ Understand the impact of play on both convergent and divergent problem solving.

✦ Identify the personality characteristics of creative children and recognize the connection between children's play and childhood creativity.

Despite the fact that easy answers may not be forthcoming, the question of the role of play in children's intellectual development is an important one, and it is to that question that this chapter is devoted. We begin with a discussion of some of the play materials that are usually available to preschool children in our society. It is not possible to discuss all play materials, of course; nor is it possible to discuss specific toys. The materials we cover might be thought of as broad categories. For example, blocks come in a huge variety of forms (floor blocks, table blocks, Legos, Lincoln Logs), but all are construction toys that stimulate the young child's imagination. Similarly, the properties and benefits of clay pertain to ceramic clay, play dough, backyard mud, snow, and a variety of other formless materials. We shall then discuss language play and end with a discussion of the relationship among play, creativity, and problem solving.

PLAY MATERIALS

Play materials are invariably connected to young children's intellectual development, as they are to all areas of children's development. According to Vygotsky (1978), the value of play materials is that they help children separate themselves from concrete reality and distinguish between actual objects and what they are intended to represent. Representational ability is, of course, a central characteristic of intellectual functioning in early childhood, and symbolic play is the most cognitively dependent of all forms of play.

Recognizing their significance, adults who work with young children use play materials that are appropriate for their particular goals. For example, a therapist might use materials, such as toy weapons or family dolls, that are the most effective in allowing children to express themselves. We shall discuss play as a form of therapy in Chapter 10. A teacher or a parent might choose materials that enhance intellectual development and are interesting to children as well as manageable in a classroom or home environment (Sutterby & Frost, 2006). Even within the realm of intellectual development, teachers might choose materials that meet the objectives of their particular programs. In programs that focus heavily on academic learning, teachers would probably use close-ended materials, such as books, crafts, construction toys, and puzzles, while in programs that are less adult directed and emphasize creativity and problem solving, they would probably use open-ended materials, such as blocks, clay, water, and props for dramatic play (Frost, Wortham, & Reifel, 2005; Sutterby & Frost).

Many psychologists and educators have addressed the issue of the relationship of specific toys to specific areas of intellectual development in preschool children. An interesting framework for this discussion was provided by Wolfgang and Stakenas (1985). They divided commonly found preschool children's toys into several categories and correlated their uses with performance on subsections of the McCarthy Scales of Children's Abilities, a well-known intelligence test for children. They found that toys with different functions contributed in different ways to children's overall cognitive growth.

Fluid construction toys are those with a fluid quality, such as paints and clay, which can be used to create an unspecified product. It was found that these contribute mostly to perceptual performance (drawing, block building, puzzle forming, right-left orientation). *Structured construction* toys (e.g., blocks, Legos, puzzles) are those that retain their structure as they are used to make something; these contribute mostly to children's verbal, perceptual, quantitative, and memory development. *Microsymbolic* toys are miniature life toys, such as cars and trucks, dolls, and toy buildings; these were found to enhance children's memory. Finally, *macrosymbolic* toys include child-size play equipment, such as props for dramatic play. These were found to influence memory, perceptual performance, and quantitative skills (Wolfgang & Stakenas, 1985).

Psychologists who study children's intellectual development report that numerous underlying cognitive skills are enhanced during play. Rather than attempting to explain these cognitive skills out of context by referring to relevant examples from children's play, we shall look at some of the play materials and activities commonly found in preschool classrooms and attempt to describe them in terms of specific intellectual benefits, with particular reference to the skills mentioned above.

Blocks

Blocks may be the most appealing of all toys for young children. They are safe, clean, sturdy, and familiar. What is more, blocks are astonishingly versatile in terms of their age appropriateness. From the 1.5-year-old who simply stacks small

---

PUTTING THEORY INTO PRACTICE 8.1

Allowing Children to Discover in Play

Allow children to discover the properties of objects and to learn on their own such skills as classification, measurement, balance, and conservation. If adults are too involved in directing the play, the intellectual benefits for children will be limited.

Play should be a process that allows children to discover answers to their own questions. Discovery is the most effective form of learning because children can take ownership of what they've learned. Consider the following short interactions between a young child and two adults, one of whom encourages discovery while the other does not:

Phil and Sarah are building with blocks, and Phil notices that Sarah's tower is taller than his. He asks a nearby adult how many more blocks he will need to make a tower as tall as Sarah's.

> *Adult 1: I think two more should do it. In fact, you'd better get three.*
> *Adult 2: I'm not sure. Why don't you go and bring back as many as you think you'll need?*

Phil returns and says the other children have used all the long blocks, so now he won't be able to make his building as tall as Sarah's.

> *Adult 1: The long blocks are gone, but you can use shorter blocks to make your building.*
> *Adult 2: Well, is there any other way you can think of to make your building as tall as Sarah's?*

Phil responds by asking how many of the smaller blocks he'll need to make his tower as tall as Sarah's.

> *Adult 1: Why don't you try six of the smaller blocks?*
> *Adult 2: Well, how many small blocks are the same as one long block?*

Phil finally gets his blocks, but as he starts adding the small blocks to his tower, he doesn't place them directly on top of one another, and it becomes clear that adding one more block will make his tower fall.

> *Adult 1: Phil, I wouldn't put any more on. It'll fall over.*
> *Adult 2: (Says nothing. The tower falls over.)*

cubes or drags floor blocks around the room to the 5-year-old who plans and executes sophisticated building projects with wooden blocks of various shapes to the 12-year-old who plays with Legos containing hundreds of tiny parts that can be made into elaborate and intricate designs, children of *all* ages enjoy block play. Perhaps adults continue to do so as well.

Not only are blocks appealing, but they also have the potential to teach a variety of quantitative and spatial concepts to the child. In the first place, blocks teach about measurement. In order to measure correctly, one must understand the concepts of *unit iteration* and *subdivision* (Piaget, 1962). Unit iteration is the ability to realize that a number of individual parts can be put together to make a whole, as when one realizes that 12 units of distance called inches can be put together to make a unit known as a foot. Subdivision is the ability to separate distances mentally into smaller segments; one can estimate, for example, the number of individual yards into which a playing field can be subdivided.

Children playing with blocks can acquire an understanding of measurement principles because they use blocks as arbitrary measures (Schwartz, 2005). They can regularly perform acts of unit iteration and subdivision without direct instruction on the part of an adult. For example, 5-year-old Katie wants to build a road that extends from one end of the block corner to the other, but how many blocks will she need to do the job? She examines the length of one rectangular block; observes the distance she wants to span, mentally subdividing it into block lengths; and then selects six blocks to build her road. As it turns out, Katie's estimate is low; six blocks take her only halfway across the space, so now she must determine how many more are needed to fill the remaining space. Katie's measurement error and her self-correcting behavior provide a valuable learning experience.

Related to measurement is the mathematical concept of **equivalency**, the recognition that space can be divided into different-size units and that a certain number of units of one size corresponds to a different number of units of another. For example, Brian is building a "raft," in the process using all the 24-inch rectangular blocks in the block corner. Todd wants to make an

Blocks are safe, clean, sturdy, and familiar, as well as astonishingly versatile in terms of their age appropriateness. Even a very young child can use blocks to practice grasping skills.

© Eyewire

identical raft but must rely on blocks of different shapes. How many 6-in. rectangles correspond to the long blocks that make up a side of Brian's raft? How many blocks arranged in a lengthwise fashion will correspond to one of Brian's blocks laid widthwise? This is a problem requiring an understanding of equivalency.

Children at play with blocks learn much about spatial concepts. A mature understanding of space is what Piaget and Inhelder (1956) called a **Euclidean spatial concept**; that is, space is thought of as an overall network, independent of the number or the arrangement of elements within it. The amount of space in a room, for example, remains the same regardless of the arrangement of furniture within it. A mature spatial concept allows people to imagine their own positions within the context of an overall spatial grid and to measure space on three dimensions.

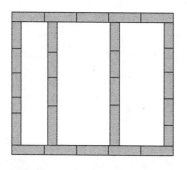

Figure 8.1   Grid Patterns Made With Floor Blocks

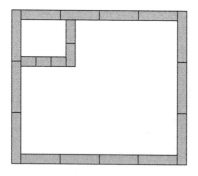

Figure 8.2   The Use of Blocks to Divide Enclosed Space Into Smaller Spaces

The ability to look at space from this broader perspective is not usually found in children until the age of 7 or 8 years, so preschoolers experience confusion on spatial tasks (Piaget & Inhelder, 1956). Block play, however, helps children come to understand space better because they are constantly building up and out in all directions. They also spontaneously form both horizontal and vertical grid patterns with floor blocks (see Figure 8.1), enclose space horizontally and vertically, divide enclosed spaces into smaller spaces (see Figure 8.2), and are able to stand back from—and above—their block creations and acquire experience in getting the lay of the land. They gain a better understanding of two- and three-dimensional space, the concepts of area and volume, because they create two- and three-dimensional structures (Kersh, Casey, & Young, 2008). In addition, playing with blocks has been found to develop the spatial skills of visualization and mental rotation, both of which are necessary for understanding mathematical concepts (Casey et al., 2008; Casey, Bobb, Sarama, & Clements, 2003). Spatial visualization is the ability to hold an impression of a shape in one's mind and find it in a more complex pattern or to combine two shapes in one's mind to create a design. Mental rotation is the ability to imagine how a two- or three-dimensional shape would look if rotated in space (Kersh et al.).

Even the experience of putting one's blocks away after playing with them can offer opportunities for intellectual growth. Blocks are typically organized according to size and shape in the block area, and many classrooms have templates indicating where the various blocks should be placed. When children return them to their proper places, they are learning to attend to the differences among them and learning to sort them according to their logically defining properties, a skill that is referred to as logical classification.

In order to classify objects, children must be able to perceive the logical similarity among them and then to sort them according to their common features. Preschool children often fail to use logic when they classify and instead rely only on perception. That is, they sort objects not in relation to one another but in relation to an overall pattern of which each object forms a part. Inhelder and Piaget (1964) referred to this immature type of sorting as graphic collections (see Chapter 5), which are pleasing or interesting arrangements of the figures (see Figure 8.3). Give a preschooler a group of different-size blocks in the shapes of squares, rectangles, and circles, and the child may line them up and say "I made a train" or arrange them in a circle to make a necklace. An older child would sort them according to size, shape, or both.

Experience with blocks can improve children's ability to sort and classify, and these are basic processes that underlie an understanding of science (Rogers & Russo, 2003; Sarawa & Clements, 2008). If adults demonstrate for preschoolers how objects are to be sorted and then give them the opportunity to practice what they have seen, their classification ability has been found to improve considerably. Even the everyday experience of putting blocks back in

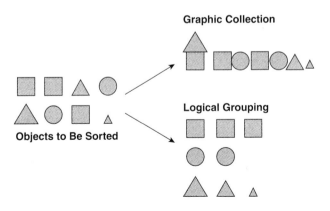

Figure 8.3   Graphic Collections: Pleasing Arrangements of Figures Produced by
Preschool Children When Asked to Group Objects

their proper locations after playing with them, an activity that encourages children to be responsible, can teach them how to classify objects in a logical way: The child must sort the blocks into groups based on shape (e.g., squares, rectangles, ramps, switches) before putting them back in their places on the shelf.

Block play experience is also related to the development of mathematical ability, and block play is recommended for teaching a variety of mathematical concepts to preschoolers (Kersh et al., 2008; Ness & Farenga, 2007; Saracho & Spodek, 2008; Williams, Cunningham, & Lubawy, 2005). We should point out, however, that in many studies the results are correlational and do not demonstrate a clear cause-and-effect relationship and in some studies the connection between block play and mathematical ability does not appear immediately. For example, in one study it was found that preschool children who are the most skilled at playing with Legos score higher on mathematics achievement tests in middle school and high school but not in elementary school (Wolfgang, Stannard, & Jones, 2003).

The mere availability of various play materials does not guarantee that they will be of intellectual benefit, since much depends on the ways materials are used and the attitudes of the adults in a child's surroundings. When engaged in block play, children seem to derive the most benefit when adults give them a lot of opportunity to explore, gently suggest problem-solving tasks, and provide a good deal of supportive verbal scaffolding (Gregory, Kim, & Whiren, 2003; Kersh et al., 2008). On the other hand, adults should not be too controlling. How likely is it that a child will learn to measure by playing with blocks if, when he or she tries to estimate the number of blocks needed to span a given space, a supposedly helpful adult quickly makes suggestions or—even worse—goes to fetch the blocks for the child? Will a child learn as efficiently about spatial concepts if his or her block play is excessively restricted in terms of numbers of blocks or available play space? And, finally, what opportunities for practicing logical classification skills will be lost if the children are not required to pick up after themselves?

Clay

Aaron is busily playing with a large lump of clay. He pounds it repeatedly against the table and then pulls off a large piece, breaks it into several smaller pieces, and rolls them into balls. He soon grows tired of rolling, so he flattens the balls into pancakes, which he distributes to each of the other three children seated at his table. Later he collects his pancakes and stretches them into hot dogs. Then he rolls them into balls again. Next he takes some of the balls, breaks them in half, and makes smaller balls of the broken pieces. Finally, when he begins to tire of the clay, he rolls the balls together in the following manner: First, he combines two small ones into a larger one; then he repeatedly adds another ball to the growing mass until he has a fairly large lump, which he proceeds to join to the original lump of clay that the teacher had given him.

In the process of playing with his clay, Aaron is learning a good deal about the concept of quantity, or amount. Such learning is important in the acquisition of what Piaget (1983) described as **conservation**, a skill that emerges as children move from a stage of intuitive, prelogical thinking that characterizes the preschool years to a stage of logical thinking that is typical of grade-school children.

A true understanding of quantity, which clay and other play materials and experiences can help a child acquire (Rubin, Fein, & Vandenberg, 1983), involves an awareness that, regardless of changes in physical appearance, the amount of a substance remains the same if no material is added or subtracted. A simple in-home experiment can illustrate developmental differences in the ability to conserve. Break a cookie in half and ask a child if there is still as much cookie as there was before. A preschool child may decide that now there is more than there was before because two pieces *look* like more than one piece. An older child will realize, of course, that no matter how the pieces of the cookie are arranged—in halves, in quarters, or even if the cookie is reduced to crumbs—the amount remains exactly the same. Unlike the younger child, the older child is said to conserve quantity, to recognize that the amount does not change simply because of a change in the physical appearance of the material. It is for this reason that Piaget (1983) referred to this ability as conservation.

Let us now return to Aaron's experience at the clay table to see how his understanding of quantity can be influenced by his play. Aaron is constantly changing the appearance of the clay, even though he realizes he is working with a predetermined amount provided by his teacher. He changes the shape of the clay and later reverses the process; he divides it into smaller and smaller parts and puts it together again. In the process of changing shapes and reversing the changes, dividing and then combining again, Aaron is learning something about the fundamental nature of matter: that appearance changes do not mean quantity changes. In that sense, he is learning that appearances can be deceiving, and such learning can help bring about the transition from what cognitive psychologists see as the perception-based thinking of early childhood to the logical thinking of older children and adults.

Water Play

Young children, whether at home or in a nursery school or group care setting, engage in a considerable amount of water play. For example, in most nursery schools, water play can be found indoors in the housekeeping area (sinks, doll

© Photodisc

Water play is a pleasing sensory experience for young children and offers a preschool child the opportunity to practice intellectual skills, such as measurement and an understanding of quantity.

baths) and outdoors when children play with mud or engage in gardening activities. Water is also an essential part of the cleanup routine (Wellhousen & Crowther, 2003). When children play at a water table—or, for that matter, in a bathtub or a sink—there is an opportunity for a considerable amount of learning to occur. For example, they can come to understand something about the principle of flotation as they analyze the properties of their play materials that float and compare them to those that do not. When bubbles are involved in the play, children often become sculptors, creating a variety of shapes, many of which will form a basis for sociodramatic play and all of which contribute to the ego building that Hartley, Frank, and Goldenson (1952) described as a benefit inherent in bubble play.

One of the major intellectual contributions of water play is that children can enhance their ability to use principles of measurement, much as they can when they play with clay. When children play with water, they typically have available a variety of containers of different sizes and shapes, as well as tubes, funnels, strainers, egg beaters, plungers, and droppers. A teacher might also want to add other interesting items to the water-play area on a regular basis to maintain the interest of the children in exploring water, and this might include plastic and PVC tubing, bucket-type pan balances, colanders, sieves, funnels, hand pumps, and sponges (Church, 2006).

A part of their enjoyment is the constant pouring of the water back and forth from container to container and through the assorted props they have been provided with. As they do so, they measure the liquid. How many small jars of water will be needed to fill up the large one? Will the water from one jar overflow if poured through a funnel into a jar that differs in size?

In addition to measurement, the child at the water table can acquire a greater appreciation of what Piaget (1983) spoke of as conservation of liquid, an understanding of quantity in a fluid medium. Children who are successful on tests of conservation of liquid realize that, regardless of the size, shape, or number of containers used, the amount of liquid remains the same so long as none is added or taken away. Nonconservers, on the other hand, seem to believe that the actual amount may change when the container changes. Many a parent has experienced the frustration of trying to convince preschool children that they are receiving equal amounts of juice when the juice is offered in differently shaped glasses, one short and wide, for example, and another tall and thin. Even if the nonconserving child actually watches as the juice is poured from its bottle and carefully measured out, he or she may still insist that one glass (usually the taller one) has more because it looks bigger.

When children are engaged in water play, they often pour water from one container to another and in doing so learn that sometimes containers actually do hold the same amount of liquid even though they are different in appearance. They come to realize that the height of a container is not the only dimension of relevance but that the width must be considered at the same time—a realization that is essential for the development of an understanding of quantity.

Children playing with water can also acquire **reversibility** in their thinking, a critical underlying element in logical reasoning. As an example of reversibility in water play, consider the actions of two 5-year-old children, Jack and Helen. The children establish the goal of emptying a large plastic container that is filled with water, and they begin by pouring some of the water into a plastic cup approximately one-fifth the size of the original container. Soon the cup is full, but a considerable amount of water still remains in the container. Jack and Helen pour some of it into a second cup. In a short while, another cup is needed, as is another; not until they have filled a fifth cup is the large container finally empty. Their goal accomplished, Jack and Helen now decide to fill the plastic container again, using the water in the five cups. One by one, the water is poured back until the large container is full again. The two children have learned that, if certain of their actions are reversed, the material they are working with can be returned to its original state.

Creative Movement

Many cognitive theorists, including Jean Piaget, Jerome Bruner, and Howard Gardner, have suggested that physical activity is an essential component of knowledge acquisition. It was Piaget's (1983) contention, for example, that the earliest forms of thinking and problem solving are of a sensory and a physical nature and that the child's earliest concepts are consistent action patterns, which he referred to as schemes. For example, infants might possess a sucking scheme, meaning that they would categorize, as it were, by their actions upon them certain objects as things to be sucked on and others as things not to put in one's mouth. Bruner (1974) spoke of the concept of enactive representation, by which he meant that information about the world can be encoded in physical movement instead of, or as well as, mentally. This concept is illustrated by the knowledge people have of riding a bicycle, typing, shifting the gears of an automobile, playing a piano, or tying a knot in a necktie. Gardner (1993, 1999) introduced the concept of multiple intelligences, which are 10 areas of intelligence that all people have in varying degrees. One of them is bodily-kinesthetic intelligence, by which we learn through physical experience.

Considering the importance of motor activity in the acquisition of knowledge, it seems clear that creative movement as a form of play can be an enriching intellectual experience. What is creative movement? It is the use of one's body in a completely open-ended way; there are no correct or incorrect ways of doing it. In a sense, creative movement is at the core of much of young children's play (Bradley & Szegda, 2006). When engaged in sociodramatic play, for example, children use their bodies as well as their words to act out their roles. Similarly, when children are pretending with their bodies to "be" clouds, willow trees, snakes, or rag dolls or pretending to act out a mood or a feeling, they are free to be inventive. There is no correct way to do it. Every willow tree may be different, and in the process of expressing themselves, children may learn about the properties of clouds, willow trees, snakes, and rag dolls.

Contrast what is called creative movement with other forms of movement in children. When a child is learning a physical skill, such as a sport or a specific dance step, this is not creativity. However, when the movement is mastered, creativity can come into play. Dance provides an interesting example of creative and noncreative movement because there are different philosophical approaches to children's dance instruction. When comparing the experience of children taught by an imitative approach with that of children taught by an open-ended approach (e.g., "Tell me a story with your dance"), it was found that children in the latter group saw dance as play and enjoyed the experience more than did the children in the imitative group (Lindqvist, 2001).

The learning potential of creative movement is such that many psychologists and educators suggest that almost any academic subject can be taught through the medium of movement (Bradley & Szegda, 2006; McMahon, Rose, & Parks, 2003; Werner & Burton, 1979). For example, McMahon and colleagues (2003) worked in Chicago elementary schools and compared the reading achievement scores of pupils taught reading in the traditional way to those of pupils involved in a drama-based reading instruction program. In the drama program, the pupils read stories. Later they were asked to act out the sensations and perceptions of characters in the stories in a creative way. For example, they might be asked to show with their bodies how a certain character felt after standing in the hot sun all day. Still later they were interviewed as if they were characters in the stories and asked questions that required them to make inferences about the characters. The result was that the children in the drama groups showed greater gains in reading ability than did the children taught in the traditional way.

An example provided by Werner and Burton (1979) illustrates how principles of physics can be taught through creative movement. The specific topic is friction, and the teacher wants to demonstrate that friction is necessary to start and stop the motion of an object. The children are organized into two teams, each of which must run through an obstacle course in the gym, one wearing tennis shoes and the other wearing only socks. The children in socks will slip and slide as they run the course, making the process slower for them, while friction will prevent the group wearing shoes from sliding. After the game, the teacher can discuss the results attributable to the characteristics of friction, which can be helpful when a person tries to start, stop, or change directions. This exercise indicates that children can learn about the properties of physical matter by using their bodies in a most enjoyable way. The information is encoded in physical movement as well as mentally and will in all likelihood be easier to remember as a result. More important, the activity is pleasurable. The teacher's goal may be to transmit academic subject matter, but for the children the lesson may seem like nothing other than physical play, which, in fact, it is.

PLAY AND THE DEVELOPMENT OF LITERACY

In several sections of this book, most notably in our discussions of developmental play patterns in Chapter 3 and play in children with linguistic deficits in Chapter 7, we point out that there is a strong relationship between language and make-believe play. Both language and symbolic play involve the ability to represent the world mentally. It is not surprising, therefore, that the developmental patterns of language and play are parallel and that language impairment is related to deficits in symbolic play.

It is also not surprising that play is related to literacy. Literacy, the ability to read and write, has been described as a written system of marks that fixes language so that it can be saved. Earlier views of literacy development viewed the acquisition of reading and writing as specific events that occurred when a child had reached an appropriate level of readiness. The more widely held view today is the concept of **emergent literacy**, meaning that children start to become literate long before they are actually able to read and write. From infancy onward, they have social experiences that lay the basis for later reading and writing, and those experiences are often acquired during play (DeZutter, 2007).

Even infants play with sounds and noises, as illustrated by their spontaneous babbling (Cook, 2000). Is babbling really play? Babbling can be thought of as sound play because it is an intrinsically motivated and freely chosen activity lacking external goals, and it appears, at least to an adult eye, to afford the child a good deal of pleasure. By the end of their first year of life, infants will produce a variety of playful sounds with their mouths—humming, smacking their lips, bubble blowing, and so forth. Indeed, play with the sounds of language not only occurs during the first two years of life but also can be found among older children. For example, children at about the age of 3 or 4 become fascinated with songs, chants, and rhymes and enjoy producing nonsensical rhyming patterns, and play of this type in older children is related to literacy development in that the ability to rhyme is correlated with early reading achievement (Athey, 1984).

The connection between literacy and play becomes particularly evident when we examine the make-believe play of preschool children. Both make-believe play and literacy require the ability to go beyond the immediate here and now—to spend time in a possible world rather than in the world as it really is (Roskos & Neuman, 2003; Roskos, Tabors, & Lenhart, 2004). In addition, both literacy and make-believe play involve decontextualized language, meaning that the words used often refer to objects not immediately present. For example, a child may tell her doll to "have some food," but there may not really be any food on the spoon. Both activities involve characters, roles, and plots. Finally, both involve the ability to move back and forth between multiple frames of reference. An example of this is seen in the child who one moment speaks like a mother to another child playing the role of baby and the following moment speaks to the teacher as herself about the game she's playing (DeZutter, 2007).

Make-believe play can lay the basis for literacy in another way. Such play familiarizes children with narrative, or storytelling. Preschool children may not yet be readers or writers, but they certainly create and derive meaning from stories. In the first place, when young children engage in sociodramatic play, which is group make-believe, they do not rely on a script. While not yet able to write the stories in advance, as an older child might do, preschool children make up the stories themselves, and each story is unique. Thus the experience of pretend play with other children may give preschoolers a "story schema," which is a basic understanding of how stories are structured (DeZutter, 2007).

In addition, children seem to derive more meaning from stories that are read to them if they have the opportunity to re-create the stories in dramatic play. Consider the following situation. Terry, Jill, and Mark listen to a story being read to them by their nursery school teacher. Then they are asked to assume the roles of the story characters and to enact the scenes they have just listened to. They do so, with gentle direction from their teacher. Afterward, the teacher asks a number of questions about the story to see how well the children understood it and how much of it they can remember.

Is the story more understandable to the children and easier to remember because of their experience in acting out the roles? In fact, there is experimental research to suggest that it is. Such research often takes the following form: One group of children listens to a story and then plays out the scenes, while another group either engages in discussion of the story or becomes involved in unrelated activities. Later, the children's memory for details of the story is tested. The finding that emerges consistently in studies of this type is that children who have acted out the story display the greatest understanding of and memory for the story's details (DeZutter, 2007; Pellegrini & Galda, 2000; Saracho & Spodek, 2002; Williamson & Silvern, 1991). The children in the play condition have also learned that stories can form the basis for their play and can provide them with interesting new ideas.

Not only do children remember stories better after acting them out, but the acting, which is dramatic play, enhances their linguistic and cognitive abilities in a variety of other ways as well. Their vocabulary is enriched because they use words from the stories that they would otherwise not use. Similarly, their grammatical constructions become more complex as they use new phrases while playing the roles of the characters. They improve in their ability to integrate information across the entire story and to make inferences about what the characters are thinking and feeling (McGee, 2003).

It becomes clear that make-believe play is not only an enjoyable exercise in imagination for young children but also central to the development of literacy. Of course, children do not have to play out a specific story in order to understand it completely. Many stories are understandable to children without the necessity of playing them out dramatically. However, when children regularly engage in the enactment of scenes from the stories they listen to, they seem to improve over time in their ability to draw meaning from spoken language (Williamson & Silvern, 1991). Presumably they will continue to show such improvement later on when they read stories rather than are read to.

Play, Creativity, and Problem Solving

Because children's play is spontaneous and freely chosen, it is often very imaginative. Indeed, it is sometimes described as creative. But what do we mean when we speak of creativity? As a general overview, creativity includes a number of characteristics, all of which can be observed in a typical preschool classroom. These are an ability to see things in new and different ways, an ability to learn from past experience and apply one's learning in new situations, an ability to think in nontraditional ways, the use of nontraditional approaches to problem solving, an ability to take information as a starting point and then to go beyond it, and finally the production of something that is unique and original (Duffy, 1998; Mindham, 2005).

When we examine these characteristics, we realize that creativity is not a simple concept but is complex in that it contains three related elements. First, it is a *personality characteristic,* an attitude toward oneself and the world that is characterized by mental flexibility, spontaneity, curiosity, and persistence.

PUTTING THEORY INTO PRACTICE 8.2

Encouraging Convergent and Divergent Thinking

Make sure that preschool children are given a supply of both fluid construction toys (e.g., paints, clay) and structured construction toys (e.g., Legos, puzzles).

In evaluating children's play materials, adults should be mindful of the type of thinking the materials are intended to encourage. Materials that encourage convergent thinking and problem solving are those that can be used to arrive at one correct solution. Materials that encourage divergent thinking are those that do not lead to one correct solution but instead offer a range of possibilities for their use. Children of 2 and 3 years are not yet at the stage of intentionally making anything, but many 4-year-olds and most 5-year-olds are fairly product oriented when they play. It is a false distinction to assume that children are process oriented and don't care about products while it is adults who force a product orientation on preschoolers. Product and process are both important. Single- and multiple-solution problems are both important. Therefore, for the older preschooler, an adult should keep in mind whether or not the material being used will lead the child to seek a correct solution or to recognize that there is no one correct solution.

Both convergent thinking and divergent thinking have value, and contrary to what is often believed, both are involved in the creative process. For that reason, children should have the opportunity to play with both convergent and divergent materials.

Creative children display evidence of persistence, high energy, self-confidence, independence of judgment, flexibility, openness to new experiences, tolerance of ambiguity, and a good sense of humor. In addition, they seem to be aware of and accepting of their own feelings and playfully curious about the world (Runco, 2003).

Creativity is also an *intellectual process*. It is a way of thinking and an approach to solving problems. Psychologists have always had trouble determining which intellectual skills are necessary for creativity, although most agree that these include a tendency to form unusual associations, to relax conscious thought to gain access to more primitive modes of cognition, to use analogies and metaphors in reasoning, to form rich visual images, and to ask original questions (Barron & Harrington, 1981). An aspect of the creative process that has been studied frequently in research on the play of preschool children is the ability to engage in what are called convergent and divergent problem solving. We shall explore these concepts in the following section of this chapter.

Finally, creativity results in a *creative product,* which is an original contribution to the appreciation, understanding, or improvement of the human condition (Weisberg, 1993). This is a lot to expect for a preschool child playing with paints or clay, so it may be more correct to say that children have the potential for turning out creative products than to say that they actually turn them out. In other words, the creativity of young children is likely to be reflected more in the processes of their thinking—and particularly in their approaches to problem solving—than in products they bring home from nursery school.

There has been a considerable amount of research, conducted mostly on preschool children, on the relationship between play and problem solving. More specifically, researchers have looked at the impact of either object play or fantasy play on children's ability to solve either single-solution or multiple-solution problems. The typical research design has been to (a) allow children to engage in free play with materials that they would later use to solve single-solution problems or (b) examine the relationship between make-believe play and children's ability to deal with multiple-solution problems.

Approaches to Problem Solving

The best approach to solving a problem depends to a large extent on the type of problem a person is dealing with. Some problems have only one correct solution, while others have many possible solutions. Single-solution problems

© Photodisc

Putting a puzzle together is a structured activity that can enhance a child's verbal, perceptual, quantitative, and memory skills. It demonstrates convergent thinking.

require the ability to engage in what is known as **convergent problem solving,** the ability to bring a variety of isolated pieces of information together to come up with the correct solution. It requires logic, speed, and accuracy, and it relies on prior information and previous problem-solving approaches (Cropley, 2006). Multiple-solution problems require the use of skills in **divergent problem solving.** Divergent problem solving involves the ability to be unconventional, to look at a problem in ways that others have not looked at it before, and to be able to come up with many possible solutions since there is no one correct solution. In essence, it is the ability to branch out from a starting point and consider a variety of possible solutions (Cropley). A person might be asked, for example, to list all the possible uses for a paper clip, in addition to holding pieces of paper together, of course. A child in a classroom might be asked to discuss the feelings George Washington may have had as he crossed the Delaware River, as opposed to simply providing the one correct answer to such a question as "Which major battle was he preparing to fight?"

Divergent problem solving has often been linked to the processes involved in creativity, whereas convergent problem solving has been related to performance on conventional intelligence and classroom tests, on which there are usually single correct answers (Guilford, 1967; Russ, 2003; Russ & Kaugars, 2001). The distinction is not quite so simple, however. It is likely that both convergent and divergent problem solving are applied together in many circumstances. For example, convergent problem solving may be involved in creativity in the sense that a solid knowledge base acquired by convergent problem solving may be necessary before a person can think divergently about an issue. It seems fair to say that both types of problem solving are involved to varying degrees in the creative process (Cropley, 2006; Runco, 2003).

Object Play

Young children need to develop both convergent and divergent problem-solving skills, so they should be exposed to materials that facilitate both types of thinking. Psychologists have discovered that there is a relationship between children's problem solving approaches and the characteristics of their play materials (Dansky & Silverman, 1975; Howard-Jones, Taylor, & Sutton, 2002; Pepler & Ross, 1981). Consider the findings of a classic study by Pepler and Ross, who gave 64 preschool children the opportunity to play repeatedly with convergent materials (e.g., puzzles with one correct solution) or divergent materials (e.g., blocks, which can be assembled in a variety of ways). Later, the children in the two groups were asked to solve a variety of problems. When their problem-solving approaches were examined, those who had engaged in divergent object play were more flexible and more original in their problem-solving approaches. They were quicker than those in the convergent group to abandon ineffective approaches to solving problems and to come up with new approaches. While convergent problem solving can be an appropriate and a highly effective approach, a danger is that reliance on prior ways of doing things can lead to a certain amount of rigidity (Cropley, 2006).

Similar results were found in a more recent study by Howard-Jones and colleagues (2002), who randomly divided 6- and 7-year-olds into two groups. One group was given play dough and offered no direction other than to "do whatever you want with it." An adult was present while the children played but interacted minimally with them. The second group was brought to a different room and asked to complete a handwriting exercise that involved copying text from the blackboard. After approximately a half-hour, both groups were brought together and asked to make collages using materials provided to them (colored tissue paper, glue and glue spreaders, scissors, and sheets of paper to make their collages on).

Ten judges familiar with the creative activities of young children—and unaware of the group each child had been assigned to—then evaluated the collages. The collages of the children who had been playing with the play dough were rated higher in terms of the number of pieces used, the range of colors used, and the overall creativity. When we realize that the two groups were initially no different in creativity, it becomes clear that experience can generate a creative mindset. In other words, creative activity can be nurtured or discouraged by the types of activities that are available to children in a classroom. It seems that an environment rich in play materials and with a variety of options regarding the use of those materials can facilitate divergent thinking in young children (Saracho, 2002).

Fantasy Play

Object play has clearly been related to divergent problem-solving ability in young children; so, too, has make-believe, or fantasy, play (Dansky, 1980;

Saracho, 2002). For example, Dansky observed 96 preschool children in a free-play situation and categorized them as high or low in their pretend play ability. (As pointed out in Chapter 4, there is considerable variation among children in fantasy predisposition.) He then assigned them to one of three categories—(a) free play, (b) imitative play, or (c) problem-solving experience—before testing all of them on a divergent problem-solving task. Dansky found that the children in the free-play situation performed best on the divergent problem-solving task but only if they were high in their level of spontaneous make-believe play. He concluded that it is not play in itself that predicts problem-solving skill but the extent to which children become involved in make-believe when they are playing.

The link between fantasy play and divergent thinking can be found in the concept of decentration, which involves the ability to attend simultaneously to many features of the environment and to transform objects and situations while at the same time understanding their original identities. In other words, decentration allows a child to imagine things as they are and as they were at one and the same time. In pretend play, a child will know that the object he is sitting in is really a cardboard box but will pretend it is a car. In a sense, it is both a box and a car at once, and perhaps it was a garbage truck 10 minutes earlier. Make-believe play, therefore, provides evidence of a considerable amount of intellectual flexibility in the child, and flexibility is a key ingredient in the creative process.

An alternative explanation of the play–divergent thinking connection was suggested by Russ (1999; Russ & Kaugars, 2001), who maintained that emotionally charged fantasy underlies both symbolic play and creative expression. Thoughts, ideas, or fantasies that contain affective themes such as exhilaration, excitement, aggression, or anxiety are illustrations of affect-laden fantasy, and such fantasy has been related empirically to creative problem solving (Isen, 1999; Russ & Grossman-McKee, 1990). Symbolic play is characterized by both fantasy and a high degree of affect, which is sometimes positive and sometimes negative, so one might expect to find a relationship between pretend play and creativity. In fact, such a relationship has been found repeatedly in the research literature (Russ & Kaugars, 2001; Russ, Robbins, & Christiano, 1999; Russ & Schafer, 2006). Finally, we should point out that the direction of influence between play and divergent problem solving is neither simple nor direct. Instead, the relationship is both complex and reciprocal. In other words, pretend play may improve divergent problem-solving skills, but the acquisition of problem-solving skills also enhances the quality of pretend play (Wyver & Spence, 1999).

Summary

There is little in the way of experimental research indicating that certain forms of play actually bring about advances in children's intellectual development. However, there is strong evidence in support of a relationship between the various types of play and intellectual growth.

A number of play materials and activities have been identified as highly likely to stimulate intellectual growth: blocks, clay, water, music, and creative movement. Blocks teach children about measurement, the mathematical concept of equivalency, balance, and logical classification, and they help children view space in a more mature way. Clay teaches children how to recognize that amount remains the same regardless of changes in the appearance of substances, a skill described as conservation. Play with water helps children learn about flotation, measurement, and the conservation of liquid. Creative movement stimulates children to encode information about the world physically, as well as intellectually, and to realize that there are many ways of knowing.

Play and language both depend on the use of mental representation, and it is not surprising that there is a developmental relationship between the two. It is also not surprising that play is related to the development of literacy, particularly in the make-believe play of preschool children. Both make-believe play and literacy require the ability to go beyond the immediate here and now—to spend time in a possible world rather than the world as it really is. In addition, both literacy and make-believe play involve decontextualized language, meaning that the words used often refer to objects not immediately present. Finally, both involve the ability to move back and forth between multiple frames of reference.

Playing out the themes of a story that has been read to them seems to make the story more understandable and to help the listeners remember it better. When children regularly engage in the enactment of scenes from the stories they listen to, they seem to improve over time in their ability to draw meaning from spoken language.

Many psychologists believe that the experience of play with appropriate materials helps children become better convergent problem solvers, effectively using information to arrive at a single correct solution. Play with open-ended materials is thought to stimulate children to become more creative in general. Finally, a clear connection has been established between fantasy predisposition and ability to solve divergent, or multiple-solution, problems, and it is thought that the basis for the connection is the cognitive concept of decentration.

Key Terms

Conservation	p. 221	Divergent Problem Solving	p. 230
Convergent Problem Solving	p. 230	Emergent Literacy	p. 226

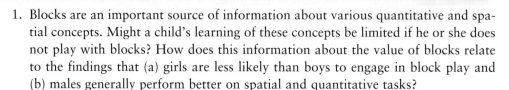

Issues for Class Discussion

1. Blocks are an important source of information about various quantitative and spatial concepts. Might a child's learning of these concepts be limited if he or she does not play with blocks? How does this information about the value of blocks relate to the findings that (a) girls are less likely than boys to engage in block play and (b) males generally perform better on spatial and quantitative tasks?

2. What are some everyday examples of learning that is encoded physically? Is it true that educators often ignore the possibility that children can learn through physical activity?

3. Some psychologists argue that children may come up with original products but aren't really creative in the sense that creativity requires an "original contribution to the appreciation, understanding, or improvement of the human condition." Do you agree that the products of young children are not really creative? What is there that's different about the creative products of adults?

4. Could we make the case that play is essential for creativity? Is there anything that might be considered "playful" in the works of well-known adult creative artists?

Chapter 9

THE SOCIAL BENEFITS OF PLAY

Paul is rolling around on the floor during free play, and Maura, his playmate, remarks that he looks like an alligator. "Yeah, I'm an alligator," says Paul, and he begins to crawl menacingly toward her. Maura shrieks, "Help! An alligator is after me!" and runs to the other side of the room, with Paul slithering after her on his belly. Both children quickly realize, however, that Paul cannot move very quickly in his alligator role, so Maura suggests that he become a bear. Paul agrees, gets up on all fours, growls once or twice, and begins to crawl rapidly after Maura.

Paul and Maura's game continues through many variations. First, Maura simply runs and hides, and Paul seeks her out and chases her from her hiding place. Then Maura begins to stand her ground and hit the bear with a pillow, making him run away from her. Later, the game is varied again as Paul begins to snatch the pillow from Maura's hands with his sharp teeth, so the outcome may be *either* the routing of the bear with a pillow or the removal of Maura's weapon, which forces Maura to flee in search of some other means of chasing Paul away.

Paul and Maura's game is an example of the social play that is so typical of the years of childhood. Indeed, we have been discussing social play, as well as the more solitary forms of play, throughout this book. In this chapter, however, we shall emphasize the specific ways in which play promotes the social development of the child, beginning with a brief discussion of the nature of social play and the underlying abilities it requires and then turning to an examination of its outcomes. We shall look at the ways in which social play facilitates parent-child attachment, social integration, group cooperation, role-taking ability, and altruism.

After reading Chapter 9, a student should be able to:

✦ Define and provide examples of the concept of social play.

✦ Understand the ways in which children at social play focus on underlying themes of social interaction and, in doing so, come to better understand such interaction.

✦ Define the concept of attachment and understand the role of social play in the facilitation of attachment between parent and child.

✦ Appreciate the value of play in promoting social integration and recognize the specific integrating functions of a variety of play materials.

✦ Understand why sociodramatic play is the most social of all forms of play and why it has the greatest impact on the development of social awareness in children.

✦ Identify the approaches taken in social skills intervention programs and be familiar with the records of success of each type of program.

WHAT IS SOCIAL PLAY?

Social play is characterized by engagement in nonliteral behaviors (an essential component of *all* forms of play) within the context of a social interaction; that is, the successive nonliteral behaviors of one child are contingent upon the nonliteral behaviors of a partner.

As an illustration of this definition, Paul and Maura both know that they are only pretending when they play; this is indicated by their willingness to change Paul's role from alligator to bear in order to make the game more exciting. Moreover, what each child does depends on what the other has done immediately before. If we were to analyze the children's behaviors sequentially, the following pattern of interaction would emerge: (a) Paul runs after Maura, (b) Maura runs and hides, (c) Paul finds Maura, (d) Maura runs to seek a new hiding place, and (e) Paul looks for Maura again. Soon the game is varied: (a) Paul finds Maura, but then (b) Maura hits Paul with a pillow, and (c) Paul runs away. In other words, there is an element of taking turns in Paul and Maura's play, with each child accommodating his or her behaviors to those just displayed by the partner.

Three abilities are essential for social play (Garvey, 1983). First, the child must have a firm grasp on reality because he or she must make a clear distinction between what is real and what is make-believe. Second, the child must be able to recognize the existence of and obey the rules for taking turns, even when these are not specifically laid out at the beginning of the game. Third, the players must share their imaginations when developing the themes of a play episode. One child may initially suggest a theme, but the script may vary as the play progresses, with all of the players eventually collaborating to determine the direction of the activity. We can see this component of the definition in Paul and Maura's game: It is impossible to determine which of the two children actually created the game as it appeared in its final form. In a very real sense the game took on a life of its own as it proceeded, with each child introducing variations at different points along the way.

BENEFITS OF SOCIAL PLAY

Social play has benefits both in a general sense and in many specific areas of socialization. In the most general sense, social play encourages children to focus on the rules that underlie the play episode and makes them aware that certain rules underlie *all* social interactions. The Soviet psychologist Lev Vygotsky (1896–1934) believed that for these reasons play was essential in the formation of the child's symbolic abilities.

In play, Vygotsky (1978) argued, all of a child's actions take on symbolic meaning, and play involves an emphasis on these meanings rather than on the specific actions that signify them. In Paul and Maura's game, for example, Maura knows that Paul does not really intend to hurt her if he catches her; nor does she intend to hurt him when she hits him with a pillow. The chasing, the hitting, and the biting are merely symbolic. Paul and Maura are acting out a ritual, the symbolic theme of which is the threat created by and the avoidance of a dangerous attacker. Their specific actions during the game—the location where Maura chooses to hide, her method of defending herself against the bear, the words the children speak to each other—are secondary in importance to the enactment of the symbolic danger theme.

The themes of social play are inherently social, with each player taking cues from the immediately preceding behaviors of a partner. This emphasis in social play on symbolic social themes not only encourages children to make up the rules to govern their own interactions but also stimulates them to focus on the meaning behind all human social interaction. To understand the ways in which children at social play focus on the underlying themes of social interaction and to come to understand such interaction better, consider the following example offered by Vygotsky (1933/1976). Two little sisters, ages 5 and 7, were asked to play a game in which they assumed the roles of sisters. When they did so, their behavior toward each other differed markedly from their usual interaction pattern. Now, in trying to act out the roles of sisters, they displayed ritualistic stereotyped behaviors illustrating what sisters were conventionally supposed to be. The learning component of this experience was described as follows:

> In the game of sisters playing at sisters, they are both concerned with displaying their sisterhood; the fact that the two sisters decided to play sisters makes them both acquire *rules of behavior.* (I must always be a sister in relation to the other sister in the whole play situation.) Only actions which fit these rules are acceptable to the play situation. (pp. 541–542)

An awareness of the rules of social interaction is necessary for acceptance in any social situation. Consider the ways in which adults, like children at play, sense these rules and display behaviors contingent upon those emitted by their partners. Engaging in successful conversation requires the ability to listen, to take turns at speaking, and to make comments that are appropriate in that they are related to those just made by the person one is speaking to. Adult interaction also contains much in the way of symbolic meaning. If the person to whom one is speaking occasionally checks the time on his or her watch or makes eye contact with someone other than his or her partner in conversation, this may indicate, to a sensitive listener at least, a lack of interest in continuing the interaction.

The Facilitation of Attachment Through Social Play

In Chapter 4 we discussed the differences in play between toddlers who are securely attached to their parents and those who are not. There is another sense, however, in which attachment and play are related. Play not only provides clues to the strength of the bond between parent and preschool child but also may facilitate the attachment process itself during the first year of life. Let us now take a closer look at the role of play in the establishment of the parent-child relationship.

To understand the ways in which play facilitates attachment, one must bear in mind that, as briefly discussed in Chapter 4, attachment is not an all-or-nothing phenomenon. Instead, there are degrees of closeness between parents and their young children. In addition, there are parental characteristics that facilitate secure attachment and those that do not; a willingness to play with one's child is just one of these characteristics.

Degrees of Attachment

In an attempt to identify a range of variation in the quality of parent-infant attachment, psychologist Mary Ainsworth (1991; Ainsworth, Blehar, Waters, & Wall, 1978) developed a test known as the **Strange Situation**. The infant and its parents would be brought into a playroom that contained a variety of interesting toys, as well as an adult stranger. Shortly thereafter, the parents would leave the room and return and would do so again later in the session; at these points of departure and return, the infant's reaction would be recorded.

Babies who were the most securely attached to their parents would notice their parents' departure and briefly seek physical and emotional contact with them when they returned but would soon resume their independent play activities. A second group of babies, identified as insecure-avoidant, would react with hostility and resistance when their parents returned to the room after leaving them briefly. Finally, a third group, referred to as insecure-ambivalent, would react with anger on their parents' return to the room but would also display a great need for contact with them.

Attachment and Parental Characteristics

Parents of closely attached infants have a high degree of self-esteem and a quiet confidence in their ability to be good parents. They are interested in their babies and make themselves available whenever possible, and they are sensitive to and quickly respond to signs of infant distress (Bakermans-Kranenburg, van Ijzendoorn, & Juffer, 2003; McElwain & Booth-LaForce, 2006). They handle their babies with love and affection and are skilled in feeding and taking care of them. They make frequent eye contact, smile at their babies a good deal, and are emotionally expressive with them. One of the most relevant parental characteristics in promoting secure attachment in a child is the extent to which parents can reflect on the fact that human behavior—their own and that of their child—is influenced by underlying mental states (Fonagy, Gergely, & Target, 2007; Fonagy & Target, 2005; Slade, Grienenberger, Bernbach, Levy, & Locker, 2005). Such parents can distinguish between behaviors and intentions, and as their children mature, they are likely to discuss that distinction with them. The result is that the children come to resemble their parents in their self-awareness and self-confidence.

Parents of insecurely attached children tend to be irritable and anxious people who lack self-confidence and do not seem to enjoy parenthood. Often abrupt and mechanical in their parenting behaviors, they project a quality of general unavailability and insensitivity to their children's needs (Bretherton & Waters, 1985; Main, 1981; Sroufe, Egeland, Carlson, & Collins, 2005a, 2005b).

Attachment and Parental Playfulness

There are noticeable differences in parental willingness to initiate social play with infants, and these differences are related to variations in the quality of attachment. Consider the findings of Blehar, Lieberman, and Ainsworth (1977), who visited 26 mother-infant pairs at home every 3 weeks during the first year of each child's life. After instructing the mothers to behave as they normally would if an observer were not present, the researchers proceeded to record a variety of maternal and infant behaviors. Later, at approximately the time of their first birthdays, all of the children were observed in Ainsworth's (1979) Strange Situation procedure to obtain measures of the degree of attachment to their mothers.

© Photodisc

Parents who enjoy playing with their babies are more fun to be around and easier to form attachments to.

The researchers discovered that maternal playfulness was correlated with the closeness of attachment at the end of the child's first year. Mothers who regularly played with their babies were the most likely to have securely attached 1-year-olds. Perhaps those parents who enjoy playing are simply more fun to be around, and as a result, their babies are more likely to form close attachments to them (Beckwith, 1986). Infants are certainly more responsive to playful parents than to nonplayful ones: They look and smile at them and gesture to them more often than do children of parents who rarely play. By contrast, infants whose mothers are depressed seem to display more anger and sadness and have less interest in face-to-face play (Tronick, Beeghly, Weinberg, & Olson, 1997; Weinberg, Olson, Beeghly, & Tronick, 2006). The degree of positive affect, on the part of both parent and child, appears to be related to the ease with which the social bond is formed.

A second strong predictor of quality of attachment is the contingent pacing of social interaction by the mother: the extent to which she allows her infant's behavioral cues to influence her own behavior (Blehar et al., 1977). This contingent pacing is an indicator of maternal sensitivity.

The connections between playfulness, contingent pacing, and attachment suggest that parents are easier to bond to if (a) they like to play and (b) they are sensitive enough to their children's needs to pace their play activities accordingly. Such a parent is quick to sense, for example, that a child is bored and needs additional stimulation or that a child is overly excited and needs to be calmed down. They know when to offer a new toy, as well as when to let their child continue playing with the one he or she already has. They know when to initiate a play routine and when to end it. And they know when their child does not want to play at all.

Parents of children who are anxious and insecure engage less often in social play because of either an inability or an unwillingness to do so (Blehar et al., 1977). In fact, a common finding is that these parents seem to lack an attitude of playfulness in their demeanor. When they are interacting with their babies, they appear to be serious, silent, and unsmiling, displaying an amazing lack of facial expression (Ainsworth, 1979). What is more, on the occasions when these parents do play, they seem to be insensitive to their infants' interests and social cues. Apparently unable to keep their babies at an optimal level of arousal, they instead under- or overstimulate them. For example, they initiate games in which the infant is a passive object rather than an active participant, and their idea of play may be simply to tickle or tease the child for long periods of time (Beckwith, 1986).

The link between play and attachment raises interesting questions about cultural differences in parental playfulness. You may recall that in Chapter 3 it was pointed out that siblings in many cultures (e.g., Mexico, Indonesia, East Africa) are more actively involved in the care of and play with younger brothers and sisters than are siblings in the United States. And in those same cultures, parents are less inclined than American parents to see themselves as playmates to their children. For example, compared with American mothers, Indonesian mothers are quieter, more reserved, and decidedly less playful (Farver & Wimbarti, 1995). Mothers in a variety of countries (e.g., India, Guatemala, Mexico, Korea) tend to view play as inappropriate for adults or as unimportant to their children's development (Farver & Howes, 1993; Gaskins, 1999; Goncu, Mistry, & Mosier, 2000).

Should we expect, on the basis of research on U.S. populations, that children in Indonesia, Mexico, or Guatemala would have attachment difficulties because their parents are not playful? As a matter of fact, children in those countries show evidence of no particular attachment difficulties, although they may distinguish between their primary attachment figure (a parent) and their playmates (siblings); when stressed, they tend to seek out a parent, but when in good spirits, they will look for a playmate (Bretherton & Waters, 1985). It is interesting, though, that in societies in which older siblings rather than parents assume the primary playmate role, sibling relationships are reported to be particularly close (Farver & Wimbarti, 1995). The distinction between playmate and attachment figure is not a clear one. For young children in the United States, the two roles are typically combined into one person—the parent. Perhaps they must be combined because, as pointed out in Chapter 3, American older siblings assume neither the role of caretaker nor that of primary playmate.

In summary, it seems that social play between infants and their parents may facilitate attachment in the sense that (a) playful parents display the greatest amount of positive affect (they are the most likeable and the most fun to be with), (b) their warmth and likeability seems to generate greater amounts of infant responsiveness and positive affect, and (c) the combination of parental likeability and infant responsiveness increases the probability of a close bond between parent and child (Beckwith, 1986).

Impact of Attachment on Children's Development

Playful, sensitive, and responsive parents seem to raise children who are securely attached, but how are these children different from those with insecure attachments? In a 30-year longitudinal study, a group of researchers at the University of Minnesota (Sroufe, 2005; Sroufe et al., 2005a, 2005b) found that attachment differences were obvious throughout childhood and adolescence. For example, teachers and camp counselors rated securely attached children as more self-confident, higher in self-esteem, and better able to regulate their emotions to suit their surroundings. For example, they could be excited and enthusiastic on the playground but able to sit still and attend when in the classroom or when engaged in structured activities. Securely attached children were more playful, more likely to respond positively to others, and more likely to enjoy themselves when they played. They were also judged to be more curious than insecurely attached children, more willing to explore, less anxious, and better able to handle stress. In both preschool and elementary school, they were likely to participate more actively in the peer group and less likely to be socially isolated. Perhaps this is related to the fact that compared with insecurely attached children they were less often seen whining or being fussy.

When observed at play in preschool settings, securely attached children showed greater signs of empathy and had closer friendships. In elementary school, they were more likely to have close reciprocated friendships and were more attuned to the rules and expectations of the peer group. In adolescence, those who had been securely attached children with histories of secure attachment were more successful when interacting with their mixed-gender peer group, displayed leadership qualities more often, and seemed to be more successful in all types of social encounters. They were more likely to be chosen as group leaders or spokespersons, and their peers were more likely to turn to them for their opinions when involved in group discussions.

Physical Play and Social Competence

Physical play between parent and child, which begins during the early months of infancy, peaks between the ages of 1 and 4 years, and then diminishes gradually, is thought to have important socializing functions (Carson, Burks, & Parke, 1993; Pellegrini, 2005). Specifically, a number of psychologists have found a relationship between the amount of physical play in the home and children's competence with peers: Children rated as popular by their teachers are the most likely to have parents—and particularly fathers—who engage in a good deal of physical play with them (Carson et al.; Parke et al., 2004; Salmon & Shackelford, 2008).

To understand the relationship between parent-child roughhouse activity and peer competence, consider what is required of a child in an episode of physical play. Since play of this sort is usually intensely stimulating, the child is highly aroused, and more important, the high arousal level must be sustained for the duration of the play. When the play is over, however, the child is admonished to "settle down." Thus the player learns to become intensely engaged with another person, to stay engaged, and to disengage when the activity comes to an end.

Popular children are more likely to engage in high levels of physical play with peers and to display a high degree of positive affect while doing so. They are also likely to be flexible in their play, meaning that they are willing to deviate from traditional roles and activities. Rejected children, on the other hand, seem to have difficulty with the intensity of a physical play interaction. Lacking the self-control required for an intensely stimulating activity, they often become overstimulated and "out of control." Since they are not as sensitive to social cues as popular children are, their rough-and-tumble play often degenerates into aggressive behavior. Sometimes they are unable to sustain a play activity for very long. Sometimes, fearing the intense stimulation of physical play, they simply avoid play entirely (Carson et al., 1993; Pellegrini, 2005; Sutterby & Frost, 2006).

Parent-child physical play may teach more than self-control. It may help the child learn to "decode" the emotional states of another person, to read the moods from the facial expressions displayed by the parent—happy, sad, angry, playful, and so forth. It may also help children learn to "encode" their own emotional states, to communicate their feelings with appropriate facial expressions. The ability to encode one's own emotional states and decode the emotional states of other people is useful in any type of social relationship, and in fact, such skills are related to popularity later in childhood; children who are the best liked by peers are the best at sending and receiving nonverbal communications (Carson et al., 1993).

It seems, therefore, that parents who play physically with young children may be doing considerably more than simply enjoying themselves. They may be teaching important skills that will benefit the child in later social interactions with peers.

Play Activities and Social Integration

It is clear that the playfulness of the home can predispose children to engage in successful social interactions with peers. Sometimes, however, the play itself, the materials used, or the activities engaged in can help timid or socially awkward children gain entrance into their peer groups. Let us now discuss how some of the materials and activities typically found in preschool classrooms can be particularly helpful in promoting social integration.

Blocks

Often considered to be among those types of play that contribute the most to the overall development of the preschool child, block play is an activity that greatly enhances children's social development. Playing with blocks encourages conversation, joint activity, and social interaction in preschool children (Brassard & Boehm, 2007).

We can see how block play facilitates social integration by looking at a child who is totally lacking in social skills or interests. Hartley, Frank, and Goldenson (1952) described the case of 3.5-year-old Lonnie, a child unwanted by his parents and abandoned to the care of a succession of housemaids. When Lonnie arrived at nursery school in the morning, he would typically begin smashing any object he could get his hands on, smearing the walls with paint or food, and attacking other children. His outdoor play was so aggressive and antisocial that he typically spent that time in the director's office instead. He rarely spoke but would shriek and scream when he could not have his way, and if told by a teacher that she liked him, he would answer, "No, you don't, damn you!"

Now let us observe Lonnie in the block corner, and we will see that, at least for those brief moments when he is under the spell of the blocks, this troubled little boy appears to be normal in his degree of socialization:

PUTTING THEORY INTO PRACTICE 9.1

Using Play to Encourage Social Integration

Never force young children to participate in activities in a group if participation is obviously painful for them. Instead, use play to draw them gradually into the group.

Identify and rate the play materials and activities available to the children you are working with in terms of their potential for social involvement. Make a chart, using Mildred Parten's (1932) classification of social play (discussed in Chapter 4) as a convenient framework. The key questions to keep in mind are:

- How many levels of social involvement will the material or activity support?
- Does the material or activity allow for the possibility of social integration?
- Does it inhibit social interaction?
- Does it force children to interact with one another?
- Does it actually facilitate a transition from solitary to parallel to associative to cooperative play?

You will observe that some activities require social interaction. Others tend to be solitary by definition. For example, dressing up and assuming a make-believe role usually works better as a group activity and may intimidate a socially withdrawn child. Painting at an easel or creating sculptures with clay usually works better as a solitary activity and may not afford a shy child the opportunity to interact with peers. If a child has difficulty interacting with peers, an inherently solitary activity may never allow opportunities for social development, while an activity that requires social interaction may frighten him or her into further withdrawal.

Can you identify activities that facilitate but do not force social involvement? Can you identify activities that children may derive great satisfaction from as forms of solitary play, as forms of parallel play, as opportunities for associative play, or as intense cooperative group interactions?

The teacher walks to the block shelf. "Anyone care to build?" she asks and places the blocks on the floor near the shelf. Lonnie relaxes, slides down from the windowsill to the stove, and from the stove to the floor using the broom for support. [The teacher] says in an encouraging tone, "Lonnie is going to build something for us." Lonnie removes his thumb from his mouth. Charlie [one of Lonnie's classmates] follows him, quickly gets down on his knees, and pulls the long blocks from the bottom shelf to the floor. Lonnie's expression changes to one of anticipation and a happy smile lights up his pale little face. He squats down on the floor next to Charlie, picks up a long block, and props it up on the floor, long end up. "Sit up, block," he says happily. He laughs loudly, and sings, "Happy Birthday to You" to the block. Charlie rests one side of the long block on the shelf and the other side on the floor, then adds others to build an incline. The block slips. Lonnie does not seem to mind. Charlie stands up, picks a small green car from the top of the shelf, stoops over and slides it down the incline. Both boys laugh loudly. "Do it again?" he asks Lonnie. Lonnie happily answers, "Yep." They send car after car down the ramp. Both boys are now laughing so loudly that they are bending over clasping their stomachs. (Hartley et al., 1952, pp. 139–140)

For an ordinary 3-year-old, the episode described above would be unremarkable. For Lonnie, who was usually unable to engage in any type of social play with peers, the degree of social integration displayed during the block episode was unusual indeed. But what is there about block play that can have a socializing influence even on a child who is ordinarily a social isolate? Hartley and colleagues (1952) suggested that blocks are an ideal first medium for children because (a) their appeal is universal, (b) they are sturdy and clean and are therefore seen as safe, and (c) they offer the possibility of a broad spectrum of social interaction.

Children at play with blocks can choose a level of social participation that is most appropriate for them. They can play in total isolation, since blocks require no cooperative efforts. They can play in parallel, as when two or more young children share the block corner, aware of each other's presence but engaged in separate activities. And blocks, of course, allow for extensive forms of cooperation, as when children share responsibility for building towers, roads, entire cities, or ramps and racetracks like those assembled by Charlie and Lonnie.

Furthermore, it is not unusual in childhood for an activity that begins in total solitude to evolve gradually into one that is inherently social, and this transition may occur even without the realization of the children involved. In that sense block play not only allows timid or socially immature children to acquire needed social skills by watching the play of more sophisticated peers but also can seduce them into increasingly higher levels of social integration. Remember that Lonnie approached the block corner by himself and only then was joined by Charlie. In addition, Lonnie's initial block play, propping up the long blocks and singing to them, was a solitary activity. Only later did the shared activity of rolling the cars down the ramps begin.

While it would be difficult to demonstrate that blocks actually cause an increase in prosocial behavior among young children, it has been found that children playing with blocks rarely engage in behavior that is truly antisocial: Rogers (1985) observed a group of kindergarten children in a block corner and reported that such behaviors as hitting, threatening, throwing blocks, and grabbing another child's blocks were rare. On the contrary, prosocial behaviors such as smiling, asking, helping, and taking turns appeared more often during block play than during other types of play. Rogers also noticed that the degree of social integration depended to a certain extent on the types of blocks used. Unit blocks—small blocks in a variety of shapes—were more often used in solitary and parallel activities; the use of large hollow blocks, ideal for building, was correlated with a greater intensity of social interaction.

Clay

Psychologist Ruth Hartley spoke of the "almost magical tongue-loosening quality of clay" (Hartley et al., 1952, p. 192). By this she meant that even the most inhibited of children will often socialize freely when they play with clay. When using clay, children are allowed to be entirely alone, yet they are given the right to group membership without the pressure to socialize that might occur in the housekeeping corner. Thus clay can serve as a protective shield behind which children can hide and study their peer group until they are ready to enter the group on their own terms. However, the opportunity for shared activity, the freedom to talk, and the ease with which clay can be handled combine to invite the child into group activity. And when they do engage in social interaction while playing with clay, children often reveal their innermost thoughts and feelings as they chatter constantly to those around them.

Block play can be a solitary activity, but for the children in this photograph, it is highly cooperative. They are each contributing to a common project. Children rarely engage in antisocial behavior when playing with blocks.

© Brand X Pictures

As an illustration of the socially facilitating effects of play with clay, consider the record of 4-year-old John, who began by playing alone and soon drew other children into shared social activities:

> John had a large gob of clay in front of him. He thought for a moment and then said, "I guess I'll make a sidewalk today." Thereupon he pulled off several segments from the mound and proceeded to thoroughly flatten them into a creditable appearing sidewalk.
>
> [Later] he used [a tongue depressor] to cut thin grooves with little depth into his sidewalk. While thus engaged, Vi [another child at the clay table] handed the teacher a flattened oval hunk of clay and said, "Here's

a birthday cake." In less than a second, John called out to the teacher, "Teach, here is my birthday cake." When the teacher came over, she asked what was the matter with his sidewalk. He answered, "My sidewalk is broken." Then he called over to Phil ([a third child at the clay table] who had brought a little cement mixer), "Cement mixer man, my sidewalk is broken." Phil came over and John watched him go through the motions of mixing the cement and repairing the sidewalk. Then he spoke up, "Teacher, look! I've got a fixed street. Cement mixer fixed it." Then he proceeded to cut another long thin groove and yelled out, "Cement mixer, my street is broken." Phil came over and went through his activity under the close scrutiny of John. As soon as Phil left, John hastened to cut some more grooves, and again called out, "My street is broken, cement mixer." (Hartley et al., 1952, p. 192)

In this brief record, under the tongue-loosening influence of the clay, John began with what was essentially a solitary activity, moved into parallel play as he accepted Vi's idea of making a birthday cake for the teacher, and ended in a cooperative shared activity with Phil, with both playing different but complementary roles. John and Phil's activities typified the essence of Garvey's (1983) definition of social play as discussed at the beginning of this chapter. Each child's pretend activities were directly related to the pretend activities displayed immediately before by the play partner.

Music

Music is an integral part of the young child's life. Even young children can recognize familiar tunes and sing them with a fair degree of accuracy, and by the time they are in kindergarten, approximately 90% of children say they enjoy taking part in musical activities. When asked about specific types of musical experience, children express the greatest preference for dancing and moving freely to music (42.7%), and this is followed by singing songs (29%) and playing musical instruments (16.5%). The least preferred activities are listening to music (4.5%) and creating new songs (4.5%) (Denac, 2008). The musical activity most often in preschool programs is singing, followed by movement to music and playing musical instruments (Nardo, Custodero, Persellin, & Fox, 2006).

It seems clear that young children want to be active participants, moving freely to the rhythms of music, singing, or playing instruments, and they are less interested in passive activities such as merely listening. They want the opportunity to express themselves as individuals through the medium of music, and the most successful educational experiences are those that will allow them to do so (Bowles, 1998; Denac, 2008; Temmerman, 2000). This is not to say, however, that passive exposure to music is of no value to preschool children. In fact, young children must learn to listen to music attentively and with a degree of understanding if their program is to meet the prekindergarten National Standards for Music Education; passive listening can also provide a foundation for continued music learning and enjoyment (Sims, 2005). What is more, even background music can enhance the quality of other aspects of children's play. For example, in one study it was found that when slow, soothing music was played in the background, children were likely to spend more time in the block area, entering and exiting less often, and were more likely to engage in cooperative play with a peer (Love & Burns, 2006).

Exposure to music undoubtedly benefits the young child in numerous ways, but Hartley and colleagues (1952) considered its major social benefit to be the integration into the peer group of children who for various reasons have experienced social rejection or neglect. Children who have difficulty interacting with their peers are sometimes aggressive and uncontrolled, with the result that other children avoid them, and sometimes so timid that they voluntarily withdraw from others. Music has special benefits for children in each of the two groups.

Listening to or playing music can soothe aggressive, extremely active children. Their anxieties often temporarily disappear as they are drawn under the spell of a relaxing tune. They may become absorbed by the challenges of mastering a musical instrument or learning the words to a song. At rhythms they may throw themselves freely and safely around the room as they listen to a lively musical selection.

Illustrating the soothing qualities music offers to an overactive child is the case of 3.5-year-old Bud, whose mother has placed him in his preschool group because she feels that she cannot handle him. Bud is indeed a difficult child who fights constantly with the other children and regularly destroys play materials in the classroom. Now observe this overly active, destructive little boy as he listens to music:

> The teacher has brought her accordion. Bud has not left the phonograph or made a sound during the entire half hour of listening. He is sitting on the table, swinging one leg as he watches the group almost going wild as they listen to various rhythms. . . . The teacher says, "I'll bet Bud would make a good horsie." Although he has apparently been dreaming, with a far-off gaze, he almost falls off the table in his eagerness, throwing himself on the floor on all fours, and progressing noisily and bumpily in a sort of strenuous hop. (Hartley et al., 1952, p. 307)

It should be pointed out that Bud's immediate response to the teacher's suggestion represents an extremely rare form of cooperation for the boy. His usual behavior is decidedly uncooperative. Observe Bud again at a later point in the same session:

Everyone . . . is tired, and someone suggests "Rock-a-Bye Baby." The teacher takes Jack's hands [Jack is another child in the preschool group] and swings his arms back and forth to the song. Watching them, Bud looks about eagerly for a partner. He goes to one boy and says "You want to rock?" and without waiting for an answer, he grabs him and says forcefully, "Rock, play rockabye." He seems clumsy and has a rhythm all his own, not related to the music, but enjoys himself in this quieting manner. (Hartley et al., 1952, p. 307)

The other children who gain the most social benefit from the musical experience are those who are timid and withdrawn. Music can make these children feel more vigorous, more capable, and more powerful. It can make them feel as if they truly are a part of the group. At the age of 5, for example, Molly is timid, overly controlled, and adult oriented; her play is mostly of the solitary variety. In the following exercise, Molly is integrated into the group because the various children are assigned musical roles to play:

Molly kneels on the floor and holds her ankles. The children are singing, and when they begin to sing loudly, she continues singing in the same tone. The teacher gets the toy instruments. Molly: "I'll play the bells." She puts the bells on her wrists and shakes them, smiling at Patsy. The teacher plays "Jingle Bells" on the piano as the children begin to sing. The teacher says, "Now, bells. . . . Good, Molly!" Molly swings her hands in and out, "Like this?" She shakes her wrists up and down vigorously. The teacher plays the piano once more and tells the children only to sing this time. Molly sings along. Teacher: "Now, jingle bells, play with me." Molly swings her arms out and in with lips slightly parted. She now slaps her hands on her knees to make the bells ring, then claps her hands, and shakes her wrists once more. (Hartley et al., 1952, pp. 315–316)

Creative Movement

As pointed out in the previous section, play with music often involves movement as well, although it need not do so. Much of a child's play, whether musical or not, involves movement of one sort or another. In fact, it will be remembered that during infancy, before the ability to represent the world symbolically has developed, physical, or sensorimotor, play predominates, and play of a physical nature (e.g., rough-and-tumble play) continues to constitute a large part of an older child's play activities. Creative movement, also referred to as creative dance, involves the use of the body to express symbolically one's ideas, feelings, and sense impressions. There is no correct way to do this, and each child uses his or her own spontaneous, original, and individual approach (Joyce, 1994). In the process of doing so, children learn more about themselves, improve their self-confidence, discover the value of physical movement as a way to communicate and to interpret the communications of other people, and experience gains in their overall social competence (Caf, Kroflic, & Tancig, 1997; Lobo & Winsler, 2006; Von Rosseberg-Gempton, Dickinson, & Poole, 1998).

Most of the evidence that experience with creative movement/dance can enhance social competence is in the form of testimonials from instructors. However, one recent study (Lobo & Winsler, 2006) used an experimental design and provided empirical evidence that a creative movement program has benefits in terms of social competence. Children in a Head Start program were randomly assigned to one of two groups. One group was taken from the classroom to participate twice a week for 8 weeks in a movement/dance program, where the children were allowed to improvise as much as possible. For example, in one segment of the program the instructor read a story or a poem to the children, who were then asked to act out the story in an improvised dance. The other group of children simply went to a different room and played with a variety of toys. It was found that those who participated in the movement/dance program showed significant improvement in social skills and a significant decrease in problem behavior, as reported by their teachers who didn't know which group the children had been assigned to. The group that simply played in another room showed no such improvements.

The consistent finding of improvement in children's social competence after involvement in dance or movement programs does not explain exactly why these improvements occur. Perhaps there are a variety of reasons. Perhaps the increase in self-confidence that is often reported for children in creative movement programs makes it easier for them to relate to others. Perhaps the experience of creative physical expression brings children out of their shell and eliminates some of their social awkwardness. Perhaps they are discovering new ways to communicate. They are learning to speak and to listen with their bodies instead of just with words, and more effective communicators are more socially competent. Consider the following example of a physical communication exercise, which begins when the teacher speaks:

I'm going to say a feeling or mood word and I want you to show me a body shape or action that expresses this word. My first word is "surprise." First show me a surprised face. Then add your arms and whole body. Show me surprise with whatever word I say. With a jump. With a stretch. With a twist. With fast moves. With slow, sustained moves. Make up a sequence of movements that show your surprise.

Next show me how you laugh. With your head. With your whole body. Can you change your level while you laugh? Can you move about while you laugh? Can you laugh a little? Change, show me a big side-splitting belly laugh. Exaggerate your laugh with really big movements to show me how funny it is. (Werner & Burton, 1979, p. 52)

Another exercise developed by the same authors (Werner & Burton, 1979) is more advanced, requiring children to use their entire bodies to express a theme or concept. For example, a child might be asked to act out nonverbally the role of a person trapped in a stalled elevator and beginning to panic, a creature from another planet arriving on Earth, or a person hanging out clothes to dry on a windy day. Such exercises represent quite a challenge, but the social benefits are considerable. Activities of this sort teach that communication can be nonverbal as well as verbal and, if other children in the group are asked to guess the meaning of the pantomime, can become part of an enjoyable game that sensitizes youngsters to the unspoken messages of the body.

Sociodramatic Play

In Chapter 4 we pointed out that sociodramatic play, in which children assume various roles while engaged in various action sequences, is the most social form of play and that it has the greatest impact on the development of social awareness in children (Hartley et al., 1952). In a case of the "rich getting richer," securely attached preschool children engage in the most competent and most imaginative forms of play because they are able to control their feelings, take turns, communicate effectively, and generate creative ideas. In turn, their involvement in sociodramatic play enhances their ability to cooperate with a group, participate in social activities, and understand human relationships. In that sense, the sophistication of children's play shows where they have come from and where they are going (Creasey & Jarvis, 2007). Perhaps it should not be surprising that children who engage in sociodramatic play with elaborate and complex themes are better liked than children who do not engage in such activities (Creasey & Jarvis, 2003; Creasey, Jarvis, & Berk, 1998).

There are two basic explanations for the social benefits of sociodramatic play. The first is that such play requires group cooperation. It is by definition a group activity and a cooperative one. A child can certainly engage in acts of make-believe that are not group oriented, but sociodramatic play is organized make-believe in a social setting, with a set of rules to ensure cooperation on the part of the players.

Not only do children behave cooperatively while actually engaged in sociodramatic play, but it appears that they may generalize this cooperative attitude to other areas of social interaction as well. This generalized cooperation was illustrated by the findings of Rosen (1974), who worked with kindergartners described as deficient in dramatic play skills. She provided them with toys—such as medical kits and firefighter's and police officer's hats—that were designed to stimulate role-playing. She actually joined the children in play, asking leading questions and offering suggestions whenever appropriate. For example, if she saw a child playing aimlessly with a truck, she would model truck driver behavior and encourage the child to join her in the activity.

Rosen (1974) found that children trained in sociodramatic play showed improvements in what she called group productivity. This was defined by the ability to work with other children as a team to create specific objects out of interlocking blocks, a task that required planning, cooperation, and the ability to avoid disagreements and acts of aggression. In addition, members of the training group improved in their ability to assume the perspectives of other children and to predict the wants and preferences of others when those wants and preferences differed from their own.

The second socialization benefit of dramatic play is that it allows children to experiment with a variety of roles; to try on those roles, as it were, and determine their appropriateness; and to develop a better understanding of the roles of other people. If children are to become successful in social interactions, they must get beyond their self-centered perspectives and try to see the world through the eyes of other people. This ability to assume the roles, or viewpoints, of others is necessary for the establishment of close interpersonal communication, and practice at taking the perspective of other people seems to enhance a child's overall social understanding (Lillard, 2002).

In the section dealing with children with autism in Chapter 7, we discussed the concept of a theory of mind, which allows a child to understand that there may be a difference between a person's feelings, thoughts, and beliefs about reality and actual reality itself. This ability, typically acquired between 3 and 5 years of age, allows the toddler to go from literally observing human behavior to understanding that there is motivation behind it (Slaughter & Repacholi, 2003). We pointed out that a theory of mind is an important component of overall social understanding that is essential for making sense of and predicting other people's behavior (Colle, Baron-Cohen, & Hill, 2007).

In sociodramatic play, children take on roles and observe other children doing the same thing. They know that there is a difference between their own thoughts and feelings and the thoughts and feelings of the characters they are playing, and they know that the same distinction applies as well to the children they are playing with. It is not surprising, therefore, that the experience of socio-dramatic play is related to the development of a theory of mind. Group fantasy play helps children appreciate that there can be a difference between feelings and behaviors, and this appreciation significantly enhances their ability to inter-act socially with others (Ellis & Bjorklund, 2004; Kavanaugh, 2006; Taylor & Carlson, 1997; Wellman, 2002; Youngblade & Dunn, 1995).

Why are some children better role takers than others? Level of development is obviously an important variable. There is no point during childhood at which an appreciation of the viewpoints of others suddenly emerges. Instead, there is a gradual progression through a series of increasingly sophisticated stages of role-taking ability (Selman, 1980).

Another variable responsible for individual differences in role-taking ability is the approach parents take in childrearing. When they discipline, parents of skillful role takers are likely to stress the impact of the child's undesirable behaviors on other people (Ruffman, Perner, & Parkin, 1999): "It makes me happy to see you sharing your toys" or "Scott is very sad because you don't seem to want to play with him" rather than "Nice children always share their toys with their friends" or "You'll play with Scott because I told you to do so."

Might the experience of play with peers in itself help children become more sensitive role takers? Psychologists Susan Burns and Charles Brainerd (1979) attempted to answer this question. As a measure of affective perspective taking, they showed preschool children three pairs of pictures and read them a short story about each pair. Each set of pictures told a story about two children, one of whom clearly represented the child being tested; the events in the stories were such that they produced completely opposite emotional reactions in the two story characters.

Each preschooler was then asked how the two characters, the one represent-ing the child being tested and the one representing another child, were feeling. It was expected that a child skilled at role taking would realize that the story characters had opposite feelings (e.g., one was happy, and one was sad), while a less capable role taker would respond egocentrically that both characters shared the feelings of the character representing him or her.

Burns and Brainerd (1979) then exposed some of the children to a construc-tive group play condition, others to a sociodramatic play condition, and the control group to no experimental treatment at all. In the constructive condition, cooperative play was encouraged; the children were told to work together to make something (e.g., a house, a wagon) out of materials provided and to discuss their work plans as a group. In the dramatic play condition, the researcher suggested a play theme, and the children were asked to discuss how the theme would be enacted and which of them would play each of the various roles. Then they played out their make-believe scenes at length.

At the end of the treatment phase, the affective perspective-taking test was again administered to see if any changes in role-taking ability resulted from the play experiences. Burns and Brainerd (1979) found that children in both play groups, which emphasized group cooperation in constructive play and required the enactment of dramatic scenes, improved in their role-taking abilities; the children in the control group did not.

The findings of the Burns and Brainerd (1979) study, as well as those of other studies of this type, suggest that role-taking skills can be improved not only by direct adult intervention but also by gently supervised forms of social play. Most of the research points to the necessity of an adult social director to stimulate children to play in a way that enriches perspective-taking ability, although some psychologists suggest that role-taking ability may be enhanced by social play that is totally spontaneous and not at all influenced by adults. In any case, it seems clear that play can serve as a vehicle by which young children can learn that other people see the world from perspectives different from their own. Considering the importance of perspective taking as a basis for successful social interaction, it is obvious again that play plays a central role in the social development of the child.

Play and Peer Group Acceptance

Even by the age of 3 years, some children are already well liked by their peers, while others are not. Well-liked preschoolers engage in a lot of cooperative play, and they are successful in social conversation, making relevant and appropriate comments to other children and offering constructive suggestions. Disliked children often make inappropriate statements in conversation (i.e., remarks not related to the immediately preceding statement made by another child) and negative comments about what others are doing without offering constructive alternatives (Hazen & Black, 1989).

Play and acceptance by the childhood peer group are intimately connected for two reasons. First, as discussed in Chapter 4, their play is increasingly social rather than solitary as children progress through the preschool years. Second, most of the peer interactions of young children occur within the context of play. As a result, there is the danger of creating an unfortunate cycle. The child who is liked by peers will have a good deal of opportunity to engage in social play

---

PUTTING THEORY INTO PRACTICE 9.2

Using Play to Evaluate Social Skills

When young children play, they reveal much about their social skills. The types of play they engage in (e.g., solitary or cooperative), as well as the quality of their social interactions when they play, can help adults identify children who have social difficulties.

Adults who work with children should become thoroughly familiar with the characteristics that result in rejection by peers, such as:

- Making irrelevant statements in conversation. These are statements that do not relate to the comments that directly precede them.

- Frequently being critical or negative in their remarks about the play of other children.

- Never offering constructive or helpful suggestions to other players.

- Being overly aggressive in play.

- Lacking basic social skills, such as saying nice things to other children, praising others, and calling them by their names.

- Taking things from others without asking.

- Failing to display signs of initiative or leadership in play.

- Being unable to engage in sustained cooperative play.

- Having difficulty sharing.

- Barging into an existing play group and trying to change the activity the other children are engaged in.

and in doing so will enhance his or her social skills, which are already well developed. On the other hand, the child who is not accepted by peers will experience serious disruptions in play, will fail to develop the skills to play successfully, and will undoubtedly face continued rejection.

As an illustration of the connection between play and peer group acceptance, consider what happens when a child joins a group of other children who are already at play. Let us say that Jack is a popular child, while his classmate Jake has difficulty being accepted by his peers. Popular Jack sizes up the situation and determines how he can best fit into the ongoing activity. In other words, he tries to share the framework of the other children, just as he is likely to share

---

Play as a Measure of Social Success

Much of the research linking play and social interaction skill is correlational in nature. That is, psychologists have discovered connections between children's play and their degree of acceptance within the peer group, but it is difficult to determine the direction of cause and effect. Does social play actually cause children to be more successful in their social interactions, or do successful socializers simply play differently than their less popular peers?

Despite the difficulty in making causal connections, the findings from research of this type are quite instructive in the sense that children's play may offer clues to their degree of social acceptance. It has been found, for example, that children in the age range of 4 to 6 years who engage in a large amount of solitary play in which they simply manipulate objects are also rated by teachers as socially incompetent and are disliked by peers (Rubin & Clark, 1983). By way of contrast, children of the same age who engage in a good deal of group activity that involves games with rules, the most socially advanced form of play, tend to be rated as the most popular, the most socially mature, and the most sophisticated in their social sensitivity (Rubin, 1986).

Psychologist Kenneth Rubin (1986) developed the **Play Observation Scale**, which can be used to study children's behaviors when they are at play and, he believes, to identify children who may be at risk in terms of their social development. Various categories of play can be recorded on the scale for an individual child, and drawing on the play-socialization relationship that is commonly found, clues might emerge about a child's social success. In that sense, play can be used as a diagnostic instrument.

If 6-year-old Toni rarely interacted with other children during the play periods recorded, if she never engaged in games of any sort, and if she typically played alone, she would fit the profile of a child with social interaction problems. It is possible, of course, that Toni is a socially well-adjusted child who is having a difficult day. No firm conclusions can be drawn from one—or even a few—limited samples of behavior. Nevertheless, the behavior recorded on the Play Observation Scale might at least suggest that further questions should be asked about Toni's social development.

---

his time and his toys when he plays. If Jack does not find the activity particularly appealing, he will not force the play in a new direction but may make helpful suggestions. Jack speaks his mind clearly and responds appropriately to the social gestures of the other children in the play group.

When unpopular Jake enters the play group, the other children see him as loud and disruptive. He may talk too much, may boast ("I can play this game better than you"), or may actually try to direct the group toward an activity that he prefers. If conflict arises, Jack will attempt to negotiate and compromise and will make efforts to see that everyone is satisfied with the outcome. Jake may argue constantly, may actually fight, or may simply walk away (Rubin, Coplan, Chen, Buskirk, & Wojslawowicz, 2005).

The recognition that the quality of children's interactions during play is related to their overall acceptance by the peer group has led psychologists and educators to wonder if intervention programs could facilitate such acceptance. Can a child like Jake be helped? In fact, there has been growing interest among professionals in helping unpopular children become better liked by their peers. Rather than using the traditional method of pressuring the group to accept the child, newer approaches involve working directly with the isolated child to coach him or her in specific social skills necessary for group acceptance, and the vehicle used in such coaching has often been play.

The format used in social intervention programs is typically in one of the following categories: modeling, coaching, or shaping (Ladd, Herald, & Andrews, 2006). *Modeling* programs use videos of adults or other children involved in a variety of social situations, and the behaviors that are modeled include illustrations of sharing, cooperating, being supportive of another person, and communicating effectively. *Coaching* involves specific instruction in a variety of social skills, rehearsal of those skills, and then feedback informing the children of how successful they were in using the skills. *Shaping* involves rewarding children for displaying the types of skills that are likely to make them more successful in the peer group. Of the three, modeling seems to be the least effective in that the acquired behaviors are not likely to last, and shaping works well but only when used in conjunction with other approaches. Coaching is the most effective, and many researchers have found evidence to support the view that coaching children in a variety of social skills (e.g., sharing, cooperating, initiating friendships, making conversation, playing games) can lead to advances in peer acceptance. It is encouraging to realize that social skills that are used in play can be taught to children deficient in them and that increases in the sophistication of social play can lead to greater overall acceptance by the peer group (Ladd, 2005).

Summary

Social play is characterized by engagement in nonliteral behaviors within the context of a social interaction; that is, the successive nonliteral behaviors of one child are contingent upon the nonliteral behaviors of a partner. Three abilities are essential for social play. First, the child must have a firm grasp on reality because he or she must make a clear distinction between what is real and what is make-believe. Second, the child must be able to recognize the existence of and obey the rules for taking turns, even when these are not specifically laid out at the beginning of the game. Third, the players must share their imagination when developing the themes of a play episode.

In the most general sense, social play encourages children to focus on the rules that underlie the play episode and makes them aware that certain rules underlie *all* social interactions. More specifically, social play has benefits in many particular areas of a child's life. In the first place, parent-infant play seems to be important in the attachment process, as indicated by the fact that maternal playfulness is correlated with the closeness of attachment at the end of the child's first year. Mothers who regularly involve their infants in play, enjoy doing so, and are sensitive enough to pace the play activity in response to the child's needs are the most likely to have securely attached 1-year-olds.

Social play facilitates children's integration into their peer groups, a particular benefit for a child who is socially withdrawn. Certain types of play materials and activities—blocks, clay, music, creative movement, and sociodramatic play—have been found to be especially helpful in promoting social integration.

Social forms of play help children learn how to cooperate with one another and get beyond their self-centered perspectives to try to see the world through the eyes of other people. This ability to assume the roles, or viewpoints, of others is necessary for the establishment of close interpersonal communication and, among older children, is related to altruistic, or helping, behavior.

Key Terms

Play Observation Scale	p. 257
Strange Situation	p. 239

Issues for Class Discussion

1. Some parents fail to play with their infants at all, others play in a rather insensitive manner, and still others play sensitively and enthusiastically. What are some of the possible reasons for these individual parental differences?

2. If maternal playfulness predicts parent-infant attachment in American populations, what can be said of the strength of attachment in cultures (Indonesia, Guatemala, Mexico) in which mothers do not see themselves as playmates for their children? Are children in those cultures not as closely attached to their parents as American children are? Are those children not as well adjusted? Are we being fair when we judge other cultures by our own standards of desirable behavior?

3. The play materials that promote social integration in children share a common feature: All afford the possibility of a considerable range of social participation so that

the child is gently encouraged to interact with others but never forced to. What are some social play activities that force children's participation, and how may such pressure further alienate the socially withdrawn child?

4. By watching children at play over a period of time, a sensitive teacher can learn much about the degrees of acceptance by their peers. Any one or two play episodes, however, may present a distorted picture of the social network, so teachers must be careful not to draw conclusions from a limited amount of observation. Why might a limited number of observations provide a totally inaccurate impression of a child's social integration?

Chapter 10 THE USES OF PLAY IN THERAPY

War is a phenomenon that stimulates the imagination of many young children, but it is confusing and frightening to them as well. It is particularly frightening when it has a direct personal impact on their lives. Let us look at the effects of war on a generally happy and socially outgoing little boy named Stewart, who is, in fact, the most popular child in his nursery school. Lately, however, he has been moody. He is troubled by the fact that two of his uncles are serving in the armed forces and the country has recently gone to war. Although obviously anxious about the safety of his uncles, he is unwilling and probably unable to talk about his fears with his parents or his nursery school teacher. Notice, however, how clearly Stewart communicates his feelings about war in this brief excerpt from a play session with psychotherapist Clark Moustakas (1959, pp. 70–71):

(Stewart gathers the soldiers and lines them up in the sandbox. He plays silently for ten minutes.)

S.: Junk.

T.: Junk?

S.: Yes, the war is junk. Where is that garbage truck? *(S. locates the truck and places soldiers in it.)* I'll put them in the junkyard. They will all burn up.

T.: You think that will stop the war to burn them all up?

S.: Yes. He's going in and he's going too. They all fight—even ladies and little girls fight.

Learning Objectives

After reading Chapter 10, a student should be able to:

✦ Recognize the potential value of play when it is incorporated into various forms of therapy with children.

✦ Identify the reasons why play is seen as an essential component of child psychotherapy.

✦ Describe the essential characteristics of psychoanalytic play therapy, the history of its use by Freudian therapists, and the differences between Anna Freud's and Melanie Klein's uses of play in the treatment of children.

✦ Identify and be able to explain Virginia Axline's eight principles of relationship play therapy.

✦ Recognize the benefits of incorporating creative art into the process of therapy with children, as well as the cautions that must be observed in the interpretation of children's art.

T.: So you're taking them all to the junkyard to be burned.

S.: I'm going to put them in the sandbox. They are all getting burned. *(S. puts the truck in the sandbox and pours sand on the figures.)* They all get buried, see? *(S. takes the soldiers out of the truck and buries them in the sand.)* Everyone will be buried and die.

T.: Is that how you feel about soldiers and war?

S.: Yeah. They're all getting buried. I'm putting more sand on and they're all going to get buried under this hill. *(Pause)* Can I get buried, too?

T.: That's up to you.

S.: I'm almost all buried, but not quite. *(S. gets out of the sandbox.)* Here is a little girl, but I won't bury her.

T.: You bury all the soldiers but not the little girl.

S.: Yeah. If they're buried, they can't use their guns.

T.: You bury them so there will be no more killing with guns.

S.: This one I'm going to free. He'll work on a farm. This one, too. None of them are buried. They aren't in a trap. They are all freed.

T.:   You want them to go back to their own work on the farms and cities.

S.:   Yeah. They all have to stand up and go back to their families.

The therapist (Moustakas, 1959) observed that in the very brief play sessions he shared with Stewart, the child struggled constantly with the implications of war and its effects on individuals and on families. He expressed the fear that not only men will kill one another but ultimately women and children may be destroyed as well. It is a sign of Stewart's maturity that, although he entertained the possibility of putting an end to war by killing all the soldiers, he realized the futility of that solution and instead returned the soldiers to their homes in the cities and on the farms.

A theme frequently expressed throughout this book has been that play allows a child to communicate when no other forms of communication are possible. A related theme is that such communication is beneficial for children. After a few play sessions, for example, Stewart seemed to come to terms with his anxieties about war, and his behavior in the classroom reflected that resolution (Moustakas, 1959). The point is that play can be an extremely therapeutic activity for any child (or adult), so in this final chapter we turn specifically to a discussion of the therapeutic benefits of play.

THE THERAPEUTIC VALUE OF PLAY

As will be seen in a later section, a number of different approaches have been taken to the psychotherapy of children. Regardless of its particular orientation, however, virtually every school of psychotherapy shares one common belief: that the use of play or a play setting is an indispensable feature of the diagnosis and treatment of children who have problems. Why is play so essential to the psychotherapy of children? Throughout the years, a number of psychologists (Guerney, 2000; Russ, 2004; Schaefer & Kaduson, 2007; Thompson & Henderson, 2007) have articulated the reasons:

- Play is a natural form of expression for children, and it allows them to communicate their feelings effectively.

- Play allows adults to enter the world of children and to show children that they are recognized and accepted. When an adult plays with a child, there is a temporary equalization of power, and the child is less likely than usual to feel threatened by the adult.

- Observing children at play helps adults understand them better.

- Since play is enjoyable for children, it encourages them to relax and thereby reduces their anxiety and defensiveness.

- Play gives children opportunities to release feelings, such as anger and fear, that might be difficult to express otherwise; it allows them to take out their frustrations on play materials without fear of censure from adults.

- Play affords children the opportunity to develop social skills that might be useful in other situations.

- Play gives children a chance to try out new roles and to experiment in a safe setting with a variety of problem-solving approaches.

APPROACHES TO PLAY THERAPY

Let us turn now to an examination of three general approaches to the uses of play in therapy. It should be noted that there are both similarities and differences among the three and that each subsumes a variety of specific approaches too numerous to mention here. The three general approaches that will be concentrated on are the psychoanalytic approach, the relationship approach, and the structured approach.

The Psychoanalytic Approach

To understand why psychoanalytic therapists felt the need to incorporate play into their therapy with children, we must first be aware of three conditions seen as essential to successful psychoanalysis. First, patients must be highly motivated to change. They must come into therapy with a clear recognition that they have a problem, a commitment to seeking a solution, and a belief that the therapist will be able to help them deal with their difficulties. Second, patients must be able to achieve **transference** with their therapists. That is, a patient must be open to the possibility of thinking of the therapist as a substitute for someone of great significance in his or her life—as a mother, father, husband, or wife figure, for example. Third, patients must be able to engage in the process of **free association**. They must be verbal enough to put into words, in the presence of their therapist, their innermost thoughts and feelings; they must be able to speak openly about anything on their mind at a given moment.

Each of the three essential characteristics of psychoanalysis is more difficult to achieve with a child patient than it is with an adult. According to Anna Freud

---

PUTTING THEORY INTO PRACTICE 10.1

Using Play Materials for Expression

Make available play materials, such as dolls and miniature toys, that reflect a child's real world. This will allow the child to express his or her feelings most easily.

While children can express their feelings using such fluid materials as clay and paints and even such structured materials as blocks, they will have an easier time if the materials more closely resemble features of their everyday world. Based on their belief that children's problems are related to family functioning, therapists usually make available miniature houses and family dolls, including baby dolls. Children can more easily express their aggressive feelings if toy weapons are made available, although these may not be appropriate for a nursery school class-room. Baby dolls and baby bottles may allow a child to express feelings about a new baby in the household and may also allow the child to express his or her own feelings of dependency.

Sometimes the most appropriate play materials depend on a particular issue that the child is facing in his or her own life. For example, a child who will soon face or has recently experienced a medical procedure may benefit from having medical toys available, including toy syringes, stethoscopes, or ambulances. In this way the child can become familiar with the materials and may reverse roles by performing procedures on a doll or stuffed animals. Similarly, a child with anxiety about starting school could benefit from having toys that represent school activities.

(1968), the first difficulty in the analysis of children is that they often lack the necessary motivation to change. It is typically not they but their parents who make the decision that therapy is needed, and the therapist must often force from the child recognition of a problem and a commitment to change. In the following passage, Freud describes the challenge she faced in motivating one of her small patients:

> The little girl already knew two children who were being analyzed by me, and she came the first time to the appointment with her slightly older friend. I said nothing special to her and merely left her to gain a little confidence in her strange surroundings. The next time, when I had her alone, I made the first attack. I said that she knew quite well why her two friends came to me . . . and I wondered whether she too had been sent to me for some such reason. At that she said quite frankly, "I have a devil in me. Can it be taken out?" Certainly it could, I said, but it would be no light work

[and] she would have to do a lot of things which she would not find at all
agreeable. . . . She replied, "If you tell me that it is the only way to do it,
then I shall do it that way." Thereby of her own free will she bound herself by the essential rule of psychoanalysis. We ask nothing more of an
adult patient at the outset. (pp. 6–7)

A second potential obstacle to the psychoanalysis of children is that transference is often difficult to achieve. Adults in therapy achieve transference
more easily than children because the significant person whom the therapist
represents is no longer actively involved in the role the therapist assumes. For
example, an adult patient may readily allow a therapist to become a substitute
father because her own father no longer fulfills that authoritative role in her
life. Children, however, already have strong parent figures and are often reluctant to allow the therapist to assume a similar role.

As an illustration of the problem of achieving transference in the psychoanalysis of children, consider the following case of a patient of Freud's (1968),
who refused to transfer to the therapist the feelings she had toward her nanny;
notice the effort required to persuade the child to transfer her feelings of dependency and trust from the nanny to her therapist:

I once analyzed an unusually gifted and sensitive child who cried too easily. She
wanted to get over this tendency with the help of analysis. But the work
with me always stuck at a certain stage. At that point there emerged as an
obstruction a tender attachment to a nurse, who was not friendly towards
analysis. The child indeed believed me as to what emerged from the analysis and what I said, but only up to a certain point—a stage to which she had
allowed herself to go and where her loyalty to her nurse began.

Then I began a keen and sustained battle with the nurse for the child's
affection, conducted on both sides with every possible expedient; in it I
awakened her criticism, tried to shake her blind dependence, and turned
to my account every one of the little conflicts which occur daily in the
nursery. I knew that I had won when one day the little girl told me again
the story of such an incident which had affected her at home, but this time
she added "Do you think she's right?" (pp. 12–13)

Freud (1968) went on to say that it was only then, after she had succeeded
in getting the child to transfer to her the feelings of attachment and trust that
had been reserved for the nanny, that the therapy was able to progress.

Finally, children do not easily engage in free association, the third essential
component in the therapy of adults. Children lack both the self-awareness and

the verbal skills necessary to free-associate as adults do, so other approaches to free association must be tried with children. How is it possible to encourage children to communicate freely to a psychotherapist their innermost thoughts, feelings, and needs? Is there another, nonverbal means of communication available to them? Indeed there is, and that form of expression is their play.

Remember from Chapter 1 that psychoanalytic theorists view play as an activity that helps children cope with objective and instinctual anxieties. Play allows children to repeat and work through specific life experiences that were too threatening, too overwhelming, and too difficult to assimilate when they first occurred (Freud, 1968). It follows, then, that play can offer insights into the mental life, both conscious and unconscious, of the child. Play can offer clues about the problems children are coping with and the mechanisms they are using to cope.

The Play Analysis of Melanie Klein

The therapist Hermine Hug-Hellmuth is generally recognized as the first to incorporate play into psychoanalytic therapy with children. Nevertheless, it was Melanie Klein who, beginning in 1919, used play extensively to deeply explore the child's unconscious mind (Russ, 2004). Play was for Klein the childhood equivalent of free association. In play, she felt, children divulge all of their secrets—their feelings about the important people in their lives, their likes and dislikes, their fears, their joys, and the causes of their hostilities.

One of the assumptions underlying what Klein (1932) referred to as her **play analysis** was that most of a child's play activities are symbolic expressions of sexual conflict or aggression that pertain to the relationship between the child and his or her parents. A child's feelings toward his or her parents often consist of many contradictions and confusions. There are combinations of love and hatred, hostility and resentment, and dependency and frustration at being dependent. Such a complex array of feelings would be difficult enough for an adult to articulate; they are nearly impossible for a child to make sense of, let alone put into words. The child, however, can play out this tangle of feelings with dolls, puppets, toy trains, and trucks.

Since she believed play was the language in which children express themselves most easily, Klein (1932) equipped her therapy room with a large variety of toys and particularly those that encouraged self-expression; many of these toys (e.g., parent dolls, baby dolls, household furnishings) were suggestive of, or pertained in some way to, family interactions. When one of her little patients entered her office, Klein would unlock his or her private drawer and take out a variety of playthings, including little wooden figures representing human beings and animals, houses, cars, balls, marbles, and various creative materials, such as paints, pencils, and clay.

As the child played, Klein (1932) would observe carefully to hear what he or she was *really* saying and would then translate into words the underlying symbolic messages of the play. If a little boy was playing with a family of dolls and regularly buried the father doll in the sand, Klein might remark that the boy felt anger toward his own father; if another child regularly caused the trucks she was playing with to collide, Klein might suggest that this action referred to the child's vision of a sexual union that was significant in her life. In short, every action took on some symbolic meaning.

It was the child's reaction to her interpretive comments that would tell Klein whether she was correct in her interpretation. For example, the validity of her comments might be indicated if the little boy burying figures in the sand looked knowingly at her or smiled in response to her comment about his hatred for his father or if the little female patient responded with vehement denials to Klein's suggestion that her truck collisions had sexual implications. The therapist would assume that a sharp denial on the part of the child was evidence that she had struck a nerve.

The success of Klein's interpretive play analysis was predicated upon two assumptions. The first was that children will have the insight to recognize the meaning of their behaviors if the symbolism is clearly pointed out to them. Actually, this assumption is controversial. On the one hand, many child analysts argue that children's capacity for insight is even greater than that of adults. Critics of Klein's approach, such as Anna Freud (1968), suggested on the other hand that children are not capable of understanding the hidden meaning of their play even when it is pointed out to them, and even if they could have such understanding, insight alone is not adequate to solve their problems.

Klein's (1932) second assumption was that, once her young patients better understood their feelings and needs, they would begin to develop new adaptive behaviors that were more effective than those that resulted from their seeking the help of a therapist in the first place.

Anna Freud's Use of Play in Therapy

Even among psychoanalytic therapists, there was a lack of total agreement on the value of Melanie Klein's (1932) interpretive approach to the play of children. Anna Freud (1968), for example, expressed serious reservations about that component of Klein's work. Freud contended that play lacks the element of purpose that is necessary in a therapeutic situation since children, whether at home or in a therapist's office, do not play for external reasons. Children play because it is enjoyable to do so and not because they want to rid themselves of emotional problems. As mentioned earlier, successful therapy requires that patients realize the purpose of the activity and want to be helped by their therapists.

Freud (1968) went on to say that, because play lacks the purposeful attitude of free association, there is no justification for treating the two as analogous. And if indeed they are not equivalent, the interpretations offered by Klein might easily stray far from the mark. For example, a child who causes two trucks to crash might simply be playing out a scene she witnessed on the street the day before! The child who greets a female visitor to his home by opening the woman's purse might not be symbolically expressing curiosity about whether his own mother's womb conceals a new baby brother or sister; he might only be looking to see if the visitor has brought a present for him.

Despite her view that Klein's particular uses of play in therapy were somewhat inappropriate and her interpretations often excessive and extreme, Freud did not deny that play can contribute much to the psychoanalytic treatment of children. The major therapeutic value of children's play, she felt, was that it allowed the therapist to gather useful information about the child. By carefully watching a child at play, an adult can see in one stroke the whole of a child's psychological world in the limited space of the therapy room. The observation of children at play in a therapist's office can actually provide *more* information than can be gotten from observing them in their natural surroundings. Why? Toys are controllable, and children can carry out actions with them that are possible only in fantasy in the large and uncontrollable everyday world.

Freud (1968) typically used play in the early stages of therapy with a child as an information-gathering technique that could be supplemented with material supplied by the parents during the course of interviews. She used interpretive feedback more sparingly than Klein and only at a much later point in the therapy, and she maintained that while children's play is sometimes imbued with meaningful symbolism, it is often symbolic of nothing at all.

During the 1930s, psychoanalytic play therapy was still in its infancy, but already there was a growing disagreement over the extent to which the patient's activities should be structured. Some psychologists advocated a nondirective approach in which toys were provided but the therapist did not specify which toys should be played with or how. In addition, the child at play was free to include or exclude the therapist; if included by the child, the therapist, in keeping with the psychoanalytic tradition, would feel free to offer interpretations and encouragement. Nondirective psychoanalytic therapy was later to shed its psychoanalytic emphases (e.g., the use of play as a basis for interpretation of dreams, fantasies, and past experiences) and evolve in the 1940s and 1950s into what is known as relationship therapy, sometimes referred to as the humanistic approach. In opposition to those who advocated nondirective play therapy were many therapists who argued the need for a certain amount of direction. These therapists would decide in advance what the child's problem was and then tailor the therapy to the patient's specific needs. The directive therapist would not offer the child the choice of any toy to play with but would present specific toys and make suggestions for play activities. As will be seen, active play therapy exists today in many forms, some of which will be discussed in the section dealing with structured approaches.

The Relationship Approach

Inspired by the work of psychotherapist Carl Rogers, the relationship approach to psychotherapy with children puts great emphasis on the quality of the interaction between the therapist and the child (Landreth, 2002; Schaefer & Kaduson, 2007). The therapist strives to create an atmosphere of total acceptance. The therapist does not criticize the child or attempt to force the therapy in any particular direction; instead, he or she is nondirective and attempts to communicate a feeling of warmth, openness, and respect. Respect for the client is essential because a general assumption of such therapy is that it is the child and not the therapist who will find the means of bringing his or her self-image "out of the shadow land and into the sun" (Axline, 1969, p. 13). When this has been done and the child is able to identify, express, and accept his or her own feelings, the child will be better able to integrate and make sense of those feelings. A major goal of relationship therapy, therefore, is the achievement of self-awareness and self-direction on the part of the child (Schaefer & Kaduson).

Why would a child need a therapist in the first place? The assumption of nondirective relationship therapy is that the climate of acceptance, or what is referred to as unconditional positive regard, is not available in the child's everyday life. Instead of accepting the child's feelings as genuine expressions of the self, parents or others reject certain feelings and thereby reject the child. Take as an example the case of 3-year-old Paul, who came to resent the presence of his new baby sister in the home. Paul told his parents that he hated the baby and asked them to return her to the hospital. His parents responded that they couldn't believe that such a nice little boy could really hate the new baby; he might *think* that he hated her, but actually he loved her as much as they did. Now Paul became confused. The hatred he felt was genuine, but people told him that he was misreading his own feelings and, more significantly, that certain of his feelings were not acceptable. One can imagine Paul as the years went by, disguising his genuine anger and resentment toward his sister, as well as toward other people and situations in his life, until he himself no longer knew what he was feeling. Many children—and adults—do not even recognize their feelings of anger, fear, or sadness because in the course of time they have lost contact with them.

Psychotherapist Virginia Axline (1950) described the heartbreaking case of a 7-year-old boy who was hospitalized for an operation and, not surprisingly, was very frightened. The child transformed his inexpressible fears into anger and became aggressive and hostile toward the hospital staff. His parents, who had never done much to help the boy express and cope with his feelings, were ashamed of their son's behavior and told him so; he was an embarrassment to them, and they hoped he would learn to "behave like a man." Then they bribed him with an offer of a new bicycle if he would stop behaving badly, assuring him that, in any case, there was nothing to be afraid of. The child obeyed his parents and kept his feelings in check; he also developed a case of asthma as his body expressed the fear and sadness that he could not outwardly display.

According to Carl Rogers (1951), it is difficult to accept another human being fully, and rejection takes a number of forms. Rejection occurs when, as in the case of little Paul, who was adjusting to the presence of a new sibling, adults deny the child's feelings. Rejection also occurs when adults criticize children for what they feel, as opposed to criticizing them only for what they do. It is one thing to punish a child for fighting, but it is quite another matter when a child is punished for *feeling* angry enough to fight. Finally, rejection occurs when adults try to change or to reinterpret a child's feelings: "You say you hate your brother, but I think the problem is that you're nervous about the exam you will take in school tomorrow."

As might be expected, nondirective relationship therapists try to provide in their therapy sessions the ingredients that have been missing in other areas of the child's life. Let us now examine the therapeutic approach of one of the best known child psychotherapists, Virginia Axline, whose treatment of a little boy named Dibs has become familiar to millions of readers since the book of the same name appeared in 1946.

Virginia Axline's Nondirective Therapy

Virginia Axline (1947), a psychotherapist and a professor at Ohio State University, outlined eight basic principles of her relationship therapy.

First, the therapist must establish a warm and friendly relationship with the child, and the child must come to see the therapy room as a comfortable and inviting place to play. The therapist might greet the child, or children in the case of group therapy, with a friendly smile or another expression of genuine interest. Axline pointed out, however, that rapport is not always easy to establish since the child in therapy may be unaccustomed to following the established rules of social behavior. A friendly smile from the therapist may be repaid with a scowl from a child who resents having to be involved in therapy in the first place.

A second principle is that the therapist must accept the child completely for what he or she is, without praise and without criticism. Such total acceptance often requires a considerable amount of patience on the therapist's part, especially if the child and the therapist are at cross purposes, as when the therapist wants to be of help but the child does not want any help. Axline described such a circumstance with reference to the case of 12-year-old Jean, who responds to the therapist's friendly greeting with stony silence and reacts with indifference to suggestions that there are a lot of wonderful things to play with in the therapy room. Jean sits in silence. The therapist tries to be accepting of the child's attitude but, because of her own inexperience, is having difficulty doing so. Finally, she says, "You know, Jean, I'm here to help you. I want you to consider me your friend. I wish you would tell me what bothers you." Jean responds with a sigh, "Nothing bothers *me!*"—a perceptive remark in that she knows that it is the therapist who is upset. The therapist has not accepted Jean's feelings, and the therapy is blocked.

Axline's third principle is that the therapist must establish a climate of permissiveness. The materials in the room and the time are to be used as the child wants to use them. When the therapist remarks that their time together belongs to the child and may be used as the child sees fit, he or she must be totally sincere. There must be no attempt to force the child to use the materials in any particular way. For example, the therapist may realize that Paul has been stressed because of his parents' constant fighting in the home and may feel that the child might develop insights into his problems by playing with the family dolls, but she should not pressure him to do so.

Similarly, there must be no probing questions that pertain to the child's life experiences. Axline (1947, p. 95) described the consequences of such probing in the case of May, a 5-year-old who is in therapy trying to deal with her reactions to a traumatic hospital experience. May is playing with a family of dolls, and the therapist, hoping to be of help, begins to push too hard. When May puts a little girl doll in a wagon and pushes her across the floor, the therapist asks, "Is the little girl going to the hospital?" May answers that she is. "Is she afraid?"

the therapist asks. Again, May responds in the affirmative. "Then what happens?" asks the therapist. May simply gets up and goes over to the window, where she stands with her back to the therapist and asks, "How much longer?"

A fourth principle is that the therapist recognizes the child's feelings and attempts to reflect them back to the child. The reflection of children's feelings, as they are expressed in words, gestures, or the symbolic meaning of the play, is intended to help them gain insight into those feelings. Even when the feelings are expressed in words, the therapist must be careful to recognize exactly what the child is saying and to avoid reading into the child's statements more than was intended. Jack says, "I spit on my brother. I spit on my father. I spit right in their very faces. They wouldn't give me my toys. He broke my gun. I'll show them. I'll spit on them." The therapist responds, "You are very angry with your brother and your father. You would like to spit right in their faces because of the way they have treated you" (Axline, 1969, p. 101).

When feelings are expressed symbolically through play, the therapist must exercise even greater caution. Axline (1947) pointed out that the recognition and the interpretation of a feeling are two different processes, but in reacting to the patient's play, it is difficult to separate the two. In marked contrast to the interpretive approach often used by psychoanalytic therapists, Axline warned against the overuse of interpretation. Interpretation should be used very sparingly, she said, for two reasons. First, any particular interpretation can be in error, particularly if made by an inexperienced therapist. Second, even if an interpretation is on target, the therapist may be pushing the patient along faster than the patient wants to go. If, however, the interpretation is both accurate and timely, the child advances in the therapy, and the therapist can actually see the patient gaining insight into his or her problems.

The fifth play therapy principle expressed by Axline is that the therapist always maintains respect for the child and recognizes that the child is capable of solving his or her own problems. The responsibility for the success of the therapy rests with the child, and in that sense the therapy is centered in the child and not in the therapist. As children realize that the responsibility is theirs, they gain a measure of self-confidence and self-respect that would not be possible if they came to rely totally on the therapist to help them.

Sixth, the therapist recognizes that in therapy, the child leads the way and the therapist follows. As indicated earlier, nondirective therapy involves no probing questions, no directions, no suggestions, no prompting, no criticism, and no approval of the child's actions. Axline (1969) believed that approval, like criticism, is a form of manipulation and may result in children's behaving in certain ways simply to please the therapist rather than because the behaviors are right for them.

The seventh principle is that the therapy must not be hurried. Many times the progress of the therapy will not be obvious, particularly if the child sits and plays quietly in session after session, but if progress is not immediately evident, that does not mean it is not occurring. Hurrying the child in therapy violates many of the principles described thus far. It may damage the rapport that has been built up between therapist and child, it does not indicate a climate of permissiveness, it does not show respect for the child, and it hardly suggests that it is the child who leads the way.

Finally, an important principle of nondirective therapy is that limits must be set. No area of a child's life is totally free of limits, and this includes the therapy session. Limits anchor children in reality and help them realize that they have responsibilities to fulfill. Limits and structure also provide a sense of security. The limits of nondirective therapy are generally of three kinds. First, the children are not allowed to harm themselves or the therapist. Second, they are not allowed to cause damage to the materials in the playroom. And third, while they may use their time with the therapist in any way they want to, the children must leave the room when the session is at an end. Observe the way in which nondirective therapist Clark Moustakas (1959, pp. 17–18) establishes, kindly but firmly, the time limit on his session with 5-year-old Tim:

T.:   In a short while, we'll have to leave.

Tim: No. I'm going to stay.

T.:   I can see you're not ready to stop, but we have only so much time to be here, and when that time is up we must leave.

Tim: My mommy can play with me.

T.:   I know your mommy can play with you, but I must close the room.

Tim: I'm not going.

T.:   You are determined to stay, but I must ask you to leave soon.

Tim: I'm going to tell my mommy; she'll come and play with me.

T.:   I guess she would, but not here. When you walk out the door, I'm turning off the lights and closing the room.

It will be noticed that the therapist accepts Tim's feelings as valid, reflects the sentiments back to the child, and offers no criticism at all. Yet he makes very clear to Tim that the rules of the playroom must be obeyed.

Structured Approaches

As we have seen, the early psychoanalytic approach to play therapy was very directive in its willingness to offer interpretations, while the relationship approach was firmly rooted in the principle that it is the child, not the therapist, who takes the lead. The current trend in thinking about the uses of play in therapy, however, represents a sort of compromise between these two extremes of directiveness. This recent tendency to seek the middle ground in psychotherapy with children is exemplified by changes in the psychoanalytic approach since the time of Melanie Klein (Russ, 2004; Thompson & Henderson, 2007; Tuma & Russ, 1993). The psychoanalytic approach has evolved into what is today referred to as the psychodynamic

---

PUTTING THEORY INTO PRACTICE 10.2

Using Play as a Diagnostic Tool

Regard a child's play as offering clues about the child's feelings and needs. Unless you are a trained psychologist, never attempt to diagnose a problem on the basis of a child's play and never draw any conclusions from isolated behaviors.

At what point should a layperson consider seeking the help of a trained psychologist? The key issue is one of balance. All children have good and bad days. On a particular day a child who is usually calm may appear to be anxious, aggressive, or depressed. He or she may be withdrawn, may spend a lot of time sucking on a baby bottle, or may engage in unusually aggressive or even destructive play. He or she may draw pictures of violence, may be fascinated by toys that could be seen as weapons, or may involve toy cars and trucks in horrendous crashes.

However, children who might need professional help never seem to have good days. Their fantasy themes are always aggressive, and they see violence and destruction everywhere. They never draw happy pictures. They always choose dark and depressing colors for their artwork. They always seem to gain more satisfaction from destroying their block structures and their clay figures than from creating them. They may seem especially anxious and dependent and may always seek out a nursing bottle and suck on it for long periods of time. Their rough-and-tumble play often results in hurting other children.

The main point for anyone who works with children to remember is that play is a highly expressive activity that offers clues to the emotional life of the player. However, it never offers conclusive proof about any underlying mental state.

approach. Even though it is still based on psychoanalytic principles, the psychodynamic approach is different in the following ways:

- An emphasis on shorter and less frequent treatments, with specific goals and strategies clearly outlined at the beginning of therapy.

- A focus on present realities rather than on unconscious mechanisms rooted in the past.

- An avoidance of the use of heavily symbolic interpretation.

- A stress on the importance of the relationship between therapist and child.

- A tendency to use a larger number of therapeutic techniques, such as a reliance on the expressive arts (music, literature, drama, puppetry, and free play).

Modern child psychotherapists of every philosophical orientation continue to use various materials and forms of play in their treatment. Dolls are used with younger children, as are puppets, miniature life toys, art materials, punching toys, and sandbox play; with older children there are also board games, construction materials, paper-and-pencil games, and even computer games. However, the ways that play materials and activities are currently used differ considerably from what was seen in the past. The tendency today is to avoid both the excessive interpretation that was characteristic of the early psychoanalytic therapists and the extremely permissive atmosphere favored by relationship therapists. In fact, instead of following a general set of theoretical principles, the modern therapist usually tailors the treatment to the needs of the individual child. The amount of structure provided by the therapist, including the extent of the limits, the particular toys made available, and the play activities suggested, depends on the child's level of development and personal characteristics, as well as on the specific goals of the therapy (Thompson & Henderson, 2007).

Another development that differentiates earlier forms of play therapy from what is often practiced today is the involvement of parents as therapists in the therapy sessions. Filial play therapy was developed in the 1960s in recognition of the fact that there were not enough professional therapists to deal with the number of problems children were facing (Guerney, 2000). In its earliest form, filial play therapy required the parents to attend training sessions under the supervision of a therapist for 12 months, during which they were conducting therapy sessions for their own children at home. In the past 20 years, filial therapy has been practiced more and more widely, in part because the training sessions for parents have become more manageable. It is typical today that parents attend 10 sessions, meet in a 2-hr weekly support group, and videotape their home sessions for the therapist to evaluate (Bratton, Ray, Rhine, & Jones, 2005;

Landreth, 2002). Even if filial therapy is not appropriate, therapists will some-times train parents to simply play with their children without directing the activity, making demands, or telling them what to do (VanFleet, 2005).

As we now examine some of the more widely used structured approaches to play in therapy, notice that all contain as a common element the recognition that play allows a child to communicate even the most complicated and most painful feelings from a safe distance: The child at play speaks, as it were, from behind a curtain of make-believe.

Storytelling

The telling of stories serves many important functions in human culture, and storytelling is at the heart of much of children's play (Schaefer & Kaduson, 2007). For example, children tell stories with words, but stories are also told through the use of clay, miniature life toys, blocks, and other materials, and stories form the basis of sociodramatic play. Parents sometimes use stories to influence the behavior of young children, such as by telling a child about past misbehavior as a reminder not to behave that way again. Stories help us make sense of the environment. They allow us to transmit the beliefs, the values, and the wisdom of a culture, or of a family, from one generation to another. They allow us to reveal information about ourselves, to express our needs, and to solve many of the problems that confront us. People often find their troubles easier to talk about if, instead of referring directly to themselves, they can describe the problems of a hypothetical "friend." Sometimes while describing the problems of this surrogate, the narrator gains valuable insights into his or her own emotional difficulties. Such storytelling affords people the safety of distance from their own lives and allows them to develop objectivity about and perspective on the issues that are troubling them (Thompson & Henderson, 2007).

An interesting variation on the storytelling technique was developed by psychotherapist Richard Gardner (1972, 1986, 1993). Instead of simply telling a story to a child and asking for reactions, Gardner engaged in what he described as **mutual storytelling.** He would first ask the child to make up an unusual and exciting story, and as the child spoke, he would try to identify whom the story's characters were intended to represent and what was the symbolic significance of the setting and the theme. Then, on the assumption that an adult who speaks in the child's own language has the best chance of being heard, Gardner would retell the story in a revised version in which any conflicts expressed in the original story were resolved in constructive ways. The child would then realize that there might be more effective ways of dealing with problems than those already being used.

Illustrative of Gardner's approach is his work with 12-year-old Frank, who suffered from anxiety, excessive guilt, and hypersensitivity to criticism (Gardner, 1972). Frank's parents were cold and inflexible people who tolerated no signs of weakness or insubordination in their son. Here is Frank's story:

> This story is about a man who killed his wife for her money. This man was greedy and he got so greedy with his money that he thought he was the best guy going. He knew that he had a lot of money, so he went and bet on a lot of different things. One night he bet and he lost all his money because he was conceited and selfish, and now he's on a street corner begging for money.
>
> The moral of the story is: don't brag about yourself because only something bad is going to happen. (p. 67)

The therapist identified the theme of Frank's story as that of excessive deprivation. The wife's money in the story represented the mother's love that Frank wanted so desperately but apparently could not have. The fact that the character killed his wife for her money is indicative of the rage Frank felt toward his mother, but interestingly enough, even by killing his wife, the story character achieved little satisfaction. The money he wanted so much was eventually lost. Frank seemed to realize that his anger toward his mother served little purpose and to believe that, just as his fictitious character lost the money because of his own personal shortcomings, he himself was unworthy of the love that he needed so much.

What follows is Gardner's (1972) retelling of Frank's story:

> Once upon a time there was a guy [whose] mother was a very selfish person. She had a lot of money but she wouldn't part with a penny. . . . This poor guy felt starved for money and he felt very bad. He wanted to buy things. Other kids got allowances, other kids had a little extra bit of spending money to buy themselves things, and he was really sad. At times he would get so sad and mad that he would feel like killing her, but he realized that this would accomplish nothing.
>
> So what he did was he decided to get a job. The first thing he did was to get a newspaper route and he was able to earn some money with that. As he got older, he was able to get bigger jobs. He went to school and he got trained in something so that he could earn a living. And then when he earned it on his own he met a wonderful girl whom he married. She had some earnings, and he earned, and they pooled their money together. They had a very good relationship, and they spent their life pleasurably.

The moral of that story is: if somebody is not giving you something that you want from them, don't kill them for it. Don't knock yourself out. Don't try to bug them when they can't give it. Try to find it elsewhere. Another way of saying the moral of that story is the old saying of W. C. Fields, "If at first you don't succeed, try, try again." After that if you still don't succeed, forget about it. Don't make a damn fool of yourself. The end. (p. 68)

Gardner (1972) began his story by acknowledging Frank's pain and deprivation. He also recognized Frank's underlying rage but indicated that anger alone would not solve the problem. Then he symbolically suggested to Frank that constructive approaches are more beneficial. The therapist let the boy know that instead of dwelling on what he was missing in life, he should realize that his mother might be unable to give him what he needed and truly deserved. He might be wise, therefore, to look for love elsewhere.

The point of this meaningful exchange between Frank and his therapist is that it probably would not have occurred without the safe, nonliteral element of make-believe. If he had to speak directly about his own life, Frank could never have been as eloquent in describing his problems. And to use the therapist's own phrase, if he had not replied to Frank in the boy's own language, he would have had a lesser chance of being heard.

Bibliotherapy

Many of us have had the experience of reading a story in which a character's life so closely resembled our own that we were comforted to discover that we are not so unusual after all. In fact, reading about the experiences of others often helps people gain insights into their own lives. This phenomenon forms the rationale for **bibliotherapy,** in which troubled children are asked to read books about people whose life circumstances are similar to theirs or to listen while a book is read aloud to them by a counselor and then are encouraged to discuss with their counselor the characters' behaviors, thoughts, feelings, and problems (Cohen, 1994).

The major goals of bibliotherapy are the following:

- To encourage children to express their problems openly.

- To teach children to be able to analyze their own feelings and behaviors.

- To stimulate children to consider a variety of possible alternatives in the solution to their problems.

© Comstock

Reading about the experiences of others often helps people gain insights into their own lives. This phenomenon forms the rationale for the form of psychotherapy known as bibliotherapy.

- To allow children to realize that their problems are not unique to them and thus to give them the comfort of knowing that they are not alone.

- To teach children to be constructive and positive in their thinking.

An underlying assumption of bibliotherapy is that if a character in a story has problems similar to those of a child in treatment, the child will identify with and gain insights from the character's experiences. Story lines are specifically selected to mirror the life experiences of the child and include such themes as making friends, dealing with separation within the family, understanding the self, or finding love. Because it is only a story, children can talk safely about what the characters think and feel. They are not threatened as they might be if asked to talk about their own feelings. However, children in therapy can gain insights into themselves by analyzing fictional characters whose lives and problems are similar to theirs (Crawford, Brown, & Crawford, 2004). Bibliotherapy seems to be particularly effective when the story characters have a breakthrough in their ability to solve a problem or deal with a difficult situation (Androutsopoulou, 2001). The recognition that bibliotherapy is beneficial for all children—those in therapy and those simply dealing with everyday life stress—is exemplified by the fact that a picture book is available for young children containing stories about stressful life events (Golding, 2006).

Art Therapy

When children are given materials that are unstructured and open-ended in that there is no obviously correct way to use them, they are free to create in any way they want. For example, with clay, paints, or crayons and paper there is no specific product required, so the child is free to be a creative artist. The experience of creating art has significant benefits for all children. Art has been described as a process that "enables children to look with open eyes, to encounter the world without fear, to acquire a perceptual vocabulary that helps them organize their experiences" (Rubin, 2005, p. 312). Art allows for the expression of feelings for which the child may not have words or that may be too painful to speak about even if the words are available. It is for these reasons that the practice of art therapy was developed to help troubled children.

Art therapy is defined by the American Art Therapy Association (n.d.) as the use of the creation of art to improve and enhance physical, mental, and emotional well-being. The assumption on which art therapy is based is that artistic expression helps people of all ages resolve conflicts, deal effectively with their problems, develop social skills, control their behavior, reduce stress, increase self-esteem and self-awareness, and achieve insight. Art therapy requires a trained therapist with a background in art, human development,

© Photodisc

When children draw, paint pictures, or sculpt figures, they may reveal useful information about their moods, inner conflicts, and overall self-images, so a major value of art is as a tool for assessment of a child's mental states.

and counseling. Originating in psychiatric settings in the 1940s, art therapy has expanded rapidly and is now used in a wide variety of environments, such as schools, hospitals, hospices, detention centers, and specialized treatment centers (Rubin, 2005).

When children draw, paint pictures, or sculpt figures, they often reveal to the therapist useful information about their moods, inner conflicts, and overall self-images. In that sense, a major value of art is as a tool for *assessment* of a child's mental states. The therapist can learn much simply by observing the process of making art. Does the child use bold, aggressive strokes or careful, delicate lines? Does she use color or restrict herself to black-and-white drawings? Does he pound the clay aggressively or handle it nervously, as if afraid to get dirty? Does she paint a colorful scene and then proceed to cover it completely with black paint, as if afraid that the original painting revealed too much about herself?

There is a danger in overanalyzing children's art, and one creative work is never enough to tell the whole story about a child's psychological life. Nevertheless, consistently repeated patterns can be quite revealing. For example, the size of characters in a child's drawings could be informative. Children who draw huge figures may be extroverted, while small figures may be produced by withdrawn, insecure, or depressed children. The relative size of figures may be important as well. If a child figure in family drawings is disproportionately small, the artist may be revealing something about his or her sense of worth compared with that of other family members.

The themes that children produce in their art are sometimes obvious and sometimes very subtle but often quite revealing. For example, one little girl drew for her therapist a picture of two houses, located near one another and connected by a bridge across the sky. She labeled one house with her own name and the other with the name of the therapist. Since the child's family was planning a 4-week vacation in the near future, the therapist interpreted the drawing as indicating the child's need for reassurance that, even though they would be separated for a month, the connection between herself and the little girl would remain (Brems, 1993).

In addition to helping a therapist understand a troubled child, art is a form of catharsis, allowing for the expression of feelings that cannot be expressed in any other way. The very act of self-expression can be beneficial to the child—getting out on paper or canvas one's angers, fears, or conflicted feelings of love and hatred for the people in one's life. Finally, art is a vehicle for emotional growth in that it helps children learn creative ways to solve problems (Rubin, 2005). Just as they realize that a number of different possibilities are available in the process of creating a painting or a sculpture, children come to see that numerous possibilities are available for the solution of any problem they face in life. In addition, the very process of manipulating materials and creating with them provides children with a sense of accomplishment and nurtures a sense of self-esteem that is often lacking in troubled children.

DOES PLAY REALLY HELP?

We have seen that play is a tool used by child psychotherapists of vastly different philosophical orientations. Now we close by asking whether there exists scientific proof of its therapeutic effectiveness. Before attempting to draw conclusions about the therapeutic effectiveness of play, we should remember that play, unlike psychoanalysis, behavioral therapy, or relationship therapy, is not in itself a particular philosophy of therapy. It is difficult, therefore, to determine precisely the effectiveness of play therapy in the sense of offering statistical proof of its usefulness. Perhaps it is difficult to prove scientifically the effectiveness of any form of therapy since techniques that work extremely well for one client may not work at all for another. Play is no exception to this general rule; exactly how and when play is incorporated into therapy seems to depend on the needs of the individual client.

In an analysis of the results of 94 different controlled studies conducted between 1953 and 2000, it was discovered that play therapy has an impressive record of success (Bratton et al., 2005). Children who underwent play therapy performed better on the various outcome measures than children who did not. The outcome measures of success varied from study to study, of course, but they included such factors as reduction in anxiety, behavioral change, improved self-concept, more successful interpersonal relationships within the family, and better overall social adjustment.

We have seen in this chapter that play therapy comes in many forms, and in addition to knowing that such treatment is effective, researchers have attempted to discover what it is about play therapy that works for children. Are some types of therapy more effective than others? It was found that, while all forms of therapy are effective, the nondirective approaches (e.g., the relationship approach) seem to result in more significant improvements than do the directive approaches (Bratton et al., 2005). In other words, children in therapy are more likely to improve if they are allowed to play freely than if restrictions or suggestions are placed on their play.

We have also discussed the fact that an increasingly common practice is for therapists to train parents or teachers in therapeutic techniques (filial play therapy) so that they may conduct the therapy. It has been discovered that therapy conducted by parents has been more effective than therapy conducted by professionals. It is important to keep in mind, however, that therapists extensively trained these parents before and during the time they were engaged in play therapy with their children. Finally, there was a relationship between the success of play therapy and the number of sessions conducted. The most effective treatment seemed to involve 35 to 40 sessions, and the results were less impressive in those cases when more or fewer sessions were conducted (Bratton et al., 2005).

In summary, there appears to be little doubt that play has a number of curative powers. Play releases tensions and pent-up emotions. It allows a child to compensate in fantasy for the hurtful experiences of reality. It encourages self-discovery. It provides the possibility for children to learn alternative—and more successful—methods for dealing with their problems. Finally, it is a child's natural medium for communication, and because of this, play has been incorporated successfully into virtually every form of psychotherapy that is practiced on children today.

Summary

Because it allows children to communicate when no other forms of communication are possible, play has been found to be an extremely valuable asset in the process of child psychotherapy. Play provides a rare opportunity for adults to understand the world from the child's point of view, and since the activity is so enjoyable for them, play encourages children to relax, let down any defenses they might have, and express their feelings openly. It also helps them develop useful social skills and try a variety of new problem-solving approaches.

Psychoanalytic therapists agree that play is an aid to therapy but disagree on the specific ways it should be used. Melanie Klein (1932), for example, treated play as the equivalent of free association. She believed that children at play will divulge all of their innermost feelings not directly but symbolically. In her work with children, Klein would observe their play and continuously translate into words what she perceived to be the underlying symbolic messages. She assumed that children have enough insight to recognize the meaning of their behaviors if the symbolism is pointed out to them and that, as children come to understand their needs and feelings better, they gradually develop new and more effective ways of adapting to the world around them.

Anna Freud (1968) rejected the analogy of play as free association and was critical of what she saw as Klein's overreliance on interpretation. Such interpretations can often be incorrect, she argued. Instead, Freud used play primarily to diagnose a child's problems. She felt that the observation of children at play could allow adults to see in one stroke the whole of the child's psychological world in the limited space of the therapy room.

The relationship approach to psychotherapy emphasizes the importance for the therapist of creating an atmosphere of total acceptance of the child and refraining from criticism, communicating instead a feeling of warmth, openness, and respect. A basic assumption of such therapy is that children have within themselves the motivation and the ability to change their lives for the better, but they can do so only after they have identified, expressed, and accepted their own feelings. The goal of therapy is self-awareness and self-direction on the part of the child.

A number of the basic principles of nondirective relationship therapy were articulated more than 40 years ago by psychotherapist Virginia Axline. Axline (1947) believed that the therapist must establish a friendly relationship with the child; accept the child completely, neither praising nor criticizing; communicate an attitude of permissiveness; recognize and reflect the child's feelings; respect the child's ability to solve his or her own problems; and be patient enough to allow the child to lead the way in therapy. The therapist must also keep the child anchored in reality even in the very permissive playroom by setting limits on time and on the possibility of damage to the materials or harm to the child or the therapist.

Modem psychotherapists are likely to use a variety of different approaches to the incorporation of play into their therapy. Guided less by a particular philosophical orientation and more by the practical constraints of reality, they tend to prefer a middle road between the extremes of directiveness represented by the early psychoanalytic therapists on the one hand and the relationship therapists on the other. Thus, we have a variety of structured approaches in which the therapist identifies the client's problem and play materials and/or activities are suggested that are most relevant in dealing with the problem. Among the most often used structured approaches to play in therapy are release therapy—which is based on the assumption that a child needs to release pent-up emotions in order to learn how to deal with them most effectively—storytelling, and bibliotherapy.

The effectiveness of play as an adjunct to therapy has been well established. The nondirective approach seems to be more effective than directive approaches, and the results are more impressive if parents trained in therapeutic procedures work directly with their own children. The curative powers of play have been widely documented.

Key Terms

Bibliotherapy	p. 279	Play Analysis	p. 267
Free Association	p. 265	Transference	p. 265
Mutual Storytelling	p. 277		

Issues for Class Discussion

1. Why do adult-oriented therapies not work well with children? What do children lack that is necessary for successful psychotherapy?

2. Looking at the differences between psychoanalytic and relationship play therapies, what can we conclude about differences in their views of human nature? What do psychoanalysts and relationship therapists assume about the abilities of people to solve their emotional problems?

3. Most child psychotherapists refuse to commit themselves to only one therapeutic approach and instead maintain that they tailor their treatment to the needs of the individual child. Why do you think this eclectic approach is favored? Might some therapies work better with some children than with others? What type of child might respond best to each approach? What type of child might not respond well to each approach?

4. Many educators and psychologists worry that when adults are aware of the therapeutic values of play, they tend to read too much into children's play behaviors. They interpret and analyze instead of merely appreciating play for what it usually is, a pleasurable recreational activity. Do you think there is a danger in knowing too much about the value of play as therapy?

Glossary

Accommodation In Jean Piaget's cognitive theory, the adjustment of the intellectual structures in response to the incorporation of new information from the outside world.

Activity/Recreation Play Programs Hospital play programs that emphasize doing things, such as arts-and-crafts projects, so that the child can gain the sense of accomplishment that comes from being busy and productive.

Arousal Modulation Theory The theory of children's play that assumes some optimal level of central nervous system arousal that a human being tries to maintain, with play being a way of maintaining this level.

Assimilation In Jean Piaget's cognitive theory, the taking of new material from the outside world and fitting it into a person's already existing intellectual structures.

Associative Play A form of play in which each child is engaged in a separate activity but there is a considerable amount of cooperation and communication.

Autocosmic Play According to psychoanalytic theorist Erik Erikson, a type of play that occurs during the first year of life, centering on the exploration of the child's own body.

Behaviorism The psychological theory developed by John B. Watson, who believed that the mind is a blank slate at birth, that people grow to be what they are made to be by the environment, and that the only legitimate area of inquiry for psychologists is the study of behavior.

Bibliotherapy A form of therapy in which troubled children are asked to read books about people whose life circumstances are similar to their own or to listen while such a book is read aloud to them by a counselor and are then encouraged to discuss with their counselor the characters' behaviors, thoughts, feelings, and problems.

Character Roles Dramatic play roles based on characters that are either stereotyped or fictional.

Child Development Play Programs Hospital play programs that include curricula ordinarily found in preschool or elementary school classrooms.

Child Life Play Programs Hospital play programs that focus on all aspects of the hospitalized child's development, seen in both an individual and a social context.

Collectivism A societal philosophy that stresses the importance of group goals, group loyalty, and group identification; encourages communal labor and communal property; and discourages the formation of potentially divisive allegiances to subgroups like the family.

Concrete Operations In Jean Piaget's theory of cognitive development, the stage at which the child has a logical system to organize representational acts but is limited in the use of logic to reason about concrete situations or events.

Congenital Adrenal Hyperplasia (CAH) A condition in which the adrenal glands produce excessively high levels of male sex hormones in a female fetus, which has a pronounced masculinizing effect on a genetically female child.

Conservation The ability to realize that even though the physical appearance changes, the amount of matter remains the same if nothing is added or taken away.

Contextual Theory A theory that is rooted in the belief that a child's development cannot be fully understood without referring to the social-cultural and historical setting in which it occurs.

Convergent Problem Solving The ability to bring a variety of isolated pieces of information together to come up with the one correct solution.

Cooperative Play A form of play that occurs when two or more children are engaged in a play activity with a common goal.

Decentration The underlying element of symbolic play that refers to the degree to which a child is able to shift the focus of its interest from the self to external objects. More generally, the ability to attend simultaneously to two or more features of the environment.

Decontextualization The underlying element of symbolic play that refers to the use of one object as a substitute for another.

Divergent Problem Solving The ability to branch out from a starting point and consider a variety of possible solutions.

Diversionary Play Programs Hospital play programs characterized by an implicit assumption that children are better off if they do not directly confront the stressful experience of hospitalization.

Emergent Literacy The view that children start to become literate long before they are actually able to read and write and that even from infancy they have social experiences that lay the basis for later reading and writing.

Enactive Representation Physical encoding of information about the world, illustrated by the way a person learns to ride a bicycle or tie a knot in a necktie.

Equivalency The recognition that space can be divided into different-size units and that a certain number of units of one size corresponds to a different number of units of another.

Euclidean Spatial Concept A conception of space as an overall network, independent of the number or the arrangement of elements within it.

Family Roles Dramatic play roles of family members, the most common roles assumed by preschool children.

Formal Operations In Jean Piaget's theory of cognitive development, the highest stage, occurring during adolescence and adulthood. Formal thinkers are able to deal with abstract, hypothetical propositions.

Free Association An essential characteristic of psychoanalysis in which patients put into words, in the presence of their therapist, their innermost thoughts and feelings.

Functional Roles Dramatic play roles that are defined by specific plans of action.

Games of Chance Competitive games in which the outcome is determined by sheer blind luck.

Games of Construction A type of play that Jean Piaget saw as representing an area of transition between symbolic play and "nonplayful activities, or serious adaptation" (Piaget & Inhelder, 1969, p. 59).

Games of Physical Skill Competitive games in which the outcome is determined solely by the physical skills of the players.

Games of Strategy Competitive games in which the outcome is determined by the rational choices made by the players and that require a degree of intellectual skill for success.

Games With Rules The games of elementary school children that involve competition between two or more players and are governed by a set of regulations agreed to in advance by all the players.

Gender Consistency The recognition that gender always remains the same, regardless of surface physical changes in appearance.

Gender Identity The preschool child's realization that males and females are different on the basis of their physical characteristics.

Gender Stability The realization that gender will always remain the same and that boys and girls will grow up to become either men or women.

Graphic Collections Pleasing or interesting arrangements of figures that are produced by preschool children when they are asked to sort objects into groups.

Hypothetico-Deductive Reasoning A type of problem solving in which the formal thinker sets up a variety of hypotheses, or "if-then" statements; ranks them in order of probability; and then tests them out systematically in sequence.

Identity The adolescent stage of personality development, according to Erikson, in which teenagers test themselves in a variety of ways as they seek deeper levels of self-awareness.

Individualism A societal philosophy characterized by a belief that loyalty to self comes before group loyalty, that people should develop their own individual identities rather than identifying with the group, that the purpose of work is more to benefit individual workers and their families than to benefit the state, and that individuals have a right to own property.

Industry In Erik Erikson's theory, the need that grade school children have to apply themselves to a variety of skills and tasks that are necessary for success in the larger world of adults.

Instinctual Anxiety In psychoanalytic theory, a type of anxiety that occurs when children recognize in themselves instincts that would be disapproved of by society at large. These forbidden feelings, whether or not they are translated into behaviors, trigger an anxiety reaction.

Integration The underlying element of symbolic play that refers to the child's ability to organize play into increasingly complex patterns during the second year of life.

Macrosphere Play According to psychoanalytic theorist Erik Erikson, a type of play that appears during the preschool years, as children at play begin to acquire mastery in social interactions.

Microsphere Play According to psychoanalytic theorist Erik Erikson, a type of play that appears during the second year of life, in which the child begins to acquire mastery over objects.

Mutual Storytelling Richard Gardner's therapeutic technique of asking children to make up a story, identifying the story's symbolic significance, and retelling the story in a revised version in which conflicts expressed in the original story are resolved constructively.

Naturalism A philosophical theory expressed by Jean-Jacques Rousseau in the 18th century that stressed the natural goodness of human beings, suggested that nature equips children with a plan for their development, and questioned the need for firm direction in childrearing.

Objective Anxiety Fear of the external world that results when a young child realizes the degree of his or her helplessness.

Onlooker Play Play in which a child watches another child or other children at play and is definitely involved as a spectator, even to the point of asking questions or offering suggestions, but does not become an active participant.

Parallel Play A form of activity in which children play separately at the same activity at the same time and in the same place.

Play Analysis The directive and interpretive form of play therapy that was originally used by the psychoanalyst Melanie Klein.

Play Observation Scale An instrument developed by psychologist Kenneth Rubin to study children's behaviors when they are at play to identify children who may be at risk in terms of their social development.

Primary Circular Reaction One of the earliest forms of sensorimotor play, a behavior that occurs when a baby accidentally discovers an interesting sensory or motor experience related to its own body, apparently enjoys it, and later continues to repeat it.

Recapitulation Theory G. Stanley Hall's early-20th-century belief that each person's development reflects the evolutionary progression of the entire human species.

Reversibility The ability to mentally reverse an action, a characteristic of thinking that does not appear before the age of 5 or 6 years.

Rough-and-Tumble Play A form of play that is characterized by play fighting, including hitting and wrestling, and chasing with the intent of fighting.

Schemes The consistent action patterns found in infancy that Jean Piaget viewed as the sensorimotor equivalents of concepts.

Secondary Circular Reaction A type of sensorimotor play that appears after the age of 4 months and involves infants' repetition of behaviors that bring about pleasing effects on their surrounding world.

Sensorimotor Play Also referred to as practice play, the sensorimotor play of the infant involves the repetition of already assimilated sensory or motor activities for the sheer pleasure of repeating them.

Sociodramatic Play A form of pretend play that involves intense group interaction, with each group member taking a role that complements the roles played by all others in the group.

Solitary Play A form of play in which the child is completely involved in an activity and is physically and/or psychologically isolated from other children.

Strange Situation An instrument developed by psychologist Mary Ainsworth to determine the degree of attachment between parent and child.

Surplus Energy Theory The belief of philosopher Herbert Spencer that the function of play is to allow children to discharge pent-up energy.

Symbolic Play Make-believe, or pretend, play that first appears at the beginning of the infant's second year of life and continues as the dominant form of play throughout the preschool years.

Tabula Rasa A blank slate, the term often used to refer to theories of human development that described human beings as empty organisms at birth who develop under the influence of the environment.

Tertiary Circular Reaction A characteristic sensorimotor activity in the second year of life, the infant's repetition of behaviors that bring about pleasing effects on the surrounding world but are now accompanied by an attempt to vary the activity instead of repeating it precisely.

Theory of Mind The ability to impute mental states to oneself and other people and to understand that there is sometimes a difference between one's feelings, thoughts, and beliefs about reality and actual reality itself.

Therapeutic Play Programs Hospital play programs based on the assumption that children cope better with a hospital stay if they can release their feelings freely.

Transference A necessary condition of psychoanalysis: A patient must be open to the possibility of thinking of the therapist as a substitute for someone of great significance in his or her life.

Vigorous Activity Play A form of solitary or social play that is characterized by intense physical activity but does not contain elements of aggression.

Zone of Proximal Development According to Lev Vygotsky, the distance between a child's actual performance when working alone and his or her potential ability in a different social context.

References

Ainsworth, M. (1991). Attachments and other affectional bonds across the life cycle. In C. Parkes, J. Stevenson-Hinde, & P. Marris (Eds.), *Attachment across the life cycle* (pp. 33–51). London and New York: Routledge.

Ainsworth, M. D. S. (1979). Attachment as related to mother-infant interaction. In J. S. Rosenblatt, R. A. Hinde, C. Beer, & M. Busnell (Eds.), *Advances in the study of behavior* (Vol. 9). New York: Academic Press.

Ainsworth, M. D. S., Blehar, M. C., Waters, E., & Wall, S. (1978). *Patterns of attachment: A psychological study of the Strange Situation.* Hillsdale, NJ: Erlbaum.

Allesandri, S. M. (1991). Play and social behavior in maltreated preschoolers. *Development and Psychopathology, 3,* 191–205.

American Academy of Pediatrics (2006). *Pediatrics, 118*(4), 1757–1763.

American Art Therapy Association (n.d.). *About art therapy.* Retrieved November 22, 2008, from http://www.arttherapy.org/aboutart.htm

American Psychiatric Association (2000). *Diagnostic and statistical manual of mental disorders* (4th ed., text rev.). Washington, DC: Author.

Anderson, C. A. (2004). An update on the effects of playing violent video games. *Journal of Adolescence, 27,* 113–122.

Anderson, C. A., & Bushman, B. J. (2001). Effects of violent video games on aggressive behavior, aggressive cognition, aggressive affect, physiological arousal, and prosocial behavior: A meta-analytic review of the scientific literature. *Psychological Science, 12,* 353–359.

Androutsopoulou, A. (2001). Fiction as an aid to therapy: A narrative and family rationale for practice. *Journal of Family Therapy, 23,* 278–295.

Anshel, M. H., Muller, D., & Owens, V. L. (1986). Effect of a sports camp experience on the multidimensional self-concepts of boys. *Perceptual and Motor Skills, 63,* 363–366.

Aries, P. (1962). *Centuries of childhood: A social history of family life.* New York: Knopf.

Athey, I. (1984). Contributions of play to development. In T. D. Yawkey & A. D. Pellegrini (Eds.), *Child's play: Developmental and applied* (pp. 9–28). Hillsdale, NJ: Erlbaum.

August, R. L., & Forman, B. D. (1989). A comparison of sexually abused and nonsexually abused children's responses to anatomically correct dolls. *Child Psychiatry and Human Development, 20,* 39–47.

Axline, V. (1946). *Dibs: In search of self.* New York: Ballantine Books.

Axline, V. (1950). Emotions and how they grow. *Childhood Education, 27,* 104–108.

Axline, V. (1969). *Play therapy* (rev. ed.). New York: Ballantine Books.

Axline, V. M. (1947). *Play therapy.* Boston: Houghton Mifflin.

Bailey, D., & Wolery, M. (1984). *Teaching infants and preschoolers with handicaps.* Columbus, OH: Merrill.

Baird, G., Charman, T., Cox, A., Baron-Cohen, S., Swettenham, J., Wheelwright, S., et al. (2001). Screening and surveillance for autism and pervasive developmental disorders. *Archives of Diseases in Childhood, 84,* 468–475.

Bakermans-Kranenburg, M. J., van Ijzendoorn, M. H., & Juffer, F. (2003). Less is more: Meta-analyses of sensitivity and attachment interventions in early childhood. *Psychological Bulletin, 129,* 195–215.

Bandura, A. (1977). *Social learning theory.* Englewood Cliffs, NJ: Prentice-Hall.

Barbour, A. (1999). The impact of playground design on the play behaviours of children with differing levels of physical competence. *Early Childhood Research Quarterly, 14*(1), 75–98.

Baron-Cohen, S. (1987). Autism and symbolic play. *British Journal of Developmental Psychology, 5,* 139–148.

Baron-Cohen, S., Leslie, A. M., & Frith, U. (1985). Does the autistic child have a "theory of mind"? *Cognition, 21,* 37–46.

Baron-Cohen, S., & Swettenham, J. (1997). Theory of mind in autism: Its relationship to executive function and central coherence. In D. Cohen & F. Volkmar (Eds.), *Handbook of autism and pervasive developmental disorders* (2nd ed., pp. 880–893). New York: Wiley.

Barr, R., & Hayne, H. (2003). It's not what you know, it's who you know: Older siblings facilitate imitation during infancy. *International Journal of Early Years Education, 11,* 7–21.

Barrett, D., & Radke-Yarrow, M. (1985). Effects of nutritional supplementation on children's responses to novel, frustrating, and competitive situations. *American Journal of Clinical Nutrition, 42,* 102–120.

Barron, F., & Harrington, D. M. (1981). Creativity, intelligence, and personality. *Annual Review of Psychology, 32,* 439–476.

Bayley, N. (2005). *The Bayley Scales of Infant Development.* New York: Psychological Corporation.

Beal, C. R. (1994). *Boys and girls: The development of gender roles.* New York: McGraw-Hill.

Beckwith, L. (1986). Parent-infant interaction and infants' social-emotional development. In A. W. Gottfried & C. C. Brown (Eds.), *Play interactions: The contributions of play materials and parental involvement to children's development* (pp. 279–292). Lexington, MA: Heath.

Beckwith, L., Rodning, C., Norris, D., Phillipsen, L., Khandari, P., & Howard, J. (1994). Spontaneous play in two-year-olds born to substance-abusing mothers. *Infant Mental Health Journal, 15,* 189–201.

Beh-Pajooh, A. (1991). Social interactions among severely handicapped children, non-handicapped children, and their mothers in an integrated playgroup. *Early Child Development and Care, 74,* 83–94.

Bekoff, M. (1972). The development of social interaction, play, and metacommunication in mammals: An ethological perspective. *Quarterly Review of Biology, 47,* 412–434.

Bekoff, M., & Allen, A. (1998). Intentional communication and social play: How and why animals negotiate and agree to play. In M. Bekoff & J. A. Byers (Eds.), *Animal play: Evolutionary, comparative and ecological perspectives* (pp. 97–114). Cambridge, England: Cambridge University Press.

Belsky, J. (2001). Emanuel Miller lecture: Developmental risks (still) associated with early child care. *Journal of Child Psychology and Psychiatry, 42*(7), 845–859.

Belsky, J., Garduque, L., & Hrncir, E. (1984). Assessing performance, competence, and executive capacity in infant play: Relations to home environment and the security of attachment. *Developmental Psychology, 20,* 406–417.

Belsky, J., & Steinberg, L. D. (1978). The effects of day care: A critical review. *Child Development, 49,* 929–949.

Benbow, C. P. (1986). *Home environments and toy preferences of extremely precocious students.* Paper presented at the annual meeting of the American Educational Research Association, San Francisco.

Bensoussan, S., Batchie, M., Catania, P., Del Vasto, R., Marchese, S., & Derevensky, J. (1992, June). *Game preferences in children: A contemporary analysis.* Paper presented at the annual meeting of the Canadian Psychological Association, Quebec City.

Berenbaum, S. A., & Hines, M. (1992). Early androgens are related to childhood sex-typed toy preferences. *Psychological Science, 3,* 203–206.

Berk, L. E. (1989). *Child development.* Boston: Allyn and Bacon.

Berlyne, D. E. (1969). Laughter, humor, and play. In G. Lindzey & E. Aronson (Eds.), *Handbook of social psychology* (Vol. 3). Reading, MA: Addison-Wesley.

Berndt, T. J. (1982). The features and effects of friendship in early adolescence. *Child Development, 53,* 1447–1460.

Bianchi, B. D., & Bakeman, R. (1978). Sex-typed affiliation preferences expressed in preschoolers: Traditional and open school differences. *Child Development, 49,* 910–912.

Bigelow, A. E., MacLean, K., & Proctor, J. (2004). The role of joint attention in the development of infants' play with objects. *Developmental Science, 7*(5), 518–526.

Bigham, S. (2008). Comprehension of pretence in children with autism. *British Journal of Developmental Psychology, 26*(2), 265–280.

Bigham, S., & Bourchier-Sutton, A. (2007). The decontextualization of form and function in the development of pretence. *British Journal of Developmental Psychology, 25*(3), 335–351.

Birney, D. P., Citron-Pousty, J. H., Lutz, D. J., & Sternberg, R. J. (2005). The development of cognitive and intellectual abilities. In M. E. Lamb & M. H. Bornstein (Eds.), *Developmental science: An advanced textbook* (5th ed., pp. 327–358). Mahwah, NJ: Lawrence Erlbaum Associates.

Bishop, S. L., & Lord, C. (2006). Autism spectrum disorders. In J. L. Luby (Ed.), *Handbook of preschool mental health: Development disorders, and treatment* (pp. 252–282). New York: Guilford.

Bjorklund, D. F., & Ellis, B. J. (2004). Evolutionary psychology and child development: An emerging synthesis. In B. J. Ellis & D. F. Bjorklund (Eds.). *Origins of the social mind: Evolutionary psychology and child development* (pp. 3–18). New York: Guilford.

Blatchford, P., Baines, E., & Pellegrini, A. D. (2003). The social context of school playground games: Sex and ethnic differences and changes over time after entry into junior school. *British Journal of Developmental Psychology, 21,* 459–471.

Blehar, M. C., Lieberman, A. F., & Ainsworth, M. D. S. (1977). Early face-to-face interaction and its relation to later mother-infant attachment. *Child Development, 48,* 182–194.

Blurton-Jones, N. G. (1967). An ethological study of some aspects of social behavior of children in nursery school. In D. Morris (Ed.), *Primate ethology.* London: Weidenfeld and Nicholson.

Blurton-Jones, N. G., & Konner, M. J. (1973). Sex differences in behavior of London and Bushman children. In R. P. Michael & J. H. Crook (Eds.), *Comparative ethology and behavior of primates.* New York: Academic Press.

Bock, J. (2002). Learning, life history, and productivity: Children's lives in the Okavango Delta of Botswana. *Human Nature, 13,* 161–198.

Bock, J., & Johnson, S. E. (2004). Subsistence ecology and play among the Okavango Delta peoples of Botswana. *Human Nature, 15,* 63–81.

Bodrova, E., & Leong, D. J. (1996). *Tools of the mind: The Vygotskian approach to early childhood education.* Englewood Cliffs, NJ: Prentice-Hall.

Bolig, R. (1984). Play in hospital settings. In T. D. Yawkey & A. D. Pellegrini (Eds.), *Child's play: Developmental and applied* (pp. 323–346). Hillsdale, NJ: Erlbaum.

Bonta, B. D. (1996). Conflict resolution among peaceful societies: The culture of peacefulness. *Journal of Peace Research, 33*(4), 403–420.

Borge, A. I. H., Rutter, M., Côté, S., & Tremblay, R. E. (2004). Early childcare and physical aggression: Differentiating social selection and social causation. *Journal of Child Psychology & Psychiatry, 45*(2), 367–376.

Borgh, K., & Dickson, W. P. (1986). Two preschoolers sharing one computer: Creating prosocial behavior with hardware and software. In P. F. Campbell & G. G. Fein (Eds.), *Young children and microcomputers* (pp. 37–44). Englewood Cliffs, NJ: Prentice-Hall.

Borstelmann, L. J. (1983). Children before psychology. In P. H. Mussen (Ed.), *Handbook of child psychology.* New York: Wiley.

Bourgeois, K. S., Khawar, A. W., Neal, A. S., & Lockman, J. J. (2005). Infant manual exploration of objects, surfaces, and their interrelations. *Infancy, 8,* 233–252.

Bowden, V. R., & Greenberg, C. S. (2008). *Pediatric nursing procedures.* Philadelphia: Lippincott, Williams, & Wilkins.

Bowker, A. (2004). Predicting friendship stability during early adolescence. *Journal of Early Adolescence, 24,* 85–112.

Bowlby, J. (1988). *A secure base: Clinical applications of attachment theory.* London: Routledge.

Bowles, C. L. (1998). Music activity preferences of elementary students. *Journal of Research in Music Education, 46*(2), 193–207.

Boyatzis, C. J. (1987). The effects of traditional playground equipment on preschool children's dyadic play interaction. In G. A. Fine (Ed.), *Meaningful play, playful meaning* (pp. 101–109). Champaign, IL: Human Kinetics Publishers.

Boyatzis, C. J., & Watson, M. W. (1993, March). *Levels of reality and correlates of toddlers' and preschoolers' fantasy play.* Paper presented at the Biennial Meeting of the Society for Research in Child Development, New Orleans, LA.

Boyd, M. P., & Yin, Z. (1996). Cognitive-affective sources of sport enjoyment in adolescent sports participants. *Adolescence, 31,* 383–396.

Bradley, C. B., McMurray, R. G., Harrell, J. S., & Deng, S. (2000). Changes in common activities of 3rd through 10th graders: The CHIC study. *Medicine & Science in Sports & Exercise, 32,* 2071–2078.

Bradley, K., & Szegda, M. (2006). The dance of learning. In B. Spodek & O. N. Saracho (Eds.), *Handbook of research on the education of young children* (2nd ed., pp. 243–250). Mahwah, NJ: Lawrence Erlbaum Associates.

Brassard, M. R., & Boehm, A. E. (2007). *Preschool assessment: Principles and practices.* New York: Guilford.

Bratton, S. C., Ray, D., Rhine, T., & Jones, L. (2005). The efficacy of play therapy with children: A meta-analytic review of treatment outcomes. *Professional Psychology: Research and Practice, 36,* 376–390.

Bredekamp, S. (1987). *Developmentally appropriate practice in early childhood programs serving children from birth through age 8: Expanded edition.* Washington, DC: National Association for the Education of Young Children.

Bredekamp, S. (1993). Myths about developmentally appropriate practice: A response to Fowell and Lawton. *Early Childhood Research Quarterly, 8,* 117–119.

Bredemeier, B., & Shields, D. (1986). Moral growth among athletes and non-athletes: A comparative analysis of males and females. *Journal of Genetic Psychology, 147,* 7–18.

Bredemeier, B. J., & Shields, D. L. (1985, October). Values and violence in sports today: The moral reasoning athletes use in their games and in their lives. *Psychology Today, 19,* 23–31.

Bredemeier, B. J., Shields, D. L., Weiss, M. R., & Cooper, B. A. B. (1986). The relationship of sport involvement with children's moral reasoning and aggression tendencies. *Journal of Sport Psychology, 8,* 304–318.

Brems, C. (1993). *A comprehensive guide to child psychotherapy.* Boston: Allyn and Bacon.

Brenner, J., & Mueller, E. (1982). Shared meaning in boy toddlers' peer relations. *Child Development, 53,* 380–381.

Bretherton, I. (1984). Representing the Social World in Symbolic Play: Reality and Fantasy. In I. Bretherton (Ed.), *Symbolic Play: The Development of Social Understanding* (pp. 3–41), New York: Academic Press.

Bretherton, I. (1986). Representing the social world in symbolic play: Reality and fantasy. In A. W. Gottfried & C. C. Brown (Eds.), *Play interactions: The contributions of play materials and parental involvement to children's development* (pp. 119–148). Lexington, MA: Heath.

Bretherton, I., & Waters, E. (Eds.) (1985). Growing points of attachment theory and research. *Monographs of the Society for Research in Child Development, 50* (1 & 2, Serial No. 209).

Brindley, C., Clarke, C., Hutt, P., Robinson, I., & Wehtli, E. (1973). Sex differences in the activities and social interactions of nursery school children. In R. P. Michael & J. H. Crook (Eds.), *Comparative ethology and behavior of primates.* New York: Academic Press.

Brinton, B., & Fujiki, M. (2004) Social and affective factors in children with language impairment. In C. Stone, E. Silliman, B. Ehren, & K. Apel (Eds.), *Handbook of language and literacy development and disorders* (pp. 130–153). New York: Guilford.

Brody, G. H., Graziano, W. G., & Musser, L. M. (1983). Familiarity and children's behavior in same-age and mixed-age peer groups. *Developmental Psychology, 19,* 568–576.

Brody, G. H., & Stoneman, Z. (1981). Selective imitation of same-age, older, and younger peer models. *Child Development, 52,* 717–720.

Brooks, R., & Meltzoff, A. N. (2002). The importance of eyes: How infants interpret adult looking behavior. *Child Development, 38,* 958–966.

Brown, S. (1998). Play as an organizing principle: Clinical evidence and personal observations. In M. Bekoff & J. A. Byers (Eds.), *Animal play: Evolutionary, comparative and ecological perspectives* (pp. 243–259). Cambridge, England: Cambridge University Press.

Brownell, C. A. (1986). Convergent developments: Cognitive-developmental correlates of growth in infant/toddler peer skills. *Child Development, 57,* 275–286.

Brownell, C. A., & Kopp, C. B. (2007). Transitions in toddler socioemotional development. In C. A. Brownell & C. B. Kopp (Eds.), *Socioemotional development in the toddler years: Transitions and transformations* (pp. 1–42). New York: Guilford.

Brownell, C. A., Ramani, G. B., & Zerwas, S. (2006). Becoming a social partner with peers: Cooperation and social understanding in one- and two-year-olds. *Child Development, 77*(4), 803–821.

Bruck, M., Ceci, S. J., & Francoeur, E. (2000). Children's use of anatomically detailed dolls to report genital touching in a medical examination: Developmental and gender comparisons. *Journal of Experimental Psychology: Applied, 6,* 74–83.

Bruner, J. S. (1972). The nature and uses of immaturity. *American Psychologist, 27,* 687–708.

Bruner, J. S. (1973). Going beyond the information given. In J. M. Anglin (Ed.), *Beyond the information given* (pp. 218–240). New York: Norton.

Bruner, J. S. (1974). The growth of representational processes in children. In J. M. Anglin (Ed.), *Beyond the information given* (pp. 313–324). New York: Norton.

Bruner, J. S. (1983). *Child's talk.* New York: Norton.

Burg, K. (1984, March). The microcomputer in the kindergarten. *Young Children, 39*(3), 28–33.

Burghardt, G. M. (2005). *The genesis of animal play.* Cambridge, MA: MIT Press.

Burnham, D. K., & Harris, M. B. (1992). Effects of real gender and labeled gender on adults' perceptions of infants. *Journal of Genetic Psychology, 153*(2), 165–183.

Burns, S. M., & Brainerd, C. J. (1979). Effects of constructive and dramatic play on perspective-taking in very young children. *Developmental Psychology, 15,* 512–521.

Bussey, K., & Bandura, A. (1999). Social cognitive theory of gender development and differentiation. *Psychological Review, 106,* 676–713.

Buysse, V., Goldman, B. D., & Skinner, M. L. (2002). Setting effects on friendship formation among young children with and without disabilities. *Exceptional Children, 68*(4), 503–518.

Caf, B., Kroflic, B., & Tancig, S. (1997). Activation of hypoactive children with creative movement and dance in primary school. *The Arts in Psychotherapy, 24,* 355–365.

Caldera, Y. M., Huston, A. C., & O'Brien, M. (1989). Social interactions and play patterns of parents and toddlers with feminine, masculine, and neutral toys. *Child Development, 60,* 70–76.

Callanan, M., & Sabbagh, M. (2004). Multiple labels for objects in conversations with young children: Parents' language and children's developing expectations about word meanings. *Developmental Psychology, 40,* 746–763.

Cameron, E., Eisenberg, N., & Tryon, K. (1985). The relations between sex-typed play and preschoolers' social behavior. *Sex Roles, 12,* 601–615.

Campbell, A., Shirley, L., & Caygill, L. (2002). Sex-typed preferences in three domains: Do two-year-olds need cognitive variables? *British Journal of Psychology, 93,* 203–217.

Campbell, A., Shirley, L., Heywood, C., & Crook, C. (2000). Infants' visual preference for sex-congruent babies, children, toys and activities: A longitudinal study. *British Journal of Developmental Psychology, 18,* 479–498.

Carpenter, M., Call, J., & Tomasello, M. (2005). Twelve- and 18-month-olds copy actions in terms of goals. *Developmental Science, 8,* 13–20.

Carson, J., Burks, V., & Parke, R. D. (1993). Parent-child physical play: Determinants and consequences. In K. MacDonald (Ed.), *Parent-child play: Descriptions and implications* (pp. 197–220). Albany: State University of New York Press.

Casey, B., Bobb, B., Sarama, J., & Clements, D. (2003). The power of block building. *Teaching Children Mathematics, 10*(2), 98–102.

Casey, B. M., Andrews, N., Schindler, H., Kersh, J. E., Samper, A., & Copley, J. (2008). The development of spatial skills through interventions involving block building activities. *Cognition & Instruction, 26*(3), 269–309.

Celeste, M. (2006). Play behaviors and social interactions of a child who is blind: In theory and practice. *Journal of Visual Impairment & Blindness, 100*(2), 75–90.

Celeste, M. (2007). Social skills intervention for a child who is blind. *Journal of Visual Impairment & Blindness, 101*(9), 521–533.

Chalmers, N. (1984). Social play in monkeys: Theories and data. In P. K. Smith (Ed.), *Play in animals and humans* (pp. 119–146). Oxford, England: Basil Blackwell.

Chalmers, N., & Locke-Hayden, J. (1985). Correlations among measures of playfulness and skillfulness in captive common marmosets (*Callithrix jacchus jacchus*). *Developmental Psychobiology, 17,* 191–208.

Chance, P. (1979). *Learning through play.* Piscataway, NJ: Johnson & Johnson.

Chandler, D., & Griffiths, M. (2000). Gender-differentiated production features in toy commercials. *Journal of Broadcasting & Electronic Media, 44*(3), 503.

Chavez, A., & Martinez, C. (1984). Behavioral measurements of activity in children and their relation to food intake in a poor community. In E. Pollitt & P. Amante (Eds.), *Energy intake and activity.* New York: Liss.

Chen, X., & Kaspar, V. (2004). Cross-cultural research on childhood. In U. Gielen & J. Roopnarine (Eds.), *Childhood and adolescence: Cross-cultural perspectives and applications* (pp. 46–80). Westport, CT: Praeger.

Chera, P., & Wood, C. (2003). Animated multimedia "talking books" can promote phonological awareness in children beginning to read. *Learning and Instruction, 13,* 33–52.

Cherney, I., & London, K. (2006). Gender-linked differences in the toys, television shows, computer games, and outdoor activities of 5- to 13-year-old children. *Sex Roles, 54*(9/10), 717–726.

Children's Defense Fund (1990). *S.O.S. America! A children's defense budget.* Washington, DC: Author.

Church, E. B. (2006). Experiment with water and ice. *Early Childhood Today, 20*(4), 4.

Clarke-Stewart, A. (1984). Day care: A new context for research and development. In M. Perlmutter (Ed.), *The Minnesota Symposia on Child Psychology: Vol. 17* (pp. 61–100). Hillsdale, NJ: Erlbaum.

Clarke-Stewart, K., & Allhusen, V. D. (2002). Nonparental caregiving. In M. H. Bornstein (Ed.), *Handbook of parenting: Vol. 3. Being and becoming a parent* (2nd ed., pp. 215–252). Mahwah, NJ: Lawrence Erlbaum Associates.

Clearfield, M. W., & Nelson, N. M. (2006). Sex differences in mothers' speech and play behavior with 6-, 9-, and 14-month-old infants. *Sex Roles, 54*(1/2), 127–137.

Clements, D. H., & Sarama, J. (2002). The role of technology in early childhood learning. *Teaching Children Mathematics, 8*(6), 340.

Coakley, J. (2002). Using sports to control deviance and violence among youths: Let's be critical and cautious. In M. Gatz, M. Messner, & S. Ball-Rokeach (Eds.), *Paradoxes of youth and sport* (pp. 13–30). Albany: State University of New York Press.

Coats, P. B., & Overman, S. J. (1992). Childhood play experiences of women in traditional and nontraditional professions. *Sex Roles, 26,* 261–271.

Cohen, L. J. (1994). Bibliotherapy: A valid treatment modality. *Journal of Psychosocial Nursing and Mental Health Services, 32*(9), 40–44.

Cohn, D. (1991). Anatomical doll play of preschoolers referred for sexual abuse and those not referred. *Child Abuse and Neglect, 15,* 455–466.

Cole, H., & Griffiths, M. D. (2007). Social interactions in massively multiplayer online role-playing gamers. *CyberPsychology & Behavior, 10*(4), 575–583.

Cole, M. (2005). Culture in development. In M. H. Bornstein & M. E. Lamb (Eds.), *Developmental psychology: An advanced textbook.* (5th ed., pp. 73–123). Mahwah, NJ: Lawrence Erlbaum Associates.

Colle, L., Baron-Cohen, S., & Hill, J. (2007). Do children with autism have a theory of mind? A non-verbal test of autism vs. specific language impairment. *Journal of Autism & Developmental Disorders, 37*(4), 716–723.

Colwell, M., & Lindsey, E. (2005). Preschool children's pretend and physical play and sex of play partner: Connections to peer competence. *Sex Roles, 52*(7/8), 497–509.

Connolly, J., Doyle, A., & Ceschin, E. (1983). Forms and functions of social fantasy play in preschoolers. In M. B. Liss (Ed.), *Social and cognitive skills: Sex roles and children's play* (pp. 71–92). New York: Academic Press.

Connolly, J. A. (1980). *The relationship between social pretend play and social competence in preschoolers: Correlational and experimental studies.* Unpublished doctoral dissertation, Concordia University, Montreal, Quebec, Canada.

Connor, J. M., & Serbin, L. A. (1977). Behaviorally based masculine and feminine activity—reference scales for preschoolers: Correlates with other classroom behaviors and cognitive tests. *Child Development, 48,* 1411–1416.

Cook, G. (2000). *Language play, language learning.* London: Oxford University Press.

Cordes, C., & Miller, E. (Eds.). (2000). Fool's gold: A critical look at computers in childhood. Available from the Alliance for Childhood Web site: http://www.alliance forchildhood.net/projects/computers/computers_reports.htm

Crawford, R., Brown, B., & Crawford, P. (2004). *Storytelling in therapy.* Cheltenham, England: Nelson Thornes.

Creasey, G., & Jarvis, P. (2003). Play in children: An attachment perspective. In O. N. Saracho & B. Spodek (Eds.), *Contemporary perspectives on play in early childhood education* (pp. 133–151). Greenwich, CT: Information Age Publishing.

Creasey, G., & Jarvis, P. (2007). Attachment in the preschool years: Implications for social learning. In O. N. Saracho & B. Spodek (Eds.), *Contemporary perspectives on social development and socialization in early childhood education* (pp. 39–58). Greenwich, CT: Information Age Publishing.

Creasey, G. L., Jarvis, P. A., & Berk, L. E. (1998). Play and social competence. In O. N. Saracho & B. Spodek (Eds.), *Multiple perspectives on play in early childhood education* (pp. 116–143). Albany: State University of New York Press.

Creasey, G. L., & Myers, B. J. (1986). Video games and children: Effects on leisure activities, schoolwork, and peer involvement. *Merrill-Palmer Quarterly, 32,* 251–262.

Crombie, G., & Desjardins, M. J. (1993, March). *Predictors of gender: The relative importance of children's play, games, and personality characteristics.* Paper presented at the Biennial Meeting of the Society for Research in Child Development, New Orleans, LA.

Cropley, A. (2006). In praise of convergent thinking. *Creativity Research Journal, 18*(3), 391–404.

Csikzentmihalyi, M., & Larson, R. (1984). *Being an adolescent.* New York: Basic Books.

Custer, W. L. (1996). A comparison of young children's understanding of contradictory representation in pretense, memory, and belief. *Child Development, 67,* 678–688.

Custer, W. L. (1997, April). Young children's use of mental state awareness and voice intonation as cues to pretense. In J. Wooley & A. Lillard (symposium chairs), *A synthesis of current findings on young children's understanding of pretense.* Symposium presented at the Biennial Meeting of the Society for Research in Child Development, Washington, DC.

Cutter, J. (2007). *Independent movement and travel in blind children: A promotion model.* Charlotte, NC: Information Age Publishing.

Damast, A. M., Tamis-LeMonda, C. S., & Bornstein, M. H. (1993, March). *Timing and content in maternal play suggestions during mother–toddler interactions.* Paper presented at the Biennial Meeting of the

Society for Research in Child Development, New Orleans, LA.

Damon, W. (1983). *Social and personality development*. New York: Norton.

Dansky, J. L. (1980). Make-believe: A mediator of the relationship between play and associative fluency. *Child Development, 51*, 576–579.

Dansky, J. L., & Silverman, I. W. (1975). Play: A general facilitator of associative fluency. *Developmental Psychology, 11*, 104.

Darwish, D., Esquivel, G. B., Houtz, J. C., & Alfonso, V. C. (2001). Play and social skills in maltreated and non-maltreated preschoolers during peer interactions. *Child Abuse and Neglect, 25*, 13–31.

Davis, D. L., Wooley, J. D., & Bruell, M. J. (2002). Young children's understanding of the roles of knowledge and thinking in pretense. *British Journal of Developmental Psychology, 20*, 25–45.

Davis, G. (1976). *Childhood and history in America*. New York: Psychohistory Press.

DeLoache, J. S. (1995). Early understanding and use of symbols: The model model. *Current Directions in Psychological Science, 4*, 109–113.

Denac, O. A. (2008). Case study of preschool children's musical interests at home and at school. *Early Childhood Education Journal, 35*(5), 439–444.

DePietro, J. A. (1981). Rough-and-tumble play: A function of gender. *Developmental Psychology, 17*, 50–58.

DeZutter, S. (2007). Play as group improvisation: A social semiotic, multimodal perspective on play and literacy (pp. 217–242). In O. N. Saracho & B. Spodek (Eds.), *Contemporary perspectives on social learning in early childhood education*. Charlotte, NC: Information Age Publishing.

Diamond, K. E., & Hestenes, L. L. (1994). Preschool children's conceptions of disabilities: The salience of disability in children's ideas about others. *Topics in Early Childhood Special Education, 16*(4), 458–475.

Diaz, R. M., & Berndt, T. J. (1982). Children's knowledge of a best friend: Fact or fancy? *Developmental Psychology, 18*, 787–794.

Din, F., & Calao, J. (2001). The effects of playing educational video games on kindergarten achievement. *Child Study Journal, 31*(2), 95–102.

Doyle, A., Ceschin, F., Tessier, O., & Doehring, P. (1991). The relation of age and social class factors in children's social pretend play to cognitive and symbolic ability. *International Journal of Behavioral Development, 14*, 395–410.

Doyle, A. B., Connolly, J., & Rivest, L. P. (1980). The effect of playmate familiarity on the social interactions of young children. *Child Development, 51*, 217–223.

Driscoll, C., & Carter, M. (2004). Spatial density as a setting event for the social interaction of preschool children. *International Journal of Disability, Development and Education, 51*(1), 7–37.

Duda, J. L. (2007). Motivation in sports settings: A goal-perspective approach. In D. Smith & M. Bar-Eli (Eds.), *Essential readings in sport and exercise psychology* (pp. 78–93). Champaign, IL: Human Kinetics Publishers.

Duda, J. L., & Nicholls, J. (1992). Dimensions of achievement motivation in schoolwork and sport. *Journal of Educational Psychology, 84*, 290–299.

Duda, J. L., & Ntoumanis, N. (2005). After-school sport for children: Implications of a task-involving motivational climate. In J. L. Mahoney, R. W. Larson, & J. S. Eccles (Eds.), *Organized activities as contexts of development: Extracurricular activities, after-school and community programs* (pp. 311–330). Mahwah, NJ: Lawrence Erlbaum Associates.

Duda, J. L., & White, S. A. (1992). The relationship of goal orientations to beliefs about success among elite skiers. *The Sport Psychologist, 6*, 334–343.

Dudley, S. K., & Carr, J. M. (2004). Vigilance: The experience of parents staying at the bedside of hospitalized children. *Journal of Pediatric Nursing, 19*(4), 267–275.

Duffy, B. (1998). *Supporting imagination and creativity in the early years*. Buckingham, England: Open University Press.

Dunn, J. (1983). Sibling relationships in early childhood. *Child Development, 54*, 787–811.

Dunn, J., Cutting, A. L., & Fisher, N. (2002). Old friends, new friends: Predictors of children's perspective on their friends at school. *Child Development. 73*(2), 621–635.

Dunphy-Lelii, S., & Wellman, H. (2004). Infants' understanding of occlusion of others' line of sight: Implications for an emerging theory of mind. *European Journal of Developmental Psychology, 1*, 49–66.

Dyer, S., & Moneta, G. B. (2006). Frequency of parallel, associative, and cooperative play in British children of different socioeconomic status. *Social Behavior & Personality: An International Journal, 34*(5), 587–592.

Edwards, C. P., & Whiting, B. B. (1993). "Mother, older sibling, and me": The overlapping roles of caregivers and companions in the social world of two- to three-year-olds in Ngeca, Kenya. In K. MacDonald (Ed.), *Parent–child play: Descriptions and implications* (pp. 305–329). Albany: State University of New York Press.

Ehrhardt, A. A., & Baker, S. W. (1974). Fetal androgens, human central nervous system differentiation, and behavioral sex differences. In R. C. Friedman, R. M. Richart, & R. L. Vande Wiele (Eds.), *Sex differences in behavior* (pp. 33–51). New York: Wiley.

Ehrhardt, A. A., & Meyer-Bahlburg, H. F. L. (1981). Effects of prenatal sex hormones on gender-related behavior. *Science, 211*, 1312–1318.

Einon, D., & Potegal, M. (1991). Enhanced defense in adult rats deprived of playfighting experience as juveniles. *Aggressive Behavior, 17*, 27–46.

Eisenberg, N. (1983). Sex-typed toy choices: What do they signify? In M. B. Liss (Ed.), *Social and cognitive skills: Sex roles and children's play* (pp. 45–70). New York: Academic Press.

Eisenberg, N., Boothby, R., & Matson, T. (1979). Correlates of preschool girls' feminine and masculine toy preferences. *Developmental Psychology, 15*, 354–355.

Eisenberg, N., Murray, E., & Hite, T. (1982). Children's reasoning regarding sex-typed toy choices. *Child Development, 53*, 81–86.

Eisenberg, N., Tryon, K., & Cameron, E. (1984). The relation of preschoolers' peer interaction to their sex-typed toy choices. *Child Development, 55*, 45–70.

Eisenberg, N., Wolchik, S. A., Hernandez, R., & Pasternack, J. F. (1985). Parental socialization of young children's play. *Child Development, 56*, 1506–1513.

Elias, C. L., & Berk, L. E. (2002). Self-regulation in young children: Is there a role for sociodramatic play? *Early Childhood Research Quarterly 17*(2), 216–238.

Elkind, D. (1981). *The hurried child: Growing up too fast too soon*. Reading, MA: Addison-Wesley.

Elkind, D. (1987). *Miseducation: Preschoolers at risk*. New York: Knopf.

Ellis, B. J., & Bjorklund, D. F. (2004). *Origins of the social mind: Evolutionary psychology and child development*. New York: Guilford.

Ellis, M. J. (1973). *Why people play*. Englewood Cliffs, NJ: Prentice-Hall.

Emery, R. (1999). *Marriage, divorce, and children's adjustment* (2nd ed.). Thousand Oaks, CA: Sage Publications.

Erikson, E. (1963). *Childhood and society* (2nd ed.). New York: Norton.

Erwin, E. J. (1993). Social participation of young children with visual impairments in specialized and integrated environments. *Journal of Visual Impairment and Blindness, 87*, 138–142.

Escalona, S. (1968). *The roots of individuality*. Chicago: Aldine.

Espinosa, M. P., Sigman, M. D., Neumann, C. G., Bwibo, N. O., & McDonald, M. A. (1992). Playground behaviors of school-age children in relation to nutrition, family characteristics, and schooling. *Developmental Psychology, 28*, 1188–1195.

Esposito, B. G., & Koorland, M. A. (1989). Play behavior of hearing impaired children: Integrated and segregated settings. *Exceptional Children, 55*, 412–419.

Etaugh, C. (1983). Introduction: The influence of environmental factors on sex differences in children's play. In M. B. Liss (Ed.), *Social and cognitive skills: Sex roles and children's play*. New York: Academic Press.

Everson, M. D., & Boat, B. W. (2002). The utility of anatomical dolls and drawing in child forensic interviews. In M. L. Eisen, J. A. Quas, & G. S. Goodman (Eds.), *Memory and suggestibility in the forensic interview* (pp. 383–408). Mahwah, NJ: Lawrence Erlbaum Associates.

Ewing, M. E., Gano-Overway, L. A., Branta, C. F., & Seefeldt, V. D. (2002). The role of sports in youth development. In M. Gatz, M. Messner, & S. Ball-Rokeach (Eds.), *Paradoxes of youth and sport* (pp. 31–48). Albany: State University of New York Press.

Fabes, R. A., Martin, C. L., & Hanish, L. D. (2003). Young children's play qualities in same-, other-, and mixed-sex peer groups. *Child Development, 74*, 921–932.

Fagen, R. M. (1984). Play and behavioural flexibility. In P. K. Smith (Ed.), *Play in animals and humans* (pp. 159–174). Oxford, England: Basil Blackwell.

Fagen, R. M. (1993). Primate juveniles and primate play. In M. E. Pereira & L. A. Fairbanks (Eds.), *Juvenile primates: Life history, development, and behavior* (pp. 182–196). New York: Oxford University Press.

Fagen, R. M. (1995). Animal play, games of angels, biology, and Brian. In A. D. Pellegrini (Ed.), *The future of play theory* (pp. 23–44).

Albany: State University of New York Press.

Fagen, R. M., & George, T. K. (1977). Play behavior and exercise in young ponies. *Behavioral Ecology and Sociobiology, 2*, 267–269.

Fagot, B. I. (1978). The influences of sex of child on parental reactions to toddler children. *Child Development, 49*, 459–465.

Fagot, B. I. (1984). The child's expectations of differences in adult male and female interactions. *Sex Roles, 11*, 593–600.

Fagot, B. I., Hagan, R., Leinsbach, M. D., & Kronsberg, S. (1985). Differential reactions to assertive and communicative acts of toddler boys and girls. *Child Development, 56*, 1499–1505.

Fagot, B. I., Hagan, R., Youngblade, L. M., & Potter, L. (1989). A comparison of the play behaviors of sexually abused, physically abused, and nonabused children. *Topics in Early Childhood Special Education, 9*, 88–100.

Faller, K. C. (2007). *Interviewing children about sexual abuse: Controversies and best practice*. New York: Oxford University Press.

Farver, J. (1999). Activity setting analysis: A model for examining the role of culture in development. In A. Goncu (Ed.), *Children's engagement in the world: Sociocultural perspectives* (pp. 99–127). Port Chester, NY: Cambridge University Press.

Farver, J. M. (1993). Cultural differences in scaffolding pretend play: A comparison of American and Mexican mother-child and sibling-child pairs. In K. MacDonald (Ed.), *Parent-child play: Descriptions and implications* (pp. 349–366). Albany: State University of New York Press.

Farver, J. M., & Howes, C. (1993). Cultural differences in American and Mexican mother-child pretend play. *Merrill-Palmer Quarterly, 39*, 344–358.

Farver, J. M., Kim, Y. K., & Lee, Y. (1995). Cultural differences in Korean- and Anglo-American preschoolers' social interaction and play behaviors. *Child Development, 66,* 1088–1099.

Farver, J. M., & Shin, Y. L. (1997). Social pretend play in Korean- and Anglo-American pre-schoolers. *Child Development, 68*(3), 544–556.

Farver, J. M., & Wimbarti, S. (1995). Indonesian children's play with their mothers and older siblings. *Child Development, 66,* 1493–1503.

Fazzi, D. L., & Klein, M. D. (2002). Cognitive focus: Developing cognition, concepts, and language. In R. L. Pogrund & D. L. Fazzi (Eds.), *Early focus: Working with young children who are blind or visually impaired and their families* (2nd ed., pp. 107–153). New York: AFB Press.

Fein, G. G. (1981). Pretend play: An integrative review. *Child Development, 52,* 1095–1118.

Fein, G. G., Campbell, P. F., & Schwartz, S. S. (1987). Microcomputers in the preschool: Effects on social participation and cognitive play. *Journal of Applied Developmental Psychology, 8,* 197–208.

Fein, G. G., & Fryer, M. G. (1995). Maternal contributions to early symbolic play competence. *Developmental Review, 15,* 367–381.

Fein, G. G., Johnson, D., Kosson, N., Stork, L., & Wasserman, L. (1975). Stereotypes and preferences in the toy choices of 20-month-old boys and girls. *Developmental Psychology, 11,* 527–528.

Feldman, J. (1997a, April). *Self-directed age-mixed interactions: How children explicitly and implicitly structure their activities.* Poster presented at the 68th Annual Meeting of the Eastern Psychological Association, Boston.

Feldman, J. (1997b, April). *The educational opportunities that lie in self-directed age-mixed play among children and adolescents.* Poster presented at the Biennial Meeting of the Society for Research in Child Development, Washington, DC.

Feldstein, J. H., & Feldstein, S. (1986). Sex differences on televised toy commercials. *Sex Roles, 8,* 581–587.

Fenson, L. (1986). The developmental progression of play. In A. W. Gottfried & C. C. Brown (Eds.), *Play interactions: The contribution of play materials and parental involvement to children's development* (pp. 53–66). Lexington, MA: Heath.

Fenson, L., Kagan, J., Kearsley, R. B., & Zelazo, P. R. (1976). The developmental progression of manipulative play in the first two years. *Child Development, 47,* 232–236.

Fenson, L., & Ramsay, D. S. (1980). Decentration and integration of play in the second year of life. *Child Development, 51,* 171–178.

Fewell, R., & Ogura, T. (1997). The relationship between play and communication skills in young children with Down syndrome. *Topics in Early Childhood Special Education, 17*(1), 103–119.

Fewell, R. R., Casal, S. G., Glick, M. E., Wheeden, C. A., & Spiker, D. (1996). Maternal education and maternal responsiveness as predictors of play competence in low birth weight, premature infants: A preliminary report. *Developmental and Behavioral Pediatrics, 17,* 100–104.

Fewell, R. R., Glick, M. P., & Spiker, D. (1994). *The relationship between play and expressive language in low birth weight toddlers.* Poster presented at the 9th International Conference on Infant Studies, Paris.

Fields, W. (1979). *Imaginative play of four-year-old children as a function of toy realism.* Unpublished master's thesis, Merrill-Palmer Institute, Detroit, MI.

File, N. (1994). Children's play, teacher-child interactions, and teachers' beliefs in integrated early childhood programs. *Early Childhood Research Quarterly, 9,* 223–240.

Fisher, S. (1995). The amusement arcade as a social space for adolescents: An empirical study. *Journal of Adolescence, 18,* 71–86.

Flavell, J. H. (1985). *Cognitive development* (2nd ed.). Englewood Cliffs, NJ: Prentice-Hall.

Fletcher-Flinn, C. M., & Gravatt, B. (1995). The efficacy of computer assisted instruction (CAI): A meta-analysis. *Journal of Educational and Computing Research, 12,* 219–242.

Fogel, A. (1979). Peer vs. mother-directed behavior in 1- to 3-month-old infants. *Infant Behavior and Development, 2,* 215–216.

Fonagy, P., Gergely, G., & Target, M. (2007). The parent–infant dyad and the construction of the subjective self. *Journal of Child Psychology & Psychiatry, 48*(3/4), 288–328.

Fonagy, P., & Target, M. (2005). Bridging the transmission gap: An end to an important mystery of attachment research? *Attachment & Human Development, 7*(3), 333–343.

Fontenelle, S. A., Kahrs, B. A., Neal, S. A., Newton, A. T., & Lockman, J. L. (2007). Infant manual exploration of composite substrates. *Journal of Experimental Child Psychology, 98*(3), 153–167.

Fraser-Thomas, J., & Côté, J. (2006, September). Youth sports: Implementing findings and moving forward with research. *Athletic Insight, 8*(3). Retrieved November 22, 2008, from http://www.athleticinsight.com/Vol8Iss3/YouthSports.htm

Fredricks, J. A., Simpkins, S., & Eccles, J. S. (2005). Family socialization, gender, and participation in sports. In C. R. Cooper, C. G. Coll, W. T. Barko, H. M. Davis, & C. Chatman (Eds.), *Developmental pathways through middle childhood: Rethinking contexts and diversity as resources* (pp. 41–62). Mahwah, NJ: Lawrence Erlbaum Associates.

Freeman, C. (1995). Planning and play: Creating greener environments. *Children's Environments, 12,* 381–388.

Freeman, N. (2007). Preschoolers' perceptions of gender appropriate toys and their parents' beliefs about genderized behaviors: Miscommunication, mixed messages, or hidden truths? *Early Childhood Education Journal, 34*(5), 357–366.

Freidemann, V., & Morgan, M. (1985). *Interviewing sexual abuse victims using anatomical dolls: The professional's guide book.* Eugene, OR: Migma Designs.

French, V. (1977). History of the child's influence: Ancient Mediterranean civilizations. In R. Q. Bell & L. V. Harper (Eds.), *Child effects on adults.* Hillsdale, NJ: Erlbaum.

Freud, A. (1968). *The psychoanalytical treatment of children.* New York: International Universities Press.

Freud, A. (1974). *The ego and the mechanisms of defense.* New York: International Universities Press.

Friedrich, W. N., Fisher, J. L., Dittner, C., Acton, R., Berliner, L., Butler, J., et al. (2001). Child Sexual Behavior Inventory: Normative, psychiatric, and sexual abuse comparisons. *Child Maltreatment, 6*(1), 37–50.

Friedrich, W. N., & Trane, S. T. (2002). Sexual behavior in children across multiple settings. *Child Abuse & Neglect, 26*(3), 243–246.

Frost, J., & Jacobs, R. J. (1995). Play deprivation: A factor in juvenile violence. *Dimensions of Early Childhood, 23*(3), 14–20.

Frost, J., Wortham, S., & Reifel, S. (2005). *Play and child development.* Upper Saddle River, NJ: Merrill, Prentice-Hall.

Frost, J. L., & Campbell, S. (1977). *Play and equipment choices of second-grade children on two types of playgrounds.* Unpublished manuscript, University of Texas–Austin.

Frost, J. L., & Klein, B. L. (1979). *Children's play and playgrounds.* Boston: Allyn and Bacon.

Gandelman, R. (1992). *Psychology of behavioral development.* New York: Oxford University Press.

Ganea, P. A., Lillard, A. S., & Turkheimer, E. (2004). Preschooler's understanding of the role of mental states and action in pretense. *Journal of Cognition & Development, 5*(2), 213–238.

Gardner, H. (1993). *Multiple intelligences: The theory in practice.* New York: Basic Books.

Gardner, H. (1999, July). *Multiple intelligences for the new millennium.* Paper presented at the Eighth International Conference on Thinking, Edmonton, Alberta, Canada.

Gardner, R. (1972, March). Once upon a time there was a doorknob . . . *Psychology Today, 5*(10), 67–71.

Gardner, R. (1986). *Therapeutic communication with children: The mutual storytelling technique.* New York: Science House.

Gardner, R. A. (1993). *Storytelling in psychotherapy with children.* Lanham, MD: Rowman & Littlefield.

Gariepy, N., & Howe, N. (2003). The therapeutic power of play: Examining the play of young children with leukaemia. *Child: Care, Health and Development, 29,* 523–537.

Garvey, C. (1977). *Play.* Cambridge, MA: Harvard University Press.

Garvey, C. (1983). Some properties of social play. In W. Damon (Ed.), *Social and personality development: Essays on the growth of the child.* New York: Norton.

Garvey, C., & Berndt, R. (1977). *Organization of pretend play.* Paper presented at the meeting of the American Psychological Association, Chicago.

Gaskins, S. (1994). Symbolic play in a Mayan village. *Merrill-Palmer Quarterly, 40,* 344–359.

Gaskins, S. (1996). How Mayan parental theories come into play. In S. Harkness & C. Super (Eds.), *Parents' cultural belief systems* (pp. 345–363). New York: Guilford.

Gaskins, S. (1999). Children's daily lives in a Mayan village: A case study of culturally constructed roles and activities. In A. Goncu (Ed.), *Children's engagement in the world: Sociocultural perspectives.* Cambridge, England: Cambridge University Press.

Gaskins, S. (2000). Children's daily activities in a Mayan village: A culturally grounded description. *Cross-Cultural Research, 34,* 375–389.

Giddings, M., & Halverson, C. F. (1981). Young children's use of toys in home environments. *Family Relations, 30,* 69–74.

Gleason, T. R. (2004). Imaginary companions: An evaluation of parents as reporters. *Infant and Child Development, 13,* 199–215.

Gleason, T. R., Sebanc, A. M., McGinley, J., & Hartup, W. (1997, April). *Invisible friends and personified objects: Qualitative differences in relationships with imaginary companions.* Poster presented at the Biennial Meeting of the Society for Research in Child Development, Washington, DC.

Glick, M. P., & Fewell, R. R. (1995). *Play skills of low birthweight toddlers: Effects of intervention and maternal education.* Poster presented at the Biennial Meeting of the Society for Research in Child Development, Indianapolis, IN.

Glick, M. P., Wheeden, A., & Spiker, D. K. (1997, April). *Predicting play and language skills of low birthweight toddlers: The influence of maternal directiveness and turn taking.* Poster presented at the Biennial Meeting of the Society for Research in Child Development, Washington, DC.

Golding, J. (2006). *Healing stories: Picture books for the big & small changes in a child's life.* New York: M. Evans & Company.

Goldstein, H., & Cisar, C. L. (1992). Promoting interaction during sociodramatic play: Teaching scripts to typical preschoolers and classmates with disabilities. *Journal of Applied Behavior Analysis, 25,* 265–280.

Golomb, C., & Kuersten, R. (1996). On the transition from pretence play to reality: What are the rules of the game? *British Journal of Developmental Psychology, 14,* 203–217.

Goncu, A., Mistry, J., and Mosier, C. (2000). Cultural variations in the play of toddlers. *International Journal of Behavioral Development, 24*(3), 321–329.

Goodman, G. S., Quas, J. A., Batterman-Faunce, J. M., Riddlesberger, M. M., & Kuhn, J. (1997). Children's reactions to and memory for a stressful event: Influences of age, anatomical dolls, knowledge, and parental attachment. *Applied Developmental Science, 1,* 54–75.

Goodman, J. F. (1994). "Work" versus "play" and early childhood care. *Child and Youth Care Forum, 23*(3), 177–196.

Goodwin, M. H. (2006). *The hidden life of girls: Games of stance, status, and exclusion.* Malden, MA: Blackwell.

Gosso, Y., Morais, M. L., & Otta, E. (2007). Pretend play of Brazilian children: A window into different cultural worlds. *Journal of Cross-Cultural Psychology, 38,* 539–558.

Gosso, Y., Otta, E., Morais, M. L. S., Ribeiro, F. J. L., & Bussab, V. S. R. (2005). Play in hunter-gatherer society. In A. D. Pellegrini & P. K. Smith (Eds.), *The nature of play* (pp. 213–253). New York: Guilford.

Gottman, J. M. (1977). Toward a definition of social isolation in children. *Child Development, 48,* 513–517.

Gottman, J. M., & Mettetal, G. (1986). Speculations about science and affective development: Friendship and acquaintanceship throughout adolescence. In H. C. Triandis & J. W. Berry (Eds.), *Handbook of cross-cultural psychology* (Vol. 2, pp. 25–55). Boston: Allyn and Bacon.

Gould, J. (1986). The Lowe and Costello Symbolic Play Test in socially impaired children. *Journal of Autism and Developmental Disorders, 16,* 199–213.

Goy, R. W., & McEwen, B. S. (1980). *Sexual differentiation of the brain.* Cambridge, MA: MIT Press.

Grantham-McGregor, S. (2005). Can the provision of breakfast benefit school performance? In O. Galal, C. Neumann, & J. Hulet (Eds.), *Proceedings of the International Workshop on Articulating the Impact of Nutritional Deficits on the Education for All Agenda, 26*(2), 144–158.

Grantham-McGregor, S., Powell, C., Walker, S., Chang, S., & Fletcher, P. (1994). The long-term follow-up of severely malnourished children who participated in an intervention program. *Child Development, 65,* 428–439.

Gregory, K. M., Kim, A. S., & Whiren, A. (2003). The effect of verbal scaffolding on the complexity of preschool children's block constructions. In D. E. Lytle (Ed.), *Play and educational theory and practice.* Westport, CT: Praeger.

Griffiths, M. D., Davies, M. N. O., & Chappell, D. (2004a). Demographic factors and playing variables in online computer gaming. *CyberPsychology & Behavior, 7*(4), 479–487.

Griffiths, M. D., Davies, M. N. O., & Chappell, D. (2004b). Online computer gaming: A comparison of adolescent and adult gamers. *Journal of Adolescence, 27*(1), 87.

Grinder, E. L., & Liben, L. S. (1989). *Quality of same- and cross-sex toy play in young children.* Paper presented at the Biennial Meeting of the Society for Research in Child Development, Kansas City, MO.

Groos, K. (1901). *The play of man.* New York: Appleton.

Grossman, K. (1997). *Infant father attachment relationship: A play situation, not the Strange Situation, is the pivot situation.* Poster presented at the Biennial Meeting of the Society for Research in Child Development, Washington, DC.

Guerney, L. (2000). Filial therapy into the 21st century. *International Journal of Play Therapy, 1*(1), 31–42.

Guerney, L. F. (1997). Filial therapy. In K. J. O'Connor & L. M. Braverman (Eds.), *Play therapy theory and practice: A comparative presentation* (pp. 139–159). New York: Wiley.

Guilford, J. P. (1967). *The nature of human intelligence.* New York: McGraw-Hill.

Guralnick M. J. (1996). Future directions in early intervention for children with Down syndrome. In J. A. Rondal, J. Perera, L. Nadel, & A. Comblain (Eds.), *Down syndrome: Psychological, psychobiological and socioeducational perspectives* (pp. 147–162). London: Colin Whurr.

Guralnick, M. J. (1999). The nature and meaning of social integration for young children with mild developmental delays in inclusive settings. *Journal of Early Intervention, 22,* 70–86.

Guralnick, M. J. (2002). Involvement with peers: Comparisons between young children with and without Down's syndrome. *Journal of Intellectual Disability Research, 46*(5), 379–393.

Guralnick, M. J., Connor, R. T., Hammond, M., Gottman, J. M., & Kinnish, K. (1996). Immediate effects of mainstreamed settings on the social interactions and social integration of preschool children. *American Journal on Mental Retardation, 100*(4), 359–377.

Guralnick, M. J., Hammond, M. A., Connor, R. T., & Neville, B. (2006). Stability, change, and correlates of the peer relationships of young children with mild developmental delays. *Child Development, 77*(2), 312–324.

Guralnick, M. J., Neville, B., Hammond, M. A., & Connor, R. T. (2007). The friendships of young children with developmental delays: A longitudinal analysis. *Journal of Applied Developmental Psychology, 28*(1), 64–79.

Gustafson, G. E., Green, J. A., & West, M. J. (1979). The infant's changing role in mother–infant games: The growth of social

skills. *Infant Behavior and Development, 2,* 301–308.

Haight, W., Masiello, T., Dickson, K. L., Huckeby, E., & Black, J. E. (1993, April). *The contexts and social functions of spontaneous mother-child pretend play in the home.* Paper presented at the Biennial Meeting of the Society for Research in Child Development, New Orleans, LA.

Haight, W., & Miller, P. J. (1992). The development of everyday pretend play: A longitudinal study of mothers' participation. *Merrill-Palmer Quarterly, 38,* 331–347.

Haight, W., & Miller, P. J. (1993). *Pretending at home: Early development in sociocultural context.* Albany: State University of New York Press.

Haight, W., Parke, R., & Black, J. (1997). Mothers' and fathers' beliefs about and spontaneous participation in their toddlers pretend play. *Merrill-Palmer Quarterly, 42,* 271–290.

Haight, W., Parke, R., Black, J. E., & Trousdale, T. (1993, March). *Mothers' and fathers' beliefs about pretend play.* Paper presented at the Biennial Meeting of the Society for Research in Child Development, New Orleans, LA.

Haight, W. L., Wang, X., Fung, H. H., Williams, K., & Mintz, J. (1999). Universal, developmental, and variable aspects of young children's play: A cross-cultural comparison of pretending at home. *Child Development, 70,* 1477–1488.

Hall, G. S. (1883). The contents of children's minds. *Princeton Review, 2,* 249–272.

Hanna, E. (1993, March). *Sex differences in play and imitation in toddlers.* Paper presented at the Biennial Meeting of the Society for Research in Child Development, New Orleans, LA.

Harkness, S., & Super, C. M. (1983). *The cultural structuring of children's play in a rural*

African community. Paper presented at the annual meeting of the Association for the Anthropological Study of Play, Baton Rouge, LA.

Harlow, H. F., & Harlow, M. K. (1962). Social deprivation in monkeys. *Scientific American, 207*, 137–146.

Harlow, H. F., & Suomi, S. J. (1971). Social recovery by isolation-reared monkeys. *Proceedings of the National Academy of Sciences, 68*, 1534–1538.

Harris, P. L., & Kavanaugh, R. D. (1993). Young children's understanding of pretense. *Monographs of the Society for Research in Child Development, 58* (1, Serial No. 231).

Harrower, J. K., & Dunlap, G. (2001). Including children with autism in general education classrooms: A review of effective strategies. *Behavior Modification, 2*, 762–784.

Hartley, R. E. (1971, November). Play: The essential ingredient. *Childhood Education, 48*, 80–84.

Hartley, R. E., Frank, L. K., & Goldenson, R. M. (1952). *Understanding children's play.* New York: Columbia University Press.

Hartley, R. E., & Goldenson, R. M. (1963). *The complete book of children's play* (rev. ed.). New York: Crowell.

Hartup, W. W. (1986). On relationships and development. In W. W. Hartup & Z. Rubin (Eds.), *Relationships and development*. Hillsdale, NJ: Erlbaum.

Hartup, W. W., & Stevens, N. (1997). Friendships and adaptation in the life course. *Psychological Bulletin, 121*, 355–370.

Hatch, A., Bowman, B., Jordan, J. R., Morgan, C. L., Hart, C., Soto, L. D., et al. (2002). Developmentally appropriate practice: Continuing the dialogue. *Contemporary Issues in Early Childhood, 3*(3), 439–457.

Hauser-Cram, P., & Howell, A. (2003). Disabilities and development. In R. M. Lerner, M. Easterbrooks, & J. Mistry (Eds.), *Handbook of psychology: Vol. 6 Developmental psychology* (pp. 513–534). New York: Wiley.

Hawkins, J., Sheingold, K., Gearhart, M., & Berger, C. (1982). Microcomputers in schools: Impact on the social life of elementary school classrooms. *Journal of Applied Developmental Psychology, 3*, 361–373.

Hay, D. L., Pederson, J., & Nash, A. (1982). Dyadic interaction in the first year of life. In K. H. Rubin & H. S. Ross (Eds.), *Peer relationships and social skills in childhood* (pp. 11–40). New York: Springer-Verlag.

Hazen, N. L., & Black, B. (1989). Preschool peer communication skills: The role of social status and interaction context. *Child Development, 60*, 867–876.

Heaton, K. (1983). *A study of rough-and-tumble play and serious aggression in preschool children.* Unpublished bachelor's thesis, University of Sheffield, England.

Hedenbro, M., Shapiro, A., & Gottman, J. M. (2006). Play with me at my speed: Describing differences in the tempo of parent-infant interactions in the Lausanne triadic play paradigm in two cultures. *Family Process, 45*(4), 485–498.

Hendon, C., & Bohon, L. M. (2008). Hospitalized children's mood differences during play and music therapy. *Child: Care, Health & Development, 34*(2), 141–144.

Henninger, M. L. (1994). Computers and preschool children's play: Are they compatible? *Journal of Computing in Early Childhood Education, 5*, 231–239.

Herrera, G., Alcantud, F., Jordan, R., Blanquer, A., Labajo, G., & De Pablo, C. (2008). Development of symbolic play through the use of virtual reality tools in children with autistic spectrum disorders: Two case studies. *Autism: The International Journal of Research & Practice, 12*(2), 143–157.

Hestenes, L. L., Carroll, D., Whitley, J., & Stephenson, A. (1997, April). *Young children's play interactions and benefits in inclusive preschool settings.* Paper presented at the Biennial Meeting of the Society for Research in Child Development, Washington, DC.

Hetherington, E. M., Bridges, M., & Insabella, G. M. (1998). What matters? What does not? Five perspectives on the association between marital transitions and children's adjustment. *American Psychologist, 53*(2), 167–184.

Hetherington, E. M., Cox, M., & Cox, R. (1979). Play and social interaction in children following divorce. *Journal of Social Issues, 35,* 26–49.

Hewlett, B. S. (2003). Fathers in forager, farmer and pastoral cultures. In M. E. Lamb (Ed.), *The role of the father in child development,* (4th ed., pp. 182–195). New Jersey: Wiley.

Hilgers, L. (2006, July 5). Youth sports drawing more than ever [Special to CNN.com]. Retrieved November 25, 2008, from http://www.cnn.com/2006/US/07/03/rise.kids.sports/index.html

Hines, M. (2004). *Brain gender.* New York: Oxford University Press.

Hines, M., & Green, R. (1991). Human hormonal and neural correlates of sex-typed behavior. *Review of Psychiatry, 10,* 536–555.

Hoffman, J. R., Kang, J., Faigenbaum, A. D., & Ratamess, N. A. (2005). Recreational sports participation is associated with enhanced physical fitness in children. *Research in Sports Medicine, 13*(2), 149–161.

Horowitz, L., Westlund, K., & Ljungberg, T. (2007). Aggression and withdrawal related behavior within conflict management progression in preschool boys with language impairment. *Child Psychiatry & Human Development, 38*(3), 237–253.

Howard-Jones, P., Taylor, J., & Sutton, L. (2002). The effect of play on the creativity of young children during subsequent activity. *Early Child Development & Care, 172*(4), 323–328.

Howes, C. (1988). Peer interaction of young children. *Monographs of the Society for Research in Child Development, 53* (Serial No. 17).

Howes, C., & Matheson, C. C. (1992). Sequences in the development of competent play with peers: Social and social pretend play. *Developmental Psychology, 28,* 961–974.

Howes, C., & Olenick, M. (1986). Family and child care influences on toddlers' compliance. *Child Development, 57,* 202–216.

Howes, C., & Rodning, C. (1992). Attachment security and social pretend play negotiations: Illustrative study #5. In C. Howes, O. Unger, & C. C. Matheson (Eds.), *The collaborative construction of pretend: Social pretend play functions* (pp. 89–98). Albany: State University of New York Press.

Howes, C., & Tonyan, H. (2003). Peer relations. In L. Balter & C. S. LeMonda (Eds.), *Child psychology: A handbook of contemporary issues* (pp. 143–157). New York: Psychology Press.

Howes, C., Unger, O. A., & Matheson, C. C. (1992). *The collaborative construction of pretend.* Albany: State University of New York Press.

Hughes, C., & Dunn, J. (2007). Children's relationships with other children. In C. Brownell & C. Kopp (Eds.), *Socioemotional development in the toddler years: Transitions and transformation* (pp. 177–200). New York: Guilford.

Hughes, F. (1998). Play in special populations. In O. Saracho & B. Spodek (Eds.), *Multiple perspectives on play in early childhood education* (pp. 171–193). Albany: State University of New York Press.

Hughes, M., & Hutt, C. (1979). Heartrate correlates of childhood activities: Play, exploration, problem-solving, and day-dreaming. *Biological Psychology, 8,* 253–263.

Hull, C. L. (1943). *Principles of behavior.* New York: Appleton-Century-Crofts.

Hultsman, W. (1992). Constraints to activity participation in early adolescence. *Journal of Early Adolescence, 12,* 280–299.

Humphreys, A. P. (1983). *The developmental significance of rough-and-tumble play in children.* Final report to Foundation for Child Development, New York.

Humphreys, A. P., & Smith, P. K. (1984). Rough-and-tumble in preschool and playground. In P. K. Smith (Ed.), *Play in animals and humans* (pp. 241–270). London: Basil Blackwell.

Hundert, J., & Houghton, A. (1992). Promoting social interaction of children with disabilities in integrated preschools: A failure to generalize. *Exceptional Children, 58,* 311–320.

Hungerford, A. (2005). The use of anatomically detailed dolls in forensic investigations: Developmental considerations. *Journal of Forensic Psychology Practice, 5*(1), 75–87.

Huston, A. C. (1983). Sex typing. In P. H. Mussen (Ed.), *Handbook of child psychology* (4th ed., Vol. 4, pp. 387–467). New York: Wiley.

Illick, J. E. (1974). Child-rearing in seventeenth-century England and America. In L. DeMause (Ed.), *The history of childhood.* New York: Psychohistory Press.

Inglehart, R., & Norris, P. (2003). *Rising tide—Gender equality and cultural change around the world.* New York: Cambridge University Press.

Inhelder, B., & Piaget, J. (1964). *The early growth of logic in the child.* New York: Norton.

Isen, A. (1999). On the relationships between affect and creative problem solving. In S. Russ (Ed.), *Affect, creative experience, and psychological adjustments* (pp. 3–17). Philadelphia: Brunner/Mazel.

Jampole, L., & Webber, M. K. (1987). An assessment of the behavior of sexually abused victims with anatomically correct dolls. *Child Abuse and Neglect, 11,* 187–192.

Jennings, N. A., & Wartella, E. A. (2007). Advertising and consumer development. In N. Pecora, J. P. Murray, & E. Wartella (Eds.), *Children and television: 50 years of research* (pp. 149–182). Mahwah, NJ: Lawrence Erlbaum Associates.

Jenvey, V. B., & Jenvey, H. L. (2002). Criteria used to categorize children's play: Preliminary findings. *Social Behavior & Personality, 30*(8), 733.

Joffe, L. S., & Vaughn, B. E. (1982). Infant-mother attachment: Theory, assessment, and implications for development. In B. B. Wolman (Ed.), *Handbook of developmental psychology* (pp. 190–207). Englewood Cliffs, NJ: Prentice-Hall.

Johnson, F. L., & Young, K. (2002). Gendered voices in children's television advertising. *Critical Studies in Media Communication, 19,* 461–480.

Johnson, J. E., & Ershler, J. (1981). Developmental trends in preschool play as a function of classroom program and child gender. *Child Development, 52,* 995–1004.

Johnson, J. E., & Roopnarine, J. L. (1983). The preschool classroom and sex differences in children's play. In M. B. Liss (Ed.), *Social and cognitive skills: Sex roles and children's play* (pp. 193–218). New York: Academic Press.

Johnson, J. O. (2005). Who's minding the kids? Child care arrangements: Winter 2002. *Current Population Reports* (P70–101, October). Washington, DC: U.S. Department of Commerce.

Joseph, R. M. (1998). Intention and knowledge in preschoolers' conception of pretend. *Child Development, 69,* 455–468.

Joyce, M. (1994). *First steps in teaching creative dance to children.* Mountain View, CA: Mayfield Publishing Company.

Jukes, M. (2005). The long-term impact of preschool health and nutrition on education. In O. Galal, C. Neumann, & J. Hulet (Eds.), *Proceedings of the International Workshop on Articulating the Impact of Nutritional Deficits on the Education for All Agenda, 26*(2), 193–201.

Kagan, S., & Madsen, M. C. (1972). Experimental analyses of cooperation and competition of Anglo-American and Mexican children. *Developmental Psychology, 6,* 49–59.

Kanner, L. (1971). Follow-up study of eleven autistic children originally reported in 1943. *Journal of Autism and Childhood Schizophrenia, 1,* 217–250.

Kasari, C., Freeman, S., & Paparella, T. (2006). Joint attention and symbolic play in young children with autism: A randomized controlled intervention study. *Journal of Child Psychology and Psychiatry, 47,* 611–620.

Kasari, C., Paparella, T., Freeman, S., & Jahromi, L. B. (2008). Language outcome in autism: Randomized comparison of joint attention and play interventions. *Journal of Consulting & Clinical Psychology, 76*(1), 125–137.

Kavanaugh, R. D., & Cinquegrana, E. A. (1997, April). *A longitudinal study of collaborative pretend play.* Paper presented at the Biennial Meeting of the Society for Research in Child Development, Washington, DC.

Kavanaugh, R. L. (2006). Pretend play. In B. Spodek & O. N. Saracho (Eds.), *Handbook of research on the education of young children* (2nd ed., pp. 269–278). Mahwah, NJ: Lawrence Erlbaum Associates.

Keenan, T. (2003). Individual differences in theory of mind: The preschool years and beyond. In B. Repacholi & V. Slaughter (Eds.), *Individual differences in theory of mind: Implications for typical and atypical development* (pp. 121–142). New York: Psychology Press.

Keller, H. (2003). Socialization for competence: Cultural models of infancy. *Human Development, 46,* 288–311.

Kersh, J., Casey, B. M., & Young, J. M. (2008). Research on spatial skills and block building in girls and boys: The relationship to later mathematics learning. In O. N. Saracho & B. Spodek (Eds.), *Contemporary perspectives on mathematics in early childhood education* (pp. 233–252). Charlotte, NC: Information Age Publishing.

King, N. R. (1979). Play: The kindergartner's perspective. *Elementary School Journal, 80,* 81–87.

Kinsman, C. A., & Berk, L. E. (1979). Joining the block and housekeeping areas: Changes in play and social behavior. *Young Children, 35,* 66–75.

Kirkby, M. (1989). Nature as refuge in children's environments. *Children's Environments Quarterly, 6*(1), 7–12.

Klein, M. (1932). *The psycho-analysis of children.* London: Hogarth Press.

Klein, M. (1955). The psychoanalytic play technique. *American Journal of Orthopsychiatry, 55,* 223–227.

Kline, S. (1995). The promotion and marketing of toys. In A. D. Pellegrini (Ed.), *The future of play theory* (pp. 165–185). Albany: State University of New York Press.

Knight, G. P., & Kagan, S. (1977). Acculturation of prosocial and competitive behaviors among second- and third-generation Mexican-American children. *Journal of Cross-Cultural Psychology, 8,* 273–284.

Kohlberg, L. (1966). A cognitive-developmental analysis of children's sex-role concepts and attitudes. In E. Maccoby (Ed.), *The development of sex differences* (pp. 82–173). Stanford, CA: Stanford University Press.

Konijn, E. A., Bijvank, M. N., & Bushman, B. J. (2007). I wish I were a warrior: The role of wishful identification in the effects of violent video games on aggression in adolescent boys. *Developmental Psychology, 43*(4), 1038–1044.

Krafft, K. C., & Berk, L. (1998). Private speech in two preschools: Significance of open-ended activities and make believe play for verbal self-regulation. *Early Childhood Research Quarterly, 13,* 637–648.

Kugelmass, J. W. (1989). The "shared classroom": A case study of interactions between early childhood and special education staff and children. *Journal of Early Intervention, 13,* 36–44.

Labrell, F. (1996). Paternal play with toddlers: Recreation and creation. *European Journal of Psychology and Education, 11,* 43–54.

Ladd, G., & Kochenderfer, B. J. (1996). Linkages between friendship and adjustment during early school transitions. In W. M. Bukowski, A. F. Newcomb, & W. W. Hartup (Eds.), *The company they keep: Friendship in childhood and adolescence* (pp. 322–345). New York: Cambridge University Press.

Ladd, G. W. (2005). *Children's peer relations and social competence: A century of progress.* New Haven, CT: Yale University Press.

Ladd, G. W. (2007). Social learning in the peer context. In O. N. Saracho & B. Spodek (Eds.), *Contemporary perspectives on social development and socialization in early childhood education* (pp. 133–164). Greenwich, CT: Information Age Publishing.

Ladd, G. W., Herald, S. L., & Andrews, R. K. (2006). Young children's peer relations and social competence. In B. Spodek & O. N. Saracho (Eds.), *Handbook of research on the education of young children* (2nd ed., pp. 23–54). Mahwah, NJ: Lawrence Erlbaum Associates.

Ladd, G. W., Herald, S. L., Slutzky, C. B., & Andrews, R. K. (2004). *Preventive interventions for peer group rejection.* Hillsdale, NJ: Erlbaum.

Ladd, G. W., & Price, J. M. (1987). Predicting children's social and school adjustment following correct dolls use in interviews of young children suspected of having been sexually abused. *Pediatrics, 84,* 900–906.

Lamb, M. E. (1978). The development of sibling relationships in infancy: A short-term longitudinal study. *Child Development, 49*(4), 1189–1196.

Lamb, M. E. (2004). *The role of the father in child development* (4th ed.). New York: Wiley.

Lamb, M. E., Frodi, A. M., Hwang, C. P., Frodi, M., & Steinberg, J. (1982). Mother- and father-infant interactions involving play and holding in traditional and nontraditional Swedish families. *Developmental Psychology, 18,* 215–221.

Lambert, E. B., & Clyde, M. (2003). Putting Vygotsky to the test. In D. E. Lytle (Ed.), *Play and educational theory and practice.* Westport, CT: Praeger.

Landreth, G. L. (2002). *Play therapy: The art of the relationship.* London: Taylor & Francis Books.

Langer, J. L. (1969). *Theories of development.* New York: Holt.

Langlois, J. H., & Downs, A. C. (1980). Mothers, fathers, and peers as socialization agents of sex-typed play behaviors in young children. *Child Development, 51,* 1217–1247.

Larson, M. S. (2001). Interactions, activities and gender in children's television commercials: A content analysis. *Journal of Broadcasting and Electronic Media, 45*(1), 41–56.

Larson, R., Kubey, R., & Colletti, J. (1989). Changing channels: Early adolescent media choices and shifting investments in family and friends. *Journal of Youth and Adolescence, 18,* 583–599.

Larson, R. W., & Verma, S. (1999). How children and adolescents spend time across the world: Work, play, and developmental opportunities. *Psychological Bulletin, 125*(6), 703–736.

Lease, A. M., Musgrove, K. T., & Axelrod, J. L. (2002). Dimensions of social status in preadolescent peer groups: Likability, perceived popularity, and social dominance. *Social Development, 11*(4), 508–533.

Lederberg, A. R., Chapin, S. L., Rosenblatt, V., & Vandell, V. L. (1986). Ethnic, gender, and age preferences among deaf and hearing peers. *Child Development, 57,* 375–386.

Lehman, D. R, Chiu, C., & Schaller, M. (2004). Psychology and culture. *Annual Review of Psychology, 55,* 689–714.

Leigh, R. (1931, May). Must boys fight? *Parents, 6,* 25.

Leventhal, J. M., Hamilton, J., Rekedal, S., Tebano-Micci, A., & Eyster, C. (1989). Anatomically correct dolls used in interviews of young children suspected of having been sexually abused. *Pediatrics, 84*(5), 900–907.

Lever, J. (1976). Sex differences in the games children play. *Social Problems, 23,* 478–487.

Levykh, M. G. (2008). The affective establishment and maintenance of Vygotsky's zone of proximal development. *Educational Theory, 58*(1), 83–101.

Lewis, V., Boucher, J., Lupton, L., & Watson, S. (2000). Relationships between symbolic play, functional play, verbal and non-verbal ability in young children. *International Journal of Language and Communication Disorders, 35,* 117–127.

Liber, D. B., Frea, W. D., & Symon, J. B. G. (2008). Using time-delay to improve social play skills with peers for children with autism. *Journal of Autism & Developmental Disorders, 38*(2), 312–323.

Lieber, J. (1993). A comparison of social pretend play in young children with and without disabilities. *Early Education and Development, 4,* 148–161.

Lifter, K., Sulzer-Azaroff, B., Anderson, S. R., & Cowdery, G. E. (1993). Teaching play activities to preschool children with disabilities: The importance of developmental considerations. *Journal of Early Intervention, 17,* 139–159.

Lillard, A. (2002). Pretend play and cognitive development. In U. Goswami (Ed.), *Blackwell handbook of childhood cognitive development* (pp. 188–205). London: Blackwell Publishing.

Lillard, A., & Witherington, D. C. (2004). Mothers' behavior modifications during pretense and their possible signal value for toddlers. *Developmental Psychology, 40*(1), 95–113.

Lillard, A. S. (1996). Body or mind: Children's categorizing of pretense. *Child Development, 67,* 1717–1734.

Lillard, A. S. (1997). *Wanting to be it: Children's understanding of intentions underlying pretense.* Unpublished manuscript, University of Virginia, Charlottesville.

Lindqvist, G. (2001). The relationship between play and dance. *Research in Dance Education, 2*(1), 41–52.

Lindsay, G. (2007). Educational psychology and the effectiveness of inclusive education/ mainstreaming. *British Journal of Educational Psychology, 77*(1), 1–24.

Ljung-Djärf, A. (2008). The owner, the participant and the spectator: Positions and positioning in peer activity around the computer in pre-school. *Early Years: Journal of International Research & Development, 28*(1), 61–72.

Lloyd, B., & Smith, C. (1985). The social representation of gender and young children's play. *British Journal of Developmental Psychology, 3*, 65–73.

Lobo, Y. B., & Winsler, A. (2006). The effects of a creative dance and movement program on the social competence of Head Start preschoolers. *Social Development, 15*(3), 501–519.

Locke, J. (1964). *Some thoughts concerning education* (Abridged by F. W. Garforth, Ed.). Woodbury, NY: Barron's Educational Series. (Original work published 1693)

Lockheed, M. E. (1986). Reshaping the social order: The case of gender segregation. *Sex Roles, 14*, 617–628.

Logan, R. D. (1977). Sociocultural change and the emergence of children as burdens. *Child and Family, 16*, 295–304.

Lombardino, L., & Sproul, C. (1984). Patterns of correspondence and non-correspondence between play and language in developmentally-delayed preschoolers. *Education and Training of the Mentally Retarded, 19*, 5–14.

Lombardino, L. L., Stein, J. E., Kricos, P. B., & Wolf, M. A. (1986). Play diversity and structural relationships in the play and language of language-impaired and language-normal preschoolers: Preliminary data. *Journal of Communication Disorders, 19*, 475–489.

Lord, C., Risi, S., & Pickles, A. (2004). Trajectory of language development in autism spectrum disorders. In M. Rice & S. Warren (Eds.), *Developmental language disorders: From phenotypes to etiologies* (pp. 7–29). Mahwah, NJ: Lawrence Erlbaum Associates.

Love, A., & Burns, M. S. (2006). "It's a hurricane! It's a hurricane!": Can music facilitate social constructive and sociodramatic play in a preschool classroom? *Journal of Genetic Psychology, 167*(4), 383–391.

Lozoff, B., Corapci, F., Burden, M., Kaciroti, N., Angulo-Barroso, R., Sazawal, S., et al. (2007). Preschool-aged children with iron deficiency anemia show altered affect and behavior. *Journal of Nutrition, 137*(3), 683–689.

Lubeck, S. (1994). Children in relation: Rethinking early childhood education. *The Urban Review, 26*(3), 153–172.

Lutz, D. J., & Sternberg, R. J. (1999). Cognitive development. In M. H. Bornstein & M. E. Lamb (Eds.), *Developmental psychology: An advanced textbook*. (4th ed., pp. 275–311). Mahwah, NJ: Lawrence Erlbaum Associates.

Lyytinen, P., Poikkeus, A.-M., Laakso, M.-L., Eklund, K., & Lyytinen, H. (2001). Language development and symbolic play in children with and without familial risk of dyslexia. *Journal of Speech, Language, and Hearing Research, 44*, 873–885.

Ma, L., & Lillard, A. S. (2006). Where is the real cheese? Young children's ability to discriminate between real and pretend acts. *Child Development, 77*(6), 1762–1777.

Maccoby, E. E. (1998). *The two sexes: Growing up apart, coming together*. Cambridge, MA: Harvard University Press.

MacDonald, K. B., & Parke, R. D. (1986). Parent-child physical play: The effects of sex and age of children and parents. *Sex Roles, 15*, 367–378.

Madsen, M. C. (1971). Developmental and cross-cultural differences in the cooperative and competitive behaviors of young children. *Journal of Cross-Cultural Psychology, 2*, 365–371.

Madsen, M. C., & Shapira, A. (1970). "Cooperative and Competitive Behavior of Urban Afro-American, Anglo-American, Mexican-American, and Mexican Village Children," *Developmental Psychology, 3*, pp. 6–20.

Main, M. (1981). Avoidance in the service of attachment: A working paper. In K. Immelmann, G. Barlow, L. Petrinoviich, & M. Main (Eds.), *Behavioral development: The Bielefeld Interdisciplinary Project* (pp. 651–693). New York: Cambridge University Press.

Malone, D. (2006). Contextually influenced patterns of play-developmental age associations for preschoolers with and without mental retardation. *Early Childhood Education Journal, 34*(3), 215–225.

Mann, B. L. (1984). Effects of realistic and unrealistic props on symbolic play. In T. D. Yawkey & A. D. Pellegrini (Eds.), *Child's play: Developmental and applied* (pp. 359–376). Hillsdale, NJ: Erlbaum.

Mann, L. R. (1984). Play behaviors of deaf and hearing children. In D. S. Martin (Ed.), *International Symposium on Cognition, Education, and Deafness.* Washington, DC: Gallaudet College Press.

Maratsos, M. P. (2007). Commentary. *Monographs of the Society for Research in Child Development, 72*(1), 121–126.

Markus, H. J., & Nurius, P. S. (1984). Self-understanding and self-regulation in middle childhood. In W. A. Collins (Ed.), *Development during middle childhood: The years from six to twelve* (pp. 147–183). Washington, DC: National Academy Press.

Martin, C. L., Ruble, D. N., & Szkrybalo, J. (2002). Cognitive theories of early gender development. *Psychological Bulletin, 128,* 903–933.

Marvick, E. W. (1974). Nature versus nurture: Patterns and trends in seventeenth-century French childrearing. In L. DeMause (Ed.), *The history of childhood.* New York: Psychohistory Press.

Matson, J. L., Fee, V. E., Coe, D. A., & Smith, D. (1991). A social skills program for developmentally delayed preschoolers. *Journal of Clinical Child Psychology, 20,* 428–433.

Matthews, W. S. (1977). Modes of transformation in the initiation of fantasy play. *Developmental Psychology, 13,* 212–216.

Maynard, A. E. (2002). Cultural teaching: The development of teaching skills in Maya sibling interactions. *Child Development, 73*(3), 969.

McCabe, P. C., & Marshall, D. J. (2006). Measuring the social competence of preschool children with specific language impairment: Correspondence among informant ratings and behavioral observations. *Topics in Early Childhood Special Education, 26*(4), 234–246.

McConnell, S. R. (2002). Interventions to facilitate social interaction for young children with autism: Review of available research and recommendations for educational intervention and future research. *Journal of Autism and Developmental Disorders, 32,* 351–372.

McCune, L. (1986). Play-language relationships: Implications for a theory of symbolic development. In A. W. Gottfried & C. C. Brown (Eds.), *Play interactions: The contribution of play materials and parental involvement to children's development* (pp. 67–80). Lexington, MA: Heath.

McCune, L. (1995). A normative study of representational play at the transition to language. *Developmental Psychology, 31*(2), 198–206.

McCune-Nicolich, L., & Fenson, L. (1984). Methodological issues in studying early pretend play. In T. D. Yawkey & A. D. Pellegrini (Eds.), *Child's play: Developmental and applied* (pp. 81–104). Hillsdale, NJ: Erlbaum.

McDonald, M. A., Sigman, M., Espinosa, M. P., & Neumann, C. G. (1994). Impact of a temporary food shortage on children and their mothers. *Child Development, 65,* 404–415.

McElwain, N. L., & Booth-LaForce, C. (2006). Maternal sensitivity to infant distress and nondistress as predictors of infant-mother attachment security. *Journal of Family Psychology, 20*(2), 247–255.

McGee, L. M. (2003). Book acting: Storytelling and drama in the early childhood classroom. In D. M. Barone & L. M. Morrow

(Eds.), *Literacy and young children: Research-based practices* (pp. 157–174). New York: Guilford.

McLoyd, V. (1980). Verbally expressed modes of transformation in the fantasy play of black preschool children. *Child Development, 51,* 1133–1139.

McLoyd, V. C. (1983). The effects of the structure of play objects on the pretend play of low-income preschool children. *Child Development, 54,* 626–635.

McLoyd, V. C. (1986). Social class and pretend play. In A. W. Gottfried & C. C. Brown (Eds.), *Play interactions: The contribution of play materials and parental involvement to children's development* (pp. 175–196). Lexington, MA: Heath.

McMahon, S. D., Rose, D. S., & Parks, M. (2003). Basic reading through dance program. *Evaluation Review, 27*(1), 104–126.

McMeeking, D., & Purkayastha, B. (1995). "I can't have my Mom running me everywhere": Adolescents, leisure, and accessibility. *Journal of Leisure Research, 27,* 360–378.

Meaney, M. J. (1988). The sexual differentiation of social play. *Trends in Neuroscience, 7,* 54–58.

Meenan, A. L. (2007). Internet gaming: A hidden addiction. *American Family Physician, 76*(8), 1116–1117.

Mellou, E. (1994). The values of dramatic play in children. *Early Child Development and Care, 104,* 105–114.

Meltzoff, A. (1995). Understanding the intentions of others: Re-enactment of intended acts by 18-month-old children. *Developmental Psychology, 31,* 1–16.

Miller, C., & Garvey, C. (1984). Mother-baby role play. In I. Bretherton (Ed.), *Symbolic play.* New York: Academic Press.

Miller, C. F., Trautner, H. M., & Ruble, D. N. (2006). The role of gender stereotypes in children's preferences and behavior. In L. Balter & C. Tamis-LeMonda (Eds.), *Child psychology: A handbook of contemporary issues* (2nd ed., pp. 293–323). New York: Psychology Press.

Mindham, C. (2005). Creativity and the young child. *Early Years: Journal of International Research & Development, 25*(1), 81–84.

Money, J., & Ehrhardt, A. A. (1972). *Man and woman: Boy and girl.* Baltimore: Johns Hopkins University Press.

Moore, R., & Wong, H. (1997). *Natural learning: Creating environments for rediscovering nature's way of teaching.* Berkeley, CA: MIG Communications.

Moore, R. C. (1989). Plants as play props. *Children's Environments Quarterly, 6*(1), 3–6.

Morelock, M. J., Brown, M. P., & Morrissey, A. (2003). Pretend play and maternal scaffolding: Comparisons of toddlers with advanced development, typical development, and hearing impairment. *Roeper Review, 6*(1), 41–51.

Moustakas, C. (1959). *Psychotherapy with children: The living relationship.* New York: Ballantine Books.

Naber, F. B. A., Bakermans-Kranenburg, M. J., van Ijzendoorn, M. H., Swinkels, S. H. N., Buitelaar, J. K., Dietz, C., et al. (2008). Play behavior and attachment in toddlers with autism. *Journal of Autism & Developmental Disorders, 38*(5), 857–866.

Nardo, L., Custodero, L. A., Persellin, D. C., & Fox, D. B. (2006). Looking back, looking forward: A report on early childhood music education in accredited American preschools. *Journal of Research in Music Education, 54*(4), 278–292.

Nash, A., & Fraleigh, K. (1993, March). *The influence of older siblings on the sex-typed toy play of young children.* Paper presented at the Biennial Meeting of the Society for Research in Child Development, New Orleans, LA.

Nawrotzki, K. (2006). Froebel is dead; long live Froebel! The National Froebel Foundation and English Education. *History of Education, 35*(2), 209–223.

Nebel-Schwalm, M. S., & Matson, J. L. (2008). Differential diagnosis. In J. L. Matson (Ed.), *Clinical assessment and intervention for autism spectrum disorders* (pp. 91–130). Burlington, MA: Academic Press.

Nelson, A. (2005). Children's toy collections in Sweden—A less gender-typed country? *Sex Roles, 52*(1/2), 93–102.

Ness, D., & Farenga, S. J. (2007). *Knowledge under construction: The importance of play in developing children's spatial and geometric thinking.* Lanham, MD: Rowman & Littlefield.

New, M. I. (1998). Diagnosis and management of congenital adrenal hyperplasia. *Annual Review of Medicine, 49,* 311–328.

Nikolopoulou, K. (2007). Early childhood educational software: Specific features and issues of localization. *Early Childhood Education Journal, 35*(2), 173–179.

Nordenstrom, A., Servin, A., Bohlin, G., Larsson, A., & Wedell, A. (2002). Sex-typed toy play behavior correlates with the degree of prenatal androgen exposure assessed by CYP21 genotype in girls with congenital adrenal hyperplasia. *Journal of Clinical Endocrinology and Metabolism, 87,* 5119–5124.

Novak, M. A., & Harlow, H. F. (1975). Social recovery of monkeys isolated for the first year of life: 1. Rehabilitation and therapy. *Developmental Psychology, 11,* 453–465.

O'Brien, M., & Huston, A. C. (1985). Development of sex-typed play behavior in toddlers. *Developmental Psychology, 21,* 866–871.

O'Connell, B., & Bretherton, I. (1984). Toddlers' play alone and with mothers. In I. Bretherton (Ed.), *Symbolic play.* New York: Academic Press.

Odom, S., Brantlinger, E., Gersten, R., Horner, R. H., Thompson, B., & Harris, K. R.

(2005). Research in special education: Scientific methods and evidence-based practice. *Exceptional Children, 71,* 137–148.

Odom, S. L., Brown, W. H., Frey, T., Karasu, N., Smith-Canter, L. L., & Strain, P. S. (2003). Evidence-based practices for young children with autism: Contributions fo single subject design research. *Focus on Autism & Other Developmental Disabilities, 18,* 166–175.

Odom, S. L., McConnell, S. R., McEvoy, M. A., Peterson, C., Ostrosky, M., Chandler, L. K., et al. (1999). Relative effects of interventions supporting the social competence of young children with disabilities. *Topics in Early Childhood Special Education, 19*(2), 75–92.

Odom, S. L., Peterson, C., McConnell, S., & Ostrosky, M. (1990). Ecobehavioral analysis of early education/specialized classroom settings and peer social interaction [Special issue: Organizing caregiving environments for young children with handicaps]. *Education and Treatment of Children, 13,* 316–330.

Odom, S. L., Skellenger, A., & Ostrosky, M. (1993, March). *Ecobehavioral analysis of activity engagement in early childhood education and special education classrooms.* Paper presented at the Biennial Meeting of the Society for Research in Child Development, New Orleans, LA.

Odom, S. L. K., Viztum, J., Wolery, R., Lieber, J., Sandall, S., Hanson, M. J., et al. (2004). Preschool inclusion in the United States: A review of research from an ecological systems perspective. *Journal of Research in Special Educational Needs, 4,* 17–49.

Ommundsen, Y., Roberts, G. C., & Kavussanu, M. (1998). Perceived motivational climate and cognitive and affective correlates among Norwegian athletes. *Journal of Sport Sciences, 16,* 153–164.

Opie, I., & Opie, E. (1957). Nursery rhymes. In W. Targ (Ed.), *Bibliophile in the nursery.* In

W. Targ (Ed.), *Bibliophile in the nursery* (pp. 266–284). Cleveland, OH: World.

O'Toole, C., & Chiat, S. (2006). Symbolic functioning and language development in children with Down syndrome. *International Journal of Language & Communication Disorders, 41*(2), 155–171.

Page, T., & Bretherton, I. (2003). Gender differences in stories of violence and caring by preschool children in post-divorce families: Implications for social competence. *Child and Adolescent Social Work Journal, 20*(6), 485–508.

Palmer, C. F. (1989). The discriminating nature of infants' exploratory actions. *Developmental Psychology, 25*(6), 885–893.

Panksepp, J., Burgdorf, J., Turner, C., & Walter, M. (1997). A new animal model for ADHD: Unilateral frontal lobe damage in neonatal rats. *Society for Neuroscience Abstracts, 23,* 691.

Panksepp, J., Normansell, L. A., Cox, J. F., & Siviy, S. (1995). Effects of neonatal decortication on the social play of juvenile rats. *Physiology and Behavior, 56,* 429–443.

Paquette, D. (1994). Fighting and playfighting in captive adolescent chimpanzees. *Aggressive Behavior, 20,* 49–65.

Park, R. J. (1982). Too important to trust to the children: The search for freedom and order in children's play. In J. Loy (Ed.), *The paradoxes of play* (pp. 96–104). Champaign, IL: Leisure Press.

Parke, R. D., Dennis, J., Flyr, M. L., Morris, K. L., Killian, C., McDowell, D. J., et al. (2004). Fathering and children's peer relationships. In M. E. Lamb (Ed.), *The role of the father in child development* (pp. 307–340). New York: Wiley.

Parke, R. D., & Tinsley, B. J. (1987). Family interaction in infancy. In J. D. Osofsky (Ed.), *Handbook of infant development* (2nd ed.). New York: Wiley.

Parker, J. G., & Gottman, J. M. (1989). Social and emotional development in a relational context. In T. J. Berndt & G. W. Ladd (Eds.), *Peer relationships in child development* (pp. 95–131). New York: Wiley.

Parker, S. T. (1984). Playing for keeps: An evolutionary perspective on human games. In P. K. Smith (Ed.), *Play in animals and humans* (pp. 271–294). Oxford, England: Basil Blackwell.

Parkinson, C. (1987). *Where children play.* Birmingham, England: Playboard Association for Children's Play and Recreation.

Parsons, S. (1986a). Function of play in low vision children (part 1): A review of the research and literature. *Journal of Visual Impairment and Blindness, 80,* 627–630.

Parsons, S. (1986b). Function of play in low vision children (part 2): Emerging patterns of behavior. *Journal of Visual Impairment and Blindness, 80,* 777–784.

Parten, M. (1932). Social play among preschool children. *Journal of Abnormal and Social Psychology, 28,* 136–147.

Pasterski, V., Brain, C., Geffner, M. E., Hindmarsh, P., Brook, C., & Hines, M. (2005). Prenatal hormones and postnatal socialization by parents as determinants of male-typical toy play in girls with congenital adrenal hyperplasia. *Child Development, 76*(1), 264–278.

Pasterski, V., Hindmarsh, P., Geffner, M., Brook, C., Brain, C., & Hines, M. (2007). Increased aggression and activity level in 3- to 11-year-old girls with congenital adrenal hyperplasia (CAH). *Hormones & Behavior, 52*(3), 368–374.

Patrick, G. T. W. (1916). *The psychology of relaxation.* Boston: Houghton Mifflin.

Peck, J., & Goldman, R. (1978, March). *The behaviors of kindergarten children under selected conditions of the physical and social environment.* Paper presented at the meeting of the American Educational Research Association, Toronto, Ontario, Canada.

Pecora, N. (2007). The changing nature of children's television: Fifty years of research. In N. Pecora, J. P. Murray, & E. Wartella (Eds.), *Children and television: 50 years of research* (pp. 1–40). Mahwah, NJ: Lawrence Erlbaum Associates.

Pederson, D. R., Rook-Green, A., & Elder, J. L. (1981). The role of action in the development of pretend play in young children. *Developmental Psychology, 17,* 756–759.

Pellegrini, A. D. (Ed.). (1995). *The future of play theory.* Albany: State University of New York Press.

Pellegrini, A. D. (1985). Social-cognitive aspects of children's play: The effects of age, gender, and activity centers. *Journal of Applied Developmental Psychology, 6,* 129–140.

Pellegrini, A. D. (1990). Elementary school children's playground behavior: Implications for children's social-cognitive development. *Children's Environments Quarterly, 7,* 8–16.

Pellegrini, A. D. (1995). Boys' rough-and-tumble play and social competence: Contemporaneous and longitudinal relations. In A. D. Pellegrini (Ed.), *The future of play theory* (pp. 107–126). Albany: State University of New York Press.

Pellegrini, A. D. (2003). Perceptions and functions of play and real fighting in early adolescence. *Child Development, 74,* 1522–1533.

Pellegrini, A. D. (2005). *Recess: Its role in education and development.* Mahwah, NJ: Lawrence Erlbaum Associates.

Pellegrini, A. D. & Archer, J. (2004). Sex differences in competitive and aggressive behavior: A view from sexual selection theory. In B. J. Ellis & D. F. Bjorklund (Eds.), *Origins of the social mind* (pp. 219–244). New York: Guilford.

Pellegrini, A. D., & Bjorklund, D. F. (2004). The ontogeny and phylogeny of children's object and fantasy play. *Human Nature, 15*(1), 23–43.

Pellegrini, A. D., Dupuis, D., & Smith, P. K. (2007). Play in evolution and development. *Developmental Review, 27*(2), 261–276.

Pellegrini, A. D., & Galda, L. (2000). Cognitive development, play, and literacy: Issues of definition and developmental function. In K. Roskos & J. F. Christie (Eds.), *Play and literacy in early childhood: Research from multiple perspectives* (pp. 63–74). Mahwah, NJ: Lawrence Erlbaum Associates.

Pellegrini, A. D., & Smith, P. K. (1998). Physical activity play: The nature and function of a neglected aspect of play. *Child Development, 6,* 577–598.

Pellis, S. M., & Pellis, V. C. (1987). Play fighting differs from serious fighting in both target of attack and tactics of fighting in the laboratory rat *Rattus norvegicus. Aggressive Behavior, 13,* 227–242.

Pellis, S. M., & Pellis, V. C. (1998). Structure-function interface in the analysis of play fighting. In M. Bekoff & J. A. Byers (Eds.), *Animal play: Evolutionary, comparative and ecological perspectives* (pp. 115–140). Cambridge, England: Cambridge University Press.

Pepler, D. J., & Ross, H. S. (1981). The effects of play on convergent and divergent problem-solving. *Child Development, 52,* 1202–1210.

Perkins, D. F., Jacobs, J. E., Barber, B. L., & Eccles, J. S. (2004). Childhood and adolescent sports participation as predictors of participation in sports and physical fitness activities during young adulthood. *Youth & Society, 35*(4), 495–520.

Perry, D. G., White, A. J., & Perry, L. C. (1984). Does early sex-typing result from children's attempts to match their behavior to sex-role stereotypes? *Child Development, 55,* 2114–2121.

Phillips, C. A., Rolls, S., Rouse, A., & Griffiths, M. D. (1995). Home video game playing in school-children: A study of incidence and patterns of play. *Journal of Adolescence, 18,* 687–691.

Phillips, D., McCartney, K., & Scarr, S. (1987). Child-care quality and children's social development. *Developmental Psychology, 23,* 537–543.

Phillipsen, L. C. (1999). Associations between age, gender, and group acceptance and three components of friendship quality. *Journal of Early Adolescence, 19,* 438–464.

Piaget, J. (1962). *Play, dreams, and imitation in childhood.* New York: Norton.

Piaget, J. (1963). *The origins of intelligence in children.* New York: Norton.

Piaget, J. (1965). *The moral judgment of the child.* New York: Free Press.

Piaget, J. (1970). Piaget's theory. In P. H. Mussen (Ed.), *Handbook of child psychology* (pp. 703–732). New York: Wiley.

Piaget, J. (1983). Piaget's theory. In P. H. Mussen (ed.), *Handbook of child psychology.* New York: Wiley.

Piaget, J., & Inhelder, B. (1956). *The child's conception of space.* London: Routledge & Kegan Paul.

Piaget, J., & Inhelder, B. (1969). *The psychology of the child.* New York: Basic Books.

Pickett, P. L., Griffith, P. L., & Rogers-Adkinson, D. (1993). Integration of preschoolers with severe disabilities into daycare. *Early Education and Development, 4,* 54–58.

Picone, M., & McCabe, P. C. (2005). The reliability and discriminant validity of the Social Interactive Coding System with language impaired preschoolers. *Journal of Early Childhood and Infant Psychology, 1,* 113–128.

Pierce-Jordan, S., & Lifter, K. (2005). Interaction of social and play behaviors in preschoolers with and without pervasive developmental disorder. *Topics in Early Childhood Special Education, 25(1),* 34–47.

Pike, J., & Jennings, N. (2005). The effects of commercials on children's perceptions of gender appropriate toy use. *Sex Roles, 52*(1/2), 83–91.

Pinchbeck, L., & Hewitt, M. (2005). Childhood and family in pre-Restoration England. In N. Frost (Ed.), *Child welfare: Major themes in health and social welfare* (pp. 169–202). London: Taylor & Francis Books.

Pine, K., & Nash, A. (2002). Dear Santa: The effects of television advertising on young children. *International Journal of Behavioral Development, 26*(6), 529–539.

Plato (1961). The laws. In E. Hamilton & H. Cairns (Eds.), *The collected dialogues.* New York: Pantheon Press. (Original work published 360 BC)

Plomin, R. (1990). *Nature and nurture: An introduction to behavioral genetics.* Pacific Grove, CA: Brooks/Cole.

Plowman, L., & Stephen, C. (2005). Children, play, and computers in pre-school education. *British Journal of Educational Technology, 36*(2), 145–157.

Plowman, L., & Stephen, C. (2007). Guided interaction in pre-school settings. *Journal of Computer Assisted Learning, 23*(1), 14–26.

Pollitt, E. (1994). Poverty and child development: Relevance of research in developing countries to the United States. *Child Development, 65,* 283–295.

Pollitt, E., Gorman, K. S., Engle, P. L., Martorell, R., & Rivera, J. (1993). Early supplementary feeding and cognition: Effects over two decades. *Monographs of the Society for Research in Child Development, 58* (6, Serial No. 255).

Poulin-Dubois, D., & Forbes, J. (2002). Toddlers' attention to intentions-in-action in learning novel action words. *Developmental Psychology, 38,* 104–114.

Power, T. G. (1985). Mother- and father-infant play: A developmental analysis. *Child Development, 56,* 1514–1524.

Power, T. G. (2000). *Play and exploration in children and animals.* Mahwah, NJ: Lawrence Erlbaum Associates.

Power, T. G., & Parke, R. D. (1980). Play as a context for early learning: Lab and home analyses. In I. E. Sigel & L. J. Laosa (Eds.),

The family as a learning environment (pp. 147–178). New York: Plenum.

Power, T. G., & Parke, R. D. (1982). Play as a context for early learning: Lab & home analyses. In L. M. Laosa & I. E. Sigel (Eds.), *Families as learning environments for children* (pp. 147–178). New York: Plenum.

Power, T. G., & Parke, R. D. (1986). Patterns of early socialization: An analysis of mother- and father-infant interaction in the home. *International Journal of Behavioral Development, 9,* 331–341.

Pulaski, M. A. (1973). Toys and imaginative play. In J. L. Singer (Ed.), *The child's world of make-believe.* New York: Academic Press.

Quay, L. C., & Jarrett, O. S. (1986). Social reciprocity in handicapped and non-handicapped children in a dyadic play situation. *Journal of Applied Developmental Psychology, 7,* 383–390.

Rabinowitz, F. M., Moely, B. E., Finkel, N., & McClinton, S. (1975). The effects of toy novelty and social interaction on the exploratory behavior of preschool children. *Child Development, 46,* 286–289.

Recchia, S. L. (1987). *Learning to play—Common concerns for the visually impaired child.* Los Angeles: Blind Children's Center. (ERIC Document Reproduction Service No. ED 292240)

Recchia, S. L. (1997). Play and concept development in infants and young children. *Journal of Visual Impairment & Blindness, 91*(4), 401–407.

Repetti, R. L. (1984). Determinants of children's sex-typing: Parental sex-role traits and television viewing. *Personality and Social Psychology Bulletin, 10,* 457–468.

Rettig, M. (1994, September/October). The play of young children with visual impairments: Characteristics and interventions. *Journal of Visual Impairment and Blindness, 88*(5), 410–420.

Reynolds, P. C. (1981). *On the evolution of human behavior: The argument from animals to man.* Berkeley: University of California Press.

Rheingold, H. L., & Cook, K. V. (1975). The contents of boys' and girls' rooms as an index of parents' behavior. *Child Development, 46,* 459–463.

Richard, J. F., Fonzi, A., Tani, F., Tassi, F., Tomada, G., & Schneider, B. H. (2002). Cooperation and competition. In P. K. Smith & C. H. Hart (Eds.), *Blackwell handbook of social development* (pp. 515–532). London: Blackwell Publishing.

Richard, J. F., & Schneider, B. H. (2005). Assessing friendship motivation during preadolescence and early adolescence. *Journal of Early Adolescence, 25*(3), 367–385.

Risi, S., Lord, C., Gotham, K., Corsello, C., Chrysler, C., Szatmari, P., et al. (2006). Combining information from multiple sources in the diagnosis of autism spectrum disorders. *Journal of the American Academy of Child and Adolescent Psychiatry, 45*(9), 1094–1103.

Robert, M., & Héroux, G. (2004). Visuo-spatial play experience: Forerunner of visuo-spatial achievement in preadolescent and adolescent boys and girls? *Infant and Child Development, 13,* 49–78.

Roberts, C., Pratt, C., & Leach, D. (1991). Classroom and playground interaction of students with and without disabilities. *Exceptional Children, 57,* 212–224.

Robinson, C. C., & Morris, J. J. (1986). The gender-stereotyped nature of Christmas toys by 36-, 48-, and 60-month-old children: A comparison between nonrequested vs. requested toys. *Sex Roles, 15,* 21–32.

Rogers, A., & Russo, S. (2003). Blocks: A commonly encountered play activity in the early years, or a key to facilitating skills in science, maths and technology? Investigating. *Australian Primary & Junior Science Journal, 19*(1), 17–21.

Rogers, C. R. (1951). *Client-centered therapy.* Boston: Houghton Mifflin.

Rogers, D. L. (1985). Relationships between block play and the social development of children. *Early Child Development and Care, 20,* 245–261.

Roggman, L., Boyce, L., Cook, G., Christiansen, K., & Jones, D. (2004). Playing with Daddy: Social toy play, early head start, and developmental outcomes. *Fathering, 2,* 83–108.

Roggman, L. A. (1989, April). *Age differences in the goals of toddler play.* Kansas City, MO: Society for Research in Child Development.

Roggman, L. A. (1992). Fathers with mothers and infants at the mall: Parental sex differences. *Early Child Development and Care, 79,* 65–72.

Rogoff, B. (2003). *The cultural nature of human development.* New York: Oxford University Press.

Romance, T. (1984). *A program to promote moral development through elementary school physical education.* Unpublished doctoral dissertation, University of Oregon, Eugene.

Roopnarine, J. L. (1986). Mothers' and fathers' behaviors toward the toy play of their infant sons and daughters. *Sex Roles, 14,* 59–68.

Roopnarine, J. L., Ahmeduzzaman, M., Donnely, S., Gill, P., Mennis, A., Arky, L., et al. (1992). Social-cognitive play behaviors and playmate preferences in same-age and mixed-age classrooms over a six-month period. *American Educational Research Journal, 29,* 757–776.

Roopnarine, J. L., & Johnson, J. E. (1984). Socialization in a mixed-age experimental program. *Developmental Psychology, 20,* 828–832.

Rosen, C. E. (1974). The effects of sociodramatic play on problem-solving behavior among culturally disadvantaged preschool children. *Child Development, 45,* 920–927.

Rosenblatt, D. (1977). Developmental trends in infant play. In B. Tizard & D. Harvey (Eds.), *The biology of play.* Philadelphia: Lippincott.

Roskos, K., & Neuman, S. B. (2003). Environment and its influences for early literacy teaching and learning. In S. B. Neuman & D. K. Dickinson (Eds.), *Handbook of early literacy research* (pp. 281–294). New York: Guilford.

Roskos, K. A., Tabors, P. O., & Lenhart, L. A. (2004). *Oral language and early literacy in preschool: Talking, reading, & writing.* Newark, DE: International Reading Association.

Ross, H. S. (1982). Toddler peer relations: Differentiation of games and conflicts. *Canadian Journal of Behavioural Science, 14*(4), 364–379.

Ross, H. S., & Lollis, S. P. (1987). Communication within infant social games. *Developmental Psychology, 23,* 241–248.

Rousseau, J. J. (2007). *Emile, or on education.* Sioux Falls, SD: NuVision Publications, LLC. (Original work published 1762)

Rozanski, A., & Kubzansky, L. (2005). Psychologic functioning and physical health: A paradigm of flexibility. *Psychosomatic Medicine, 67,* 47–53.

Rubin, J. A. (2005). *Child art therapy: 25th anniversary edition.* New York: Wiley.

Rubin, K. A., Bukowski, W., & Parker, J. G. (2006). Peer interactions, relationships, and groups. In W. Damon (Series Ed.), N. Eisenberg (Vol. Ed.), *Handbook of child psychology* (6th ed., Vol. 3, pp. 571–645). New York: Wiley.

Rubin, K. H. (1980). Fantasy play: Its role in the development of social skills and social cognition. In K. H. Rubin (Ed.), *Children's play* (pp. 69–84). San Francisco: Jossey-Bass.

Rubin, K. H. (1982). Non-social play in preschoolers: Necessary evil? *Child Development, 53,* 651–657.

Rubin, K. H. (1986). Play, peer interaction, and social development. In A. W. Gottfried & C. C. Brown (Eds.), *Play interactions: The contribution of play materials and parental involvement to children's development* (pp. 163–174). Lexington, MA: Heath.

Rubin, K. H., & Clark, L. (1983). Preschool teachers' ratings of behavioral problems. *Journal of Abnormal Child Psychology, 11,* 273–285.

Rubin, K. H., Coplan, R. J., Chen, X., Buskirk, A. A., & Wojslawowicz, J. C. (2005). Peer relationships in childhood. In M. H. Bornstein & M. E. Lamb (Eds.), *Developmental science: An advanced textbook* (5th ed., pp. 469-512). London: Taylor & Francis Books.

Rubin, K. H., Coplan, R. J., Nelson, L. J., Cheah, C. S. L., & Lagace-Seguin, D. G. (1999). Peer relationships in childhood. In M. H. Bornstein & M. E. Lamb (Eds.), *Developmental psychology: An advanced textbook.* (4th ed., pp. 451–496). Mahwah, NJ: Lawrence Erlbaum Associates.

Rubin, K. H., Fein, G. C., & Vandenberg, B. (1983). Play. In P. H. Mussen (Ed.), *Handbook of child psychology* (4th ed., pp. 693–774). New York: Wiley.

Rubin, K. H., & Pepler, D. J. (1982). Children's play: Piaget's views reconsidered. *Contemporary Educational Psychology, 7,* 289–299.

Ruble, D. N., & Martin, C. L. (1998). Gender development. In W. Damon (Series Ed.) & N. Eisenberg (Vol. Ed.), *Handbook of child psychology: Vol. 3. Social, emotional, and personality development* (5th ed., pp. 933–1016). New York: Wiley.

Ruble, D. N., Taylor, L. J., Cyphers, L., Greulich, F. K., Lurye, L. E., & Shrout, P. E. (2007). The role of gender constancy in early gender development. *Child Development, 78*(4), 1121–1136.

Ruff, H. A. (1984). Infants' manipulative exploration of objects: Effects of age and object characteristics. *Developmental Psychology, 20,* 9–20.

Ruff, H. A., & Saltarelli, L. M. (1993). Exploratory play with objects: Basic cognitive processes and individual differences. In M. H. Borstein & A. W. O'Reilly (Eds.), *The role of play in the development of thought* (pp. 5–15). San Francisco: Jossey-Bass.

Ruffman, T., Perner, J., & Parkin, L. (1999). How parenting style affects false belief understanding. *Social Development, 8*(3), 395–411.

Runco, M. A. (Ed.). (2003). *Critical creative processes.* Cresskill, NJ: Hampton.

Russ, S. W. (1999). Play, affect, and creativity: Theory and research. In S. Russ (Ed.), *Affect, creative experience, and psychological adjustment* (pp. 57–75). Philadelphia: Brunner/Mazel.

Russ, S. W. (2003). Play and creativity: Developmental issues. *Scandinavian Journal of Educational Research, 47*(3), 291–304.

Russ, S. W. (2004). *Play in child development and psychotherapy: Toward empirically supported practice.* Mahwah, NJ: Lawrence Erlbaum Associates.

Russ, S. W., & Grossman-McKee, A. (1990). Affective expression in children's fantasy play, primary process thinking on the Rorschach, and divergent thinking. *Journal of Personality Assessment, 54,* 756–771.

Russ, S. W., & Kaugars, A. S. (2001). Emotion in children's play and creative problem solving. *Creativity Research Journal, 13*(1), 211–219. Retrieved November 25, 2008, from http://www.informaworld.com/smpp/title~content=t775653635~db=all~tab=issueslist~branches=13#v13

Russ, S. W., Robbins, D., & Christiano, B. (1999). Pretend play: Longitudinal prediction of creativity and affect and fantasy in children. *Creativity Research Journal, 12,* 129–139.

Russ, S. W., & Schafer, E. D. (2006). Affect in fantasy play, emotion in memories, and divergent thinking. *Creativity Research Journal, 18*(3), 347–354.

Rutter, M. (1978). Language disorder and infantile autism. In M. Rutter & E. Schopler (Eds.), *Autism: A reappraisal of concepts and treatment* (pp. 85–104). New York: Plenum.

Rutter, M. (1983). Cognitive deficits in the pathogenesis of autism. *Journal of Child Psychology and Psychiatry, 24,* 513–531.

Sagi, A., Lamb, M. E., Shoham, R., Dvir, R., & Lewkowicz, K. S. (1985). Parent-infant interaction in families on Israeli kibbutzim. *International Journal of Behavioral Development, 8,* 273–284.

Salguero, R. A., Moran, T., & Bersabe, R. M. (2002). Measuring problem video game playing in adolescents. *Addiction. 97,* 1601–1606.

Salmon, C., & Shackelford, T. K. (2008). *Family relationships: An evolutionary perspective.* New York: Oxford University Press.

Saracho, O. (2002). Young children's creativity and pretend play. *Early Child Development & Care, 172*(5), 431–438.

Saracho, O. N., & Spodek, B. (1995). Children's play and early childhood education: Insights from history and theory. *Journal of Education, 177*(3), 129.

Saracho, O. N., & Spodek, B. (2002). *Contemporary perspectives in literacy in early childhood education.* Charlotte, NC: Information Age Publishing.

Saracho, O. N., & Spodek, B. (2003). Understanding play and its theories. In O. N. Saracho & B. Spodek (Eds.), *Contemporary perspectives on play in early childhood education* (pp. 1–20). Greenwich, CT: Information Age Publishing.

Saracho, O. N., & Spodek, B. (Eds.). (2008). *Contemporary perspectives on mathematics in early childhood education.* Charlotte, NC: Information Age Publishing.

Sarawa, J., & Clements, D. H. (2008). Mathematics in early childhood. In O. N. Saracho & B. Spodek (Eds.), *Contemporary perspectives on mathematics in early childhood education* (pp. 67–94). Charlotte, NC: Information Age Publishing.

Schaefer, C. E., & Kaduson, H. G. (2007). *Contemporary play therapy: Theory, research, and practice.* New York: Guilford.

Schindler, P. J., Moely, B. E., & Frank, A. L. (1987). Time in day care and social participation of young children. *Developmental Psychology, 23,* 255–261.

Schneekloth, L. H. (1989). Play environments for visually impaired children. *Journal of Visual Impairment and Blindness, 83,* 196–201.

Schneider, B., Soteras de Toro, M., Woodburn, S., Fulop, M., Cervino, C., Bernstein, S., et al. (2006). Cross-cultural differences in competition among children and adolescents. In X. Chen, D. French, & B. Schneider (Eds.), *Peer relationships in cultural context* (pp. 310–338). Cambridge, MA: Cambridge University Press.

Schwartz, L. A., & Markham, W. T. (1985). Sex stereotyping in children's toy advertisements. *Sex Roles, 12,* 157–170.

Schwartz, S. L. (2005). *Teaching young children mathematics.* Westport, CT: Praeger.

Schwartzman, H. B. (1984). Imaginative play: Deficit or difference? In T. D. Yawkey & A. D. Pellegrini (Eds.), *Child's play: Developmental and applied* (pp. 49–62). Hillsdale, NJ: Erlbaum.

Schwebel, D. C., Rosen, C. S., & Singer, J. L. (1999). Preschoolers' pretend play and theory of mind: The role of jointly constructed pretense. *British Journal of Developmental Psychology, 17,* 333–348.

Segers, E., & Verhoeven, L. (2002). Multimedia support of early literacy learning. *Computer & Education, 39,* 207–221.

Selman, R. L. (1980). *The growth of interpersonal understanding.* New York: Academic Press.

Serbin, L. A., & Conner, J. A. (1979). Sex-typing, children's play preferences, and patterns of cognitive performance. *Journal of Genetic Psychology, 134,* 315–316.

Serbin, L. A., Conner, J. A., Burchardt, C. J., & Citron, C. C. (1979). Effects of peer presence on sex-typing of children's play behavior. *Journal of Experimental Child Psychology, 27,* 303–309.

Serbin, L. A., Tonick, I. J., & Sternglanz, S. H. (1977). Shaping cooperative cross-sex play. *Child Development, 48*, 924–929.

Servin, A., Nordenstrom, A., Larsson, A., & Bohlin, G. (2003). Prenatal androgens and gender-typed behavior: A study of girls with mild and severe forms of congenital adrenal hyperplasia. *Developmental Psychology, 39*, 440–450.

Shannon, J. D., Tamis-LeMonda, C. S., London, K., & Cabrera, N. (2002). Beyond rough-and-tumble: Low-income fathers' interactions and children's cognitive development at 24 months. *Parenting: Science and Practice, 2*, 77–104.

Shantz, C. U. (1983). Social cognition. In P. H. Mussen (Ed.), *Handbook of child psychology* (4th ed., Vol. 3, pp. 495–555). New York: Wiley.

Shapira, A. (1976). Developmental differences in competitive behavior in kibbutz and city children in Israel. *Journal of Social Psychology, 98*, 19–26.

Shapira, A., & Madsen, M. C. (1974). Between and within group cooperation and competition among kibbutz and non-kibbutz children. *Developmental Psychology, 10*, 1–12.

Shapiro, L. J., Ho, K., & Fernald, A. (1997, April). *Mother-toddler play in the United States and Japan: Contrasts in content and approach.* Paper presented at the Biennial Meeting of the Society for Research in Child Development, Washington, DC.

Shepherd, J. T., Brollier, C. B., & Dandrow, R. L. (1994). Play skills of preschool children with speech and language delays. *Physical and Occupational Therapy in Pediatrics, 14*(2), 1–20.

Shields, D. L., & Bredemeier, B. J. (1995). *Character development and physical activity.* Champaign, IL: Human Kinetics Publishers.

Shields, D. L., & Bredemeier, B. J. (2007). Can sports build character? In D. Smith & M. Bar-Eli (Eds.), *Essential readings in sport and exercise psychology* (pp. 423–432). Champaign, IL: Human Kinetics Publishers.

Shimada, S., Sano, R., & Peng, F. C. C. (1979). A longitudinal study of symbolic play in the second year of life. *The Research Institute for the Education of Exceptional Children, Research Bulletin.* Tokyo: Gakugei University.

Sidorowicz, L. S., & Lunney, G. S. (1980). Baby X revisited. *Sex Roles, 6*, 67–73.

Sigman, M., Neumann, C., Carter, E., Cattle, D., D'Souza, S., & Bwibo, N. (1988). Home interactions and the development of Embu toddlers in Kenya. *Child Development, 59*, 1251–1261.

Sigman, M., Neumann, C., Jansen, A. A. J., & Bwibo, N. (1989). Cognitive abilities of Kenyan children in relation to nutrition, family characteristics, and education. *Child Development, 60*, 1463–1474.

Sigman, M., Whaley, S. E., Neumann, C. G., Bwibo, N., Guthrie, D., Weiss, R. E., et al. (2005). Diet quality affects the playground activities of Kenyan children. In O. Galal, C. Neumann, & J. Hulet (Eds.), *Proceedings of the International Workshop on Articulating the Impact of Nutritional Deficits on the Education for All Agenda, 26*(2), 202–212.

Sigman, S., & Sena, R. (1993). Pretend play in high-risk and developmentally delayed children. In M. H. Bornstein & A. W. O'Reilly (Eds.), *The role of play in the development of thought* (pp. 43–53). San Francisco: Jossey-Bass.

Simon, T. (1985). Play and learning with computers. *Early Child Development and Care, 19*, 69–78.

Sims, W. L. (2005). Effects of free versus directed listening on duration of individual music listening by prekindergarten children. *Journal of Research in Music Education, 53*(1), 78–86.

Singer, D. G., & Singer, J. L. (1976). Family television viewing habits and the spontaneous play of preschool children. *American Journal of Orthopsychiatry, 46,* 496–502.

Singer, J. L. (Ed.) (1973). *The child's world of make-believe: Experimental studies of imaginative play.* New York: Academic Press.

Singer, J. L. (1995). Imaginative play in childhood: Precursor of subjunctive thought, daydreaming, and adult pretending games. In A. D. Pellegrini (Ed.), *The future of play theory* (pp. 187–219). Albany: State University of New York Press.

Singer, J. L., & Streiner, B. F. (1966). Imaginative content in the dreams and fantasy play of blind and sighted children. *Perceptual and Motor Skills, 22,* 475–482.

Singer, L. K., & Lythcott, A. E. (2004). Fostering school achievement and creativity through sociodramatic play in the classroom. In E. F. Zigler, D. G. Singer, & S. F. Bishop-Josef (Eds.), *Children's play: The roots of reading* (pp. 77–94). Washington, DC: Zero-to-Three.

Skellenger, A. C., & Hill, E. W. (1994). Effects of a shared teacher-child play intervention on the play skills of three young children who are blind. *Journal of Visual Impairment and Blindness, 88*(5), 433–445.

Slade, A. (1987). Quality of attachment and early symbolic play. *Developmental Psychology, 23,* 78–85.

Slade, A., Grienenberger, J., Bernbach, E., Levy, D., & Locker, A. (2005). Maternal reflective functioning, attachment, and the transmission gap: A preliminary study. *Attachment & Human Development, 7*(3), 283–298.

Slaughter, V., & Repacholi, B. (2003). Individual differences in theory of mind: What are we investigating? In B. Repacholi & V. Slaughter (Eds.), *Individual differences in theory of mind: Implications for typical and atypical development* (pp. 1–12). New York: Psychology Press.

Smilansky, S. (1968). *The effects of sociodramatic play on disadvantaged preschool children.* New York: Wiley.

Smith, C., & Lloyd, B. (1978). Maternal behavior and perceived sex of infant: Revisited. *Child Development, 49,* 1263–1266.

Smith, P. B., Bond, M. H., & Kagitcibasi, C. (2006). *Understanding social psychology across cultures: Living and working in a changing world.* London: Sage.

Smith, P. K. (1983). Differences or deficits? The significance of pretend and sociodramatic play. *Developmental Review, 3,* 6–10.

Smith, P. K. (1989, April). *Rough-and-tumble play and its relationship to serious fighting.* Paper presented at the Biennial Meeting of the Society for Research in Child Development, Kansas City, MO.

Smith, P. K., & Connolly, K. J. (1980). *The ecology of preschool behavior.* Cambridge, England: Cambridge University Press.

Smith, T. L. (1986). Self-concepts of youth sports participants and nonparticipants in Grades 3 and 6. *Perceptual and Motor Skills, 62,* 863–866.

Snow, M., Jacklin, C., & Maccoby, E. (1983). Sex-of-child differences in father-child interaction at one year of age. *Child Development, 54,* 227–232.

Sobel, D. M. (2006). How fantasy benefits young children's understanding of pretense. *Developmental Science, 9*(1), 63–75.

Somerville, J. (1982). *The rise and fall of childhood.* Beverly Hills, CA: Sage.

Spencer, H. (1873). *Principles of psychology.* New York: Appleton-Century-Crofts.

Spencer, M., & Baskin, L. (1997). *Microcomputers and young children.* Urbana, IL: ERIC Clearinghouse on Elementary and Early Childhood Education. (ERIC Document Reproduction Service No. ED 327295 83)

Spodek, B., & Saracho, O. N. (2003). Early childhood educational play. In O. N. Saracho & B. Spodek (Eds.), *Contemporary perspectives on play in early childhood education* (pp. 171–180). Greenwich, CT: Information Age Publishing.

Sroufe, L. A. (2005). Attachment and development: A prospective, longitudinal study from birth to adulthood. *Attachment & Human Development, 7*(4), 349–367.

Sroufe, L. A., Egeland, B., Carlson, E., & Collins, W. A. (2005a). *The development of the person: The Minnesota study of risk and adaptation from birth to adulthood.* New York: Guilford.

Sroufe, L. A., Egeland, B., Carlson, E., & Collins, W. A. (2005b). Placing early attachment experiences in developmental context. In K. E. Grossmann, K. Grossmann, & E. Waters (Eds.), *The power of longitudinal attachment research: From infancy and childhood to adulthood* (pp. 48–70). New York: Guilford.

Stanley, G. C., & Konstantareas, M. M. (2007). Symbolic play in children with autism spectrum disorder. *Journal of Autism & Developmental Disorders, 37*(7), 1215–1223.

Steinkamp, M. W. (1989). Factors mediating the relationships between preschool children's play patterns and peer ratings: Verbal communication styles. *Journal of Applied Developmental Psychology, 10,* 505–525.

Stern, M., & Karraker, K. H. (1989). Sex stereotyping of infants: A review of gender labeling studies. *Sex Roles, 20,* 501–522.

Stevenson, H., Azuma, H., & Hakuta, H. (Eds.). (1986). *Child development and education in Japan.* New York: Wiley.

Stevenson, M. B., Leavitt, L. A., Thompson, R. H., & Roach, M. A. (1988). A social relations model analysis of parent and child play. *Developmental Psychology, 24,* 101–108.

Strassburger, V. C., & Wilson, B. J. (2002). *Children, adolescents, and the media.* Thousand Oaks, CA: Sage Publications.

Stratton, G., Marsh, L., & Moores, J. (2000). Promoting children's physical activity in primary school: An intervention study using playground markings. *Ergonomics, 43*(10), 1538–1546.

Strein, W., & Kachman, W. (1984). Effects of computer games on young children's cooperative behavior: An exploratory study. *Journal of Research and Development in Education, 18,* 40–43.

Suomi, S. J. (1991). Early stress and adult emotional reactivity in rhesus monkeys. *Ciba Foundation Symposium, 156,* 171–189.

Suomi, S. J. (2005). Genetic and environmental factors influencing the expression of impulsive aggression and serotonergic functioning in rhesus monkeys. In R. E. Tremblay, W. W. Hartup, & J. Archer (Eds.), *Developmental origins of aggression* (pp. 63–82). New York: Guilford.

Sutterby, J. A., & Frost, J. (2006). Creating play environments for early childhood: Indoors and out. In B. Spodek & O. N. Saracho (Eds.), *Handbook of research on the education of young children* (2nd ed., pp. 305–322). Mahwah, NJ: Lawrence Erlbaum Associates.

Sutton-Smith, B. (1967). The role of play in cognitive development. *Young Children, 22,* 361–370.

Sutton-Smith, B. (1979). The play of girls. In C. B. Kopp & M. Kirkpatrick (Eds.), *Becoming female: Perspectives on development.* New York: Plenum.

Sutton-Smith, B. (1980). Children's play: Some sources of play theorizing. In K. H. Rubin (Ed.), *Children's play.* San Francisco: Jossey-Bass.

Sutton-Smith, B. (1985). The child at play. *Psychology Today, 19,* 64–65.

Sutton-Smith, B., & Kelly-Byrne, D. (1984). The idealization of play. In P. K. Smith (Ed.), *Play in animals and humans* (pp. 305–322). Oxford, England: Basil Blackwell.

Sutton-Smith, B., & Roberts, J. M. (1971). The cross-cultural and psychological study of games. *International Review of Sport Sociology, 6,* 79–87.

Sutton-Smith, B., & Roberts, J. M. (1981). Play, games, and sports. In H. C. Triandis & A. Heron (Eds.), *Handbook of cross-cultural psychology: Developmental psychology* (Vol. 4). Boston: Allyn and Bacon.

Tamis-LeMonda, C. S. (2004). Conceptualizing fathers' roles: Playmates and more. *Human Development, 47*(4), 220–227.

Tamis-LeMonda, C. S., & Bornstein, M. H. (1989). Habituation and maternal encouragement of attention in infancy as predictors of toddler language, play, and representational competence. *Child Development, 60,* 738–751.

Tamis-LeMonda, C. S., & Bornstein, M. H. (1990). Language, play, and attention at one year. *Infant Behavior and Development, 13,* 85–98.

Tamis-LeMonda, C. S., & Bornstein, M. H. (1991). Individual variation, correspondence, stability, and change in mother and toddler play. *Infant Behavior and Development, 14,* 143–162.

Tamis-LeMonda, C. S., Bornstein, M. H., Cyphers, L., Toda, S., & Ogino, M. (1992). Language and play at one year: A comparison of toddlers and mothers in the United States and Japan. *International Journal of Behavioral Development, 1,* 19–42.

Tamis-LeMonda, C. S., & Damast, A. M. (1993, April). *Individual differences in mothers' play actions and beliefs: Correspondence to toddler-play competence.* Paper presented at the Biennial Meeting of the Society for Research in Child Development, New Orleans, LA.

Tamis-LeMonda, C. S., Damast, A. M., & Bornstein, M. H. (1993, March). *Individual differences in mother's play actions and beliefs: Correspondence to toddler play competence.* Paper presented at the Biennial Meeting of the Society for Research in Child Development, New Orleans, LA.

Tamis-LeMonda, C. S., Damast, A. M., & Bornstein, M. H. (1994). What do mothers know about the developmental nature of play? *Infant Behavior and Development, 17,* 341–345.

Tassi, F., & Schneider, B. H. (1997). Task-oriented versus other-referenced competition. *Journal of Applied Social Psychology, 27,* 1557–1580.

Taylor, A. F., Wiley, A., Kuo, F. E., & Sullivan, W. C. (1997). *Growing up in the inner city: Green spaces as places to grow.* Paper presented at the Biennial Meeting of the Society for Research in Child Development, Washington, DC.

Taylor, M., & Carlson, S. M. (1997). The relation between individual differences in fantasy and theory of mind. *Child Development, 68,* 436–455.

Temmerman, N. (2000). An investigation of the music activity preferences of preschool children. *British Journal of Music Education, 17*(1), 51–60.

Tessier, O., de Lorimier, S., & Doyle, A. (1993, March). *The quality of social involvement in social play: The effects of mode of play, relationship, and age.* Paper presented at the Biennial Meeting of the Society for Research in Child Development, New Orleans, LA.

Theokas, C., Ramsey, P. G., & Sweeney, B. (1993, March). *The effects of classroom interventions on young children's cross-sex contacts and perceptions.* Paper presented at the Biennial Meeting of the Society for Research in Child Development, New Orleans, LA.

Thierry, K. L., Lamb, M. E., Orbach, Y., & Pipe, M. (2005). Developmental differences in the function and use of anatomical dolls during interviews with alleged sexual abuse victims. *Journal of Consulting & Clinical Psychology, 73*(6), 1125–1134.

Thomas, N., & Smith, C. (2004). Developing play skills in children with autistic spectrum disorders. *Educational Psychology in Practice, 20*(3), 195–206.

Thompson, C. L., & Henderson, D. A. (2007). *Counseling children.* Belmont, CA: Thomson/Brooks/Cole.

Thompson, K. M., & Haninger, K. (2001). Violence in E-rated video games. *Journal of American Medical Association, 286,* 591–598.

Tietjen, A. M. (2006). Cultural influences on peer relations: An ecological perspective. In X. Chen, D. French, & B. Schneider (Eds.), *Peer relationships in cultural context* (pp. 52–74). Cambridge, England: Cambridge University Press.

Toqueville, A. de. (1946). *Democracy in America* (H. Reeves, Trans.). New York: Knopf. (Original work published in 1835)

Tracy, D. M. (1987). Toys, spatial ability, and science and mathematics achievement: Are they related? *Sex Roles, 17,* 115–138.

Trapolini, T., Ungerer, J. A., & McMahon, C. A. (2008). Maternal depression: Relations with maternal caregiving representations and emotional availability during the preschool years. *Attachment & Human Development, 10*(1), 73–90.

Tronick, E. Z., Beeghly, M., Weinberg, M. K., & Olson, K. L. (1997). Postpartum exuberance: Not all women in a highly positive emotional state in the postpartum period are denying depression and distress. *Infant Mental Health Journal, 18,* 406–423.

Troster, H., & Brambring, M. (1994). The play behavior and play materials of blind and sighted infants and preschoolers. *Journal of Visual Impairment & Blindness, 88*(5), 421–433.

Tucker, M. J. (1974). The child as beginning and end: Fifteenth and sixteenth century English childhood. In L. DeMause (Ed.), *The history of childhood* (pp. 229–230). New York: Psychohistory Press.

Tuma, J., & Russ, S. W. (1993). Psychoanalytic psychotherapy with children. In T. Kratochwill & R. Morris (Eds.), *Handbook of psychotherapy with children and adolescents* (pp. 131–161). Boston: Allyn and Bacon.

Umek, L. M., & Musek, P. L. (2001). Symbolic play: Opportunities for cognitive and language development in preschool settings. *Early Years: Journal of International Research & Development, 21*(1), 55–64.

Ungerer, J. A., Zelazo, P. R., Kearsley, R. B., & O'Leary, K. (1981). Developmental changes in the representation of objects in symbolic play from 18 to 34 months of age. *Child Development, 52,* 186–195.

U.S. Census Bureau (2008). *Child care arrangements of preschoolers under 5 years old living with mother, by employment status of mother and selected characteristics: Spring 2005.* Retrieved November 25, 2008, from http://www.census.gov/population/socdemo/child/ppl-2005/tab01A.xls

Valentino, K., Cicchetti, D., Toth, S. L., & Rogosch, F. A. (2006). Mother-child play and emerging social behaviors among infants from maltreating families. *Developmental Psychology, 42*(3), 474–485.

Valkenburg, P. M. (2000). Media and youth consumerism. *Journal of Adolescent Health, 27*(2), 52–56.

Vandenberg, B. (1978). Play and development from an ethological perspective. *American Psychologist, 33,* 724–738.

Vandenberg, B. (1998). Real and not real: A vital developmental dichotomy. In O. N. Saracho & B. Spodek (Eds.), *Multiple perspectives on play in early childhood education* (pp. 295–305). Albany: State University of New York Press.

VanFleet, R. (2005). *Filial therapy: Strengthening parent-child relationships through play.* Harrisburg, PA: Professional Resource Press.

Venuti, P., de Falco, S., Giusti, Z., & Bornstein, M. H. (2008). Play and emotional availability in young children with Down syndrome. *Infant Mental Health Journal, 29*(2), 133–152.

Vernadakis, N., Avgerinos, A., Tsitskari, E., & Zachopoulou, E. (2005). The use of computer assisted instruction in preschool education: Making teaching meaningful. *Early Childhood Education Journal, 33*(2), 99–104.

Vibbert, M., & Bornstein, M. H. (1989). Specific associations between domain of mother–child interaction and toddler referential language and pretense play. *Infant Behavior and Development, 12,* 163–184.

Viernickel, S. (1997, April). *Gender segregation and peer interaction in toddler playgroups.* Poster presented at the Biennial Meeting of the Society for Research in Child Development, Washington, DC.

Vig, S. (2007). Young children's object play: A window on development. *Journal of Developmental & Physical Disabilities, 19*(3), 201–215.

Von Rosseberg-Gempton, I., Dickinson, J., & Poole, G. (1998). Creative dance: Potentiality for enhancing social functioning in frail seniors and young children. *The Arts in Psychotherapy, 26,* 313–327.

Vygotsky, L. S. (1962). *Thought and language.* Cambridge, MA: MIT Press.

Vygotsky, L. S. (1976). Play and its role in the mental development of the child. In J. Bruner, A. Jolly, & K. Sylva (Eds.), *Play: Its role in development and evolution* (pp. 537–554). New York: Basic Books. (Original work published 1933, *Soviet Psychology, 5,* 6–18)

Vygotsky, L. S. (1978). *Mind in society: The development of higher psychological processes.* Cambridge, MA: Harvard University Press.

Wachs, T. D. (1993). Multidimensional correlates of individual variability in play and exploration. In M. H. Bornstein & A. W. O'Reilly (Eds.), *The role of play in the development of thought* (pp. 43–53). San Francisco: Jossey-Bass.

Wachs, T. D., Moussa, W., Bishry, Z., Yunis, F., Sobhy, A., McCabe, G., et al. (1993). Relations between nutrition and cognitive performance in Egyptian toddlers. *Intelligence, 17*(2), 151–172.

Waldron, J., & Krane, V. (2005). Motivational climate and goal orientation in adolescent female softball players. *Journal of Sport Behavior, 28*(4), 378–391.

Walka, H., Pollitt, E., Triana, N., & Jahari, A. B. (1997, April). *Early supplemental feeding and spontaneous play in West Java, Indonesia.* Paper presented at the Biennial Meeting of the Society for Research in Child Development, Washington, DC.

Walzer, J. F. (1974). A period of ambivalence: Eighteenth century American childhood. In L. deMause (Ed.)., *The history of childhood* (pp. 351–382). New York: Psychohistory Press.

Warneken, F., & Tomasello, M. (2007). Helping and cooperation at 14 months of age. *Infancy, 11*(3), 271–294.

Warren, D. H. (1984). *Blindness and early childhood development.* New York: American Foundation for the Blind.

Watson, J. B. (1925). *Behaviorism.* New York: Norton.

Watson, J. B. (1928). *Psychological care of infant and child.* New York: Norton.

Watt, N., Wetherby, A., & Shumway, S. (2006). Prelinguistic predictors of language outcome at 3 years of age. *Journal of Speech, Language & Hearing Research, 49*(6), 1224–1237.

Webster, A. A., & Carter, M. (2007). Social relationships and friendships of children with developmental disabilities: Implications for inclusive settings. A systematic review. *Journal of Intellectual & Developmental Disability, 32*(3), 200–213.

Wei, R. (2007). Effects of playing violent videogames on Chinese adolescents' pro-violence attitudes, attitudes toward others, and aggressive behavior. *CyberPsychology & Behavior, 10*(3), 371–380.

Weinberg, M. K., Olson, K. L., Beeghly, M., & Tronick, E. Z. (2006). Making up is hard to do, especially for mothers with high levels of depressive symptoms and their infant sons. *Journal of Child Psychology & Psychiatry, 47*(7), 670–683.

Weinberger, L. A., & Starkey, P. (1994). Pretend play by African-American children in Head Start. *Early Childhood Research Quarterly, 9*, 327–343.

Weisberg, R. W. (1993). *Creativity: Beyond the myth of genius.* New York: W. H. Freeman.

Wellhousen, K., & Crowther, I. (2003). *Creating effective learning environments.* Clifton Park, NY: Delmar.

Wellman, H. M. (2002). Understanding the psychological world: Developing a theory of mind. In U. Goswami (Ed.), *Blackwell handbook of childhood cognitive development* (pp. 167–187). London: Blackwell Publishing.

Wellman, H. M., Phillips, A. T., & Spelke, E. S. (2002). Infants' ability to connect gaze and emotional expression to intentional action. *Cognition, 85*, 53–78.

Werner, H., & Kaplan, B. (1983). *Symbol formation.* New York: Wiley.

Werner, P. H., & Burton, E. C. (1979). *Learning through movement: Teaching cognitive content through physical activities.* St. Louis, MO: Mosby.

Wesley, J. (1768). A short account of the school in Kingswood, near Bristol. In T. Jackson (Ed.), *Works* (Vol. 13, pp. 460–464). Grand Rapids, MI: Baker Book House.

White, P. C., New, M. I., & Dupont, B. (1987). Congenital adrenal hyperplasia. *New England Journal of Medicine, 316*, 1519–1524.

White, S., Strom, G. A., Santilli, G., & Halpin, B. M. (1986). Interviewing young sexual abuse victims with anatomically correct dolls. *Child Abuse and Neglect, 10*, 519–529.

White, S. A. (1998). Adolescent goal profiles, perceptions of the parent-initiated motivational climate, and competitive trait anxiety. *The Sport Psychologist, 12*, 16–28.

Whiting, B., & Edwards, C. P. (1973). A cross-cultural analysis of sex differences in the behavior of children aged three through eleven. *Journal of Social Psychology, 91*, 171–188.

Whiting, J. W., & Whiting, H. W. (1968). *Proverbs, sentences, and proverbial phrases from English writings mainly before 1500.* Cambridge, MA: Harvard University Press.

Will, J. A., Self, P. A., & Datan, N. (1976). Maternal behavior and perceived sex of infant. *American Journal of Orthopsychiatry, 46*, 135–139.

Williams, B., Cunningham, D., & Lubawy, J. (2005). *Preschool math.* Beltsville, MD: Gryphon House.

Williamson, P. A., & Silvern, S. B. (1991). Thematic-fantasy play and story comprehension. In J. F. Christie (Ed.), *Play and early literacy development* (pp. 69–90). Albany: State University of New York Press.

Wilson, B. J., & Weiss, A. J. (1992). Developmental differences in children's reactions to toy advertisements linked to a toy-based cartoon. *Journal of Broadcasting and Electronic Media, 36*, 371–394.

Wilson, J. M. (1986). Parent-child play interaction in hospital settings. In A. W. Gottfried & C. C. Brown (Eds.), *Play interactions: The contribution of play materials and parental involvement to children's development* (pp. 213–224). Lexington, MA: Heath.

Wing, L., Gould, J., Yeates, S. R., & Brierly, L. M. (1977). Symbolic play in severely mentally retarded and in autistic children. *Journal of Child Psychology and Psychiatry, 18, 167–178.*

Winner, E. (1982). *Invented worlds: The psychology of the arts.* Cambridge MA: Harvard University Press.

Wohlwill, J. F. (1984). Relationships between exploration and play. In T. D. Yawkey & A. D. Pellegrini (Eds.), *Child's play: Developmental and applied* (pp. 143–170). Hillsdale, NJ: Erlbaum.

Wolery, M., Holcombe-Ligon, A., Brookfield, J., Huffman, K., Schroeder, C., Martin, C. G., et al. (1993). The extent and nature of preschool mainstreaming: A survey of general early educators. *The Journal of Special Education, 27,* 222–234.

Wolfberg, P., & Schuler, A. (1993, March). *A case illustration of the impact of peer play on symbolic activity in autism.* Paper presented at the Biennial Meeting of the Society for Research in Child Development, New Orleans, LA.

Wolfgang, C. H., & Stakenas, R. G. (1985). An exploration of toy content of preschool children's home environments as a predictor of cognitive development. *Early Child Development and* Care, *19,* 291–307.

Wolfgang, C. H., Stannard, L., & Jones, I. (2003). Advanced constructional play with Legos among preschoolers as a predictor of later school achievement in mathematics. *Early Child Development & Care, 173*(5), 467–475.

Wright, J., & Samaras, A. (1986). Play and mastery. In G. G. Fein & P. F. Campbell (Eds.), *Young children and microcomputers* (pp. 73–86). Englewood Cliffs, NJ: Prentice-Hall.

Wyver, S. R., & Spence, S. H. (1999). Play and divergent problem solving: Evidence supporting a reciprocal relationship. *Early Education and Development, 10,* 419–444.

Yogman, M. W. (1980). Child development and pediatrics: An evolving relationship. *Infant Mental Health Journal, 1,* 89–95.

Youngblade, L. M., & Dunn, J. (1995). Individual differences in young children's pretend play with mother and sibling: Links to relationships and understanding of other people's feelings and beliefs. *Child Development, 66,* 1472–1492.

Zaijka, A. (1983). Microcomputers in early childhood education? A first look. *Young Children, 38,* 61–67.

Zarabatny, L., Hartmann, D., & Rankin, D. (1990). The psychological functions of preadolescent peer activities. *Child Development, 61,* 1067–1080.

Index

Note: In page references, p indicates photos, f indicates figures, and t indicates tables.

Child care, 78, 120–123, 121t
Child development play programs,
    206, 288
Childhood autism *See* Autism
Child life play programs, 206–207, 288
Chiu, C., 54
Christiano, B., 232
Christiansen, K., 83
Chrysler, C., 192
Church, E. B., 9, 223
Cicchetti, D., 199
Cinquegrana, E. A., 80
Cisar, C. L., 198
Citron, C. C., 118
Citron-Pousty, J. H., 132
Clark, L., 257
Clarke, C., 176
Clarke-Stewart, A., 122
Clarke-Stewart, K., 121
Classification skills, 216, 219, 220, 233
Clearfield, M. W., 84
Clements, D. H., 107, 218, 219
Clyde, M., 32
Coaching, 258
Coakley, J., 147
Coats, P. B., 180
Coe, 198
Coe, D. A., 198
Cognitive deficits, 190, 191–192
Cognitive-developmental theory,
    157–159, 181
Cognitive functioning, 114, 118
Cognitive skills, 48, 215
Cohen, 279
Cohen, L. J., 279
Cohn, 201, 202
Cohn, D., 201, 202
Cole, 133, 152
Cole, M., 152
Colle, 193, 254
Colle, L., 193, 254
Collectivism, 54, 288
Colle et al., 194
Colletti, 150
Colletti, J., 150
Collins, 240
Collins, W. A., 240
Colwell, M., 118

Communication skills
    adolescence and, 137–138, 153
    animal play and, 41
    associative play and, 102
    autism and, 192, 195
    children with disabilities and, 197
    creative movement and, 251, 252
    cultural differences and, 47, 48
    day care and, 122
    dramatic play and, 114
    infant/peer interactions and, 87–88, 90
    nonverbal, 194, 244, 252, 267
    physical play and, 243–244
    play therapy and, 284
    social play and, 259
    therapy and, 267, 277, 284, 285
    2-year-olds and, 94
    See also Language skills
Competition, 57
    adolescence and, 143
    age of playmates and, 120
    competitive games and, 50–52
    cooperation and, 52–53
    cultural predictors of, 53–57
    games with rules and, 178, 179
    gender differences and, 181
    rough-and-tumble play and, 173, 174
Complementary play, 88
Computer games, 52, 107, 276
    adolescence and, 149, 151–152, 152p
Conceptualization, 136–137, 139, 150, 153
Concrete operations, 99, 132, 133,
    137, 178, 288
Congenital Adrenal Hyperplasia (CAH),
    169–170, 288
    games with rules and, 180
    rough-and-tumble play and, 177–178
Conner, J. A., 118
Connolly, J. A., 106, 118, 170, 176
Connolly, K. J., 176
Connor, J. M., 161, 168
Connor, R. T., 197
Conservation, 216, 221, 223, 288
Contextual theory, 30, 288
Contingent pacing, 240–241
Control
    adult/infant/toddler play and, 81
    dramatic play and, 113

Greenberg, C. S., 202, 205, 206, 207
Gregory, K. M., 32, 220
Greulich, F. K., 159
Grienenberger, J., 239
Griffith, P. L., 197
Griffiths, M. D., 151, 152, 167
Grinder, E. L., 168
Groos, K., 24
Grossman-McKee, A., 232
Group interactions, 101–102, 106, 107
Guerney, L. F., 263, 276
Guilford, J. P., 230
Guralnick, M. J., 190, 196, 197
Gustafson, G. E., 86
Guthrie, D., 114

Hagan, R., 176, 200
Haight, W., 46, 48, 79, 80, 115
Hakuta, H., 47
Hall, G. S., 19, 23, 291
Halpin, B. M., 201
Halverson, C. F., 161
Hamilton, J., 201
Hammond, M. A., 197
Haninger, K., 152
Hanish, L. D., 118
Hanna, E., 165
Hanson, M. J., 197
Harkness, S., 43
Harlow, H. F., 41
Harlow, M. K., 41
Harrell, J. S., 179
Harrington, D. M., 229
Harris, K. R., 197
Harris, M. B., 161
Harris, P. L., 104
Harrower, J. K., 198
Hartley, R., 21, 96, 98, 111, 112, 222, 244, 246, 247, 248, 249, 250, 252
Hartmann, D., 150
Hartup, W. W., 109, 137
Hatch, A., 6
Hate, 136–137, 270, 271, 282
Hauser-Cram, P., 191
Hawkins, J., 107
Hay, D. L., 87
Hayne, H., 85

Hazen, N. L., 255
Health issues, 114–115
Hearing impairments, 184, 185t, 189, 209
Heaton, K., 176
Hedenbro, M., 82
Henderson, D. A., 263, 275, 276, 277
Hendon, C., 202, 205
Henninger, M. L., 107
Herald, S. L., 117, 258
Hernandez, R., 162
Heroard, J., 10, 11
Héroux, G., 169
Herrera, G., 195
Hestenes, L. L., 197
Hetherington, E. M., 106, 116, 117
Hewitt, M., 10
Hewlett, B. S., 83, 177
Heywood, C., 159
Hilgers, L., 143
Hill, E. W., 196
Hill, J., 193, 254
Hindmarsh, P., 170, 177, 180
Hines, M., 159, 170, 177, 180
Hite, T., 165
Ho, K., 47
Hoffman, J. R., 145
Holcombe-Ligon, A., 197
Hormonal factors
    biological explanations and, 180
    gender differences and, 176, 181
    masculine characteristics in females and, 169–170
    rough-and-tumble play and, 177–178, 181
    See also Feminine behavior; Masculine behavior
Hormonal theory, 158, 159
Horner, R. H., 197
Horowitz, L., 189
Houghton, A., 198
Houtz, J. C., 200
Howard, J., 77
Howard-Jones, P., 231
Howe, N., 202
Howell, A., 191
Howes, C., 77, 78, 88, 103, 104, 114, 116, 118, 122, 241
Hrncir, E., 116

About the Author

Fergus P. Hughes, PhD, is professor emeritus at the University of Wisconsin–Green Bay. From 1972 until 2004 he was a professor of human development and psychology at the University of Wisconsin–Green Bay, where he taught courses on child development, adolescent development, life span human development, and children's play. In 2004 he assumed the role of dean of Liberal Arts and Sciences, which he held until his retirement in 2007. He is currently engaged in scholarly writing and teaching courses in the university's Adult Degree Program.

He is the author or coauthor of eight books and numerous book chapters and scholarly articles dealing primarily with childhood cognition and children's play. The first edition of his book *Children, Play, and Development* appeared in 1991 and has since been translated into Chinese, Korean, and Spanish. In addition, he serves as a professional consultant and regular contributor to *Child Parenting Journal*, a national Australian parenting magazine.